George Eliot and Nineteenth-Century Science

George Eliot
and Nineteenth-Century Science

The Make-Believe of a Beginning

Sally Shuttleworth

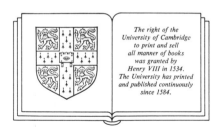

The right of the
University of Cambridge
to print and sell
all manner of books
was granted by
Henry VIII in 1534.
The University has printed
and published continuously
since 1584.

Cambridge University Press

Cambridge
London   New York   New Rochelle
Melbourne   Sydney

Published by the Press Syndicate of the University of Cambridge
The Pitt Building, Trumpington Street, Cambridge CB2 1RP
32 East 57th Street, New York, NY 10022, USA
296 Beaconsfield Parade, Middle Park, Melbourne 3206, Australia

First published 1984

Printed in Great Britain at
the University Press, Cambridge

Library of Congress catalogue card number: 83–15173

British Library Cataloguing in Publication Data
Shuttleworth, Sally
George Eliot and nineteenth-century science.
1. Eliot, George – Criticism and interpretation
2. Science in literature
I. Title
823'.8'356   PR4692.S3
ISBN 0 521 25786 7

Contents

v

For my mother and father

Acknowledgements

My warmest thanks are due to Gillian Beer who guided this project in its initial stages and has proved, throughout, a source of unfailing support and inspiration. I am also greatly indebted to Felicia Bonaparte and George Levine for their invaluable criticisms of my work, and for the generous spirit of their responses.

Amongst the many others who have contributed towards the making of this book I would like to thank my early teachers Alan Dawe and Raymond Williams, my colleague at the University of Aberystwyth, Christopher Gill, who interrupted his classical studies to aid me in my work, and my colleagues in the English Department at Princeton University who read this manuscript, either in whole or in part, and offered many helpful criticisms: Lee Mitchell, Ulrich Knoepflmacher, William Howarth, Alvin Kernan and Valerie Smith. For help with issues relating to the history of science, and for his careful scrutiny of several chapters, I am grateful to Gerald Geison of Princeton's History of Science Department. I would also like to extend my thanks to my typist, Marilyn Walden, for her unerring accuracy, and for the patient good humour with which she received my untidy drafts and endless revisions.

I was aided in this work by a fellowship from the Frank Knox Foundation which enabled me to pursue research at Harvard University from 1978–9, and by grants from the Research Council and Surdna Foundation of Princeton University.

An earlier form of Chapter 8 appeared in *Victorian Science and Victorian Values: Literary Perspectives*, edited by James Paradis and Thomas Postlewait; I am grateful to the New York Academy of Sciences for permission to reprint it. To Jonathan G. Ouvry and the Beinecke Rare Book and Manuscript Library, I am indebted for permission to reprint short extracts from George Eliot's and G. H. Lewes' diaries and journals. I would also like to record my appreciation of the invaluable help given by the staff of Dr Williams's Library, and that of all the many other libraries in which I have worked.

Finally, I would like to express my deepest gratitude to my friends, Peter Onek and Valerie Smith, for their unshakeable patience and dedicated editorial assistance in the concluding stages of this work.

Preface

In his review of *Middlemarch* Henry James expressed his distaste for what he deemed the unwarranted intrusion of science into the realm of fiction. The novel was, he observed, "too often an echo of Messrs Darwin and Huxley."[1] Other Victorian critics shared his disapprobation. A reviewer of *Romola*, for instance, pondering gloomily on the "psychologico-medical study of Baldassarre," concluded that George Eliot's scientist–companion G. H. Lewes was probably responsible for this regrettable slip in artistry.[2]

Such royal disdain of "things scientific" was not, however, universal. One noted nineteenth-century reviewer of *Middlemarch* positively acclaimed George Eliot's "profound sense of the importance of physiological conditions in human life."[3] Critics in the twentieth century have tended to share this sympathetic response. Since the publication of Bernard Paris' *Experiments in Life* in 1965, scholarly attention has been focused increasingly on the role of science in George Eliot's fiction.[4] Henry James' dogmatic distinction between the realms of art and science now appears, in the light of current research, both wrong-headed and arbitrary: a last-ditch attempt to defend the bastion of art by a writer whose novels were themselves suffused with the notions of nineteenth-century science.[5]

Although all novelists in the nineteenth century were inevitably affected by the close interdependence of social and scientific thought, George Eliot was, in this respect, remarkable. She brought to her writing a breadth of knowledge of contemporary social and scientific theory unmatched by any of her peers. Scientific ideas did not merely filter through into the metaphors and images of her work; in constructing her novels she engaged in an active dialogue with contemporary scientific thought. My aim in this work is to trace the diverse and complex ways in which her involvement with science influenced the development of her fiction. Building on earlier, largely thematic, studies of this area, I show how scientific ideas and theories of method affected not only the social vision but also the narrative structure and fictional methodology of her novels.[6]

I shall not, of course, attempt to cover in this study the entire field of nineteenth-century scientific thought since Victorian science was not, as many modern critics tend to assume, a unified body of knowledge, but rather a diffuse collection of disciplines divided internally by competing theories and intellectual schisms. Far from dispersing my energies amidst this "tempting range of relevancies called the universe," I intend to focus my attention on unravelling just one particular aspect of this web: the field of organic theory. Critics from the Victorian era onwards have spoken of George Eliot's organic conception of society, or her moral theory of organic unity, but few have defined this conception with any precision, and fewer still have traced its connections to nineteenth-century physiological theory.[7]

The organic idea is generally associated in criticism with notions of harmonious cultural integration and gradual social development – ideas that were ubiquitous in Victorian theory, and so familiar to our ears, that we have tended to ignore their historical origins and to attribute to them a timeless dimension. The Victorian theorists who stressed the dynamic interdependence of whole and part were adhering, however, to premises that were first articulated in both social and physiological thought only at the end of the eighteenth century. This era witnessed, in fact, the parallel development of social theories of organic evolution and scientific theories of dynamic, biological life.

For social theorists writing in the wake of the French Revolution, the idea of organic development offered an attractive conceptual model since it allowed them to reconcile rather threatening notions of social change with more reassuring conceptions of continuity. "Society," as G. H. Lewes observed, "is thus conceived as an Organism, in which incessant movement accompanies constant stability of form."[8] Victorian social theorists replaced the atomistic social ideas of the eighteenth century with images of organic interdependence, and subordinated the revolutionary insistence on individual rights to more "wholesome" considerations of social duty.

George Eliot, in common with so many of her contemporaries, eagerly appropriated this organicist philosophy. All her novels, despite their diversity of setting and theme, draw their moral framework from its premises. Daniel Deronda, in his yearning to become "an organic part of social life" articulates the goal of all his predecessors.[9] In each

THE HOME DEPOT 5220

AT 5270 SHADY GROVE RD, GAITHERSBURG, MD

DAVID MUCHER   MANAGER (301)-330-4800

18/12/01   5220 00034 60021

T18   05:18 PM

SPANIARD 212/2/669030   0.27

PHONE 1092180817420   8.9

JNB TOTAL   72.07

TAX WD 5.000 181   0.23   368.010

Total   82.074

XMAS 3275800847582008   70.82

BULB CODE 5377887/454749   .10

THE HOME DEPOT 2550

15740 SHADY GROVE RD. GAITHERSBURG, MD
DAVID WAGNER   MANAGER (301)-330-4900

```
             2550 00024 80481      07/21/97
SALE                        813    02:18 PM


030699142712 FASTNERS                  0.75
074108512604 PHONE                     9.67
             SUBTOTAL                 10.42
   10.42     TAX MD 5.000              0.53
             TOTAL                   $10.95
372900874263008  AMEX                 10.95
AUTH CODE 551789/6241344                 TA
```

ORIGINAL RECEIPT REQUIRED FOR REFUND
THANK YOU FOR SHOPPING AT THE HOME DEPOT
WAREHOUSE PRICES - DAY IN, DAY OUT

of George Eliot's novels, the central drama arises from a clash between the protagonist's desire for individual fulfilment, and the demands of social duty. The essential quest is always for a form of self-fulfilment which would simultaneously contribute to the harmonious development of the larger social whole. Although George Eliot changes the historical setting of the novels, and shifts the focus of attention, from ideas of political integration in *Felix Holt*, for example, to the integrative potentiality of Zionism in *Daniel Deronda*, she yet addresses, within each work, the same fundamental moral issues.

This continuity of moral theme is not reflected, however, in the novels' social vision. George Eliot's first full-length novel, *Adam Bede*, clearly conforms to the social model usually associated with the organic idea: it portrays a society that is ordered, harmoniously integrated, and fundamentally hierarchic. Yet the idyllic harmony of rural Hayslope contrasts sharply with the petty provincial life of the 1830s in *Middlemarch* and the conflict-ridden world of contemporary England in *Daniel Deronda*. This discrepancy between the moral ideal and social vision of George Eliot's later novels could be explained, in part, by her reluctance to relinquish an ideal that no longer accorded with her awareness of the actual realities of English life. Close analysis, however, reveals that the explanation is by no means so simple. The organic analogy did not, as is commonly assumed, offer a single image of society. Indeed, social interpretation of the organic idea varied in accordance with the physiological premises each theorist adopted. Thus the vitalist conceptions which sustained German Romanticism differed fundamentally from the physiological theories which underpinned the positivist philosophy of Auguste Comte. The power of the organic idea as a conceptual model lay, in fact, in the diversity of possible interpretations it offered. The movement of organicism in nineteenth-century thought should be regarded, therefore, less as a single idea than as a language that imposed a uniform structure on all who attempted to extend its vocabulary.[10]

In tracing the impact of organic theory on George Eliot's fiction, I shall be primarily concerned with the two figures who fundamentally affected her thought: Comte, and G. H. Lewes. While Comte's ideas of the evolution of the social organism influenced George Eliot's early conceptions of social development, Lewes' theories ultimately had the more significant impact on her work. Lewes, in extending the biological premises of Comte's conception of organic life, produced a radical theory of social and psychological development that also had dramatic implications for his theory of scientific method. The effects of Lewes' organicist theory can be discerned in George Eliot's changing conceptions of social order, and in the transformations in the psychological theory and narrative methods of her novels.

The evolution of George Eliot's interpretation of organic theory can best be measured by a comparison between her first and last novels. The traditional ideal of organic social harmony presented in *Adam Bede* is reflected in the psychological theory, and in the unified, cyclical narrative structure of the work. *Daniel Deronda,* by contrast, portrays both a society and characters riven by contradiction, while the unified structure of the earlier work is supplanted by a more open and fragmented narrative form which disrupts both spatial and temporal continuity. The contrast is evident, too, in George Eliot's shift in narrative stance. In *Adam Bede* she adheres to the scientific and artistic creed she had earlier outlined in her essay, "The Natural History of German Life." She adopts the role of natural historian, a passive observer of organic life, concerned only to record the unchanging details of external form. Her empiricist method sustains the novel's static conception of society and character. In *Daniel Deronda,* however, her narrative method is closer to that of the creative, experimental scientist, to whom the visionary Jew, Mordecai, is compared. The methods of natural history are replaced by those of experimental physiology. No longer a passive observer, but now an active participant, George Eliot actively creates the experiment of her novel. This change in method is reflected in the more dynamic structure of the novel, and in its social and psychological theory. Far from reflecting an image of static harmony, it actually encompasses conflict and contradiction. All these changes, I shall argue, can be correlated with transformations in contemporary scientific theories of the organic.

Through close analysis of the inter-relationship between the social and scientific aspects of organicism in George Eliot's work, I intend to challenge the assumption often made by radical historians that science is only employed in social theory to ratify the *status quo.* This argument holds true only partially for George Eliot's work since, in the later novels, scientific conceptions actually undermine dominant social theories and modes of categorisation. Similarly, in response to the recent Marxist critique of organicism, I would like to rescue concepts of the organic from an unproblematic association with notions of totality or unity, whether social, psychological, or aesthetic.[11] I am indebted to this critique for exposing the relationship between theories of historical continuity, and a unified psychological subject, and for showing how these assumptions concerning unity and continuity dictate the techniques and form of the realist novel. Analysis of George Eliot's work shows, however, that these theories fail to take account of the complexity of nineteenth-century social and scientific thought. Although George Eliot worked squarely within an organicist framework, one can yet discern, in the predominantly realist forms of her fiction, distinct changes in her theory of history, society and psychology.

The structure of this work follows George Eliot's own pattern of composition. Within each novel she examined different aspects of the social, moral, psychological, and political issues raised by organicist theory, and employed a different strategy to achieve narrative resolution. In order to capture fully the relationship between the theme and structure of each work, and to avoid repetition of material, I have chosen, therefore, not to adopt a thematic organisation but to treat each novel individually, focusing each time on a separate issue.

The first chapter examines the social, psychological, and political ramifications of organic theory in nineteenth-century European thought, while the subsequent chapters analyse the impact of the theory on the narrative structure of George Eliot's works. The chapter on *Adam Bede* addresses the relationship between the practice of natural history and the novel's narrative organisation and social vision. George Eliot's own verdict on this novel was that it was "more complete and better balanced" than her following work, *The Mill on the Floss*. She believed, however, that the latter had a "profounder veracity."[12] The "veracity" of *The Mill* perhaps stems from the fact that it confronts directly many of the problems in organic theory which were never articulated fully in the earlier novel. The chapter devoted to this work explores the internal narrative conflict between theories of organic social and psychological development and the catastrophic structure of the plot. In *Silas Marner* George Eliot seems to return once more to the harmonious social vision of *Adam Bede*, but her ambivalent response to organic theories of social evolution, suggested by *The Mill*'s concluding flood, is still in evidence. The analysis of *Silas Marner* also focuses, therefore, on the issue of internal conflict since, like *The Mill*, this novel seems to offer two different models of history, one based on theories of gradual organic development, and another which privileges notions of chance and disruption.

On completion of her "legendary tale," George Eliot turned away from her accustomed English rural setting in order to consider the issues of nineteenth-century organicism within the setting of fifteenth-century Italy. The chapter on *Romola* examines the various ways in which she employed the idealisation made possible by this temporal and cultural distance to explore the social implications of Comtean theory. In her subsequent novel, *Felix Holt*, George Eliot again adopts the clarity of historical perspective to explore contemporary social issues, but this time her setting is, once more, the transitional society of England in the 1830s. With the increased political urgency created by the proposed Second Reform Bill, the underlying political issues in *Romola* and the earlier novels are raised, in this work, to the level of explicit theme. The sixth chapter examines, in accordance with the dual structure of the novel, the political and sexual implications of organicism, tracing the relationship between political theories of social submission and duty, and Victorian ideals of womanhood.

Middlemarch, like all George Eliot's preceding novels, focuses on the individual's quest for social integration, yet it displays neither the political crudeness nor the naive idealisation of "woman's lot" found in certain sections of *Felix Holt*. Faced with apparent irreconcilable contradictions within the traditional organic model, George Eliot now adopts explicitly the complex model of organic life defined, within the novel, in Lydgate's biological theory. In the *Middlemarch* chapter I focus on the various ways in which this theory affected the social analysis and narrative practice of George Eliot's "experiment in time." The term "experiment" rightly belongs, however, to her final novel, *Daniel Deronda*, in which she develops the social and methodological implications of the dynamic model of organic life to their full extent. In this last chapter, I show how the innovative form, intricate psychological analysis and idealism of *Daniel Deronda* all stem from organicist theory.

My aim within each chapter is thus to explore the key social and political issues of nineteenth-century organic theory, and to chart the various ways in which George Eliot employed scientific theory to achieve narrative resolution of the problems addressed by the organic social metaphor.

CHAPTER 1

Science and social thought: The rise of organic theory

George Eliot opens her final novel, *Daniel Deronda*, with a reflective epigraph that links the practice of writing to that of science:

Men can do nothing without the make-believe of a beginning. Even Science, the strict measurer, is obliged to start with a make-believe unit, and must fix on a point in the stars' unceasing journey when his sidereal clock shall pretend that time is at Nought.

While it is scarcely surprising that George Eliot, with her noted interest in positivism, should draw a comparison between her own procedures and those of a scientist, the actual basis of the analogy is rather startling; the comparison rests not on the common commitment of the novelist and scientist to the objective recording of external fact, but on their shared need for imaginative construction. The observation clearly suggests the radical changes that had occurred in George Eliot's theories of scientific and fictional practice since her first novel. In *Adam Bede* she adhered to the methodology of natural history; the artist, like the natural historian, was to be guided not by theory or imagination, but by concrete observation. His function was to record, to describe truthfully what he saw. This creed of realism, with its naive view of truth, is based on the belief that the novelist, like the scientist, records a pre-given world. The opening epigraph of *Daniel Deronda*, with its reference to the "make-believe of a beginning," clearly challenges this conception. The scientist does not merely record; he actively constructs a schema within which his observations are placed. Such an act of "make-believe," or heuristic construction, threatens the comforting conception of science as the unquestionable transcription of the unchanging external world. This transformation in George Eliot's theory of scientific method and fictional practice can be correlated with her developing understanding of the social and scientific aspects of organic theory.

George Eliot's concern with ideas of organic social unity is not peculiar to her work, but rather links her thought to that of the major

1

authors of her age. Social theorists and writers throughout the nine-teenth century, from Coleridge and Wordsworth to Carlyle, Arnold, and Dickens, display a similar preoccupation. They are not, however, simply adhering to an age-old model of social development. Although comparisons between the human body and society occurred in Aristotle, Livy, Shakespeare, and Hobbes, all these analogies were fundamentally static and mechanistic and thus qualitatively distinct from those that emerged in the late-eighteenth and early-nineteenth centuries. Hobbes, for example, alternately compared the state to a body and to a watch; society, like a machine, was conceived as an artificial aggregate of dis-crete units in which the whole equalled the sum of the parts.[1] Such a model could not account either for growth or change or reciprocal interaction between the individual and the social whole. In contrast with the Hobbesian view, the idea of organic order to which George Eliot and her contemporaries adhered was a dynamic one, based on recently defined principles of physiological life.

At the close of the eighteenth century a revolution occurred, not only in the social order, but also in the natural and social sciences as the mechanistic cosmology of the preceding two centuries was overthrown. Models of explanation in scientific, social and psychological theory had, until this era, been based on mechanical laws of association. As Walter Buckley argues,

Man was regarded as a physical object, a kind of elaborate machine, whose actions and psychic processes could be analyzed in terms of the principles of mechanics. In "social mechanics," society was seen as an "astronomical system" whose elements were human beings bound together by mutual attraction or differentiated by repulsion; groups of societies or states were systems of balanced oppositions. Man, his groups, and their inter-relations thus constituted an unbroken continuity with the rest of the mechanistically interpreted universe. All were based on the interplay of natural causes, to be studied as systems of relationships that could be measured and expressed in terms of laws of social mechanics.[2]

Thus, in the physical sciences, the naturalist Buffon viewed the organism as an association of parts whose movements could be inter-preted according to the Newtonian mechanical laws of attraction, while Hume applied similar principles to explain the formation of ideas.[3] In social philosophy, theorists of the French Revolution employed the principles of association to explain the composition of society. The idea of association implies the coming together of separate parts and, for the Ideologues, society was just a collection of separate individuals, an artificial structure which, they believed, could be transformed by the rational action of men. The physiological and social principles of organic life first formulated in the last decades of the eighteenth century explicitly challenged this belief.

In 1790 Kant proposed in *Critique of Judgment* the now-classic definition of the organism as a whole in which each part is reciprocally means and end. This definition gave expression to a principle of causality which was to dominate the life sciences and social philosophy of the nineteenth century.[4] In both spheres the premises of associationism were overturned. Theories of organic interdependence now replaced those of free association, and interest in dynamic historical processes supplanted the earlier dominant preoccupation with quantitative measurement. Hitherto the natural sciences had been dominated by natural history, a science which focused on organic and inorganic phenomena alike, and was concerned with the measurement and classification of the visible surface of nature. With the development of biology, a science devoted exclusively to the study of life-processes, scientists turned their attention away from the fixed details of external form to focus on the principles of internal organisation and the laws that governed historical development.[5] The organism was no longer viewed simply as an association of organs. No element was autonomous; rather, each owed its form to its role and position within the development of the whole.

Following the upheaval of the French Revolution, European social theorists of all political persuasions turned to these principles of organic life for a model of social order. The nature of the state, Burke had contended in *Reflections on the Revolution in France*, is essentially organic; revolutionary action disrupts the natural processes of historical growth. His theories directly influenced the *Naturphilosophen* in Germany, while in France fundamentally similar arguments were offered by the conservative theologians de Maistre and de Bonald and by the later, more liberal, Comteans.[6]

Despite these thinkers' differences in political perspective, all were united in their opposition to the Ideologues' theory of society and the psychological subject: to the conception of the social contract, and the doctrine of equality and natural rights. The idea of organic interdependence and growth suggested a different theory of the "natural." The fundamental attraction of the organic conception lay in the fact that it appeared to offer a model that could reconcile the eighteenth-century ideals of individualism with the newly perceived demands of social order. On the historical plane, the idea of organic growth –

development linked to stability of form – appeared to fulfil the demands of both historical change and continuity. Rejecting the atomism of eighteenth-century philosophy, organic theorists stressed the interdependence of the whole, rather than the freedom of the parts, and the necessity for gradual cumulative growth rather than the infinite potentiality for change.

George Eliot adhered throughout her life to these principles of organic social theory. The first clear assertion of her belief occurs in her essay, "The Natural History of German Life" (1856), in which she observes that society is *"incarnate history."*[7] Though ostensibly outlining Riehl's views she is obviously in clear agreement with his belief that any attempt "to disengage [society] from its historical elements must . . . be simply destructive of social vitality."[8] Like Burke or Comte, she believes that society is not an artificial creation of men, but an organic whole whose laws of natural growth must be observed, for "What has grown up historically can only die out historically, by the gradual operation of necessary laws."[9] Organicist theories of historical development underlie the central moral and social questions George Eliot explores in her work. In a notebook essay on "Historic Guidance" she focused her discussion on the need for *"Continuity* (in human history) and *Solidarity* (in the members of the race)."[10] Her categories are drawn from Comte's definition of the consensus of the social organism which extended, he argued, to a feeling of Solidarity in the present, and a sense of Continuity with the past.[11] These two concerns structure all George Eliot's fiction, whether she is dealing with Maggie Tulliver's relations with the evolving life of St Ogg's, Romola's commitment to Florence, or Daniel Deronda's bond to his Jewish heritage.

The influence of organic theory can also be discerned in the moral categories of George Eliot's fiction, particularly in her preoccupation with the evils of egoism and the virtues of social duty. Theorists of the Revolution had stressed the importance of social equality and individual rights; but, under the light of the organic analogy, ideas of individualism were revealed to be related to a socially disruptive, and thus morally reprehensible, egoism. The doctrine of rights associated with the upheaval of the French Revolution was now replaced by one of social duties. Thus the German philosopher Johann Fichte argued, in the *Principles of Natural Right* (1791), that the distinction between an isolated man and a citizen was like that between the parts of an inorganic object and those of an organic body: "In the organic body each part constantly maintains the whole, and is in maintaining the whole thereby itself maintained, just so stands the citizen in relation to the state."[12] The principle of natural right was thus transformed to that of social duty, while the doctrine of individual interests was replaced by one of social functions. Despite the gulf which separated German Romanticism from French Positivism, Comte offered similar arguments. In the true organic society, he observed, "the vague and stormy discussions of rights would be replaced by the calm and precise discussion of duties."[13] In her novels, George Eliot sought to find the precise nature of this duty, to weigh the relative claims of individual rights and social demands. Daniel Deronda, in his longing for "some ideal task, in which I might feel myself the heart and brain of a multitude – some social captainship, which would come to me as a duty, and not be striven for as a personal prize" (Ch. 63, III, 315), articulates the value schema of all the preceding novels. Whether explicitly, like Felix and Savonarola, or implicitly like Dorothea and Maggie, all George Eliot's protagonists search for a form of social duty that would make them an organic part of social life and yet would avoid the taint of egoism or individualistic self-seeking.

In the positivist philosophy of Comte, George Eliot discovered apparent scientific foundations for a theory of social duty. Positivism, as Lewes explained, "aims at creating a Philosophy of the Sciences as a basis for a new social faith. A social doctrine is the *aim* of Positivism, a scientific doctrine the *means*."[14] George Eliot, like Comte, Lewes, and Herbert Spencer, found her articles of faith in the belief that the growth and interdependence of society – the social organism – are governed by the operation of the same immutable laws that govern physiological life. In her 1851 review of Mackay's *The Progress of the Intellect,* she communicates the excitement felt by so many of her contemporaries at the recognition "of undeviating law in the material and moral world – of that invariability of sequence which is acknowledged to be the basis of physical science, but which is still perversely ignored in our social organization, our ethics and our religion."[15] From this "invariability of sequence" she draws her understanding of "that inexorable law of consequences, whose evidence is confirmed instead of weakened as the ages advance." "Human duty," she concludes, "is comprised in the earnest study of this law and patient obedience to its teaching."[16] This doctrine of consequences is evident in the moral structure of her novels and clearly underlies the nemesis that pursues Hetty and Arthur, Godfrey Cass, Tito, Bulstrode, and all other characters who do not dutifully consider the social consequences of their actions. The premises of the doctrine are later articulated by George Eliot in her famous conversation with F. W. H. Myers, when, taking "the words *God, Immortality, Duty* – [she] pronounced, with terrible earnestness, how inconceivable was the *first*, how unbelievable the *second*, and yet how peremptory and absolute the *third*. Never, perhaps, have sterner accents affirmed the sovereignty of impersonal and unrecompensing Law."[17] Reified scientific law has taken the place of the theological word as the source of a prescriptive morality.

Though avoiding the worst excesses of her contemporaries' enthusiasm for the moral functions of scientific law, George Eliot does fall partially into the mistake, described by John Stuart Mill, of confusing the idea of a "Law of Nature," denoting observed uniformities in the occurrence of phenomena, with the ethical interpretation of "Law" as expressing "what ought to be."[18] Her conviction that science could provide the moral foundations for a theory of duty does not, however, simply reflect the decline of her religious belief. Transformations in the sciences of the period made her position possible; for, with the decline of belief in the self-evident order of the world, scientists turned from mere taxonomy to analysis of the laws that governed the processes of historical growth. The rise of faith in science accompanied this development.

The Victorians' tendency to refer to science as if it were a defined and coherent entity reflects their desire to treat it as an unproblematic source of authority. Such an assumption obscures, however, the social origins and diversity of practice of nineteenth-century science. Thus, for social theorists like Comte, Spencer, and Lewes, science was not just a uniform demonstration of law to be raided for the validation of their social beliefs. Indeed, the development of their social theories went hand in hand with that of their physiology. Comte, for example, in outlining the physiological principles upon which he founded his theory of organic social life, became, in the eyes of his later admirer the scientist, Claude Bernard, one of the great innovators in biology.[19] Far from simply appropriating a pre-defined scientific model of organic life, he actively contributed to the evolution of both social and scientific theory.

Victorian intellectuals in all spheres were intensely interested in the social ramifications of the new scientific theories. In an essay on "The Scientific Movement and Literature," the literary critic Edward Dowden draws out what he believes to be the decisive implications of the scientific discoveries of the era. Evincing the same admiration as

George Eliot for the "regularity of sequence" manifest in the world, he draws the same conclusion that these physical processes actually reveal a moral order: "But not only is nature everywhere constant, uniform, orderly in its operations; all its parts constitute a whole, an *ensemble*. Nothing is added, nothing can be lost."[20] Dowden, like most of his contemporaries, assumes that the regularity of the operation of physical law actually guarantees the mode of transformation. He takes no account of the possibility of laws governing sudden or disruptive change but assimilates notions of universal physical law directly within the social perspective of gradualism and orderly organic growth. Physical law is also used to reinforce the social doctrine of organic unity. Dowden draws on the principles of the conservation of energy that were, in 1847, extended by Helmholtz to the sphere of organic life, to sustain a theory of moral coherence throughout the natural and social realms.[21] From this argument it is but a short step to Dowden's moral conclusion that science, as it reveals the unity of the physical and social world, also declares "with increasing emphasis that duty is social."[22] Like Comte, Dowden uses science to reinforce the organicist doctrine of the primacy of the social whole. Since all individuals are also members of a larger unified social realm, "Self-surrender is therefore at times sternly enjoined, and if the egoistic desires are brought into conflict with social duties, the individual life and joy within us, at whatever cost of personal suffering, must be sacrificed to the just claims of our fellows."[23] Dowden claims the authority not only of science but also of George Eliot for this stern moral warning: "And what in effect is this statement, justified by science, of the nature of duty, but a rendering into abstract formulae of the throbbings of the heart which lives at the centre of such creations as *Romola, Armgart* and *Middlemarch*?"[24]

Dowden correctly identifies the moral issues raised by organicism that frame George Eliot's novels, but not their resolution. The question of whether self-surrender should be "sternly enjoined" is one that remains open in her work; it is not simply resolved theoretically. The poem "Armgart," to which Dowden refers, supplies a clear illustration of this point. Narrative endorsement of the ethics of submission is ambiguous. Armgart, an incomparable singer, experiences, in overcoming her egoism, a "birth from that monstrous Self."[25] The price of such a birth, however, is the loss of her one truly creative and distinctive talent, her voice. The narrative may appear to preach self-surrender and the abandonment of egoistic desire, but such sacrifice does not bring glorious integration within a unified social whole, but rather Armgart's sorrowful understanding of her membership in the "race oppressed."[26] The conclusion of the poem is dominated less by a sense of moral transcendence than by a feeling of loss and regret. Throughout George Eliot's work one can find the same ambivalence toward the ethics of self-surrender and social duty. Though the central moral issues explored in her novels are drawn from contemporary theories of organicism, narrative developments in each work in fact expose the contradictions the organic social metaphor conceals while appearing to offer a perfect reconciliation between ideas of individualism and social duty.

In social theory the organic metaphor clearly functioned as a screen which selectively filtered perceptions, focusing attention on specific issues and suppressing others.[27] Inconsistencies inevitably occurred, however, precisely in regard to issues which the metaphor was designed to resolve: the relationship of part to whole, or individual to society. The same tension between individualism and holism that occurs throughout George Eliot's works is also to be found in the work of the social theorists who influenced her. Comte, for instance, vacillated between organicist conceptions, and more individualistic premises. In initially defining his physiological and social theories, he discarded simultaneously the associationist view of the organism and of society. The organism was not, he argued, an association of independently formed parts but rather a dynamic process in which each part was defined by its membership in the whole. The social implications of this theory are manifest in his declaration that "it is necessary to strip away the last metaphysical illusions, and show what is the true human point of view, – that it is not individual but social; . . . Man is a mere abstraction, and there is nothing real but Humanity, regarded intellectually or, yet more, morally."[28] Man cannot be considered apart from his membership in the social organism. Individualist philosophy, Comte believes, is based on an illusion; the concept of the individual as an autonomous entity must be discarded. Comte's social and physiological theory are clearly in accordance here, yet at times, in order to further a social argument, he does return to an associationist model. Thus at one point he states that, "All notions of public good must be based upon those of private advantage, because the former can be nothing else than that which is common to all cases of the latter."[29] The argument is based on an associationist theory of the organism in which the whole simply equals the sum of its parts.

The internal contradictions within Comte's social thought are similar to conflicts which emerge in the work of two other figures who influenced

George Eliot: John Stuart Mill and Herbert Spencer. Mill, who was initially strongly influenced by Comte, accepts, in his *System of Logic*, the latter's theories of the historical development of the social organism and the physiological principle of consensus expressed by the idea that "there is no social phenomenon which is not more or less influenced by every other part of the condition of the same society."[30] Mill's primary orientation, however, like that of the Revolutionary theorist Condorcet, from whom he draws an epigraph, is individualistic. He is not prepared to accept fully all the social implications of the idea of consensus: that the social whole cannot be reduced to the sum of its parts. "Human beings in society," he argues, "have no properties but those which are derived from, and may be resolved into, the laws of the nature of individual man."[31] Mill wishes to avoid reifying society; he is torn between his desire to treat the individual as primary and his adherence to the organic model. Unlike Comte, his allegiance lies with an individualistic perspective. In his later more critical work, *Auguste Comte and Positivism*, he questions what he sees as the authoritarian implications of Comte's organic social model, and firmly rejects Comte's theories of government since "Liberty and spontaneity on the part of individuals form no part of the schema."[32] He dissents, as George Eliot's Maggie Tulliver was briefly to do, from what he terms the doctrines of Thomas à Kempis: that the individual should act only for the good of others, "and that we should endeavour to starve the whole of the desires which point to our personal satisfaction."[33] Mill's challenge is to the doctrine of complete self-surrender for the good of the social whole, which both Comte and Dowden believed could be demonstrated by science. George Eliot's novels reveal a similar, though less emphatic, disquiet with this doctrine. Maggie and Dorothea might ultimately wish to surrender desires for the self and to achieve full incorporation within the surrounding social organism, but George Eliot saves them from this fate. Maggie is sent to her death, and Dorothea is permitted to marry Will and move from the town of Middlemarch. Like Mill, George Eliot is unwilling to accept fully the social implications Comte draws from the organic metaphor. Within her novels she attempts to find some form of balance between her belief in the individual's right to self-fulfilment and her firm commitment to the idea of social duty.

The most extreme individualistic interpretation of the organic metaphor occurs in the work of Herbert Spencer, George Eliot's close friend and intellectual asociate of the early 1850s, and the theorist most clearly responsible for popularising ideas of the social organism in England.

Throughout his work he was concerned to combat ahistorical notions of an invariable human nature, and to demonstrate scientifically not only that "the analogy between a society and a living creature is borne out to a degree quite unsuspected by those who commonly draw it, but also, that the same definition of life applies to both."[34] Though Spencer shared with Comte and Mill the belief that physiological laws of growth and interdependence govern the development of the social organism, his moral and political theories were actually founded on the principles of individualism and *laissez-faire* economics. Like the philosophers of the eighteenth century, his primary concern lay not with duties but with rights. Thus duty is defined in *Social Statics* as the fulfilment of one's own desires. Spencer's "First Principle" is that, "Every man has freedom to do all that he wills, provided he infringes not the equal freedom of any other man."[35] He wishes to demonstrate the "ultimate identity of personal interests and social interests;"[36] that is, how pursuit of self-interest could create social harmony, and not, as Comte and Fichte believed, how the personal must be subsumed within the social. If Spencer's theory is looked at closely, one can see that though his concept of history is drawn from organicism, his theory of social interaction is based on a chemical or mechanical model. Thus in *Social Statics* he argues: "To understand humanity in its combinations, it is necessary to analyze that humanity in its elementary form – for the explanation of the compound, to refer back to the simple."[37] Understanding of society is to be drawn from that of the individual; society is conceived as an aggregate of discrete units in which the whole equals the sum of its parts. Spencer's individualism, his support of the idea of rights, is founded on a theory of mechanical association.

As the preceding discussion suggests, there was no agreement amongst George Eliot's contemporaries as to social interpretation of the organic model. Each theorist experienced internal contradictions within his work and each turned to a different biological theory to sustain his social philosophy. While Comte employed a dynamic theory of organic formation to undercut notions of individual autonomy, individualists like Mill and Spencer turned to a mechanical theory of association in order to preserve their notion of individual freedom. Their disagreements, however, define the crucial issues of George Eliot's novels. In each work she explores the moral question of whether individualistic desire can ever accord with social duty, and the wider philosophical issue of individual autonomy. The primary debate amongst Comte, Mill, and Spencer concerned the issue of individual development: to what extent the individual is determined by his incorporation within the life of the social organism. Comte, discarding associationist principles, would reply, "fully."

Comte's model of social development was one which sustained both a psychological theory of determinism and a moral theory of historical allegiance. As Lewes observes of Comte: "in regard to History I venture to say that no philosopher has ever laid so much emphasis on it, no one has more clearly seen and expressed the truth, that the past rules the present, lives in it, and that we are but the growth and outcome of the past."[38] George Eliot substantially embraces this perspective; in painting the portrait of Maggie Tulliver, for instance, she sketches both Maggie's immediate surroundings and the evolutionary history of the town of St Ogg's. Maggie's final moral stance reflects that of Comte; for, as she demands of Stephen, "If the past is not to bind us, where can duty lie?"[39] Like all George Eliot's novels, however, *The Mill on the Floss* exhibits internal tensions and contradictions which arise from her attempt to avoid the extreme deterministic implications of Comte's organicism, and to find some moral resolution compatible with ideas of individual freedom.

George Eliot's attraction to the various, even mutually contradictory, organicist theories of Comte, Lewes, and Spencer stems from their common commitment to the belief that science could provide the foundations for a system of ethical conduct. Spencer opens *Social Statics* with the dramatic exclamation: " 'Give us a guide,' cry men to the philosopher,"[40] and Lewes introduces *The Foundations of a Creed* with the observation that "The great desire of this age is for a Doctrine which may serve to condense our knowledge, guide our researches, and shape our lives, so that Conduct may really be the consequence of Belief."[41] All three philosophers turned to the principles of organic life and development to provide this surety. In defining their systems, each relied heavily on recently formulated principles of embryological theory which made it possible to explain change not as a movement towards chaos, but as a movement towards a higher state of order.

Until the mid-eighteenth century, theories of generation and growth had been predominantly preformationist; the fully formed individual was presumed present in miniature in the embryo. Development was seen, therefore, simply as a process of growth, not of change. The theory of preformation was related to the practice of natural history for, as François Jacob has observed:

As long as living organisms were perceived as combinations of visible structures, preformation provided the simplest explanation for the persistence of these structures through succeeding generations. The linear continuity of the living world in space and time required a continuity of form through the actual process of generation. The role of generation was to perpetuate visible order.[42]

Theories of preformation sustained ideas of an unchanging natural order. With the development of theories of epigenesis, however, the idea of change could be incorporated within an ordered model of the world. The theory of epigenesis, first formulated by Wolff in 1759, and later popularised by Goethe and Von Baer, explained embryonic growth as a process of constant differentiation as the embryo evolved from simplicity to complexity, from homogeneity to heterogeneity.

This theory of development was crucial to the physiological and social ideas of Comte, Lewes, and Spencer. Indeed, the social and physiological aspects appeared so interconnected for Lewes that he actually used the idea of the social division of labour to explain the organic differentiation of functions.[43] The significance of the idea of epigenesis lay in the fact that, in associating growth with change, it directed attention away from the visible surface of nature and toward the historical process. As the nineteenth-century physiologist Dollinger observed, "In this course of life and passing of existence the single phenomenon itself cannot have any significance for itself"; it is defined by its position within a larger historical process. The value of each phenomenon, therefore, "consists merely in its contribution to the establishment of a coming stage of development. Thus, the knowledge of individual human existence cannot truly be other than historical."[44] Though Dollinger is speaking of physiological analysis, his argument also clearly applies to Victorian social theory.[45] He defines the assumptions that guide George Eliot's careful analysis of her characters' relations to the social organism of which they form a part.

The development of theories of epigenesis was directly related to the general nineteenth-century transformation in attitudes towards the historical past. The eighteenth-century contempt for the past was discarded once theorists started to argue that simple or "primitive" societies could be related to complex or "civilised" societies on a developmental scale. This vision of ordered historical change prompted T. H. Buckle in his *History of Civilization in England* to proclaim grandly that it shall clearly be seen that, from the beginning there has been no discrepancy, no incongruity, no disorder, no interruption, no interference; but that all the events which surround us, even to the furthest limits of material creation, are but different parts of a single scheme, which is permeated by one glorious principle of universal and undeviating regularity.[46]

All events and changes within the physical and social worlds appeared to conform to the uniform operation of one scientific law. Buckle's sentiments are echoed in George Eliot's recognition of the "undeviating law in the material and moral world." Expressing the same idea, in her 1865 review of Lecky's *Influence of Rationalism*, she extols the "great conception of universal regular sequence, without partiality and without caprice," which study of the physical sciences had introduced to the moral and social world.[47]

Principles of epigenesis were appropriated by nineteenth-century social theorists to sustain ideas of inevitable social progress. Spencer based his whole philosophy on epigenetic premises. In his formative essay, "Progress: Its Law and its Cause" (1857), he argued that the law of organic development from homogeneity to heterogeneity governed all the spheres of natural and social science from physiology through to astronomy, anthropology, and philology.[48] Though one should not place too much trust in the thoroughness of Spencer's research, he has located the dominant explanatory strategy of the age. The sciences of the period did employ similar principles of historical explanation; in accordance with the principles of embryological theory, each part was to be considered in relation to the evolving whole.

The connection between embryology and anthropology is quite evident; the idea that "ontogeny recapitulates phylogeny" became one of the dominant assumptions guiding studies of man's history through successive civilisations. A similar structure of explanation can also be traced, though less directly, in geology. In "The Progress of the Intellect," George Eliot uses a geological analogy to explain her idea of the laws of uniform development that govern human action. She observes that "A correct generalization gives significance to the smallest detail, just as the great inductions of geology demonstrate in every pebble the working of laws by which the earth has become adapted for the habitation of man."[49] Examination of a pebble yields an understanding of the history of the stratum of which it forms a part. The geological theory to which George Eliot is undoubtedly referring is the uniformitarianism propounded by Sir Charles Lyell in *Principles of Geology* (1830–3), which was, as the book's sub-title succinctly states, "An attempt to explain the former changes of the earth's surface by reference to causes now in operation." Uniformitarian theory undermined ideas of natural fixity and theories of catastrophism, which had sought to reconcile evidence of the earth's changes with ideas of an unchanging natural order. As in theories of epigenesis, change was conceived as an ordered process.

Throughout her essays, letters, and notebooks for her novels, George Eliot draws on her wide-ranging knowledge of such diverse fields as geology, physics, astronomy, and philology to sustain social arguments.[50] Like the scientists and social philosophers of the period, she was clearly aware that similar principles of explanation were employed in each field. Social and natural scientists, in fact, drew freely on other disciplines to elucidate their theories. Thus, in *Lectures on the Science of Language*, which George Eliot described as a "great and delightful book,"[51] Max Muller compares philology to the sciences of geology and comparative anatomy. The philologist "must learn to make the best of his fragmentary information, like the comparative anatomist, who frequently learns his lessons from the smallest fragments of fossil bones."[52] In philology, as in comparative anatomy, fragments were to be considered not as isolated parts but as tokens of a complex organisation. Physiologists like Cuvier and Goethe turned from the static analysis of external forms of natural history to morphology, the study of the processes governing physiological structure.[53] Muller similarly claimed to be carrying out a "morphological classification of speech."[54] Cuvier's famous claim that, given the nail of an animal or the feather of a bird, he could reconstruct the whole, served almost as a watch cry for many nineteenth-century disciplines, from the social sciences to philology, palaeontology, and evolutionary biology. The part, it was believed, could reveal the whole, for growth occurred by a process of ordered differentiation of the parts.

Of all these sciences, the one that had the most obvious impact on social thought was evolutionary biology. George Eliot greeted the publication of Darwin's *Origin of Species* as an "epoch." His work was, she believed, "an expression of his thorough adhesion, after long years of study, to the Doctrine of Development."[55] Darwin was the first scientist to demonstrate conclusively that development, not only of the individual organism, but also of the species, occurred according to the operation of uniform law. Though Cuvier had espoused a dynamic conception of organic life, he had still clung to the idea of the fixity of species as the only way of preserving his theory of organic functional interdependence. Darwin, however, employing the theory of natural selection, showed that species development, like that of the organism, occurred through an ordered process of differentiation. In the famous closing paragraph of the *Origin of Species* he observes:

It is interesting to contemplate an entangled bank, clothed with many plants of many kinds, with birds singing on the bushes, with various insects flitting about, and with worms crawling through the damp earth, and to reflect that these elaborately constructed forms, so different from each other, and dependent on each other in so complex a manner, have all been produced by laws acting around us.[56]

The form of each species has been determined by its complex modes of interaction with the other forms of life upon the bank. As in physiology or organic social theory, the form and development of each part is dependent on that of the whole.

The role which Darwin allotted to chance in the process of natural selection has appeared, to many twentieth-century critics, to distinguish his theory from other Victorian conceptions of development. C. C. Gillispie, for instance, has argued that Darwin's theory of history was atomistic; its model was not that of the organism but rather that of the machine.[57] For most of Darwin's immediate contemporaries, however, his theory only seemed to confirm the uniform development of history. Darwin himself argued that the term chance was a "wholly incorrect expression;" though it served "to acknowledge plainly our ignorance of the cause of each particular variation" it did not suggest the breakdown of uniform law.[58] His vision of the unified life of the bank is reinforced in the text by his use of the romantic organicist image of the Tree of Life,[59] though in his notebooks he had considered the image of coral which, because it is constantly being eroded, is less positively associated with growth.[60] His final choice suggests that in presenting his work to a public audience he wished to place it within an organicist perspective.

George Eliot's reception of *Origin of Species* as another illustration of the "Doctrine of Development" is indicative of contemporary response. Few critics fully appreciated the potential implications of the actual mechanism of natural selection; the notion of chance, which threatened conceptions of ordered development, received little attention initially. Those in favour of Darwin's theories simply assimilated them into a pre-established framework of developmental thought. Thus Lewes, for instance, in an extensive review of Darwin's theories, argued that: "The laws of Natural Selection may indeed be said to be only a larger and more philosophic view of the law of Adaptation which Lamarck had imperfectly conceived."[61] The idea of natural selection was, in fact, borrowed by theorists in other disciplines to express ideas of uninterrupted historical development. George Eliot, in an unpublished essay, applied the idea of natural selection to the development of art: "Fortunate irregularities are discoveries in art; they are stages of its development, and go on living according to a natural selection."[62] Max Muller also employed the idea of a natural selection of roots to explain the development of language: "Natural selection," he suggests, "if we could but see it, is invariably rational selection."[63] For many social philosophers, Darwinian theory seemed to reinforce ideas of ordered growth. Thus Dowden believed that man's dignity could only be increased by the extended time scale. "Who would not choose to be a citizen of a nobly-ordered commonwealth rather than to be lord of a petty clan?" he demands. Darwinian theory confirmed for him "the universal presence of law. Endless variety, infinite complexity, yet through all an order."[64]

For George Eliot and her fellow Victorians, the natural and social sciences formed an inter-related network. Thus Buckle, reviewing the science of his own period, observed that "the followers of Bichat are associated in geology with the doctrine of uniformity; in zoology with that of the transmutation of the species; and in astronomy, with the nebular hypothesis."[65] Each of these scientific theories challenged conceptions of a fixed order, offering in their place an historical explanation of development. All demanded a similar stance to the world. This fact was well understood, not only by members of the scientific community, but also by the general public; thus even highly technical scientific disputes aroused enormous interest throughout British society, for they were interpreted in light of their social or religious implications. When George Eliot observes in *Middlemarch* that Lydgate adhered to the theories of Bichat, her statement would recall for her readers the bitter social and religious controversy that raged in England from 1814 to 1825 and was ostensibly based on a physiological dispute between the scientists Abernethy and Lawrence. Fundamentally, the issue was whether life, as Bichat's follower Lawrence argued, was dependent on organisation, or whether, as the vitalist Abernethy believed, it was an actual principle or substance, like electricity. Lawrence, comparing Abernethy's theory of the vital principle to the personifications of myth, went so far as to include in his attack the inspired nature of the whole Old Testament. The social outcry that arose was both religious and political in character; for, in situating life within organisation, rather than viewing it as a separate vitalising principle, Lawrence's theories appeared to challenge social and religious conceptions of established order.[66] Like Darwinian theory, or uniformitarian theories of geology, his system required no external guiding principle.

For the Victorians, then, even apparently abstruse areas of science had both ethical and social implications. Though the discussion of Lydgate's biological theories in *Middlemarch* is the only occasion on which George Eliot raises physiological or scientific theory to the level of an obvious theme in her work, the social and moral issues of all the novels are directly related to contemporary scientific concerns. George Eliot's preoccupation with the individual's relation to the social whole is a projection of the question that recurs throughout the sciences of the period, whether it concerns the relation of a pebble to a geological stratum, a linguistic root to a language, or a nail to a whole organism. Her developing understanding of this problem, however, can be linked even more explicitly to transformations in contemporary scientific theory; for the different theories of physiological organisation being formulated at that time suggested very different models of society and psychology.

Though all organicists challenged eighteenth-century conceptions of individual autonomy, their political sympathies determined whether they emphasised the rigidity of organic structure or the fluidity of process. Thus Carlyle, wishing to preserve a hierarchical society, stressed the inflexibility of the organism, rather than its potentiality for growth and change. Organic harmony could only be preserved, he believed, if each individual fulfilled the function to which he or she were born. Carlyle raged against what he termed the "mutinous serving-maids" who posed as "Distressed Needle-women."[67] Though he espoused a theory of organic historical development, he yet clung to the idea of fixed functions: each individual was defined in terms of a set social role. Theorists who, on the other hand, emphasised ideas of organic process or change, rather than structure, undermined such concepts of fixity, whether of individual or social composition.

George Eliot's notion of organic social order in her first novel, *Adam Bede*, closely resembles that of Carlyle. Ideas of organic harmony are celebrated at the conclusion of the novel, when Arthur and Adam resume their rightful roles of squire and respectful villager. There are, however, many internal contradictions in the novel, and in attempting to resolve these problems, George Eliot moves, in her later works, towards a more dynamic model of the organism which was being developed simultaneously by G. H. Lewes. The intellectual association between George Eliot and Lewes was remarkably strong. Throughout their years together, they shared their reading and studied each other's work. Indeed, George Eliot was so conversant with Lewes' philosophy that, in preparing the final series of *Problems of Life and Mind* for publication after Lewes' death, she substantively rewrote some of the sections on social psychology.[68] Her changing understanding of the social and psychological implications of organicist thought was, in fact, closely related to Lewes' own evolving social and scientific theory.

In a late essay which summarises the philosophy underlying the *Problems of Life and Mind*, Lewes defined his position as that of organicism: "Organicism is distinguishable by its consistent carrying out of the hypothesis that the organic phenomena grouped under the terms Life and Mind are activities not of any single element, in or out of the organism, but activities of the whole organism in correspondence with a physical and social medium."[69] This guiding principle affects his epistemology, psychology, and social theory. Organicism is an approach, he argues, that transcends the traditional oppositions of subject and object, mind and body, spiritualism (or vitalism) and materialism, and the political stances of Toryism and Radicalism. It reconciles the Tory demands for continuity with the radical demands for change "by showing that Progress is the development of Order."[70] The language Lewes employs here is derived from Comte, who argued in his *Positive Philosophy* that "ideas of Order and Progress are, in Social Physics, as rigorously inseparable as the ideas of Organization and Life in Biology; from whence indeed they are, in a scientific view, evidently derived."[71] For both theorists the social and scientific aspects of organic theory were clearly indivisible.

Lewes' philosophical premises are derived from Comte's physiology. In defining life, both social and organic, as a process of interaction between organism and medium, Comte had challenged equally the premises of the vitalists who invoked the idea of an animating principle to explain life, and of the materialists who sought to reduce life to the operation of chemical laws. His theory laid the foundations for Claude Bernard's later definition of life as a process of regulative interaction between an internal and an external milieu, which, it has been argued, marked the beginning of the modern era of biological thought. While vitalists like Abernethy argued that life was a substance like electricity,

Bernard asserted that life, like electricity, was an abstraction: "la vie est le résultat du contact de l'organisme et du milieu; nous ne pouvons pas la comprendre avec l'organisme seul, pas plus qu'avec le milieu seul."[72] Comte employed the same structure of explanation to argue that the idea of individual autonomy was illusory; the individual was an abstraction. As Lewes' definition of organicism suggests, Comte's theory of life undermined, on the physiological level, the traditional opposition between the organism and the environment, and on the social level, the artificial division drawn between the individual and the social medium.

Though in much of his work Lewes was working from the same premises as Comte, he drew more radical social and psychological conclusions. In *The Foundations of a Creed*, he called attention to his disagreement with Comte, who "holds that Humanity develops no attribute, intellectual or moral, which is not also to be found in Animality, whereas I hold that the attributes of Intellect and Conscience are special products of the Social Organism."[73] Lewes shared Comte's conviction that eighteenth-century theories of individualism were founded on a false premise; the individual could only fully be comprehended as part of the social organism. Lewes believed, however, that social determinism extended even to man's emotions, perceptions, and thoughts, for the Social Medium, he argues, is "the collective accumulations of centuries, condensed in knowledge, beliefs, prejudices, institutions, and tendencies."[74] It thus determines "the mode in which succeeding generations will feel and think."[75] This is the "Social Factor in Psychology" which George Eliot, referring to the work of Lewes, pronounced to be "the supremely interesting element in the thinking of our time."[76] The questions it raises render her analysis of the individual's relation to society exceedingly complex. Her works do not simply explore the relationship between an autonomous individual and an external society; social values and conceptions are actually inscribed within the personality itself. The moral dilemmas experienced by Maggie, Romola, and Mrs Transome do not arise solely from a clash between the individual and a constraining society, for social contradictions are internalised by the individual, thus creating division within the self. In working out the moral issues of her later novels, George Eliot attempts to balance her intuitive belief in individual difference with the social implications of Lewes' philosophy.

Lewes' theories of organicism profoundly affected not only George Eliot's social analysis, but also her psychological conceptions. Though

Comte had not been concerned with the psychological implications of his physiological ideas, these implications are central for Lewes. "I do not know," he observes

that any previous writer has rigorously carried out the principles of Organicism to this extent . . . But if the upholders of Organicism have not extended to Mind the principles adopted with respect to Life, the stream of tendency in modern psychological research has, I think, all pointed in this direction.[77]

Lewes was in advance of the stream, however, anticipating in his psychology later nineteenth- and twentieth-century developments. Organic theory, he believed, challenged both the idea of individual autonomy, and the related psychological conception of a unified controlling consciousness. The idea of a Psychical Principle, like the equivalent hypothesis of a Vital Principle, was, he argued, an illusion.[78] In *The Foundations of a Creed*, he observes that the notion of an ultimate unity and simplicity assigned to the Thinking Principle cannot be upheld: "In any positive meaning of the term, that Principle is not an antecedent but a resultant, not an entity but a convergence of manifold activities."[79] His theory of organic interaction undercuts the Cartesian division between mind and body and the identification of the self with conscious thought which that theory sustained. Ideas of a rational controlling ego had to be discarded, for consciousness, as Lewes observes, "is not an agent, but a symptom."[80] "Mind" defined for Lewes not a separate controlling principle but rather the "activities of the whole organism in correspondence with a physical and social medium."[81] This physiological principle gave rise to a theory of the unconscious whose premises can be discerned in George Eliot's novels, from her analysis of Maggie's internal contradictions to her later complex psychological studies of Dorothea and Gwendolen.

Lewes was not alone in formulating a theory of the unconscious. Though the term "unconscious" only came into common parlance in the early 1800s, interest in the topic was rife by mid-century; thus large numbers of popular periodical articles were devoted to the subject, while Hartmann's great synthesising work, the *Philosophy of the Unconscious*, which Lewes read in both 1869 and 1872, sold a staggering 50,000 copies throughout Europe.[82] The rise of theories of the unconscious was directly associated with the emergence of organic social theory. Under the social cosmology of the seventeenth and eighteenth centuries, conceptions of the psyche were defined by analogy with notions of material extension. Thus Locke had argued that "it is altogether as intelligible to say that a body is extended without parts, as that anything thinks without being conscious of it."[83] "Being" was identified with conscious thought: *cogito ergo sum*. This Cartesian dualism was undermined once attention was turned from the measurable surface of nature to its hidden parts; once organic theory challenged the idea that a whole must equal the sum of its parts. There was no uniformity, however, in the theories of the unconscious that emerged. Like social interpretations of the organic idea, psychological theories also varied according to the underlying physiological model employed by each theorist. In Germany, for instance, theories of the unconscious were associated with Romantic vitalist conceptions; Hartmann identified his theory with Hegel's shaping Idea, and Schopenhauer's motivating Will. The psychological theories which primarily influenced George Eliot, however, were those of a distinctly English tradition represented by physiologists such as Carpenter, Maudsley, Spencer, and Lewes. These theorists shared the belief that the principles of physiological unity also applied to the mind. Thus, as E. S. Dallas, summarising their views for his study of the impact of the unconscious on literature, observed, details lost to consciousness were not dormant; they still influenced mental processes for "the mind is an organic whole and lives in every part, even though we know it not."[84] The same interdependence defined both the psychical and physiological organism.

Lewes' fellow English theorists, however, did not carry their concepts of physiological interdependence to the same radical social or psychological conclusions. Although Herbert Spencer, for example, also included the environment in his theory of life, which he defined as "the continuous adjustment of internal relations to external relations," he assumed that the environment was static and unchanging; that progress consisted in man's movement towards greater harmony with his surroundings.[85] He did not allow for a reciprocal process of change. Similarly, though Spencer proposed a theory of unconscious activity, he argued, in line with his main theory of progress, that the development of civilisation could be related to an evolving unity of consciousness. Social progress was marked by an increasing dominance of conscious control.[86]

Spencer's theory was not unique. Theorists of the unconscious in the mid-nineteenth century tended to assume either, in vitalist fashion, that the mind was ultimately controlled by a dominating Will, or, that the unconscious was only a pre-form of rationality. Lewes, however, put forward a theory of unconscious activity that obeyed no such ordering principles. The unconscious, he believed, did not obey the seriation of conscious thought: "Every one of the unconscious processes is operant, changes the general state of the organism, and is capable of at once issuing in a discriminated sensation when the force which balances it is disturbed."[87] Consciousness is always liable to disruption. The mind is not divided into a hierarchy of levels; nor does the unconscious function to organise material for conscious use. The mind does not conform to any schema of rationality. While his fellow theorists emphasised the order and unity of the mind, Lewes stressed the individual's lack of control and the potentiality for conflict and contradiction within the psyche.

George Eliot found in Lewes' work a model of organic life that could encompass her changing assessment of the real foundations of organic unity. Lewes' theory suggested that both social and psychological life might be dominated less by harmony and control than by contradiction and disorder; for functional interdependence does not necessarily imply harmonious union. While Lewes only stated his theoretical assumptions, however, George Eliot explored fully in her novels their social and psychological implications. Thus, the social analysis of a conflict-ridden, moribund English society in *Daniel Deronda* is inseparable from the psychological study of the internal conflicts that contribute to Gwendolen's psychological make-up. In each of her novels George Eliot investigates the relationship between the moral ideals of organic theory and the actual social and psychological models which physiological theories of the organic could actually sustain.[88]

The implications of organic theory for George Eliot's work, however, are not restricted to the social or psychological realms; they also extend to the sphere of methodology. Whereas the static science of natural history had required only that the scientist be a careful observer, the development of the science of biology ushered in a new methodology. Vitalist theories had insisted that organic life was indivisible, and that experimentation was thus impossible; but Comte and Bernard, in breaking through the traditional split between vitalism and materialism, laid the foundations for a new experimental science. The role of the scientist was not simply to record and observe, but actively to construct experiments, to bring about, as Bernard observed, "the appearance of phenomena which doubtless always occur according to natural laws, but in conditions which nature has often not yet achieved."[89] The scientist not only creates the appearance of these phenomena; he also actively constructs in his mind's eye the potential results. Lewes, extending these premises, argues that the processes of fiction are indispensable to the Experimental Method, for science is "Ideal Construction."[90]

Against the vulgar objection that scientists only believe in what they can see and touch, he rhetorically asserts "the truth" that "Science mounts on the wings of Imagination into regions of the Invisible and Impalpable, peopling these regions with Fictions more remote from fact than the phantasies of the Arabian Nights are from the daily occurrences in Oxford Street."[91] Unlike the fictions of the poet, however, the fictions of the scientific thinker are not wayward caprices but are "constructed in obedience to rigorous canons, and moulded by the pressures of Reality."[92] This description, as George Levine has noted, corresponds closely to the account of Lydgate's scientific imagination in *Middlemarch*; "the delightful labour of the imagination which is not mere arbitrariness, but the exercise of disciplined power."[93] As this quotation suggests, George Eliot, in moving from the static social vision of *Adam Bede* to a more dynamic social model, also turned from the realism of natural history to a narrative practice that was more closely related to the science of Ideal Construction. The mythological elements in *Middlemarch* and the idealism of the Jewish sections of *Daniel Deronda* both stem from this new experimental methodology. Starting with the "make-believe of a beginning," George Eliot takes active responsibility for her new creative role.

George Eliot's relationship to organic theory, then, was as complex and diverse as the status of organic theory itself in nineteenth-century thought; for organicism, as I suggested earlier, should be seen less as a single idea than as a language. Within the confines of one structural framework, it offered multiple possibilities of interpretation. As a general conceptual model, however, it can be associated with the changes that occurred in social and scientific philosophy once the eighteenth-century mechanistic cosmology was displaced. In all fields and from all perspectives, organic theory was linked to an increasing interest in history as a developmental process, and in notions of interaction and interdependence. Organicist premises were associated in social and psychological theory with a decline of belief in individual autonomy and an emerging interest in the phenomena of the unconscious; and, in ethical theory, with the question of the relationship between concepts of individualism and social duty. While George Eliot structured all her fiction in accordance with organicist assumptions, she yet employed diverse scientific interpretations of the organic to support her changing conceptions of social and psychological life. In the following chapters I shall chart the complex history of her involvement with organicism.

CHAPTER 2

Adam Bede:
Natural history as social vision

Adam Bede appears at first sight a classic text of organicism. Adam, found carving a heraldic shield in the opening scene, welcomes his master home at the close. The potential threat to social order posed by the individualism of Hetty, Arthur, and Dinah has been overcome. The precise chronological dating of the novel, which stretches from the "eighteenth of June . . . 1799" to "near the end of June, in 1807," appears to signal this space of time as a segment of organic development. Yet the attention to historical detail within the novel is undercut by the eternalising nature of descriptions. Our eyes are drawn at the close to the solidity of objects, to the light falling on the cottage "much as it did . . . on that June evening nine years ago." The novel seems to describe less a process of development than the restoration of a static order.

Within the ideal organic model of history the variables of change and continuity, individuation and social integration, are balanced and reconciled. The perfect harmony of the ending of *Adam Bede* appears to suggest, however, that continuity has triumphed over change, stasis over process, and natural history over biology. The questions this ending raises concerning the relationship between George Eliot's theory of organic order, and her narrative method in *Adam Bede* can be illuminated through a comparison with her essay "The Natural History of German Life" (July, 1856). The essay, published 15 months before George Eliot commenced writing *Adam Bede*, was ostensibly a review of Riehl's *Naturgeschichte des Volks*. It became, however, a programmatic statement for her theory of fiction in that novel. Although *Adam Bede* is, obviously, not simply a literal transcription of the review's methodological premises, there are fundamental similarities between the two works. Details of peasant life from the essay recur in the novel, and in both works George Eliot confronts the essential issues raised by organic theory in nineteenth-century thought.

The fact that George Eliot endorsed Riehl's choice of the term "natural history" is in some ways rather curious, for the expression stems from a practice which had been superseded by biology, and which had originally been *ahistorical*. Natural historians, concerned only with the details of external form, drew no distinctions between the study of animate or inanimate matter. "Natural history," therefore, implied neither the study of actual life processes nor an investigation of evolutionary history. Yet in "The Natural History of German Life," George Eliot employs the term to describe Riehl's theories of social evolution, his conception of society as "incarnate history." This usage is coupled, however, with a more customary one: natural history as the precise description of external form receives equal stress and attention. The two meanings are elided by play upon the word "history"; but, since the latter meaning is radically ahistorical, a source of fundamental ambiguity is thus introduced. I intend to trace the narrative effects of this ambiguity in *Adam Bede*; to analyse whether a true synthesis is achieved between the two meanings of natural history, or whether history, as the study of change, is subordinated to the classificatory schema of natural history. The issue is one that, in light of the arguments in the preceding chapter concerning the relationship between natural history and biology, clearly holds implications for all narrative levels of the novel, from the development of plot, or history, and the narrator's stance, to the conception of society and the psychological subject.

The ambiguity of George Eliot's conception of natural history stems, in part, from her adherence, at crucial stages in her argument, to an image of historical change which corresponds closely to what A. O. Lovejoy has termed the "temporalized chain of being." In the eighteenth century, Lovejoy argues, the static concept of the chain of being was perceived as inadequate since it could not account for progress. It was therefore transposed into a temporal dimension and it "came to be conceived by some not as the inventory but as the program of nature."[1] History is only nominally incorporated into such a theory, however, for time does not play a constitutive role. Change is neither disruptive nor unforeseen. Time is incorporated into the inventory only to defuse the challenge history offers to such theories of a given order. The historian of science, Canguilhem, has reached similar conclusions concerning the relationship between theories of embryonic preformation and concepts of history:

Tenir la génération pour un simple développement (evolutio), c'est identifier génération et agrandissement, ou déploiement selon les trois dimensions de l'espace. C'est réduire la formation apparente à l'exhibition progressive d'une préformation. Les moments ou les phases d'une évolution constituent sans doute une succession, une série chronologique ordonnée, mais le temps n'existe ici que par et pour l'observateur.[2]

Time becomes another dimension of space: temporal extension does not permit change. Though nominally historical theories, the tem-polarised chain of being and the theory of preformation in natural science are fundamentally static, classificatory schema. They illustrate the possibility of extending natural history into temporality without altering its intrinsically rigid structure. Time, as Canguilhem observes, is a construct of the observer; a response to the recognition of chrono-logical succession. Thus for the reader of *Adam Bede*, the idea of temporal progression suggested by the experience of narrative con-tinuity is actually at variance with the relatively static picture of life conveyed.

In George Eliot's essay there is evident contradiction between the two forms of natural history. At one stage she appears to adopt the Comtean theory of organic social development:

What has grown up historically can only die out historically, by the gradual operation of necessary laws. The external conditions which society has inherited from the past are but the manifestation of inherited internal conditions in the human beings who compose it; the internal conditions and the external are related to each other as the organism and its medium, and development can take place only by the gradual consen-taneous development of both.[3]

In accordance with the theories of Comte, George Eliot suggests that individual and social development occurs through a process of dynamic interaction between organism and medium.[4] Neither the individual nor the surrounding social medium is a fixed quantity; both evolve through a continuous process of mutual change. George Eliot does not follow, however, the methodological premises Comte drew from this theory. In a later passage in which she outlines Comte's theory of the hierarchy of sciences she correctly observes that each science, from mathematics through to biology, involves an explanation of a higher order of complexity. She concludes, however, that Social Science has "what may be called its Biology, carrying us on to innumerable special phenomena which outlie the sphere of science, and belong to Natural History" (p. 290). Comte did *not* argue that the phenomena of biology outlie the sphere of science, and thus were not susceptible to explanation by law but, rather, that they obeyed laws of a higher complexity. George Eliot wrongly transforms Comte's theory into a justification of em-piricism. Following her illegitimate equation of Natural History and

Biology, she concludes that "a wise social policy must be based not simply on abstract social science, but on the Natural History of social bodies" (p. 290). The study of laws or processes, denigrated by the term "abstract," must be supplemented, she suggests, by a "Natural History" which concentrates on "special phenomena," the individual instance in its isolated peculiarity. In place of Comte's dynamic, biological schema, which considers social phenomena in light of the laws that govern the development of the social whole, George Eliot proposes a fundamentally static analysis of individual phenomena. This conception of natural history is clearly at odds with her earlier model of organic development which suggested the impossibility of isolating either the individual or the social medium from the process of reciprocal growth.

George Eliot's commitment to Natural History is reflected in the doctrine of art of both essay and novel, a doctrine which is recognisably based on the theory of realism which she attributed to Ruskin in a review of *Modern Painters*, written a few months before "The Natural History of German Life": [5] "The truth of infinite value that he teaches is *realism* – the doctrine that all truth and beauty are to be attained by a humble and faithful study of nature, and not by substituting vague forms, bred by imagination on the mists of feeling, in place of definite, substantial reality."[6] Eliot's antagonism to this form of imagination, and her insistence on "substantial reality," spring from the same source as her opposition to abstract social science. Though her theory of realism clearly stems from her belief in the moral responsibility of the artist, it commits her to an epistemology which is that of Natural History: a fundamentally static and isolating theory of knowledge. The role of the artist is simply to reflect, or objectively record, an unchanging external realm.

The methodology of natural history which George Eliot espoused gives rise to the empiricist demand that observation be unclouded by theory. Riehl is praised for his inductive method: "He began his investigations with no party prepossessions, and his present views were evolved entirely from his own gradually amassed observations" (p. 286). This naive realism contrasts strongly with the theoretical position of Comte who argues in his *Positive Philosophy* that "no real observation of any kind of phenomena is possible, except in as far as it is first directed, and finally interpreted, by some theory."[7] Riehl's vaunted freedom from party prepossessions would, in Comte's eyes, merely expose him to the dangers of an unguarded empiricism which he equates with the "egotism that belong[s] to our anarchical condition."[8]

Comte's antagonism to empiricism is based on the biological principles from which he drew his social philosophy. In place of the quantitative description of isolated phenomena of natural history, he proposes a relational theory of method founded on the biological concepts of process and interdependence. Observation must be subordinated, he argues, to "the statical and dynamical laws of phenomena. No social fact can have any scientific meaning till it is connected with some other social fact; without which connection it remains a mere anecdote, involving no rational utility."[9] The principles of dynamic interdependence that govern social life also determine the methodology of the scientist. The scientist's function is not simply to amass observations; he must actively intervene to construct a theory that will demonstrate the relationship between the observed "social facts." George Eliot, however, in accordance with the premises of natural history, wishes to minimise her authorial role, to insist that she is only recording a given external order. This methodological assumption affects markedly her representation of society and character in *Adam Bede*, for it leads her to stress the static nature of social order, and to view characters apart from their incorporation within the social organism. The statical and dynamical laws of phenomena were related, for Comte, to the two social ideals of "order" and "progress";[10] George Eliot's realism and confident empiricism are based on a static theory of order that tends to exclude the dimension of change or progress. The social and political implications of this position are manifest in the narrative of *Adam Bede*, where the mode of presentation is indivisible from the vision of a static, hierarchical society.

George Eliot's adherence to the methodological principles of natural history does not relate solely, however, to her political stance; her commitment also reflects the determining moral ideals of her art. In *Adam Bede* she reasserts the methodological assumptions of the essay. The declared aim of the narrator is

to give a faithful account of men and things as they have mirrored themselves in my mind. The mirror is doubtless defective; the outlines will sometimes be disturbed, the reflection faint or confused; but I feel as much bound to tell you as precisely as I can what that reflection is, as if I were in the witness-box narrating my experience on oath.[11]

Though the narrator admits defects in the mirror he still adheres to the theory of simple reflection;[12] Bacon, in laying the foundations for the inductive method, had similarly admitted defects in the mirror of the mind.[13] For George Eliot, however, the theory of reflection is a function of moral commitment. In "The Natural History of German Life,"

where authorial statement is unqualified by the ambiguities of narra-
torial role, George Eliot outlined the moral ideals which underlie the
realism of *Adam Bede*:

Art is the nearest thing to life; it is a mode of amplifying experience and
extending our contact with our fellow-men beyond the bounds of our
personal lot. All the more sacred is the task of the artist when he undertakes to paint the life of the People. Falsification here is far more pernicious
than in the more artificial aspects of life. It is not so very serious that we
should have false ideas about evanescent fashions – about the manners and
conversations of beaux and duchesses; but it *is* serious that our sympathy
with the perennial joys and struggles, the toil, the tragedy, and the humour
in the life of our more heavily-laden fellow-men, should be perverted,
and turned towards a false object instead of the true one (p. 271).

On a superficial reading the theory of art articulated in this passage
seems directly opposed to the practice of natural history: it is the extension of experience, of sympathy, which is proposed, not the neutral
activity of classification. But sympathy is claimed for "the People" – a
generic classification of a species which, like plants, has its own "perennial" life style. Significantly, George Eliot refers to *the* true object; the
singular denomination indicates the unity of the species being examined.
Thus feelings are to be evoked for the "People," conceived as a fixed,
ahistorical category. Sympathy, like classification, fixes its object.

George Eliot's simultaneous commitment to the individual and the
particular, and also to the activity of classification, is in the tradition of
natural history. Thus Buffon had argued that "There are really only
individuals in nature and genera, orders, and classes exist only in our
imagination."[14] To follow nature faithfully, there should be as many
classes as individuals; but in order to study botany, dividing lines should
be discerned, classification imposed. Concentration on phenomena in
their isolated individuality actually leads to natural history, a mode of
classification which necessarily imposes fixity on its subjects. George
Eliot does not adhere to Comte's "biological," relational epistemology;
her theory of realism is based on the premise that the role of the scientist
or novelist is to place within a preconceived framework the phenomena
observed. Both the essay and novel are founded on the belief that if
phenomena are to be shown as part of the "real" they must be demonstrably representative of a particular class.

The practice of generic classification is evident throughout essay and
novel. In "The Natural History of German Life" George Eliot observes
that, "it would be possible to give a sort of topographical statistics of
proper names, and distinguish a district by its rustic names as we do by

its Flora and Fauna" (p. 276). Within the natural history of a Linnean, a district would be characterised, not by the interactive processes of life to be found there, but simply by the occurrence of species – a topographical equivalent of still life. Though chronological history might be incorporated into George Eliot's schema it is subordinated to species identification. Thus the taxonomic practice of maintaining the same name through generations and in collateral branches of the family described in the essay is illustrated in *Adam Bede* by the specimens of Chad's Bess and Timothy's Bess. Such an easy transfer of information between essay and novel clearly indicates their common methodological premises.

Though there are regional differences, George Eliot observes in the essay, "the generic character of the German peasant is everywhere the same" (p. 286). In her examination of German peasant life, the peasants are measured against George Eliot's own conception of the "genuine" specimen: thus she observes that "In their villages they have the air and habits of genuine, sturdy peasants" (p. 275). The comments even extend to the prescriptive: "The genuine peasant is. . ." (p. 279). Judgement is based on a preconceived classificatory framework whose prescriptive nature illustrates the inherent conservatism of natural history, its inability to incorporate historical change or transformation. The narrative of *Adam Bede* exhibits a similar affirmation of taxonomic fixity. Describing the villagers congregating for Dinah's address, the narrator observes: "Villagers never swarm: a whisper is unknown among them, and they seem almost as incapable of an undertone as a cow or a stag. Your true rustic. . ." (Ch. 2, I, p. 24). "Villagers," despite the diversity of life style that term includes, are a generic type like cows or stags, or, as the verb implies, bees. The behaviour pattern of the true rustic can therefore be unequivocally stated. The mind of the villager is also a known quantity, requiring no qualitative assessment. The text is sprinkled with references to "the bucolic mind": "in those days the keenest of bucolic minds. . ." (Ch. 6, I, 116), "The bucolic mind does not readily. . . ." (Ch. 24, I, 401). The first quotation, which refers to the individualised character of Mrs Poyser, emphasises her representative function. Yet, the facetious tone of these remarks is indicative of George Eliot's unease within the relationship she has adopted towards her material. It dramatises a conflict, present throughout *Adam Bede*, between her desire to portray her characters as representative of fixed types, and her awareness that such typology cannot capture the complexity of process and change.

The rural chorus is not the only subject of generic classification. George Eliot is also anxious to portray Adam as a type. The traveller who gazes with the eye of an external observer is introduced within the text to enact the desired response of the reader:

As he reached the foot of the slope, an elderly horseman, with his portmanteau strapped behind him, stopped his horse when Adam had passed him, and turned round to have another long look at the stalwart workman in paper cap, leather breeches, and dark-blue worsted stockings. (Ch. 1, I, 15).

Adam is presented as no more and no less than an admirable specimen of the species "stalwart workman" – a classification which later narrative emphasis on the value of labour is to endorse. George Eliot is concerned that Adam should not be viewed as too distinct or individual to represent a type; the narrator later intervenes, therefore, to admit that Adam is not "an average man":

Yet such men as he are reared here and there in every generation of our peasant artisans – with an inheritance of affections nurtured by a simple family life of common need and common industry, and an inheritance of faculties trained in skilful courageous labour: they make their way upward, rarely as geniuses, most commonly as pains-taking honest men, with the skill and conscience to do well the tasks that lie before them (Ch. 19, I, 320–1).

Though the passage refers to a process of individual growth and progress it is the historical repetition of the process which is emphasised. Upward movement occurs every generation; individual change does not create social transformation, it is an intrinsic part of the process of cyclical repetition. Adam can thus be generalised to "they." The events of his life, like the villagers' habits of speech or standing, can be treated as a typical behaviour pattern conforming to a pre-established taxonomic definition. Adam's progress confirms the static, ahistoric mode of natural history.

George Eliot defines her art in *Adam Bede* in relation to the "truthfulness" of Dutch painting:

I turn, without shrinking, from cloud-borne angels, from prophets, sibyls, and heroic warriors, to an old woman bending over her flower-pot or eating her solitary dinner, while the noonday light, softened perhaps by a screen of leaves, falls on her mob-cap, and just touches the rim of her spinning-wheel, and her stone jug, and all those cheap common things which are the precious necessaries of life to her (Ch. 17, I, 268).

Significantly, George Eliot chooses the static mode of pictorial representation to illustrate the goal of her narrative. Attention is focused not on process, but on external form; the itemising of details clearly conforms to the practice of natural history. In an essay on *Adam Bede*, John Goode points, in a brilliant insight, to the way in which George Eliot employs sunlight to produce an impression of stability:

The comparison to Dutch genre painting is thus more than a plea for humble and rustic life: it really defines the procedure of fixing the core through the arrested moment. Hence the important emphasis on sunlight; E. H. Gombrich has said that Vermeer, through the use of light, gives his animate portrayals the stability of the still life, and George Eliot does the same — she fixes the world she describes through the creation of representative scenes.[15]

Goode draws attention to the persistent tendency in the early parts of the narrative "to resolve the narrative into pictures"; both Adam's workshop and the church service are fixed by sunlight. Yet it is a tendency, I would argue, which is not restricted to the early sections but is indicative of the practice of natural history throughout the whole. Thus the sunlight playing on the cottage in the Epilogue effectively undermines previously constituted impressions of historical process or instability. In addition, sunlight also appropriates its object for the realm of nature, guaranteeing it part of the natural order. Thus the sunlight on the harvest scene in chapter 53 appears to Adam to consecrate his love for Dinah as part of nature's rhythms — a perception which antipates Mr Irwine's final judgement on Adam's marriage: "and what better harvest from that painful seed-time could there be than this?" (Ch. 55, II, 372). The marriage which marks the restoration of communal order is represented, primarly, not as an instance of individual progress but as part of the unchanging rhythms of rural life.

The harvest-supper chapter clearly illustrates the ways in which theories of evolutionary development in *Adam Bede* are yet subordinated to the fixity of natural history. Though the chapter is obviously a celebration of the unchanging community of rural life, it also includes direct references to evolutionary history. The pointed discussion of the drinking song — whether it were the product of "individual genius" or "that consensus of many minds which was a condition of primitive thought, foreign to our modern consciousness" (Ch. 53, II, 350) — is clearly a reference to the theory of social evolution from homogeneity to heterogeneity. Similarly, Adam's dissent from Craig's story of the French musketeer, as distinct from Mr Poyser's "easy credence," marks his ascent along the evolutionary path of individuation and rationality. Yet the dominant mode of the scene is natural history.

George Eliot includes details of peasant life from the essay – the labourer carrying home corn in his pockets, and the argument concerning the rustic smile. It was a "prejudice" of the "artistic mind," George Eliot argued in the essay, to represent the peasant as merry (p. 269). In the novel she observes:

> The bucolic character at Hayslope, you perceive, was not of that entirely genial, merry, broad-grinning sort, apparently observed in most districts visited by artists. The mild radiance of a smile was a rare sight on a field-labourer's face, and there was seldom any gradation between bovine gravity and a laugh (Ch. 53, II, 349).

The narrator, it is implied, is not simply an artist but a natural historian – a reading reinforced by the addition of the adjective "bovine" to the original material.

The commemoration of old Kester during this scene is in accordance with the moral ideals of realism set out in the essay; it is similarly based on the typification of "such men," and the assumption that it portrays a fixed life style:

> I am not ashamed of commemorating old Kester: you and I are indebted to the hard hands of such men – hands that have long ago mingled with the soil they tilled so faithfully, thriftily making the best they could of the earth's fruits, and receiving the smallest share as their own wages (Ch. 53, II, 348).

Kester does not die but mingles with the soil, confirming his position within the cyclical rhythms of nature of which his life style is presumed to be a part. The moral indignation of the passage is defused by the assumption that the situation is fixed and unchanging. Though the anthropologist narrator draws attention to Kester's lineage, and the historical corruption of his name, reference to such linguistic change merely heightens our awareness of Kester's own immunity from history.

The harvest supper, with its celebration of historical stasis and simultaneous recognition of evolutionary progress, represents a conjunction between traditional natural history and a natural history which incorporates a temporal dimension. A similar union had occurred in the essay, where all references to historical development were employed as arguments to support social stasis. Thus the theory of individuation had illustrated the *non*-progressive nature of peasant life for "the cultured man acts more as an individual; the peasant, more as one of a group . . . many thousands of men are as like each other in thoughts and habits as so many sheep or oysters" (p. 274). The attribution of animal status is indicative of George Eliot's desire to stress that peasant life is untouched by evolutionary development. Yet the essay also contains references to the transmutation of species. Of government attempts to transform the conditions of the peasant, George Eliot observes: "He finds himself in a new element before an apparatus for breathing in it is developed in him" (pp. 281–2).

Such an early adherence to a theory of organic adaptation, and transmutation should not surprise us if George Eliot's acquaintance with the works of Spencer is borne in mind. In *The Principles of Psychology* (1855) Spencer had argued that all life had "arisen out of the lowest and simplest beginnings, by steps as gradual as those which evolve a homogeneous microscopic germ into a complex organism . . . Save for those who still adhere to the Hebrew myth, or to the doctrine of special creations derived from it, there is no alternative but this hypothesis or no hypothesis."[16] The theory of the transmutation of species was accepted and proclaimed before Darwin. George Eliot's acceptance of this theory is of less significance, however, than the purpose for which she employed it: to reinforce social conservatism. The theory of constant historical transformation is turned upon itself to support social stasis.

References to physiology or the social organism in the essay all occur in the context of arguments against social change. Government measures are criticised because they do not endeavour "to promote to the utmost the healthy life of the Commune, as an organism the conditions of which are bound up with the historical characteristics of the peasant" (p. 282). History becomes the court of appeal against change. Thus society is *"incarnate history"* (the incarnation, one feels, effectively opposes history as process) and "any attempt to disengage it from its historical elements must . . . be simply destructive of social vitality" (p. 287). The analogy is drawn from vitalist biology; the idea that death would result from the slightest alteration of an organism's condition supplied a potent image for conservative social theory. Natural history might aptly be described as "naturalising history": it supplies a "natural" justification of past events and the *status quo*. Its linguistic similarity to "natural theology" is significant: both systems seek to describe the world in terms of a reigning order.

The theory of social growth which George Eliot proposes is one that stresses rootedness in the past, not the process of change: "The nature of European men has its roots intertwined with the past, and can only be developed by allowing those roots to remain undisturbed while the process of development is going on, until that perfect ripeness of the seed which carries with it a life independent of the root" (p. 288). History is seen as a teleological process which does not require the actions of men; passivity is clearly exhorted. The idea of rootedness is also central to *Adam Bede*. Martin Poyser, articulating the dominant values of the novel, was "loath to leave th' old place, and the parish where I was bred and born, and father afore me. We should leave our roots behind us, I doubt, and niver thrive again" (Ch. 32, II, 91). Hetty, by contrast, was like "some plants that have hardly any roots: you may tear them from their native nook of rock or wall, and just lay them over your ornamental flowerpot, and they blossom none the worse" (Ch. 15, I, 230). Rootedness takes on an intrinsic ethical value. The passivity with which it is associated in social philosophy, however, seems to consort strangely with the more aggressive theories of individual development neatly summarised by the maxim of Franklin which Adam adopts as his biblical text: "God helps them as helps theirsens" (Ch. 4, I, 65).[17] This apparent conflict can be resolved by reference to Spencer's theories of organicism.

Spencer's conception of the social organism, unlike that of Comte, was founded on the principles of *laissez-faire* economics. The law of equal freedom found its correlate in the belief that duty lay in the exercise of one's faculties – a theory to which one can trace Adam's belief in the dignity and divinity of labour. Individual liberty in Spencer's theory was circumscribed, however, by the laws of economics. Like the conservative French theologians, de Maistre and de Bonald, he believed that the social organism functioned according to natural principles which men should not disturb, only the moving principle for the theologians was God, whilst for Spencer it was the laws of the market economy. Spencer could thus argue for the preservation of poverty rather than government interference; the "harsh fatalities" of suffering were "full of the highest beneficence" since they would lead, by elimination, "to a form of being capable of a happiness undiminished by these drawbacks."[18] Government interference he characterises as a "dead mechanism," one which prevents vital growth. George Eliot similarly speaks of the "evils resulting from a bureaucratic system which governs by an undiscriminating, dead mechanism" (p. 289). Both writers employ the same assumptions concerning natural ripeness. State educationalists, Spencer argues, are like children trying to pull a flower open to make it bloom; "Somewhat like this childish impatience is the feeling exhibited by not a few state-educationists. Both they and their type show a lack of faith in natural forces."[19] George Eliot similarly criticises "the false system of enlightening the peasant" adopted by the bureaucratic government which was designed to appeal "to a logical understanding which is not yet developed in him" (p. 282). In *Adam Bede* it is solely Adam who has reached the evolutionary fitness, or ripeness, for education. Of the other pupils George Eliot observes: "It was almost as if three rough animals were making humble efforts to learn how they might become human" (Ch. 21, I, 353). Significantly they are learning how to write "The corn is ripe" – their difficulty indicates the inapplicability of the phrase to their own mental development.

Spencer's theories of organic growth were founded on ideas both of necessary passivity in relation to the development of the social organism and of economic individualism. Individuation in *Adam Bede* is also primarily economic. The sole form of differentiation permitted is that of Adam's economic progress from workman to owner, a mode of transformation which merely sustains the unchanging structure of Hayslope society. Of the other individualists, Hetty is exorcised from the community, Dinah transformed into a village matron, and Arthur banished until he can truly resume his patriarchal role. Adam, who appears the sole character launched on an evolutionary path is also the figure who holds most firmly to traditional values and a static vision of the social structure. First characterised as "an uncommon favourite wi' the gentry" (Ch. 2, I, 21), it is he who demands that Arthur evolve to the perfect form of squire. He was, the narrator observes, not "a philosopher, or a proletaire with democratic ideas, but simply a stout-limbed clever carpenter with a large fund of reverence in his nature, which inclined him to admit all established claims unless he saw very clear grounds for questioning them" (Ch. 16, I, 245). The opposition between "clever carpenter" and "proletaire," who possesses no specific skills but only ideas, serves to identify Adam's respect for rank with his skill at work.

The structure of *Adam Bede* seems to confirm the belief held by both Spencer and Riehl that, as Riehl expresses it, with the division of labour "the principle of differentiation and the principle of unity are identical" (p. 296). Riehl's social stance led him to regard communistic theories as "the despair of the individual in his own manhood, reduced to a system" (p. 299), thus equating manhood with the possession of property. Adam's growth into true manhood is described both by his development of greater tenderness and his progression from foreman to owner of Burge's timber yard. Revealingly, Adam's vision of his own connection with the yard is cast in terms of images of individual work and natural, social, and economic growth:

Adam saw here an opening into a broadening path of prosperous work, such as he had thought of with ambitious longing ever since he was a lad: he might come to build a bridge, or a town-hall, or a factory, for he had always said to himself that Jonathan Burge's building business was like an acorn, which might be the mother of a great tree (Ch. 33, II, 100).

The economic differentiation of the individual creates the natural growth of the social seed.

Though the social organicism of *Adam Bede* is founded on the economic individualism of Spencer this is not, as was demonstrated in the preceding chapter, the only possible model. Comte rejected the associationist view of the organism, and the correlated social conception which formed the foundation of Spencer's sociology – that society was an association of individuals all rationally pursuing their own interests. In his dynamic conception, the social whole was greater than the sum of its parts. For Spencer, however, society was merely an aggregate of component parts, as expressed in his belief that "There is no way of coming at a true theory of society, but by inquiring into the nature of its component individuals."[20] Social unity was created through the interlocking of individual interests. It is possible to trace a correlation between this individualist conception of the social organism and the relatively static picture of society the natural history of *Adam Bede* conveys.

Spencer's theory, like traditional natural history, is founded on a mathesis: in accordance with the principles of mathematical addition, the whole equals the sum of its parts. In *Adam Bede*, Adam's progress towards economic differentiation is constantly presented in terms of a mathematical calculus. Thus Bartle Massey bewails Adam's unfortunate involvement with Hetty. Adam was his only scholar who "ever had the will or the head piece for mathematics. If he hadn't had so much hard work to do, poor fellow, he might have gone into the higher branches" (Ch. 40, II, 195). Adam's social progress is synonymous with his power of mathematical addition. It is upon this power that he bases his judgements on society, judgements rarely qualified by the narrator. Adam's moral strength and correctness are shown as the product of his mathematical reasoning. At the age of 18 he had run away with his "mensuration book in his pocket" but had returned since "It 'ud make a poor balance when my doings are cast up at the last, if my poor old mother stood o' the wrong side" (Ch. 4, I, 69). Even his religion is founded on a mathematical basis. Adam's powers of addition enable him, indirectly, to offer Arthur the only sound moral warning that he receives: "I've seen pretty clear, ever since I could cast up a sum, as you can never do what's wrong without breeding sin and trouble more than you can ever see. It's like a bit o' bad workmanship – you never see th' end o' the mischief it'll do" (Ch. 16, I, 250). It is Adam's solid grounding in the concrete reality of his work, a practical application of the principles of mathematics, which lends such decisive correctness to his moral judgements. He is not like Mr Ryde, whom he describes to the narrator in his old age as "ignorant as a woman" of "math'matics and the natur o' things" (Ch. 17, I, 273). Mr Ryde's religion had been like a mathematics learnt at the fireside, but never put into practice.

Whilst the concrete practice of carpentry guarantees the validity of Adam's mathematical, moral judgements it also reinforces a static vision of the world. As in natural history, the world is viewed as an aggregate of distinct parts which can be subject to quantitative addition; their sum, it is assumed, will never change. Thus Adam's deliberative judgement following his father's death:

"There's nothing but what's bearable as long as a man can work," he said to himself: "the natur o' things doesn't change, though it seems as if one's own life was nothing but change. The square o' four is sixteen, and you must lengthen your lever in proportion to your weight, is as true when a man's miserable as when he's happy; and the best o' working is, it gives you a grip hold o' things outside your own lot" (Ch. 11, I, 171).

The inner flux of experience is measured against an unchanging external state. Work is not seen as a means of transforming the external environment, but solely as an activity which can place one in contact with an unchanging external world. The model does not allow for the reciprocity of interaction between organism and medium. Change is merely a quality of subjective experience, for the square of four will always equal sixteen.

Adam's progress is set against the unchanging "natur o' things." His belief in the value of labour does not alter. At Arthur's birthday celebration Adam affirms allegiance both to the social hierarchy and to man's duty to work. He accepted his new employment, he states, at Captain Donnithorne's desire:

I'd wish for no better lot than to work under him, and to know that while I was getting my own bread I was taking care of his int'rests. For I believe he's one o' those gentlemen as wishes to do the right thing, and to leave the world a bit better than he found it, which its my belief every man may do, whether he's gentle or simple, whether he sets a good bit o' work going and finds the money, or whether he does the work with his own hands" (Ch. 24, I, 406).

Despite Hetty's tragedy Adam expresses the same beliefs when re-accepting the management of the woods: "I'll stay, sir: I'll do the best I can. It's all I've got to think of now – to do my work well, and make the world a bit better place for them as can enjoy it" (Ch. 48, II, 277). Support for the hierarchical class system is no longer explicit, but is implicit in the repetition of sentiments. On finding Arthur and Hetty together in the woods it had seemed to Adam "as if I'd been measuring my work from a false line, and had got it all to measure over again" (Ch. 29, II, 42–3). But, he neither takes his measurements from a new line, nor questions whether it is actually possible to measure the world from one fixed base line. Mathematical reasoning lends a rigidity to his social judgements; he cannot accept the dissolution of traditional social categories, of the fixed social hierarchy. Thus the Epilogue finds Adam rejoicing that Arthur had smiled at him, just as he had when he was a lad – before, that is, his actions had cast doubt on his fitness for the role of social patriarch. Adam's progress from foreman to master is thus ratified: guaranteed part of the eternal "natur o' things." The view of society as the fixed sum of determinate quantities seems to remain unchallenged.

There is one moment in the novel when fixed social measurement ceases to rule – when Adam and Arthur fight man to man in the woods. Physical contact breaks down the social divisions. Paradoxically, however, physical imagery of the body also ultimately naturalises the social hierarchy. Adam's view of work was that it gave one "a grip hold o' things outside your own lot." Physical control, the grip of the hand around a piece of wood, is taken as synonymous with social control. Work is abstracted out of the social process, where Arthur supplies the capital and Adam the labour. The social hierarchy is both obscured and naturalised by the physical imagery which seems to guarantee both individual autonomy and the transformative power of individual action. Adam's plans for ingenious cupboards which make a virtue out of cramped conditions would stand, perhaps, as a better image of the social grip his work permitted him. The potentiality of power conveyed through the sense of muscular strength is in fact illusory.

Adam's physical strength, and the harmonious coordination of his faculties, appear to guarantee social coordination and harmony. His problems are seen as purely individual in origin, to be overcome by physical exertion. Adam hoped to "subdue sadness by his strong will and strong arm" (Ch. 11, I, 171). The correlation proposed between physical power and psychical fulfilment is based on principles of physiological psychology formulated by Spencer and Lewes. Both thinkers believed that all activities of the mind could be traced to physiological functions. Thus Spencer, in *The Principles of Psychology* (1855)[21] and Lewes in *The Physiology of Common Life* (which he was working on whilst George Eliot was writing *Adam Bede*) both argue for the identity of physiological and psychological force. They are but two aspects of the same phenomenon; a physiological force within the organism may discharge itself either in sensation, action or thought.[22] The following passage, in which the narrator explicitly supports Adam's association of physical and mental force, is clearly founded on the arguments of physiological psychology:

The sound of tools to a clever workman who loves his work is like the tentative sounds of the orchestra to the violinist who has to bear his part in the overture: the strong fibres begin their accustomed thrill, and what was a moment before joy, vexation, or ambition, begins its change into energy. All passion becomes strength when it has an outlet from the narrow limits of our personal lot in the labour of our right arm, the cunning of our right hand, or the still, creative activity of our thought (Ch. 19, I, 318).

The orchestral imagery (later employed in connection with Caleb Garth)[23] proposes a model of social harmony which is sustained by images of physiological coherence. In accordance with the theories of Spencer and Lewes, George Eliot suggests that all sensations, whether physical or mental, share the same physiological basis in the fibres of the mind.[24] These concepts of physiological unity and harmonious transposition are then subtly associated, however, with the idea of unified social integration implied by the musical analogy. By directing his energy outwards Adam will fulfil his part in the social orchestra. Spencer argued in *The Principles of Psychology* that the substratum of all knowledge was the impression of resistance. Perception of resistance "consists in the establishment of a relation of coexistence between the muscular sensation itself and that particular state of consciousness which we call *will*."[25] George Eliot bases the correlation of Adam's strong will, and his strong arm upon the assumption of this coexistence. The muscular basis of will is illegitimately assumed to ensure the physical fulfilment of that will. Thus "all passion becomes strength," where strength carries both physical and moral connotations. Discounting the social sphere of action, George Eliot transforms the physiological strength of a sensation into a moral assessment of psychological force and social effectivity.

The relationship George Eliot assumes here between internal physiology and social action is also drawn from Spencer who argued that the process of civilisation occurs through the increased coordination of correspondences between organism and medium.[26] He concludes:

> we see that the correspondence between the internal changes and the external coexistences and sequences, must become more and more complete. The continuous adjustment of the vital activities to the activities in the environment must become more accurate and exhaustive. The life must become higher and the happiness greater – must do so because the inner relations are determined by the outer relations.[27]

Adam's capacity for directed labour, his ability to coordinate his responses to the environment, illustrates this process of social progress. There appears to be, however, a discrepancy between this theory of evolutionary progress and the vision of a stable harmonious society with which the novel ends. An explanation for this apparent conflict can also be found in the work of Spencer. Though Spencer proclaimed adherence to an interactive model of the social organism, he assumed an unchanging environment: men responded not to their environing social conditions, the product of their own labour, but to the eternal conditions of nature. The social hierarchy and conditions of labour are thus naturalised as eternal truths.

Physiological psychology is also employed within the novel in analysis of Adam's emotional growth and progress. "Let us . . . be thankful," the narrator exclaims, "that our sorrow lives in us as an indestructible force, only changing its form, as forces do, and passing from pain into sympathy" (Ch. 50, II, 302). The principle of the correlation of forces, or the conservation of energy, is invoked to explain how Adam's traumatic experiences can yet be productive of good.[28] Since energy can never be destroyed, but only transformed, pain, George Eliot argues, must eventually lead to sympathy. She describes this process in terms of the growth of new physiological fibres; thus Adam "did not know that the power of loving was all the while gaining new force within him; that the new sensibilities bought by a deep experience were so many new fibres by which it was possible, nay, necessary to him, that his nature should intertwine with another" (Ch. 50, II, 303). Physiology is employed to sustain a theory of progress which might otherwise bear a disturbing resemblance to the moral casuistry so condemned in Arthur. Nowhere is Arthur treated with such scorn as in his plans to make amends to Hetty by future patronage: "*So* good comes out of evil. Such is the beautiful arrangement of things!" (Ch. 29, II, 36). No such beauty exists, George Eliot implies; but the wonderfully symmetrical conclusion seems to point to precisely this arrangement. Physiology is employed to circumvent the paradox of the fortunate fall.[29] The discrepancy between the two perspectives points, however, as I shall argue later, to a powerful internal tension within the novel.

The physiological principles invoked to describe Adam's economic and moral progress actually illustrate the return of Hayslope to a non-progressive state of harmony. If evolution is involved it is, as in the temporalised chain of being, simply evolution to a more perfect type where progress will cease. Temporality becomes another dimension of space. The social situation in the Epilogue is that portrayed in the opening scenes of the novel, only now the potentially disruptive elements are removed. Hetty, with her lack of respect for the traditions of community life, is effectively silenced by death. Arthur, suitably chastened, has learnt to accept the boundaries of his social authority, whilst Dinah has given up preaching. She had offered a challenge, through her preaching, both to traditional sexual divisions, and to the social and "natural" order represented by Mr Irwine who "harmonised extremely well with that peaceful landscape" (Ch. 5, I, 101). It is to the harmony of this peaceful, unchanging landscape that the novel finally returns; to "the mellow evening light . . . falling on the pleasant house with the buff walls and the soft grey thatch, very much as it had when we saw Adam bringing in the keys on that June evening nine years ago" (Epilogue, II, 374). The concluding scene is dominated by the solidity of objects impervious to the passing of time. The sun plays on the house just as it did nine years ago, only now it transfixes Dinah, adding her "more matronly figure" to the natural still life of the scene. Transformed into matron, mother and submissive wife, Dinah's presence affirms the triumph of the unchanging values and life style of the organic community of Hayslope. Her possession of Arthur's watch confirms her acceptance of the "time" of the stable social hierarchy.

It is significant that George Eliot softens, in the novel, details of "natural history" which she drew from the essay. In the essay she records that "the aged father who has given up his property to his children on condition of their maintaining him for the remainder of his life, is very far from meeting with delicate attentions" (p. 280). Martin Poyser, in contrast, "was of so excellent a disposition that he had been kinder and more respectful than ever to his old father since he had made a deed of gift of all his property" (Ch. 14, I, 213). Similarly in the essay, George Eliot discriminates between the idyllic visual appearance, and the coarse laughter, triumphant taunts and drunkenness which actually characterise the haymakers (p. 269). In the novel there is the same distinction between the near and the far impact, but the attribute of coarseness now appears to distinguish the actual quality of sound rather than the cast of mind which lay behind it. The detail is employed to emphasise the socially integrative power of labour: "Men's muscles move better when their souls are making merry music" (Ch. 19, I, 313). Such transformation is indicative of the compositional process of the whole novel. Elements which threaten to disrupt the picture of the perfect continuity, and thus ahistorical nature of rural life, are deliberately suppressed, subordinated to a preconceived ideal model of organic community.

This process of suppression is not, however, complete. Although the symmetrical structure of the plot endorses ideas of social harmony, there are strong countercurrents within the novel which suggest a very different image of society. George Eliot tacitly acknowledged this problem when she remarked in a letter of 1861 that "To my feeling, there is more thought and a profounder veracity in *The Mill* than in *Adam*; but *Adam* is more complete, and better balanced."[30] The balance, or organic structure, of *Adam Bede* is achieved only at a certain cost.[31] Throughout the novel there is a tension between the ordering movement of the plot and the disruptive energies it attempts to contain. Thus Dinah replaces Hetty, completing once more the social circle of Hayslope, but her conversion is hastily sketched. The "balanced" conclusion cannot take account of the social factors which led to the rebellion of either of these two powerful, intricately connected, individualists.

The internal tensions within the novel emerge with greatest clarity in the treatment of Hetty and Arthur's relationship, for their history calls into question the validity of the hierarchical structure found within the traditional organic community. At one stage the narrator intervenes to condemn, with bitter irony, the class system which could support the exploitation and abuse of one individual by another: "and we don't inquire too closely into character in the case of a handsome generous young fellow, who will have property enough to support numerous peccadilloes" (Ch. 12, I, p. 185). The tone and observation are of a piece with the later, much bleaker, vision of *Daniel Deronda*, but they cannot be integrated fully into the rural idyll of Hayslope. George Eliot's divided responses to this organic ideal give rise in the novel to sudden shifts in perspective and narrative tone. Thus she recognises at one stage that Arthur's affair with Hetty is not a departure from, but a *product* of, the hierarchically stratified organic community. Mrs Poyser actually facilitates Arthur's approaches to Hetty: "Indeed, sir, you are very kind to take that notice of her. And I'm sure, whenever you're pleased to dance with her, she'll be proud and thankful, if she stood still all the rest o' th' evening" (Ch. 7, I, 124). Yet this detail serves less to demonstrate how Arthur's conquest is to be founded on the traditions established by generations of such proud and happy subservience, than to illustrate Mrs Poyser's sterling qualities. Her outburst against the squire similarly functions within the narrative to reaffirm, not disrupt, the unity of the community. Mrs. Poyser's "repulse of the old Squire" passes into community folklore; it distinguishes her for Irwine as "one of those untaught wits that help to stock a country with proverbs" (Ch. 33, II, 93). The generic classification defuses the potential challenge of her words. As the narrative stance shifts into natural history, critical perspective is lost.

The portrayal of Hetty displays a similar ambiguity: the initial recognition that Hetty's plight was, in part, a direct consequence of social stratification is later suppressed. At one stage a bitterness in the narrator's tone indicates a clear-sighted awareness of the nature of Hetty's exploitation by both Adam and Arthur. Both men, if they envisaged such a girl in future years, would imagine "himself being virtuously tender to her, because the poor thing is so clingingly fond of him. God made these dear women so – and it is a convenient arrangement in case of sickness" (Ch. 15, I, 229). The final clause exposes the manner in which appeals to a natural or providential order function to sustain a social formation which both contributes to men's actual dominance and self-glorification and condemns women to a subservient role in which they act out men's patronising fantasies. But the bitter irony of this passage is not maintained. Within a paragraph the narrator launches into a condemnation of Hetty for failing to possess these self-same attributes of clinging affection: "Does any sweet or sad memory mingle with this dream of the future – any loving thought of her second parents – of the children she had helped to tend – of any youthful companion, any pet animal, any relic of her own childhood even? Not one" (Ch. 15, I, 230). The values articulated here are those of rootedness and continuity, qualities exemplified by Adam, whose reverence for Arthur and love for Hetty arise from his need to create a sense of solidarity between past and present.[32] Like a shallow-rooted ornamental flower, "Hetty could have cast all her past life behind her, and never cared to be reminded of it again" (Ch. 15, I, 230). Such an easy facility for thriving appears almost an indecent flouting of nature, or rather, of the social ideology which stresses that society evolves by a slow process of growth which must not be disturbed.

In the final analysis, Hetty's tragedy seems to stem less from the inequities of social organisation than from the limitations of her own nature. Her "moral deficiencies" lie in her refusal to recognise the continuity of past and present. She is oriented, indeed, toward future rather than present reality; "as unsympathetic as butterflies sipping nectar" she is "isolated from all appeals by a barrier of dreams" (Ch. 9, I, 148). Hetty, wandering through the Chase, is indifferent to its beauty (Ch. 13, I, 201); Adam, however, is endowed with an unconscious appreciation, "hardly once thinking of it – yet feeling its presence in a certain calm happy awe which mingled itself with his busy working-day thoughts" (Ch. 27, II, 9). In contrast to Adam, whose work places him in harmony with men and nature, Hetty's hopes for the future isolate her both from human and natural contact. The "narcotic" (Ch. 9, I, 146) atmosphere in which she lives bespeaks her alienation both from the world of work and its values, and her submergence in a self-indulgence at odds with the work ethic of the novel. Hetty's indifference to the evening, to Totty, or "the round downy chicks peeping out from under their mother's wing" (Ch. 15, I, 232), prepares us for the final tragedy in which she violates that most ideologically potent symbol of natural life – the sanctity of motherhood.

Hetty's actions and fate are portrayed as the consequence of her internal constitution. The animal epithets applied to her do not simply characterise Arthur's approach, they also reflect the attitude of the narrator. George Eliot employs them to indicate Hetty's moral qualities. Thus Hetty possessed "the luxurious nature of a round, soft-coated pet animal" (Ch. 37, II, 136), whilst her soul was that of a fluttering butterfly (Ch. 13, I, 200). Elaborating on this image, George Eliot later observes that Hetty was "a woman spinning in young ignorance a light web of folly and vain hopes which may one day close round her and press upon her, a rancorous poisoned garment, changing all at once her fluttering, trivial butterfly sensations into a life of deep human anguish" (Ch. 22, I, 377). Though the imagery is drawn from the predatory animal world it does not include Arthur. Hetty is both predator and prey; her enemy, not the squire, but the limitations of her own nature.

Hetty is one of the first of a long series of George Eliot characters who regulate their actions according to chance,[33] ignoring what George Eliot termed in "The Progress of the Intellect" that "inexorable law of consequences," which establishes the foundations for moral conduct and human duty.[34] Unlike Adam, Hetty is not furnished with a rigid mathesis, a measuring line from which to assess all actions. Under the irritation of suffering she "was ready for one of those convulsive, motiveless actions by which wretched men and women leap from a temporary sorrow into a life-long misery" (Ch. 31, II, 76). Hetty's moral deficiency and lack of knowledge are conflated as George Eliot displaces moral judgement into the sphere of science. The doctrine of consequences is articulated in the novel by Mr Irwine: "Consequences are unpitying. Our deeds carry their terrible consequences, quite apart from any fluctuations that went before – consequences that are hardly ever confined to ourselves" (Ch. 16, I, 258). George Eliot, like Dowden, turns to the physical theory of the conservation of energy to support her belief in the moral uniformity of nature.[35] She employs the physical principle that each motion must produce a chain of effects to reinforce ideas of social interdependence, and to suggest, furthermore, that society is a unified *coherent* whole, not the interplay of antagonistic forces The scientific principle of the uniform *operation* of physical law is used to sustain the idea that society is, in itself, a uniform order, governed by unbreakable laws. Duty, the observation of the law of consequences, thus implies acting to preserve the established order, since any action which departed from customary patterns of behaviour would disrupt the accepted "laws" of social interaction. The doctrine of consequences supplies scientific grounding both for a critique of the actions of Hetty and Arthur, and for affirmation of the pre-established social order.

In the treatment of Arthur, George Eliot appears to go beyond the static mode of natural history. The narrator hastens to reassure readers who might be disturbed by Arthur's apparent change. He is:

The same, I assure you, only under different conditions. Our deeds determine us, as much as we determine our deeds; and until we know what has been or will be the peculiar combination of outward with inward facts, which constitutes a man's critical actions, it will be better not to think ourselves wise about his character (Ch. 29, II, 36–7).

A reproof is delivered to the natural historians who would hope to categorise a man as a fixed quantity. He is not a static entity but a process, a product of interaction between the organism and the environment. Yet George Eliot has not hereby accepted the full potentiality of transformative change. Her formulation is a modified version of natural history. Arthur remains the same, develops no new attributes; external conditions merely expose different sides of his character.[36] As Mr Irwine remarks: "A man can never do anything at variance with his own nature. He carries within him the germ of his most exceptional action" (Ch. 16, I, 257). The assumption that all character is contained in "germ" brings George Eliot's argument into close relation with Spencer's theory of social development. Spencer attempts, in *Social Statics*, to distance himself from teleological notions of social development. In the light of his theories, "civilization no longer appears to be a regular unfolding after a specific plan; but seems rather a development of man's latent capabilities under the action of favourable circumstances; which favourable circumstances, mark, were certain some time or other to occur."[37] Like George Eliot, Spencer assumes all future developments are latent, there is no transformation of character. Whilst he rejects an explicit teleology, he cannot reconcile himself to the openness of chance; his moral orientation dictates the addition of the final clause – that favourable circumstances will inevitably occur "at some time or other." Similarly, one feels with George Eliot that the minimum amount of openness sanctioned by the "latency" argument is likewise closed by the implicit moral assumption that favourable circumstances *will* always occur to expose hidden flaws. Natural history has not been fully undermined. Classification is still possible if temporality is included as one of the dimensions.

Adam Bede is not based, however, on an uncritical acceptance of the tenets of natural history. The narrator's careful correction of those readers who thought themselves wise about Arthur's character is expressive of George Eliot's desire to distance herself from natural history. Similar reproofs are repeated throughout the novel. The stranger on horseback is the subject of gentle irony, for presuming that outward form revealed inner being: "Perhaps he was one of those who think that nature has theatrical properties, and, with the considerate view of facilitating art and psychology, 'makes up' her characters, so that there may be no mistake about them" (Ch. 2, I, 30–1). George Eliot rejects the simple correlation drawn by natural historians between outer form and inner being (though, significantly, narrative developments do seem to confirm the stranger's judgement that Dinah was not meant for a preacher). The argument is later explicitly placed in the context of physiological heredity. Mrs Irwine bases her judgement of Arthur's character on his physical resemblance to her family. Her son slyly reminds her that a dog may feature the mother but possess the father's tricks. Mrs Irwine's reply is emphatic, "Nonsense, child! Nature never makes a ferret in the shape of a mastiff. You'll never persuade me that I can't tell what men are by their outsides" (Ch. 5, I, 93). And she is proved emphatically wrong. Nature, George Eliot wishes to indicate, is not so unproblematic. Adam's attempt to read Hetty's character from her face is treated more gently: "Nature has her language, and she is not unveracious; but we don't know all the intricacies of her syntax just yet, and in a hasty reading we may happen to extract the very opposite of her real meaning" (Ch. 15, I, 229). Nature can be read. Physical appearances are letters in an alphabet, the observer must simply avoid too easy a correlation; bear in mind that genetic inheritance means that eyelashes may express the disposition of one's grandmother. Natural history is not entirely rejected; nature's system is simply more complex than was previously suspected.

This degree of openness and flexibility is itself overborne, however, by other elements within the narrative. Great emphasis is placed upon the hereditary resemblance between Adam and his mother, Adam and Seth, Dinah and her two aunts, and Hetty and her father. The narrator does, at one stage, protest against placing too great a reliance on physical resemblance, for its power is often counteracted by an even greater mental division. "Family likeness," he observes, "has often a deep sadness in it. Nature, that great tragic dramatist, knits us together by bone and muscle, and divides us by the subtler web of our brains" (Ch. 4, I, 55). But narrative developments override such subtlety. Physical resemblance offers too potent an image of social continuity to be cast into an ambiguous light. The dominating values of organicism ensure that the Epilogue gives no place to the earlier recognition that Hetty's tragedy is the product of the hierarchical organic community. In similar fashion, the argument that physical resemblance provides no firm basis for a classification of generic "type" is likewise ignored in the novel's conclusion. In the opening of the final section of the novel Dinah's resemblance to her aunt is stressed, both to emphasise the lack of historical change, and to demonstrate Dinah's movement towards her natural type. The scene is placed 18 months after Adam and Arthur's parting when sunshine is once again playing on Hall Farm: "Mrs. Poyser too has on a black gown, which seems to heighten the family likeness between her and Dinah. In other respects there is little outward change now discernible in our old friends, or in the pleasant house-place, bright with polished oak and pewter" (Ch. 49, II, 282). Hetty's tragedy has had little lasting effect in a world where bright polished oak and pewter constantly reflect the solid, eternal "natur o' things." The only change is that Dinah's resemblance to her aunt is more marked. Soon the realities of the harsh life of Stonyshire will be erased, once Dinah reverts to her "natural" form of matron and wife. The reference to family resemblance prepares the reader for this transformation which will finally remove the last discordant element from the life of Hayslope. Physical resemblance is not misleading; it possesses a veracity which Dinah only finally acknowledges.

The idyllic, atemporal picture of the Epilogue similarly plays upon the guarantee of an unchanging world offered by physical resemblance. The two children are miniature copies of Adam and Dinah. The girl possesses both Dinah's physical characteristics and her passive, trusting nature while the boy features the black hair, and eyes, and forceful character of his father. Together they are visible pledges that the types of Adam and Dinah will neither be transformed nor die out. Like the unchanged cottage in the evening light, they illustrate the eternal realities of rural life and the ahistorical nature of the narrative of *Adam Bede*.

The events of *Adam Bede*, to follow Canguilhem's formulation, constitute a succession, a chronologically ordered series. The narrator, that "judicious historian" (Ch. 12, I, 188) carefully demarcates the temporal space the events occupy – from "the eighteenth of June, in the year of our Lord 1799" to "near the end of June, in 1807," thus reaffirming the impression of temporal progression created by the linear narrative sequence. But the sense of progression is, as Canguilhem argues, a creation of the external observer. The novel opens and closes in the same physical setting, in the same month of the year. If time as an active agent exists within the novel it is less progressive than cyclical; it functions solely to sustain a preordained order.

In *Adam Bede*, as in her essay "The Natural History of German Life," George Eliot engages with the fundamental issues of organicism, attempting to reconcile the four variables of change and continuity, individuation and social integration. But the perfect harmony of the conclusion displays the dominance of continuity over change, of integration over individuation, of natural history over biology. Though the creed of realism to which George Eliot adheres in *Adam Bede* reflects her theory of the moral functions of art, it commits her to a fundamentally static view of society. Her desire to demonstrate that her characters are representative specimens of the "real" restricts her art. Like the natural historian she can only detail the external order of nature, she cannot capture processes of change. Her view of society is less the dynamic historical conception of Comte which she outlines in the essay, than the fundamentally associationist model of Spencer, founded, like the science of natural history, on a mathesis.

Adam Bede does not offer, however, an unambiguous endorsement of the ideal of an unchanging hierarchical community. Although the conclusion seems to reinforce notions of organic social harmony, the internal tensions and contradictions throughout the novel suggest a more complex social vision. They reveal the disquiet George Eliot herself later voiced in her statement that the balance of *Adam Bede* was achieved at the expense of veracity. Her following novel, *The Mill on the Floss*, shows her breaking away from the narrative stance of natural history, and the social vision it implied. Her theory of organicism moves closer to the dynamic conception of Comte and Lewes, than to the theory of Spencer, while her concern with social harmony is replaced by an active exploration of the possibilities of social and psychological contradiction.

CHAPTER 3

The Mill on the Floss:
The shadowy armies of the unconscious

A wide plain, where the broadening Floss hurries on between its green banks to the sea, and the loving tide, rushing to meet it, checks its passage with an impetuous embrace.[1]

The opening passage of *The Mill on the Floss* disturbs temporal perspective. Unlike *Adam Bede,* the scene is not placed in a precise historical period. Nor is there an external objective observer to create an impression of pictorial fixity. If in *Adam Bede* the static mode of representation placed the scene outside temporal process, it is, in *The Mill on the Floss,* the very immersion in temporality which disrupts continuity. The syntactic structure of the opening sentence, which does not obey the customary division of subject, verb and object, subverts the normal linear progression of narrative. The reader is confronted not with the solidity of objects transfixed by adjectival description but with motion: "broadening," "hurries," "loving," "rushing," "checks," "impetuous embrace." The narrative, placed not in the imperfect but in the present tense, defies temporal ordering. Entry into the novel again differs from *Adam Bede* for it occurs not through the detached observations of the natural historian but through memory and dream. In the opening scene of her earlier tale, "The Sad Fortunes of the Reverend Amos Barton," George Eliot had employed memory to establish a sense of continuity and temporal perspective between the past of the novel and the present of the reader.[2] Memory in this novel, however, dissolves present into past. In "Amos Barton" memory functioned as a guarantee of ontological realism – that Shepperton Church really did exist. But in *The Mill on the Floss* Dorlcote Mill is introduced entirely through dream, through the subjective consciousness of the narrator.

Marcel Proust expressed his admiration for *The Mill on the Floss* and, as L. A. Bisson has noted, there is a marked similarity between the opening of *The Mill* and Proust's *Swann.* In both cases, memory gives the *matière première* of the novel and its technique. Furthermore, the form of memory employed in each work is not that of conscious selection but involuntary:

In George Eliot as in Proust, the physical sensation (the numbness of the down-pressed arms), with its at first imperfectly recognised stimulus (the arm of the chair = the parapet of the bridge), releases in a living and present flux an uncontrollable train of images from the experience of long ago.[3]

The qualities which distinguish the opening of *The Mill* from "Amos Barton" are precisely the unbidden and uncontrollable nature of the images which arise not from conscious social time but from the atemporal unconscious. Stress placed on the physical sensations of the narrator emphasises further the fact that the memories portrayed are not those of an objective world but derive purely from the subjective, unconscious realm of the narrator's mind.

The link with Proust is significant for it indicates the extent to which Eliot has gone beyond the empiricist theory of realism which sustained the natural history of *Adam Bede*. The social vision of *The Mill* is more complex than that of the earlier novel and the effects of this complexity can be traced in both the narrative structure and psychological theory of the novel. Though the central moral issues remain the same, the question of organic unity and continuity is peculiarly fraught in *The Mill*, for the society portrayed does not conform to the ideal harmony of life in *Adam Bede*: the world of the Tullivers and Dodsons is shown in all its "oppressive narrowness." Maggie, struggling for individual fulfilment against the constrictions imposed by the evolving social organism of which she forms a part, appears to be struggling against a society whose only virtue is that of continuity.

The central moral issue of the novel is expressed in Maggie's question to Stephen: "If the past is not to bind us, where can duty lie? We should have no law but the inclination of the moment" (Bk VI, Ch. 14, II, 329). To ignore the past, to act only according to the promptings of egoism, would be to disrupt both organic social harmony and historical continuity. The question assumes, however, a unified history and a unified self: that the past is a linear continuum and the self a united and coherent whole. Both these premises are questioned in *The Mill*. The novel portrays not only a society divided by conflict, but also an individual similarly torn. The analysis of the disjunction between the promptings of Maggie's unconscious and her social conscience gives rise to a multi-levelled theory of history which is also reflected in the narrative structure of the novel.

The Mill on the Floss possesses two beginnings and two endings: it proposes two models of history. It opens, first, with the narrator's Proust-like submergence into the world of unconscious memory, and, second, with the start of the linear, conscious narration of the story. This division is enacted in the conclusion of the novel. The first ending is the "one supreme moment" when Maggie and Tom, in their final embrace, enter the timeless world of memory and the unconscious, and recapture forever their childhood. The second is contained in the narrator's comment: "Nature repairs her ravages – but not all."

In the first conclusion Maggie and Tom finally achieve organic union: they escape from the conflict associated with the linear progress of social time through submergence in the atemporal realm of unconscious memory. Yet their union is possible only at the cost of a complete disruption of historical continuity. The concluding flood does not conform to theories of organic evolution but rather to the historical schema of catastrophism, a geological theory discredited by the 1860s which postulated a series of world disasters and successive creations in order to perpetuate the theory of the fixity of species in the face of evidence for their extinction. The second ending is in accordance with uniformitarian principles of gradual development. Yet even here the image of history is not purely that of cumulative growth; development, for George Eliot, also entails loss.

The divided narrative structure of *The Mill* must be seen in the light of George Eliot's attempts to resolve the contradictions of organicism. Science did not simply provide the moral framework of the novel; close analysis of the text reveals that contemporary scientific theories of development, particularly those of Darwin and Lewes, engaged George Eliot's interest as she sought to find a historical schema which could express her social vision. *The Mill on the Floss* was the first novel George Eliot produced after the publication of *Origin of Species*, and it is tempting to try to account for the distance between *Adam Bede* and *The Mill* in terms of the differences between natural history and evolutionary biology. Yet to do so would be to ignore the more complex attitude to time and fictional construction which the analogy with Proust has demonstrated. Uniformitarian ideas of evolutionary development could also not account for the catastrophic structure of the plot. Even if, like Gillispie, one interprets the Darwinian model of history as one which disrupts the unity of nature, "fragmenting it into discrete events connected by chance and circumstance,"[4] the theory of history which underlies the novel would remain inexplicable. The Darwinian echoes in *The Mill*, and references in George Eliot's own personal writings, reinforce the idea of gradual change (though not necessarily progress) within a unified continuum.

To understand fully the transformations which occur in George Eliot's fiction, and the apparent contradictions between the two models of history in *The Mill*, it will be helpful to consider them in the light of the distinctions Edward Said has drawn between the classic realist text and the modernist text. For Said, the classic realist text is dynastic in form, concerned with ideas of genesis and familial continuity. He sees it as mimetic, bound to sources and origins. The modernist text, however, is concerned less with continuity and origins than with discontinuity and construction. The novel is no longer seen as mimetic of a pre-existent reality: "instead of a source we have the intentional beginning, instead of a story a construction."[5]

In one sense, *The Mill on the Floss* clearly belongs to the first schema. The text displays the continuity of life; Maggie's development is related both to her originating family and to the larger life of St Ogg's. The narrator's comment that she possesses several manuscript versions of the legend of St Ogg's reinforces the idea that George Eliot wishes to make her text mimetic, bound to pre-existent sources. But this model cannot account for the role of dream and the unconscious in the novel: the distinction between the opening dream and the beginning of linear conscious narration, and the final conflict between the catastrophic ending of the plot, where Maggie's submergence into the timeless world of the unconscious disrupts narrative continuity, and the developmental perspective of the narrator's concluding comments. Maggie's history re-enacts the escape from linear time which the narrator initially achieves through dream. The notion of a dream narrative challenges ideas of mimesis, and draws attention to the fictional, constructed nature of the text. Furthermore, dream in *The Mill* establishes the idea of plural, conflicting forms of time, thus distancing the narrative again from the dynastic form of the classic realist text which was founded on a linear concept of time and a theory of a unified psychological subject.

The idea of the unconscious put forward by Freud forms, for Said, a model for the discontinuity of the twentieth-century text.[6] Indeed the loss of the idea of a unified subject is clearly associated with the retreat from realism and narrative continuity in the modernist text. The changes in George Eliot's fictional method in *The Mill on the Floss* can similarly be related to the growing complexity of her idea of society and the psychological subject as she seeks to resolve the contradictions of organicism. In place of the empiricism of *Adam Bede*, the belief in the solidity of the external world, and the cyclical rhythms of nature which dominated that text, *The Mill on the Floss* proposes its own fictionality and a multi-levelled theory of time. For the unity of the earlier novel, whether of time, society, or the subject, *The Mill* substitutes a model which can encompass conflict and contradiction.

The opening scenes of the novel illustrate the narrator's lingering awareness of her constructive role. Directions are given, as if for a stage drama, as the narrator controls the movements of her creations: "Exit Maggie, dragging her bonnet by the string, while Mr. Tulliver laughs audibly" (Bk I, Ch. 2, I, 15). The conversation also obliquely reflects the narrator's own preoccupations: it concerns the creation of an unambiguous language. The world George Eliot is presenting retains no vestiges of simple natural history. Mr Tulliver is still a natural historian – he judges books not by their content but by their covers. He is hopelessly lost, however, in a world where inner and outer do not correspond. There no longer seems the assurance of *Adam Bede* that nature does possess a syntax, and correspondence between inner and outer is merely displaced a few generations. Mr Tulliver finds the world a puzzle, and the simple mathesis of *Adam Bede* will no longer serve. Power of mathematical addition would not solve the complex equation of social life. Mr Tulliver yearns for the Eden where word and world were in harmony:

Not but what, if the world had been left as God made it, I could ha' seen my way, and held my own wi' the best of 'em; but things have got so twisted round and wrapped up i' unreasonable words, as aren't a bit like 'em, as I'm clean at fault, often an' often. Everything winds about so – the more straightforward you are, the more you're puzzled. (Bk I, Ch. 3, I, 25).

But, failing this harmony, Mr Tulliver desires that his son should, like Mr Riley, know "a good lot o' words as don't mean much, so as you can't lay hold of 'em i' law" (Bk I, Ch. 2, I, 11) in order to facilitate his own adaptation to the puzzling social world. In default of plenitude, language must become a means not of solving, but of evading the puzzle. Language is prized for its *lack* of correspondence with the world. The project of a Linnean – naming the order of the world – is no longer possible.

Mr Tulliver's preoccupation with language reflects George Eliot's awareness of her own constructive role and her belief, which runs counter to her earlier conviction in *Adam Bede*, that there is not one simple and unambiguous truth. Truth does not inhere in external appearance, it is ambiguous, often complex and contradictory. Tom, despite his father's desires, clings to a belief in the transparency of action, in opposition to the opacity of language. Dragging Maggie away from Philip he declares: "I'm not to be imposed upon by fine words: I can see what actions mean" (Bk V, Ch. 5, II, 124). It is this belief in the unambiguous truth of external appearance which is to divide him from Maggie. Yet the distinction between the two is not, as it would have been in *Adam Bede*, between truth and falsity, but between different forms of truth. Thus Maggie, "writhed under the demonstrable truth of the character he had given to her conduct, and yet her whole soul rebelled against it as unfair from its incompleteness" (Bk V, Ch. 5, II, 120). This notion of the relativity of truth, which contrasts sharply with the realism, and social mathesis of *Adam Bede*, originates within analysis of the internal conflicts created in Maggie by contradictions in the historical process. George Eliot's preoccupation with language, and the constructed nature of fiction, is directly related to the increasing complexity of her social vision.

History in *The Mill on the Floss* follows neither the cyclical pattern of *Adam Bede*, nor a simple model of linear progression. Said has argued that "the process of writing a classical novel and the course of its plot may be comprehensible within an image of time unfolding, as a family unfolds and generations are linked."[7] Though images of growth abound in *The Mill*, however, they cannot account either for the dramatic conclusion of the novel, or the actual relations between generations. Tom, like Adam, undergoes a process of economic individuation; yet his course does not exhibit the law of transformation from homogeneity to heterogeneity. His goal is simply to regain the wealth and status his father has lost. History appears to engender conflict rather than progress. Maggie experiences that same opposition between inner and outer which had so puzzled Mr Tulliver and disrupted his natural history and theology. Of the discrepancy between Maggie's dreams and her outer life the narrator observes: "No wonder, when there is this contrast between the outward and the inward, that painful collisions come of it" (Bk III, Ch. 5, I, 369). There appears an irresolvable conflict between Maggie's own desires and the demands made by the repressive society which formed her, and to which she herself also desperately wishes to belong. The narrator later remarks, in the same vein, that Maggie possessed "that early experience of struggle, of conflict between the inward impulse and outward fact, which is the lot of every imaginative and passionate nature" (Bk IV, Ch. 2, II, 11). As the narrative itself clearly shows, however, Maggie's conflict is not simply created by her passionate nature; it is a product of history, both social and biological.

George Eliot's analysis of the actual complexity of the historical process leads her to question unifying schemas: scientific theories which stress the order of nature rather than its conflicts. Darwinian imagery is therefore employed not to illustrate progressive adaptation, but to demonstrate how the mixing of Tulliver and Dodson blood rendered Maggie unfit for survival in her environment.[8] "That's the worst on't wi' the crossing o' breeds," as Mr Tulliver observes, "you can never justly calkilate what'll come on't" (Bk I, Ch. 2, I, 12). Maggie is a "mistake of nature" (Bk I, Ch. 2, I, 14), ill-adapted for survival. Philip feels "the pity of it, that a mind like hers should be withering in its very youth, like a young forest-tree, for want of the light and space it was formed to flourish in" (Bk V, Ch. 1, II, 63). Yet Maggie's case differs significantly from that of the forest tree in this illustration. The environment does not simply hinder her development; it actually aids in constituting the internal contradictions of which she is composed. Maggie, "seems to have a sort of kinship with the grand Scotch firs . . . Yet one has a sense of uneasiness in looking at her – a sense of opposing elements, of which a fierce collision is imminent" (Bk V, Ch. 1, II, 49). The collision, which is to play itself out in Maggie in her relationship with Stephen, is between her sense of self founded on memory, and past social experience, and the direct promptings of passion. If accepted as a valid contradiction, this collision would undermine the reconciliation the organic model seeks to achieve between individual and social demands, historical change and continuity. For a theory of gradual historical progress, it would substitute a model of constant conflict which would effectively forbid progress.

Maggie, Dr Kenn, and the narrator all recite the same creed, upholding the social values which will ensure continuity. When Maggie demands of Stephen where duty can lie if we are not to be bound by the past, she sets egoistic desire in firm opposition to historical solidarity. In similar vein, Dr Kenn observes of the moral life of St Ogg's: "At present everything seems tending towards the relaxation of ties – towards the substitution of wayward choice for the adherence to obligation, which has its roots in the past" (Bk VII, Ch. 2, II, 358). This moral perspective is reinforced by the narrator who crowns Maggie's defeat of temptation with the following passage: "It came with the memories that no passion could long quench: the long past came back to her, and with it the fountains of self-renouncing pity and affection, of faithfulness and resolve" (Bk VII, Ch. 5, II, 390). But with the fountains of virtue there also comes the flood of death. The internal conflict from which Maggie suffers also seems to characterise the narrative: the "official" melioristic ideology runs counter to the sense of conflict and contradiction which dictates the non-progressive ending.

This opposition is clearly revealed in the passages where George Eliot outlines her doctrine of gradual organic development, and the social composition of man. The "oppressive narrowness" of the Dodson and Tulliver life must be presented, the narrator argues, if we are to understand "how it has acted on young natures in many generations, that in the onward tendency of human things have risen above the mental level of the generation before them, to which they have been nevertheless tied by the strongest fibres of their hearts" (Bk VI, Ch. 1, II, 6). The sense of conflict is undermined once it is defined as part of the "onward tendency of human things," while Maggie's sufferings are glorified by relating them to those of victim and martyr "which belongs to every historical advance of mankind." Maggie gains an illustrious lineage, yet under the very dubious argument that suffering constitutes an historical advance. To conclude, George Eliot refers the reader to the teachings of science, a device to which she often resorts when aware of the questionable nature of her argument:

and we need not shrink from this comparison of small things with great; for does not science tell us that its highest striving is after the ascertainment of a unity which shall bind the smallest things with the greatest? In natural science, I have understood, there is nothing petty to the mind that has a large vision of relations, and to which every single object suggests a vast sum of conditions. It is surely the same with the observation of human life (Bk VI, Ch. 1, II, 6).

The power of the argument stems from the subtle transformation of the quantitative terms of natural science into qualitative assessments of value. "Greatest" refers not to size but to George Eliot's assessment of the human qualities exhibited by martyrs. Similarly the use of "petty" disguises the distinction which should be drawn between things which are petty in size and things which, according to value judgement, are petty in character. The unity for which science strives is a theoretical unity, the application of the same law to great or small phenomena. But, in this passage, the description of a unity which binds, creates the connotation of a phenomenally unified whole. George Eliot draws upon the apparent authority of science to substantiate her own value judgements; to play down the sense of contradiction between Maggie and the oppressive narrowness of her surroundings, and to reinforce the idea that society is an organic whole, and history the process of its gradual growth.

The impression created by the description of the "narrow, ugly, grovelling existence" of the Rhône villages cannot, however, be erased. The "cruel conviction that the lives these ruins are the traces of, were part of a gross sum of obscure vitality, that will be swept into the same oblivion with the generations of ants and beavers" (Bk VI, Ch. 1, II, 4–5) is not altered by George Eliot's scientific analogies. The impression remains that suffering is neither glorious nor progressive, and that life is characterised less by unity than by conflict. E. S. Dallas, writing a review of *The Mill* in *The Times,* praised George Eliot for portraying her characters in all their "intrinsic littleness." "Everybody in this tale is repelling everybody," he observes, "and life is in the strictest sense a battle."[9] George Eliot, referring to the article, stated that she found herself "rather aghast" to find the Dodsons "ticketed with such very ugly adjectives."[10] But Dallas' reading, especially the view that life is a battle, may certainly be found in the text, running counter though it does to much of the narrator's commentary.

The model of history which emerges in *The Mill on the Floss* bears little relation to Spencer's theories of progress as a "beneficient necessity." It is closer to George Eliot's own arguments in her essay, "The Antigone and Its Moral." The antagonism of valid principles found in this play is not, she argues, peculiar to polytheism: "Is it not rather that the struggle between Antigone and Creon represents that struggle between elemental tendencies and established laws by which the outer life of man is gradually and painfully being brought into harmony with his inward needs."[11] The observation is framed within a progressionist theory of history but is dominated by an overwhelming sense of almost eternal struggle. If the same principle which was valid for Antigone is valid in the nineteenth century, progress must be so slow as to be imperceptible.

George Eliot's treatment of evolutionary theory confirms the fact that her theory of history in *The Mill* is not simply that of the gradual growth of an organic whole. The characteristics which distinguish men from animals are very debatable signs of progress. Maggie is "gifted with that superior power of misery which distinguishes the human being, and places him at a proud distance from the most melancholy chimpanzee" (Bk 1, Ch. 6, I, 67). Misery is, arguably, a spiritual gain. The evidence of evolutionary "progress" exhibited by Tom, however, is that of his aggressive behaviour; his desire for mastery over the inferior animals "which in all ages has been an attribute of so much promise for the fortunes of our race" (Bk I, Ch. 9, I, 139). The same desire for mastery dictates his behaviour to Maggie, thus exposing the heavy irony in the terms "promise" and "fortune." Progress, it seems, is synonymous with brutality and insensitivity.

Appeals to the evolutionary past in the novel only demonstrate the non-progressive nature of human life. The comparison between Mrs Pullet, a fashionably dressed woman in grief, and a Hottentot, redounds to the Hottentot's advantage. The "complexity" introduced into the emotions by civilisation relates not to the quality of grief but to frivolous considerations of dress. Specific references to Darwinian concepts of adaptational theory might indicate the survival of the fittest, but certainly not of the best. Thus the narrator instructs those readers who do not believe in Mr Pullet's ignorance to "reflect on the remarkable results of a great natural faculty under favouring circumstances. And uncle Pullet had a great natural faculty for ignorance" (Bk I, Ch. 7, I, 104). Reference is made to strategies of adaptation, but only to indicate Mr Tulliver's lack of such adaptational progress:

Certain seeds which are required to find a nidus for themselves under unfavourable circumstances, have been supplied by nature with an apparatus of hooks, so that they will get a hold on very unreceptive surfaces. The spiritual seed which had been scattered over Mr. Tulliver had apparently been destitute of any corresponding provision, and had slipped off to the winds again, from a total absence of hooks (Bk IV, Ch. 1, II, 10).

In fact, all the elements in Darwin's theory which might possibly be linked with a theory of progress or directed adaptation are challenged by the narrator.

Darwin, employing a Lamarckian form of argument, observes in *Origin of Species* that animals in colder climates have thicker fur "but who can tell how much of this difference may be due to the warmest-clad individuals having been favoured and preserved during many generations, and how much to the direct action of the severe climate? for it would appear that climate has some direct action on the hair of our domestic quadrupeds."[12] The Lamarckian theory of direct adaptation sustains ideas of necessary progress. In *The Mill on the Floss* George Eliot refutes all such implications for human life. Philip's deformity and misery has not been the agent of his development of unusual virtue. "The theory that unusual virtues spring by a direct consequence out of personal disadvantages, as animals get thicker wool in severe climates, is," the narrator observes, "perhaps a little over-strained" (Bk V, Ch. 3, II, 99). George Eliot puts into question in *The Mill on the Floss* all theories of evolution which imply either some form of progress or a discernible plan in nature.

One instance of Tom's aggression, which underlies the mastery he wishes to exert over Maggie, occurs when he attempts to kill a bluebottle "which was exposing its imbecility in the spring sunshine, clearly against the views of Nature, who had provided Tom and the peas for the speedy destruction of this weak individual" (Bk I, Ch. 9, I, 131). This rationalisation of brutality according to a plan of nature is in the tradition of natural theology, as characterised by the Bridgewater Treatises, where cruelty within nature was demonstrated to be part of a divinely ordained movement towards greater order and harmony.[13] Yet its applicability is not solely restricted to natural theology but can be extended to Darwin. Darwin was strongly influenced by Paley's *Natural Theology*. As John Burrow observes, *Origin of Species* and *Natural Theology* "concentrate to a considerable extent upon the same features, particularly upon adaptation; upon the relation of structure to function and the benefit to the animal concerned."[14] The difference between their theories lies in their interpretation of these phenomena: Paley attributed them to God's plan, and Darwin to the mechanism of natural selection. Both theories, however, are based on a sense of "fitness" or "order" and Tom's viewpoint does reflect, though within a distorted mirror, Darwin's mode of explanation. Tom's survival, and the bluebottle's death, would indicate, in Darwinian terms, Tom's higher state of adaptation, providing, therefore, a retrospective teleology. George Eliot puts into question, in *The Mill on the Floss*, even this more moderate form of discovering an underlying order in nature. Mr Glegg, searching amongst the wonders of natural history in his garden for the meaning of social events, provides a delightful illustration of the absurdity of natural theology. Neither nature nor the early chapters of Genesis can supply him with a key to that mystery in the scheme of things – why Mrs Glegg is "normally in a state of contradiction" (Bk I, Ch. 12, I, 186). Though painted with playful irony this sketch does highlight the underlying distrust of unifying schemas, which attempt to conceal or deny contradiction and conflict, that runs throughout the novel.

Perhaps a clearer example of this distrust is supplied in the treatment of Mr Riley's recommendation of Mr Stelling; a recommendation offered on no firmer ground than that of having been asked to deliver an opinion. "Nature herself," the narrator observes, "occasionally quarters an inconvenient parasite on an animal towards whom she has otherwise no ill-will. What then? We admire her care for the parasite" (Bk I, Ch. 3, I, 35). Darwin, concluding *Origin of Species* with the image of the entangled bank, populated by many different forms all "dependent on each other in so complex a manner," speaks of the grandeur in this view of life, that "from so simple a beginning endless forms most beautiful and most wonderful have been, and are being, evolved."[15] Though far from endorsing Paley's natural theology, Darwin, in stepping from analysis of the mechanisms of natural selection to consider the wonders of the overall process, does evince that admiration for nature's care of the parasite, for the complex dependency of animal life, to which George Eliot refers. Yet her point is precisely that neither nature nor social life possesses such order. Nature's "care" is simply a retrospective form of explanation which creates a sense of order not actually inherent within the action, and explains an initial evil in terms of good. Concentration on adaptation and a developmental perspective focuses attention not on synchronic disorder and conflict but on the order discernible through diachronic analysis. The narrative of *The Mill on the Floss*, like that of *Origin of Species*, is internally divided between these two perspectives: the emphasis placed on ideas of ordered social growth conflicts with the simultaneous revelation of the social contradictions such a historical perspective conceals.

Analysis of George Eliot's treatment of the history of St Ogg's reveals this discrepancy. It is, the narrator states, "one of those old, old towns which impress one as a continuation and outgrowth of nature, as much as the nests of the bower-birds or the winding galleries of the white ants: a town which carries the traces of its long growth and history like a millennial tree" (Bk I, Ch. 12, I, 178). The illustration would appear to be almost a truism of social organicism. It then emerges, however, that only the buildings of the town exhibit this natural continuity. The inhabitants are ignorant of their history and show no signs of interest in improving their knowledge: "The mind of St. Ogg's did not look extensively before or after. It inherited a long past without thinking of it, and had no eyes for the spirits that walk the streets" (Bk I, Ch. 12, I, 182). Though the town itself might resemble a millennial tree, the memories which had been left behind "had gradually vanished like the receding hilltops." Darwin in *Origin of Species* had compared the process of evolution to the Tree of Life: the image was one of accumulation, the dead branches created the new surface of the earth.[16] The life cycle of the inhabitants of St Ogg's, however, appears to be purely one of erosion – the receding hilltops are not complemented by deposition in the valleys.

Whilst the life of the buildings might be that of natural growth, the life of the residents of St Ogg's is characterised by no such unity. But, like Darwin, the inhabitants are firm uniformitarians. In *Origin of Species* Darwin called attention to the similarity between his own opinions and those of Lyell:

Natural selection can only act by the preservation and accumulation of infinitesimally small inherited modifications, each profitable to the preserved being; and as modern geology has almost banished such views as the excavation of a great valley by a single diluvial wave, so will natural selection, if it be a true principle, banish the belief of the continued creation of new organic beings, or of any great and sudden modification in their structure.[17]

The mind of St Ogg's has similarly banished belief in the operation of large-scale natural forces, and in change other than by imperceptible steps:

And the present time was like the level plain where men lose their belief in volcanoes and earthquakes, thinking tomorrow will be as yesterday, and the giant forces that used to shake the earth are for ever laid to sleep (Bk I, Ch. 12, I, 182–3).

Memories of the floods have receded, and the theory of history as a level plain cannot accommodate ideas of a single diluvial wave. The uniformitarianism which supplanted catastrophe theory suddenly appears as the product of complacency, of blindness, of a refusal to recognise conflict and contradiction and the possibility of whole-scale change. This position is correlated with political conservatism. The forgotten volcano which used to shake the earth is represented by Maggie with her "volcanic upheavings of imprisoned passions" (Bk IV, Ch. 3, II, 40), which create the "sense of opposing elements, of which a fierce collision is imminent." The flood which ends the novel, disrupting all previous continuity like a diluvial wave, may be seen, on one level, as a final vindication of catastrophe theory.

In an entry in one of her notebooks of this period George Eliot asks:

Is the interpretation of man's past life on earth according to the methods of Sir Charles Lyell in geology, namely, on the principle that all changes were produced by agencies still at work, thoroughly adequate & scientific? Or must we allow especially in the earlier periods, for something incalculable by us from the data of our present experience? Even within comparatively near times & in kindred communities how many conceptions & fashions of life have existed to which our understanding & sympathy has no clue![18]

Clearly her departure from uniformitarian principles of development in the narrative structure of *The Mill on the Floss* did not stem from a deliberate rejection of scientific theory. Her quarrel with uniformitarian theory was rather that it was not scientific enough: it was too simple a formula to capture historical complexity. George Eliot's reflections on the diverse nature of social communities, and on the possibilities for variation in conceptions of life, clearly show how directly she related scientific theory to social understanding. It is from evidence of the subjective nature of our understanding of the surrounding natural and social world that she concludes that uniformitarian theory may offer only a partial explanation of the world. Like the inhabitants of St Ogg's, scientists might be contenting themselves with a form of explanation which, though satisfying in its simplicity, fails to capture the actual complexities of historical development.

Neither the plot nor the commentary of *The Mill on the Floss* wholeheartedly reinforce organicist conceptions of gradual uniform development. George Eliot displays a willingness to recognise conflict and change as fundamental features of social life which was not present in her earlier novel. In *Adam Bede* the recognition that Arthur and Hetty's tragedy was socially created was later suppressed. The condemnation of upper-class privilege was not repeated, and Hetty was rendered subhuman. With Maggie, however, passion is humanised, and tragedy and conflict are shown to be social creations. The bitterness which occasionally tinged the treatment of Arthur rises to the fore, unchecked. The narrator mockingly apologises for the "tone of emphasis" she is apt to fall into which might offend "good society" which floats "on gossamer wings of light irony" (Bk IV, Ch. 3, II, 37). There follows a vivid representation of the sufferings the majority undergo to maintain the "tone" of the minority: "condensed in unfragrant deafening factories, cramping itself in mines, sweating at furnaces, grinding, hammering, weaving under more or less oppression of carbonic acid. . ." "This wide national life," the narrator observes, "is based entirely on emphasis – the emphasis of want, which urges it into all the activities necessary for the maintenance of good society and light irony" (Bk IV, Ch. 3, II, 37).

In *Adam Bede*, George Eliot had condemned the fact that a gentleman of property could support "numerous peccadilloes" without general moral censure. There had been no real vision, however, of the actual suffering the majority of the population must necessarily endure in order to make this situation possible. *The Mill on the Floss*, by contrast, offers a clear picture of the class structure of society. The "emphasis of want" is not restricted to factory workers, a class removed from the general sphere of the novel and thus an easy object for paternalist pity. Maggie's sufferings are equated with those of the factory workers, and the plight of both groups is related to the stratification of society. The idealisation which sustained the organic form of *Adam Bede* is not operative in *The Mill on the Floss*. A minor, but telling example relates to the detail of children's behaviour to their parents which, in the passage from "The Natural History of German Life" to *Adam Bede*, had been transformed from negative to positive. In *The Mill*, Mr Tulliver purposefully wishes Tom not to be a miller so that he will not, like other sons, evict his own father. *The Mill on the Floss* is able to confront the harshness of family and social life which, in accordance with the dictates of organic harmony, had been transmuted in *Adam Bede*.

Yet *The Mill on the Floss* does have its own Eden – that of childhood. The full-scale social critique is made possible because it is not society itself which must carry the burden of the ideal, but rather childhood. Though subject originally to all the trials and passions which characterise adult life, Maggie's childhood takes on, in retrospect, the qualities of an Edenic, atemporal realm. Like *Adam Bede*, *The Mill on the Floss* does, in part, conform to a cyclical pattern. Whilst the conclusion of *Adam Bede* returns us to the solidity of the unchanging cottage, the initial ending of *The Mill* re-enacts the timeless moments of childhood. Both exclude the possibility of change. But in *The Mill* this vision of timelessness appears from one viewpoint to be an illusion: "Nature repairs her ravages – but not all" (Bk VII, Conclusion, II, 401). Nature is not cyclical; the histories of Tom and Maggie were part of a social process whose essence was change.

In childhood, in that "strangely perspectiveless conception of life" (Bk I, Ch. 7, I, 98) Tom and Maggie espoused a theory of history based on preformation, not epigenesis: their lives would simply be a process of growth, not of change and division. They had "no thought that life would ever change much for them: they would only get bigger and not go to school" (Bk I, Ch. 5, I, 57). Their lives were composed of the constant repetition of the same elements: the "same flowers," the "same hips and haws," the "same redbreasts" (Bk I, Ch. 5, I, 58). History seemed to be repetition, with no difference. Yet this perspective is not shared by the narrator: "Life did change for Tom and Maggie" (Bk I, Ch. 5, I, 58). The timeless world of Tom and Maggie is framed by the narrator's predictive knowledge. Thus Maggie's promise to Philip will be rendered void, the narrator forecasts, by her involvement within the onward movement of social process: "void as promises made in

Eden before the seasons were divided, and when the starry blossoms grew side by side with the ripening peach – impossible to be fulfilled when the golden gates had been passed" (Bk II, Ch. 7, I, 292). The narrator both reinforces this vision of plenitude, where time does not intrude to create division or differentiation, and predicts the Fall. Its occasion is their father's bankruptcy. Until this time Tom's "thoughts and expectations had been hitherto only the reproduction, in changed forms, of the boyish dreams in which he had lived three years ago. He was awakened now with a violent shock" (Bk II, Ch. 7, I, 297). Tom is awoken from the eternal repetition which characterised childhood to an awareness of the linear nature of social time. This abrupt transition re-enacts the narrator's movement in the opening chapter from submergence in dream to conscious narration. The timeless world of dream is replaced by linear progression.

The parallel between the narrator's experience, the self-reflexive awareness of the fiction, and that of Tom should warn us against placing *The Mill on the Floss* in any simplistic time schema. The novel does not follow the classic pattern of education of the *Bildungsroman* where the linear progression of the narrative displays the progress of the characters from illusion (which in this case would be that of atemporality) to knowledge (the linear nature of time.)[19] It possesses, rather, a multi-levelled model of time. The narrative proposes two equally valid endings: the "one supreme moment" in which Tom and Maggie recapture forever the whole of their childhood, and the narrator's comment that "Nature repairs her ravages – but not all." The second does not undercut the first for they belong to two different schemas, the first to the dream narrative, and the second to conscious narration. The plurality reflects George Eliot's emancipation from the theory of a unified subject. The primacy placed upon dreams and the unconscious in the novel subverts the traditional theory of man as unified rational actor which sustains theories of history as linear progression. As Anthony Wilden has argued, the "notion of linear chronological development, evolution or change" is the correlative of an atomistic view of the individual.[20] A direct parallel can indeed be drawn between Cartesian notions of a unified thinking subject, and theories of history founded on concepts of continuity or evolution.

The function of dreams and the unconscious in *The Mill on the Floss* is thus to undercut ideas both of psychological unity and of historical continuity. With the theory of an unconscious, George Eliot introduces the idea of a plurality of time scales: "Life did change for Tom and

Maggie; and yet they were not wrong in believing that the thoughts and loves of these first years would always make part of their lives" (Bk I, Ch. 5, I, 58). The differentiation made here between the two forms of time is that captured by the two distinct endings to the novel, the cyclical and the progressive. Yet both, I would argue, can be traced to the same source – social organicism. *Adam Bede*, with its underlying mathesis, and reliance on quantitative assessment, clearly belonged, at least partially, to the eighteenth- and early-nineteenth-century mechanistic cosmology. Though it was oriented around the ideal of the organic community, there was no real conception of society as an evolving whole. Associationist assumptions dominated the social and psychological vision of the novel. In *The Mill on the Floss*, however, there is a greater sense of dynamic social evolution, and of the reciprocal formation of the individual and the social organism. This organic conception reinforces theories of history and psychology based on images of growth and development. It also gives rise, however, to theories of the unconscious which, by suggesting the possibility of a differential scale, actually subvert ideas of the unified growth of the individual. The organic theory of history is in fact disrupted by the theory of psychology to which it gives birth.

The treatment of the history of St Ogg's illustrates this dual model. A distinction is drawn between the conscious mind of St Ogg's which "did not look extensively before or after. It inherited a long past without thinking of it, and had no eyes for the spirits that walk the streets" (Bk I, Ch. 12, I, 182), and its unconscious history which stands outside such temporal progression. Thus:

The shadow of the Saxon hero-king still walks there fitfully, reviewing the scenes of his youth and love-time, and is met by the gloomier shadow of the dreadful heathen Dane, who was stabbed in the midst of his warriors by the sword of an invisible avenger, and who rises on autumn evenings like a white mist from his tumulus on the hill, and hovers in the court of the old hall, by the river-side (Bk I, Ch. 12, I, 179).

The social, conscious, history of the town is distinguished from its unconscious history which is immune to change and constantly repeats itself. This distinction can also be traced in the individual life of Maggie, receiving its final embodiment in the two endings of the novel. The shadows of St Ogg's find reflection in Maggie who tries, as an early chapter titles states, to "run away from her shadow" (Bk I, Ch. 11). This image is later recalled when the narrator observes that "Maggie's life struggles had lain almost entirely within her own soul, one shadowy army fighting another, and the slain shadows forever rising again" (Bk V, Ch. 2, II, 64). The constantly repeated battles place Maggie's life outside the linear continuity of social time. Like the shadows of St Ogg's, they point to the possibility of a differential time scale, of alternative histories. They disrupt the linear continuum. Tom, who embodies the mind of St Ogg's, conceives history only according to one pattern, his attitude to past action is that " 'I'd do just the same again' . . . whereas Maggie was always wishing she had done something different" (Bk I, Ch. 6, I, 77). Maggie, the narrator later observes, "rushed to her deeds with passionate impulse, and then saw not only their consequences, but what would have happened if they had not been done, with all the detail and exaggerated circumstance of an active imagination" (Bk I, Ch. 7, I, 96). Her attitude, and conception of possible alternatives, enacts the narrator's vision of a plural history.

The idea of plurality in history, and in the individual subject can, paradoxically, be traced to organicist evolutionary theory. The principles which underpin interpretation of psychological action in *The Mill on the Floss* are to be found in Lewes' *The Physiology of Common Life* (1859) in which he sought to apply Comte's theories of social organicism to physiological and psychological life. Like Comte, Lewes departed from the atomism of eighteenth-century mechanistic physiology and psychology: "You may take a mechanism to pieces, and explain by physical laws the action and interaction of each wheel and chain; but you cannot take an organism to pieces, and explain its properties by chemical laws."[21] To explain this principle Lewes draws not, as one might expect, on Comte's physiology, but rather on his social theory: his argument that, as the social whole is greater than the sum of its parts, one can never use the unit of the family as a model for the larger social state.[22] Employing Comte's social theory of organic interdependence Lewes challenges the Cartesian division between mind and matter, arguing that "Mind is the psychical aspect of Life – that it is as much the sum total of the whole sensitive organism, as Life is the sum total of the whole vital organism."[23] Consciousness is no longer identified with thought but becomes an attribute of the whole organism. Differentiating the sensation–perception couple of eighteenth-century psychology, Lewes argues that to have a sensation and to attend to it are two different things. He employs the illustration of a mill-wheel to support this argument:

The mill-wheel, at first so obtrusive in its sound, ceases at length to excite any attention. The impressions on our auditory nerves continue; but although we hear them, we cease to think about them: the same reflex-feelings are no longer excited. It is held, indeed, that we cease to hear them, in ceasing to be "conscious" that we hear them; but this is manifestly erroneous. Let the wheel suddenly stop and there is an immediate corresponding sensational change in us; so much so, that if it occurs during sleep, we awake.[24]

The mill-wheel, which illustrates Lewes' theory of the different levels of consciousness, performs a similar function in *The Mill on the Floss*. The "dreamy deafness" it creates acts "like a great curtain of sound, shutting one out from the world beyond" (Bk I, Ch. 1, I, 5). It establishes a level of consciousness distinct from that of social life thus setting forth the two separate forms of history which are to govern Maggie's life and the narrative of *The Mill on the Floss*.

Said has argued that the loss of the thinking subject of Cartesian philosophy must be associated with problems that have arisen concerning the subject's authenticity: "For of what comfort is a kind of geological descent into identity from level to lower level of identity, if no one point can be said confidently to *be* irreducible, beginning identity?"[25] The illustration is peculiarly apt, for geology was one of the primary sciences which helped establish the theory of gradual continuous development in nature. Once Lewes sought, however, to apply principles of unified organic development to individual psychology, he created a theory which undercut notions of a unified history. The subject possesses different levels of consciousness which do not all coexist within the same linear continuum of time.

The relationship between organicist ideas of history, and theories of psychology in *The Mill on the Floss* demands careful attention since there appear to be conflicting models. The narrator's comments frequently reinforce a theory of cumulative history drawn from social organicism. Thus Maggie had "no other part of her inherited share in the hard-won treasures of thought, which generations of painful toil have laid up for the race of men, than shreds and patches of feeble literature and false history" (Bk IV, Ch. 3, II, 31). But the catastrophic ending of the novel disrupts this idea of cumulative progress. A similar ambivalence occurs in George Eliot's use of Lewes' organicist theories of psychology. Unconscious processes are associated both with Maggie's elopement with Stephen and with her final reunification with Tom; with Mr Tulliver's attack on Wakem, and with his attachment to the mill. They are linked both with egoistic action which disrupts organic continuity, and with a fundamental state of organic harmony. The idea of the unconscious, by challenging the traditional conception of the rational actor, evokes fear of man's uncontrollable nature. At the same time, however, the image of an unconscious life, which stands outside the flow of social time, also suggests an Edenic vision of a timeless, conflict-free state, a unification of past and present, inner and outer. Maggie beating her fetish, and venting her childish grief attains "a passion that expelled every other form of consciousness – even the memory of the grievance that had caused it" (Bk I, Ch. 4, I, 38). She seems thus to achieve the apotheosis of egoism, but the mill with its "resolute din, the unresting motion of the great stones" which evokes awe "as at the presence of an uncontrollable force" creates a similar isolation from the external world. The mill, source of Maggie's child-hood happiness, was for her "a little world apart from her outside every-day life" (Bk I, Ch. 4, I, 39). The isolation it offered was one of time-less harmony. This ambivalence towards unconscious absorption – whether it indicates uncontrollable, and thus socially disruptive, passion, or the ultimate possibility of organic union – is the source of a central contradiction within *The Mill on the Floss*.

A further source of ambivalence in the novel stems from George Eliot's use of Lewes' theories of organism–medium interaction. "We must constantly bear in mind," Lewes states, "that Life is possible only under the necessary conditions of an *organism*, on the one hand, and an external *medium* on the other."[26] George Eliot employs this principle in *The Mill on the Floss* to illustrate the development of the individual through interaction with the external medium. Her explanation is redo-lent with a nostalgic longing for a lost unity. In childhood:

the pattern of the rug and the grate and the fire-irons were "first ideas" that it was no more possible to criticise than the solidity and extension of matter. There is no sense of ease like the ease we felt in those scenes where we were born, where objects became dear to us before we had known the labour of choice, and where the outer world seemed only an extension of our own personality: we accepted and loved it as we accepted our own sense of existence and our own limbs (Bk II, Ch. 1, I, 234).

Since individual development occurs through a process of interaction with the environment there is, in childhood, as yet no isolated centre of self; no distinction is drawn between external objects and the inner self. The ideal union of inner and outer which Adam achieved by work is given, in the above quotation, a precise physiological basis in childhood.

This conception of personal growth serves as a foundation for the idealisation of the "organic community" where the "labour of choice" does not arise. Thus Mr Tulliver "felt the strain of this clinging affection for the old home as part of his life, part of himself" (Bk III, Ch. 9, I, 413). "Our instructed vagrancy," the narrator observes, "can hardly get a dim notion of what an old-fashioned man like Mr. Tulliver felt for this spot, where all his memories centred, and where life seemed like a familiar smooth-handled tool that the fingers clutch with loving ease" (Bk III, Ch. 9, I, 414). Though George Eliot has discarded the associationist, atomic model of psychology, the theory of organic process she adopts does not lead, as one might expect, to a dynamic theory of history, but to an argument for social stasis. Only if external conditions remain the same can inner memory and outer world reproduce that state of unity between inner and outer which characterised childhood. Mrs Tulliver's mind was "reduced to such confusion by living in this strange medium of unaccountable sorrow" (Bk III, Ch. 8, I, 401). Once her household goods are removed she feels she "would never recover her old self. . . how could she? The objects among which her mind had moved complacently were all gone" (Bk IV, Ch. 2, II, 12). Changes within the external social medium disrupt her sense of identity. Physiological psychology is thus employed to reinforce ideological conceptions of organic harmony within the traditional community. In undercutting the theory of the subject as a clear and distinct identity, however, it also simultaneously challenges ideas of linear progression in history.

George Eliot attempts, at one stage, to draw physiological psychology within a cumulative, evolutionary framework. Of childhood sorrow she remarks: "Every one of those keen moments has left its trace, and lives in us still, but such traces have blent themselves irrecoverably with the firmer texture of our youth and manhood" (Bk I, Ch. 7, I, 98). The model proposed is not that of differential levels but of one unified process. But this idea of gradual modification cannot account either for the conflict and contradiction Maggie experiences, or for the conclusion in which the past is regained in its original form. In his essay on Proust, Walter Benjamin states that there is a dual will to happiness: "The one is the unheard of, the unprecedented, the height of bliss; the other, the eternal repetition, the eternal restoration of the original, the first happiness." To the latter, he believes, Proust sacrificed in his works "plot, unity of character, the flow of the narration, the play of the imagination."[27] In *The Mill on the Floss* the final restoration of the original happiness also demands the sacrifice of plot, unity of character, and flow of the narration; but only, however, if they are conceived according to the model of organic growth conveyed in the idea of a developing texture. *The Mill on the Floss* also proposes another model of history which undercuts this conception of organic growth.

Physiological psychology does not merely furnish a model for historical development in *The Mill*. Throughout the novel even the most minor gestures of the various characters are related in physiological terms. Thus Mrs Pullet's manœuvrings through the doorway are a product of a "composition of forces" (Bk I, Ch. 7, I, 84), while Mr Glegg's mental activity, "when disengaged from the wool business, naturally made itself a pathway in other directions" (Bk I, Ch. 12, I, 186). It is noticeable that the number of physiological references increases when George Eliot attempts to explain the effects of crisis. Thus the presence of the bailiff was to Tom "a touch on the irritated nerve compared with its spontaneous dull aching" (Bk III, Ch. 2, I, 316), while his natural inclination to blame, held in abeyance by the predisposition to think his father always right, "was turned into this new channel by his mother's plaints" (Bk III, Ch. 2, I, 320). The vocabulary of forces, pathways, channels is that employed by Lewes and his fellow physiological psychologists. Life, Lewes observed, is the sum total of "all the forces at work"; thoughts make "pathways" for themselves, and sensation has a tendency to "discharge itself through the readiest channel."[28] In George Eliot's work this vocabulary conveys, not merely an eccentric delight in an idiosyncratic mode of expression, but a distinct theory of character and action which departs from the earlier mechanistic conceptions of associationist psychology.

Lewes exhibits in *The Physiology of Common Life* a detailed interest in the phenomena of irrational action, sleep and dreams. Close analysis of George Eliot's treatment of Mr Tulliver's dream reveals the extent to which it was founded on Lewes' theories: the representation of Mr Tulliver's clinging affection for the mill, and of the irrational passion in which he beats Wakem, can both be traced to the same theoretical source. The physiological analysis commences with Tom's story of his financial success:

It was well that there was this interest of narrative to keep under the vague but fierce sense of triumph over Wakem, which would otherwise have been the channel his joy would have rushed into with dangerous force. Even as it was, that feeling from time to time gave threats of its ultimate mastery, in sudden bursts of irrelevant exclamation (Bk V, Ch. 6, II, 134).

There is a disjunction between conscious attention and the workings of the unconscious, the latter disrupting the former at intervals.

Consciousness, as Lewes argued, is "the confluence of many streams of sensation."[29] George Eliot is following what Lewes termed the "Law of Sensibility": "No sensation terminates in itself; it must either discharge its excitation in some secondary sensation, or in some motor impulse. Generally it does so in both together."[30] Denied expression in Mr Tulliver's conscious mind, the sensation excited is restricted to forging chains of secondary sensation within his subconscious. "A self-terminating sensation," Lewes continues, "is as inconceivable as a self-terminating motion. The wave of force is propelled onwards, and for ever onwards, now in this direction, and now in that."[31] In Mr Tulliver's case, the wave of force continues in his sleep, to issue forth in the dream of Wakem which shocks him into wakefulness. Nor it its force spent there. It has established a channel of discharge.[32] Thus, on meeting Wakem, Mr Tulliver lapses into a dream-like state and, it is implied, enacts his dream.

This relation of dream to waking life is in full accordance with the theories propounded by Lewes. There is no true antagonism, Lewes argues, between sleep and waking: "Dreams are mental process carried on during sleep, and are closely allied to the Reveries carried on during waking hours."[33] Sleeping or waking the mind follows a train of associated ideas. Awake, the mental processes are checked and controlled by the reports of the senses; asleep, they are allowed free rein. Mr Tulliver's dream establishes a path of discharge for action which would have been rejected by his conscious mind. On meeting Wakem, the chain of association was reawakened and the corresponding action evoked.[34]

Despite its fundamental grounding in the concepts of physics, Lewes' physiological psychology has produced a model of man which bears little relation to the associationist's rational model. As the example of Mr Tulliver has shown, man might be controlled by, rather than in control of, his own mind. Yet the processes which create this loss of control are similarly those which underscore the ideal of organic harmony, the unconscious associations which link past and present, inner and outer. This contradiction is more evident in the case of Maggie who had had, George Eliot declares, "so eager a life in the triple world of Reality, Books, and Waking Dreams" (Bk IV, Ch. 2, II, 12). The quotation establishes Maggie's intimate connection with the world of dream and multiple realities, and George Eliot's own allegiance to Lewes' theory that reverie is a form of waking dream.

Maggie is in a dream state when she accomplishes her two decisive actions, the first, which cuts her ties with her former life, and the second, which reunites her irrevocably to her past. In her voyage with Stephen, and in her final reunification with Tom, she is swept along by the underlying currents of her mind, visibly symbolised in the river and flood. On both occasions she slips out of the continuum of conscious time. Drifting down the river with Stephen, Maggie is in the dream state described by Lewes, in which thought and sensation are not subject to any confrontation: "Maggie was only dimly conscious of the banks, as they passed them, and dwelt with no recognition on the villages." "Memory was excluded" and the continuity of past, present and future broken: "and thought did not belong to that enchanted haze in which they were enveloped: it belonged to the past and the future that lay outside the haze" (Bk VI, Ch. 13, II, 311). Yet, such submergence is not simply the result of "a mindless yielding to natural appetite."[35] The dream state also characterises Maggie's actions in the flood: "The whole thing had been so rapid – so dream-like – that the threads of ordinary association were broken" (Bk VII, Ch. 5, II, 393–4). The opposition between conscious, rational control and mindless passion cannot capture the complexity of George Eliot's model of the mind.

In Maggie's earlier struggles with Stephen the situation is presented as a simple division between the values of organic continuity and their polar opposite – egoism. Thus Maggie clings to her memories, to her "tranquil, tender affection for Philip, with its root deep down in her childhood" rather than respond to Stephen who appealed to her "vanity or other egoistic excitability of her nature" (Bk VI, Ch. 7, II, 225). The former is "sacred" for it creates both temporal and social unity; the latter is purely divisive. The division here is between conscious memory and uncontrolled response. Maggie's actions when she leaves Stephen, however, also partake of the dream-like state of her yielding:

Maggie was not conscious of a decision as she turned away from that gloomy averted face, and walked out of the room: it was like an automatic action that fulfils a forgotten intention. What came after? A sense of stairs descended as if in a dream – of flagstones – of a chaise and horses standing – then a street... (Bk VI, Ch. 14, II, 335).

Her "moral" action is accomplished in a state of lapsed consciousness. The automatic action conforms to the pattern outlined by Lewes: "Habits, Fixed Ideas, and what are called Automatic Actions, all depend on the tendency which a sensation has to discharge itself through the readiest channel."[36]

To appreciate the full significance of George Eliot attributing an apparently moral action not to the sphere of conscious mind and memory but to the unconscious, one must place her work in the perspective of her contemporaries' reactions. William Carpenter, who pioneered the phrase "unconscious cerebration" (and whose *Comparative Physiology* George Eliot records reading in 1855), was largely concerned with the phenomenon of unconscious action.[37] Yet he concurred with many of his contemporaries in seeing it as a threat and possible source of moral weakness. In *Principles of Mental Physiology* he speaks of the "unconscious influence of what may be called the Moral Atmosphere breathed during the earlier period of life, in forming the habits, and thereby determining the Mechanism of Thought and Feeling."[38] The statement could easily be an outline schema for *The Mill on the Floss*. But Carpenter sees this process not as a source of moral strength, but as a threat to the rational control of action:

The *unconscious* prejudices which we thus form are often stronger than the conscious; and they are the more dangerous, because we cannot knowingly guard against them. And further (as Mr. Lecky has well remarked), though the reason, in her full strength, may pierce the clouds of prejudice, and may even rejoice and triumph in her liberty, yet the conceptions of childhood will long remain latent in the mind, to reappear in every show of weakness, when the tension of the reason is relaxed, and the power of old associations is supreme.[39]

Like Carpenter, W. E. H. Lecky, in his *History of the Rise and Influence of the Spirit of Rationalism in Europe* (which George Eliot was to review, rather unfavourably, in 1865), associates the onward progress of man with the extension of rational control.[40] Unless memory of the past serves as a conscious guide it can only be disruptive. George Eliot, in attributing a moral role to the unconscious in *The Mill on the Floss*, challenges such linear theories of development.

A similar association of the unconscious with dangerous disruption occurs in the theories of Bergson. Proust's distinction between his own theories and those of Bergson could also be applied to that between George Eliot and Carpenter. It would not be exact, Proust argues, to call his novels "romans bergsoniens": "car man œuvre est dominée par la distinction entre la mémoire involontaire et la mémoire volontaire, distinction qui non seulement ne figure pas dans le philosophie de M. Bergson, mais est même contredite par elle."[41] Bisson points out that Proust in fact employs Bergson's terminology to establish this distinction, yet his intuitive sense of their opposition is correct. To Bergson, as

Bisson argues, "the processes of involuntary memory are irrelevant or dangerous. In mentioning them his tone is one of indifference, or deprecation, or even censure; they are an aberration from the normal and proper function of the memory, a hindrance to right action, a pathological symptom or a concomitant of sleep."[42] Right action, for Bergson, is action guided by conscious memory which would keep firmly in check the flood of unconscious associations. For Bergson, as for Lecky and Carpenter, surrender to the unconscious is a surrender of humanity. Yet for Proust the involuntary, uncontrollable memory offers the sole possibility of illuminating the chaos of life with meaning. Voluntary memory "qui est surtout une mémoire de l'intelligence et des yeux, ne nous donne du passé que des faces sans vérité."[43] Proust's novels, therefore, display not the linear structure of rational intelligence, but the cyclical structure of unconscious memory which unites past and present. His admiration for *The Mill on the Floss* was no doubt evoked by his recognition that he shared with George Eliot a similar conception of memory.

The dual structure of *The Mill on the Floss* – the cyclical and the progressive – is indicative of George Eliot's divided allegiances. Traces of both the Bergsonian and Proustian models are to be found in the text. The scene with Stephen in which "memory was excluded" appears to be cast in terms of the values of Carpenter, Lecky, and Bergson. The exclusion of conscious memory is a denial of human responsibility and the organic continuity of social life.[44] Yet the exclusion of memory entails precisely that loss of perspective which characterises the opening scene of the novel, and thus the narrator's stance, and Maggie's reunion with Tom. The structure of the novel cannot be explained according to a simple opposition between control–continuity and lack of control–discontinuity.

The contradictions within the novel stem primarily from the complex attitude towards organicism. In the reunion of Tom and Maggie the values of organicism are preserved, yet at the cost of organic continuity in history.[45] Ideal harmony is not, as in *Adam Bede*, to be found in society, but only by stepping out of the onward social process. For society is not static in *The Mill on the Floss*, but is characterised by change and flux. Official, narrative statement in *The Mill* sustains a theory of linear continuity. In this, as in George Eliot's other novels, the law of consequences is proclaimed to hold firm sway. Thus the narrator, employing an organic image which emphasises the interconnectedness of human lots, remarks: "we can conceive no retribution that does not spread beyond its mark in pulsations of unmerited pain" (Bk III, Ch. 7, I, 382). Furthermore, Maggie, in her social isolation, was: "unhappily quite without that knowledge of the irreversible laws within and without her, which, governing the habits becomes morality, and, developing the feelings of submission and dependence, becomes religion" (Bk IV, Ch. 3, II, 31–2). The observation, which is based on a theory of organic unity between inner and outer life, suggests a gradual, cumulative moral process throughout history. Yet this idea of historical development is at odds with the vision of the biologically and socially created contradiction within Maggie. Despite narrative emphasis on the law of consequences there is in fact a profound distrust of progressionist evolutionary theory, and of the concept of the rational actor with which it is, as in Lecky, associated.

George Eliot found in Lewes' work a dynamic model of individual development, based on Comtean principles of social evolution. In applying the premises of social organicism to individual psychology, however, Lewes created a model of mind which actually challenged notions of individual and social continuity. If individual identity is constructed through a process of interaction between organism and medium, a true state of harmony between the inner and outer realms can only be maintained in childhood, or in a society without change. In place of the model of the unified rational actor which had sustained ideas of linear social progression, Lewes proposed a model of mind which stressed the conflict of streams of sensation, and discontinuous levels of consciousness. George Eliot's divided attitude towards the operation of the unconscious can, in light of Lewes' theories, be seen as a symptom of her divided attitude towards theories of historical progress. On the one hand, submergence into the atemporal subconscious is clearly seen as disruptive: to relapse into the timeless flow of the unconscious is to break the ties which bind past and present; the continuum of history. But, on the other hand, if the experience of social life is characterised by continuous conflict, submergence offers the sole way of obtaining the desired unity, or organic harmony. The double nature of the ending, which casts its questioning shadow over the whole of the preceding narrative, enacts this division.

CHAPTER 4

Silas Marner:
A divided Eden

The divided narrative structure of *The Mill on the Floss* marks a departure from the natural history of *Adam Bede*, with its cyclical rhythms and clear character divisions. Uniting the qualities of Hetty and Dinah, Maggie internalises social contradictions which the dual ending seeks to resolve. But George Eliot's own distrust of the evasion constituted by the final vision of organic union may be inferred from "The Lifted Veil." Written during the course of the novel's composition, this "jeu de melancholie"[1] may be considered as a parallel text, only without *The Mill*'s redemptive strategy. Both texts are centrally concerned with historical continuity, but in Latimer's vision of Prague, "the dusty, weary, time-eaten grandeur of a people doomed to live on in the stale repetition of memories," *The Mill*'s positive representation of memory is challenged.[2] The inhabitants of Prague, who appear as "a swarm of ephemeral visitants infesting it for a day" (Ch. 1, p. 287), recall the narrator's "cruel conviction" that the lives of which the ruins of the Rhône villages were traces "were part of a gross sum of obscure vitality that will be swept into the same oblivion with the generations of ants and beavers." Yet Prague does not evoke an awareness of "the onward tendency of human things," but rather emphasises the futility of life. In Prague, as in St Ogg's, spirits repeat their actions, but "compelled by their doom to be ever old and undying, to live on in the rigidity of habit" (Ch. 1, p. 287), they possess none of the romance of the "Saxon hero king" or "dreadful heathen Dane." Repetition, which had characterised the childhood of Tom and Maggie, and ensured their final return to this Edenic atemporal realm, signals, in "The Lifted Veil," only sterility and death.

Like *The Mill on the Floss*, "The Lifted Veil" is a text aware of its own fictionality. The life of Latimer, its narrator, is synonymous with that of the narrative. In its cyclical structure *The Mill* moves between two timeless moments, the opening immersion in unconscious memory, and Maggie's final reattainment of original plenitude. "The Lifted

Veil" reverses the novel's procedures, commencing with a vision of the end of time which the end of the narrative fulfils. Maggie's death represents a victory over the linear progression of narrative; through immersion in the timeless world of memory, she defies the temporal truncation signalled by the narrative's close. Death for Latimer, however, does not bring the reattainment of a primal unity, but only pure negation. Starting with the words "The time of my end approaches," "The Lifted Veil" is a text which seems to exist only to confirm its own death, dramatising George Eliot's distrust of the creative authority she claimed in *The Mill on the Floss*. Though the catastrophe of the flood in *The Mill* puts into question evolutionary theories of history, an alternative cyclical model was founded on the unconscious. But in "The Lifted Veil" Latimer's forced immersion in the unconscious exposes only the world's pettiness, heightening his desire for sheer oblivion. The negativity of "The Lifted Veil" is a reflex of the idealisation of *The Mill on the Floss*, revealing the dark underside of that novel which the final vision of the "daisied fields" suppresses.[3]

In her "legendary tale," *Silas Marner*, George Eliot again addresses the issue of historical continuity.[4] Like the earlier *Adam Bede*, however, the novel seems to evade the challenge of social change and disruption. Against the flow of history, the plot moves backward in time: the dweller from the industrial city is finally incorporated into the world of "Merry England," "never reached by the vibrations of the coach-horn, or of public opinion."[5] Just as Dinah left the harsh world of Stoniton for Hayslope, so Silas leaves the industrial life of Lantern Yard for the rural village of Raveloe which, like Hayslope, stands "aloof from the currents of industrial energy and Puritan earnestness" (Ch. 3, p. 33). In *Adam Bede* George Eliot emphasised the continuity of this process of change: Dinah seemed to evolve, without undue stress, into her "natural" form of matron. In *Silas Marner*, however, following the pattern of *The Mill on the Floss*, she dramatises the conflict and discontinuity of the historical process. Maggie experienced the "clash of opposing elements" and was forced into temporary exile; Silas is abruptly cast out from his friends, work, and home.

George Eliot explores the same themes in *Silas Marner* and *The Mill*, but this time she reverses the structural pattern of the earlier novel. Opening with an evocation of the Eden of Maggie's childhood, *The Mill on the Floss* plots the growing division between Maggie's past and present life, which only the concluding catastrophe of the flood resolves. *Silas Marner*, by contrast, opens with a catastrophe which establishes an absolute and immediate break between Silas' past and future existence. Through his later relationship with Eppie, however, we trace the gradual restoration of historical continuity to his life, until he attains the final plenitude in which both the past and the realm of historical change seem to be erased. The conclusion of *Silas Marner*, like that of *Adam Bede*, confirms historical stasis. The fenced-in garden of Silas' cottage, to which the "four united people" return, symbolises, as in Medieval iconography, their Eden, a world where history and change are excluded. Surrounded by the flowers which "shone with answering gladness," they have in fact attained the "daisied fields" of Maggie's heaven.

The structural pattern of *Silas Marner* suggests that George Eliot adopted, in this novel, a more positive attitude towards ideas of historical development than in her previous work; yet, as the plot's movement backward in time reveals, she did not fully resolve her ambivalent responses. In *Silas Marner*, as in *The Mill on the Floss*, she interrogates theories of organic continuity in history, and, to this end, she explores, in each work, the relations between theories of social and psychological formation. *The Mill on the Floss* offered two models of history, based on two different patterns of psychology: the linear development of consciousness, and the atemporal unconscious. The two determining moments in Maggie's life both belonged to this latter model. When she drifted away with Stephen, and when she attempted to rescue Tom from the flood, Maggie relinquished conscious control of her actions, lapsing into the realm of the unconscious. In both cases her behaviour violated the psychological pattern associated, in contemporary theory, with linear theories of social progress; that of a rational actor, responsibly directing her actions in light of her knowledge of the "law of consequences."[6] This break from a linear model of psychology is accentuated in *Silas Marner*.[7] During the two determining moments of Silas' life he is in a state akin to death, suffering from a cataleptic fit. On each occasion, when he is framed by William Dane, and when Eppie enters his life, he is entirely without responsibility for his actions. As Eppie wanders into his cottage Silas stands by the door "arrested . . . by the invisible wand of catalepsy" (Ch. 12, p. 169). The reference to the magic wand highlights the disruptive function of Silas' disease. Despite the increased interest in abnormal states of consciousness in the mid-nineteenth century, catalepsy still remained a mystery to psychologists.[8] Inexplicable, and uncontrollable, catalepsy seemed to suggest the eruption of chance, rather than the operation of uniform law.

George Eliot's treatment of Silas' malady confirms this reading.

Once Silas' senses return, after one of his fits, he remains "unaware of the chasm in his consciousness" (Ch. 12, p. 169). The term chasm, which recalls the "sudden chasm" (Ch. 10, p. 117) created in Silas' life by the loss of his gold, suggests an image of history based on the premises of catastrophism, rather than on uniformitarian theory. Both Silas' social and psychological life conform to these premises: the breaks in his consciousness parallel the discontinuity of his social history. Powerless to control either the workings of his own mind, or the machinations of others, he is abruptly thrust out of Lantern Yard, forced to start an entirely new life. His cataleptic fits function, indeed, as one symptom of a more inclusive powerlessness. Like Maggie's lapses into the unconscious, and *The Mill*'s concluding flood, Silas' catalepsy suggests George Eliot's uncertain allegiance to ideas of uniformitarian development.

George Eliot's contemporaries were quick to note the internal conflicts within her work. Thus E. S. Dallas objected to Silas' trances since they "render[ed] him a singularly unaccountable being."[9] The pleasure of fiction, Dallas argued, "depends mainly on our being able to count upon the elements of human character and to calculate results." Thus, if an "imbecile" is brought forward, "it involves the introduction of chance and uncertainty into a tissue of events the interest of which depends on their antecedent probability."[10] Dallas' theory of narrative progression and psychological development is based upon uniformitarian principles. The enjoyment of narrative, he believed, is founded on the comforting rehearsal of rational history in which continuous order can always be discerned. Predictability is thus the key to social and psychological order. Unconscious trances clearly constitute a threat since they introduce elements not subject to control.

Dallas jibbed at Silas' fits because they seemed inconsistent with the dominant moral of the tale:

As in one fit of unconsciousness he lost his all, so in another fit of unconsiousness he obtained a recompense. In either case he was helpless, had nothing to do with his own fate, and was a mere feather in the wind of chance. From this point forward in the tale, however, there is no more chance – all is work and reward, cause and effect, the intelligent mind shaping its own destiny. The honest man bestows kindness upon the child, and reaps the benefit of it in his own increasing happiness, quickened intelligence, and social position.[11]

Chance and the unconscious are balanced against continuity and control, values which Dallas associates with the smooth functioning of economic and social life. Coopting the authority of science to support his arguments, he presents work and reward as synonymous with the principles of cause and effect. His model of society is that of the capitalist economy; each individual in control of his own destiny, freely pursuing his own interest. In personal life, as in the market place, honest investment will reap a merited reward. The idea of orderly sequence within individual life stands as a model for the larger movement of social history.

Despite the fact that Silas' life is dominated more by chance than by rational order and control, George Eliot does, as Dallas correctly observes, draw the moral framework of her novel from these latter values. In accordance with her practice in *Adam Bede* (and, indeed, in all her later novels) she condemns those who subscribe to a belief in chance. Thus the inadequacies of Lantern Yard as a social and religious community are revealed by its members' superstitious trust in the drawing of lots. The novel's two greatest villains, William Dane and Dunsey Cass, are distinguished by their faith in their own luck and the workings of chance; both, as Joseph Wiesenfarth has argued, "believe in their election to fortune."[12] Godfrey Cass is similarly tainted by this belief. He is roundly castigated by the narrator for clinging to the hope that chance might release him from the consequences of his unfortunate marriage. "Favourable Chance," the narrator gravely observes, "is the god of all men who follow their own devices instead of obeying a law they believe in" (Ch. 9, p. 112).

In adhering to a model of history which permits the intrusion of chance and randomness, Godfrey violates the moral, social and economic assumptions underpinning the Victorians' faith in uniformitarian law. Godfrey's beliefs are quickly linked to the realm of economic activity: to the self-deluding dreams of those who live outside their income, or "shirk the resolute honest work that brings wages," or, in an even more explicitly directed social commentary, attempt to move up the social ladder. Thus the narrator observes, "Let him forsake a decent craft that he may pursue the gentilities of a profession to which nature never called him, and his religion will infallibly be the worship of blessed Chance, which he will believe in as the mighty creator of success" (Ch. 9, pp. 112–13). Social mobility, like the worship of chance, poses a threat to a "naturally" ordained social order. Referring to this mode of worship the narrator concludes, "The evil principle deprecated in that religion, is the orderly sequence by which the seed brings forth a crop after its kind" (Ch. 9, p. 113). Ideas of economic and social order are here firmly grounded in a theory of natural, organic, historical growth. Yet, the narrator's declared allegiance to theories of orderly sequence and moral responsibility in action is clearly undercut by the determining role played within the novel by chance and the loss of rational control. Like its predecessor, *The Mill on the Floss*, *Silas Marner* actually offers two conflicting models of history, one based on ideas of continuity, moral order, individual responsibility and control, and another which stresses gaps and jumps in historical development, chance, individual powerlessness, and self-division.

Although *Silas Marner* is cast within an apparently simple mould, George Eliot brings to her analysis of the issues of organic development in this work all the complexity of her previous fiction. Through its legendary form she examines in concrete detail Strauss' and Feuerbach's theories of the mythic imagination, and Comte's theory of the three stages of human evolution, from the fetishism of the polytheistic stage through to the rational thought of positivism.[13] The fictional mode of the work actually functions as a commentary upon the stage of development attained by the Raveloe villagers. George Eliot's treatment of the villagers' initial reactions to Silas, and their discussions in the Rainbow and responses to the "evidence" surrounding the robbery, reveals her interest in the processes of mythological thought, and the forms of rationality current in man's various developmental stages. Like Comte, she brings to her work a profound respect for the processes of history, a firm belief that each stage is directly linked to its predecessors.[14] Thus Silas' love of his brick hearth is treated tenderly and sympathetically: "The gods of the hearth exist for us still; and let all new faith be tolerant of that fetishism, lest it bruise its own roots" (Ch. 16, p. 212). In *Silas Marner* George Eliot explores the various historical roots of man's behaviour, examining the development of an individual life within the perspective of a larger evolutionary framework. Her aim in returning to the primitive life of Lantern Yard and Raveloe is "to enter into that simple, untaught state of mind in which the form and the feeling have never been severed by an act of reflection" (Ch. 1, p. 18), and to offer, in accordance with Comtean theory, a full account of the ways in which the characters evolved through interaction with their surrounding social medium.[15] As a Victorian reviewer observed, "It is impossible to dissociate any of the characters from the village in which they were born and bred – they form an organic whole with Raveloe."[16]

In translating this theory of social organicism into its full psychological consequences, however, George Eliot encounters problems similar to those that emerged in *The Mill on the Floss*. Her analysis of the psychological effects of Silas' sudden displacement recalls narrative discussions of the devastating personal impact of the Tullivers' bankruptcy: [17]

> Even people whose lives have been made various by learning, sometimes find it hard to keep a fast hold on their habitual views of life, on their faith in the Invisible, nay, on the sense that their past joys and sorrows are a real experience, when they are suddenly transported to a new land, where the beings around them know nothing of their history, and share none of their ideas – where their mother earth shows another lap, and human life has other forms than those on which their souls have been nourished (Ch. 2, p. 20).

Silas, like Mr and Mrs Tulliver, loses his sense of identity once his familiar surrounding medium is transformed. He can neither orient himself within the strange world of Raveloe, nor relate to his own past history. He retains no sense of self distinct from his relationship to his environment. As in *The Mill on the Floss*, the theory of psychology drawn from notions of organic development and historical continuity actually subverts the idea of a unified, rational actor.

Once displaced from Lantern Yard, Silas undergoes the "Lethean influence of exile, in which the past becomes dreamy because its symbols have all vanished, and the present too is dreamy because it is linked with no memories" (Ch. 2, p. 20). As in his cataleptic fits he enters into a trance-like state, becoming incapable of ordering or imposing continuity on his life. His experience contradicts the accepted psychological pattern outlined here by Alexander Bain in his observation that "The unbroken continuity of our mental life holds together the past and the present in a sequence that we term Order in Time." For Bain, this mental continuity was both a measure and a guarantee of social order; he relates the linear sequence of the mind directly to "the sequences of nature, or the order of the world."[18] George Eliot's analysis of Silas' loss of personal identity effectively challenges such dominant assumptions of social and psychological continuity. Silas' faith in a benign, God-given order was shattered when the drawing of lots declared him guilty. George Eliot's exploration of his ensuing experience suggests that ideas of essential order in the social and psychological realms are also open to doubt.

The portrait of Silas follows the psychological theory of Lewes who differed pre-eminently from Bain and other contemporaries in his

belief that the mind had no controlling ego, no "unity of the execu-
tive."[19] Mind, he argued, like organic life, comprised the processes of
interaction between the organism and medium, thus "psychical Life has
no one special centre, any more than the physical Life has one special
centre: it belongs to the whole, and animates the whole."[20] The operations of the mind were not unified and directed by a rational ego, there
was no essential self to impose order on incoming sensations, thus mental
history need not constitute a linear continuum. In pursuing the psychological implications of Comte's theory of dynamic interaction Lewes
and George Eliot undercut Comte's determining social and moral
assumptions. Eliot's image of the relationship between the individual
and surrounding society is not one of simple reflection, where psychological continuity reflects social continuity. Neither the individual nor
society possess intrinsic coherence. In *Silas Marner* George Eliot develops the psychological insights of *The Mill on the Floss* to create a
masterly study of the growing disjunction between Silas and his surrounding world. Far from reinforcing an idealistic picture of social life,
the novel actually anticipates, in its opening sections, the later *Daniel
Deronda*, with its pessimistic vision of the conflict, and lack of communication that can actually characterise social interdependence.

Following the premises of Lewes' psychological theory, George Eliot
traces the internal effects of Silas' alienation. She reveals how, within
the rural world of Raveloe, he is reduced from human status to a
"spinning insect," until he finally takes on the qualities of an object:

he had clung with all the force of his nature to his work and his money;
and like all objects to which a man devotes himself, they had fashioned
him into correspondence with themselves. His loom, as he wrought in it
without ceasing, had in its turn wrought on him, and confirmed more and
more the monotonous craving for its monotonous response. His gold, as
he hung over it and saw it grow, gathered his power of loving together
into a hard isolation like its own (Ch. 5, p. 63).

As his own creativity is drawn from him in his increasing subjection to
his loom and his gold, Silas endows these alienated self-images with
his own active powers. Clearly he is no rational actor in charge of his
sensual steed; indeed, he is unable to establish any hierarchical differentiation between human, animal or even object life. The pattern of his
life conforms not to the Comtean theory of evolution from fetishim to
rationality, but rather to the "fetishism of commodities" described by
that other great nineteenth-century historian, Marx. In the monetary
system, Marx observes, "gold and silver, when serving as money, did

not represent a social relation between producers, but were natural objects with strange social properties."[21] Gold, for Silas, takes on these strange social properties. His relations with his fellow villagers become for him a mere function through which he can acquire more coins. Reduced into a "constant mechanical relation to the objects of his life" (Ch. 2, p. 29) he looks, for the last vestiges of human contact, towards his gold. Whilst lavishing his loving attention on his piles of coins he "thought fondly of the guineas that were only half earned by the work in his loom, as if they had been unborn children" (Ch. 2, p. 31). He comes, indeed, to believe that his coins are "conscious of him" (Ch. 2, p. 27). Social relations for Silas are displaced entirely into the realm of objects.

This powerful analysis of Silas' growing alienation inverts organicist theories of historical development. Comte believed that the evolution of society from homogeneity to heterogeneity would necessarily bring greater social solidarity. As the division of labour increased, and social interdependence developed, feelings of sympathy would arise, and altruism would supplant the more primitive emotions of egoism. Silas' presence in Raveloe signals a new increase in the division of labour, but he does not create a growing solidarity within the community. He evokes hostility, not altruism, from his neighbours, whilst he himself is precipitated into isolation and egoism, and an ever-narrowing range of response.

George Eliot's critical vision of Raveloe society is not sustained, however. Halfway through the novel the pattern of Silas' life is reversed with the arrival of Eppie. Unlike Maggie, Silas is permitted to grow, in the midst of life, into organic community with his neighbours. The change appears little short of miraculous. Like the concluding flood of *The Mill on the Floss* it suggests a disruption of uniform law. As Strauss argued in *The Life of Jesus*, "no just notion of the true nature of history is possible without a perception of the inviolability of the chain of finite causes, and of the impossibility of miracles."[22] Yet, although Eppie is compared to the angels who led men away from the city of destruction (Ch. 14, p. 201) there are in fact no miracles involved in Silas' restoration; George Eliot takes care to ensure that the natural chain of causation is not broken. In accordance with her design, the novel reveals "the remedial influences of pure, natural human relations."[23] To achieve this end she turns, perhaps surprisingly, to the principles of physiological psychology which had sustained the analysis of Silas' growing alienation. Although Lewes' theories, in their ultimate implications, undercut ideas of ordered social or psychological development, the original impetus behind his work was to affirm the reign of order throughout the physical and social realms. George Eliot's fiction is characterised by a similar duality; she employs the principles of physiological psychology initially to challenge, and ultimately to affirm conceptions of organic unity and continuity.

In accordance with physiological principles George Eliot makes Silas' first response to Eppie one of memory:

Could this be his little sister come back to him in a dream . . . ?
. . . It was very much like his little sister. Silas sank into his chair powerless, under the double presence of an inexplicable surprise and a hurrying influx of memories (Ch. 12, p. 170).

Eppie does not disrupt the continuity of Silas' life but rather stimulates the dormant channels of his mind. George Eliot's analysis in this crucial passage conforms to Lewes' conception of the mind as an "aggregate of forces" and to his theories of unconscious association. Thus the sight of the child stimulates within Silas a whole chain of associated memories: "a vision of the old home and the old streets leading to Lantern Yard – and within that vision another, of the thoughts which had been present with him in those far-off scenes" (Ch. 12, p. 170). Silas' sequence of memory illustrates the "law of attraction" defined here by Spencer: "that when any two psychical states occur in immediate succession, an effect is produced such that if the first subsequently recurs there is a certain tendency for the second to follow."[24] The physical processes of unconscious association establish continuity in personal life, a continuity which, Spencer believed, was then passed on to future generations through the physiological inheritance of "modified nervous tendencies."[25] Physiological structure seemed, to Spencer, to guarantee progressive social evolution.[26]

Although George Eliot did not entirely share Spencer's ebullient social optimism, she did attribute a key role to physiology in Silas' recovery. The physiological unity of mind, represented by his unconscious association of ideas, allows him to heal the breach in his social experience. Through his relationship with Eppie he grows once more into union with his neighbours, and into a sense of continuity with his past. Eppie's progressive development is mirrored in Silas as the underlying continuity of his history is gradually revealed: "As the child's mind was growing into knowledge, his mind was growing into memory: as her life unfolded, his soul, long stupefied in a cold narrow prison, was unfolding too, and trembling gradually into full consciousness"

(Ch. 14, pp. 193–4). The term "full consciousness" is here replete with meaning: it implies not only an integrated sense of self based on continuous memory, but also an open, accepting awareness of surrounding social life. Under the influence of Eppie Silas moves beyond the "ever-repeated circle" of thought established by his gold to look for links and ties with his neighbours. He learns to channel his previously inert feelings into "the forms of custom and belief which were the mould of Raveloe life; and as, with reawakening sensibilities, memory also reawakened, he had begun to ponder over the elements of his old faith, and blend them with his new impressions, till he recovered a consciousness of unity between his past and present" (Ch. 14, p. 213). Silas grows simultaneously into organic unity within his social and psychological life; isolation and personal disruption are replaced by integration.

Silas' change appears, on the surface, to be a dramatic transformation; but, in charting its course, George Eliot employs the same theoretical premises that lay behind her earlier analysis. Throughout the novel she examines both social and psychological life in the light of Lewes' and Spencer's theories of channelled energy. The great attraction of physiological psychology for these thinkers lay in the fact that it allowed them to extend to the mind the principles they saw operating in the social and physiological organism. They employed in their work a single vocabulary of channelled energy to describe the three different spheres of physiological, mental, and social life. George Eliot readily adopted these theories, since they allowed her to integrate her analysis of the different levels of organic life.

In her study of the effects of the Lantern Yard religion on Silas' mind George Eliot draws together the concepts of external cultural channels, and internal pathways of the mind. Thus Silas accepted the religious explanation of his fits since "culture had not defined any channels for his sense of mystery, and so it spread itself over the proper pathway of inquiry and knowledge" (Ch. 1, p. 11). The image of the force of mystery irresistibly spreading over the "proper pathway of inquiry and knowledge" is in accordance with Lewes' Law of Sensibility that "No sensation terminates in itself." Once aroused, a sensation must necessarily receive issue. The customs of Lantern Yard formed, for Silas, "the channel of divine influences" (Ch. 2, p. 21). Following his expulsion from these accustomed channels of expression, his social disruption is replicated internally in the physiological structure of his mind: "Thought was arrested by utter bewilderment, now its old narrow pathway was closed, and affection seemed to have died under the bruise that had fallen on its keenest nerves" (Ch. 2, p. 23). This sensitive description of Silas' psychological confusion is based on the physiologically precise idea of energy diverted from its usual, defined channels of discharge. It conforms to Lewes' theories concerning the contrast between the ease felt in accustomed action, and the difficulties of acquiring new patterns of behaviour:

> In learning to speak a new language, to play on a musical instrument, or to perform any unaccustomed movements, great difficulty is felt, because the channels through which each sensation has to pass have not become established; but no sooner has frequent repetition cut a pathway, than this difficulty vanishes.[27]

These principles lie behind George Eliot's analysis of Silas' alienation. His growing subjection to the numbing activity of weaving and the counting of gold is explained in terms of the ease felt in a habitual action for "Do we not wile away moments of inanity or fatigued waiting by repeating some trivial movement or sound, until the repetition has bred a want, which is incipient habit?" (Ch. 2, p. 27). This suggestion conforms to Lewes' theory that once frequent repetition has cut a pathway actions become so automatic that "if once commenced, they must continue."[28] In hoarding his gold, marking the periods of his existence only by the acquisition of his guineas, Silas' life was "narrowing and hardening itself more and more into a mere pulsation of desire and satisfaction that had no relation to any other being" (Ch. 2, p. 28). While the physical image of pulsation accurately portrays the nature of Silas' life it also suggests, in moral terms, its inadequacies: Silas' reduction from a social to a purely physical being. The physical description in fact reinforces the moral analysis.

George Eliot did not employ physiological theory solely for the sake of descriptive accuracy. Its integrated vocabulary allowed her to shift easily between different levels of analysis, combining intricate psychological analysis with wider social and moral conclusions. Thus throughout the novel she transposed physiological concepts into vivid metaphorical images to highlight their social and psychological implications.[29] Silas' lack of interest in the hedgerows he had once loved is expressed in the following poetic terms:

> these too belonged to the past, from which his life had shrunk away, like a rivulet that has sunk far down from the grassy fringe of its old breadth into a little shivering thread, that cuts a groove for itself in the barren sand (Ch. 2, p. 31).

The description is extraordinarily rich and evocative. From the hedgerow banks, which offer both a literal and symbolic image of the changes in Silas' life, it moves to the idea of river banks, and to the contrast between the lush fertility of a full river, and the stark, desert-like conditions of a drought. The passage, with its shift from an historical to a physiological definition of life, captures brilliantly the qualitative changes in the nature of Silas' existence. Reduced to a "shivering thread," Silas clearly possesses no control over the conditions of his life. Behind these striking natural images lies the physiological premise that streams of sensation, once displaced from their accustomed channels, only carve a new pathway with great difficulty. It is the "peculiar characteristic of vigorous intellects," Lewes notes, " that their thoughts are ever finding new pathways instead of moving amid old associations."[30] Silas, however, has not the vitality to affect this change. Thus, in a variation on the earlier image "his soul was still the shrunken rivulet, with only this difference, that its little groove of sand was blocked up, and it wandered confusedly against dark obstruction." (Ch. 10, p. 132). The "fountains of human love and faith" in his mind are locked up, unable to find a channel of release. The terms are still those of physiological psychology, but with the relatively simple addition of the word "soul," the physical description takes on extensive moral and social implications.

Eppie, of course, functions as the catalyst for the release of Silas' energy. Her appearance does not mark, however, the first time that Silas' memories have been awakened. George Eliot charts both the shrinking current of Silas' life, and the movements within his unconscious which lead to his later change. Early in his residence in Raveloe, the sight of Sally Oates suffering from dropsy had recalled memories of his mother and stimulated him to aid her: "In this office of charity, Silas felt, for the first time since he had come to Raveloe, a sense of unity between his past and present life." But suspicion and misunderstanding prevented its growth. Indeed, in precise physiological terms, the incident "heightened the repulsion between him and his neighbours, and made his isolation more complete" (Ch. 2, pp. 25, 26). But the precedent for his response to Eppie has been set. In telling the story of his robbery in the Rainbow, and in coming to terms with his false accusation of Jem, Silas also experienced awakened memories of his past though, as the narrator observes, "Our consciousness rarely registers the beginning of a growth within us any more than without us: there have been many circulations of the sap before we detect the smallest sign of the bud." (Ch. 7, p. 86). The passage, with its vivid organic images, prepares the reader for

Silas' future development. By establishing a differential time scale between apparent social history and the hidden life of the unconscious, it suggests how Silas' fragmentary existence will once more be brought into union. The appearance of a figure who could release his blocked emotion and reopen the channels of his mind leads inevitably to the restoration of social and psychological unity. The apparent discontinuity of his life is discounted by the stable physiological structure of his mind. History, as the moral critique of Godfrey implied, is cumulative.

Analysis of the physiological underpinnings of George Eliot's figurative language reveals the extraordinary complexity of her work. Each word and phrase was related to her larger purpose as she attempted to resolve, in concrete terms, the social issues raised by organicism.[31] The satisfying conclusion of Silas' life, however, was only possible because the shared vocabulary of organic social and psychological theory allowed George Eliot to elide these two distinct levels of analysis. Spencer and Lewes turned to physiological psychology for scientific validation of their belief in the hidden order of the world, and George Eliot, in this novel, follows their example: she employs physiology to reinforce the moral structure of her tale. In focusing on Silas' physiological growth into unity, however, she excludes reference both to his disruptive fits, and to the wider social context of his life. Ultimately, his isolation therefore appears as less a product of the social relations in Raveloe than an accident of personal circumstance, to be resolved on an individual level. This perspective is at odds, however, with the wider social analysis offered in the rest of the novel, notably in the history of Godfrey which runs in direct counterpoint to that of Silas.

After the arrival of Eppie the novel appears to move swiftly towards a happy ending. The wedding, set in the season of eternal renewal "when the great lilacs and laburnums in the old-fashioned gardens showed their golden and purple wealth above the lichen-tinted walls" (Conclusion, p. 270) and confirmed by the, for once, unanimous approval of the Raveloe chorus, certainly seems to validate the organic social ideal. The social harmony is marred, however, by the absence of Godfrey Cass; whilst forward movement of the plot is balanced by the less positive model of history suggested by the destruction of Lantern Yard. Following his "resurrection" by Eppie, Silas had turned once more to a belief in the providential government of history. Inspired by her to a sense of "presiding goodness" (Ch. 16, p. 213) he came to believe that his earlier expulsion from Lantern Yard must have been due to some error. He returned, therefore, with Eppie to Lantern Yard to see Mr Paston "a man with a deal o' light," in the hope that the minister would be able to illuminate the historical process: why the "drawing o' the lots" did not vindicate Silas' belief in an ordered universe but rather seemed to endorse the rule of chance. In place of the light and order he expected to find, however, he discovered only darkness and destruction: "Here and there a sallow, begrimed face looked out from a gloomy doorway at the strangers" (Ch. 21, p. 268). Into this gloom, so reminiscent of Eppie's origin, Lantern Yard had vanished, to be replaced by a factory, symbol of the industrial changes which, like Molly's dark history, had no discernible impact on Raveloe life. Silas failed to find order or meaning in history. Lacking historical illumination he was left in darkness: "It's dark to me Mrs. Winthrop, that is; I doubt it'll be dark to the last" (Ch. 21, p. 269). Through Eppie he found "light enough to trusten by," but not the light of historical reason he had sought.

Silas' failure highlights the internal conflicts in the novel. The tale is no simple endorsement of organicist theories of social development. As the stress on moral responsibility is balanced by the seemingly uncontrollable nature of Silas' fits, so Silas' growth into psychological continuity is offset by the seeming recalcitrance of social history; its refusal to conform to a pattern of ordered development. The dark vision of the "great manufacturing town" where the jail hides the sky suggests that the novel's Edenic conclusion can only be achieved by moving backwards in history to the pre-industrial landscape of Raveloe. Yet even here, it is questionable whether the life of a rural idyll could be attained. George Eliot's portrayal of Raveloe, is marked by the same duality that characterises the rest of the tale. On the one hand it appears a land of Edenic bounty, with "orchards looking lazy with neglected plenty" (Ch. 2, p. 21). Protected, like Hayslope, by nature "it was nestled in a snug well-wooded hollow," and centered round "a fine old church" (Ch. 1, p. 7). These images of a natural, harmonious existence are, on the other hand, offset by descriptions of the peasantry's lives as "pressed close by primitive wants. . . To them pain and mishap present a far wider range of possibilities than gladness and enjoyment: their imagination is almost barren of the images that feed desire and hope, but is all overgrown by recollections that are a perpetual pasture to fear" (Ch. 1, p. 6). The image is a grim one indeed, but, throughout the novel, George Eliot offers no direct representation of this poverty and fear. This reluctance to portray the darker side of Raveloe experience suggests George Eliot's own ambivalent response.

The bald references to the poverty and misery of Raveloe life are balanced by the detailed celebration of the organic community of the feudal order. Thus the loving attention lavished on Miss Nancy's arrival at Squire Cass', the feast and the New Year's Eve dance seems to confirm for the reader, as for the assembled community of villages, the "fitness of things": "That was as it should be – that was what everybody had been used to – and the charter of Raveloe seemed to be renewed by the ceremony" (Ch. 11, pp. 156–7). This ritual of renewal is disrupted, however, by the arrival of Silas with Eppie in his arms. For Godfrey, Silas seemed "an apparition from that hidden life which lies, like a dark by-street, behind the goodly ornamented façade that meets the sunlight and the gaze of respectable admirers" (Ch. 13, p. 174). The dark by-streets are not confined to the manufacturing town of Silas' past, but intrude even upon the gay procession in the White Parlour "where the mistletoe-bough was hung, and multitudinous tallow candles made rather a brilliant effect, gleaming from among the berried holly-boughs, and reflected in the old-fashioned oval mirrors fastened in the panels of the white wainscot" (Ch. 11, p. 156). The villagers' own belief in a harmonious natural order, celebrated here in these images of brilliant festivities, is shown to be founded on an illusion. In place of the villagers' affectionate respect for the gaiety of their superiors' lives, we should perhaps substitute the narrator's vision of our rural forefathers, "men whose only work was to ride round their land, getting heavier and heavier in their saddles, and who passed the rest of their days in the half-listless gratification of senses dulled by monotony" (Ch. 3, p. 44). George Eliot no longer endorses the social vision of *Adam Bede*. Although the earlier novel had condemned Arthur's abuse of his social position and responsibilities it had not questioned the fundamental desirability of the hierarchical social system. *Silas Marner*, however, portrays the life of the squirearchy as intrinsically negative and unproductive. Even the "order and purity" of a Nancy Lammeter cannot, it seems, bring fertility to a form of life which is essentially barren.

The significant absence of Godfrey Cass from the concluding scene suggests that the final harmony is attained only by excluding the murkier side of Raveloe life. Godfrey's history reveals the petty and even sordid nature of experience within this rural community. In *Adam Bede* George Eliot had portrayed seduction and even murder, but had not even hinted at the form of life she now reveals through Godfrey's backstairs marriage, Molly's death from opium addiction and Dunsey's blackmail and theft. Silas and Godfrey, as critics have pointed out, undergo a similar pattern of experience; both are victims of a scheming brother who plots their overthrow.[32] There is a crucial difference, however, in the mode of presentation. Whilst William Dane is only sketchily presented, we see Dunsey Cass in all his taunting, menacing glory. George Eliot offers the facts of Dane's treachery without exploring fully its causes or motivations, but in dealing with Dunsey she reveals, in careful detail, how the social conditions of the Casses' lives contribute to his behaviour. His malignancy is not an individual aberration but a direct product of his social environment. Even more clearly than in Lantern Yard, evil seems to be endemic to the structure of Raveloe life.

Throughout the novel George Eliot brings to her representation of Godfrey this same clear-eyed vision. In the parallel structure of the plot, Silas' 15 barren years are re-enacted in Godfrey's barren marriage, and Godfrey's loss of Eppie becomes, as U. C. Knoepflmacher has observed, Silas' "strange gain."[33] There exists, however, a disturbing disparity between the two stories. Whilst Silas' fall and later redemption are originally brought about by chance, Godfrey's life is rigorously governed by the operation of uniform law. Though Godfrey, like Dunsey, cares initially, "more for immediate annoyances than for remote consequences" (Ch. 4, p. 52), he comes to learn that an individual must bear responsibility for all his deeds. He becomes, indeed, a living exemplum of George Eliot's doctrine of the "inexorable law of consequences." Like Arthur Donnithorne, Godfrey takes comfort initially in casuistry. As Arthur had hoped that good could come out of evil, so Godfrey trusts that, if events turn out better than a man expects "is it not a proof that his conduct has been less foolish and blameworthy than it might otherwise have appeared?" (Ch. 13, p. 183). The narrative decisively rejects such moral relativism. Godfrey's childless marriage, and the recovery of Dunsey's body, function as moral symbols of the workings of inexorable law.

Whilst Silas receives the unexpected gift of Eppie, Godfrey is treated with all the harshness of "unrecompensing law." Arthur, despite his crimes, had been welcomed back at the close of *Adam Bede* into the community of Hayslope. Godfrey, however, learns that there are some debts that cannot be paid: "While I've been putting off and putting off, the trees have been growing – it's too late now" (Ch. 20, p. 262). The implicit moral recalls the concluding observation in *The Mill on the Floss*: "Nature repairs her ravages – but not all." In both novels this image of historical attrition stands in direct contrast to a more optimistic social vision. *Silas Marner* ends with Eppie's joyful exclamation "I think nobody could be happier than we are." But, as in *The Mill*, this joy is only to be attained at a certain cost. Maggie lost her life; Silas and Eppie lose part of their past. Silas no longer looks to integrate Lantern Yard within his present life, whilst Eppie, in an ideologically significant gesture, denies Godfrey's paternal claims, thus violating the natural chain of biological continuity.

Although strong arguments have been made for the satisfying nature of *Silas Marner*'s conclusion, its symmetry seems marred.[34] Godfrey fails to take account of the unity of the historical process and is duly punished; Silas is unaccountably blessed by chance and learns, in consequence, to relinquish his quest for order and meaning in history. He learns, instead, to trust; but, such a position implies a passivity directly at odds with the ideal of active, far-sighted responsibility for action, inculcated elsewhere in the novel. Trust, indeed, is a viable stance only within a harmonious order, a society without conflict; it would not have resolved the dilemmas of Maggie's life. Silas, unlike Maggie, is spared the conflict of irreconcilable claims, but the dual representation of Raveloe life puts into question the quality of his Eden.

The celebration of plenitude which concludes *Silas Marner* is based, like the flood in *The Mill on the Floss*, on an evasion of the preceding attempt to find within history an ordered process of growth. Like the earlier novel, *Silas Marner* offers two models of history. Order, continuity and control are set against chance, disruption and powerlessness: the fairy tale elements are balanced by the darker history of Molly or Dunsey, and the stress on moral responsibility is offset by the seemingly uncontrollable nature of Silas' fits. These divisions within the novel reveal George Eliot's ambivalent responses to theories of organic development. Clearly, it was no longer possible for her to resolve the issues raised by organicism by turning to the life of "Merry England." Thus in her next novel she abandoned her accustomed English setting, choosing to dramatise these questions in the idealised form made possible by the temporal and cultural distance of Renaissance Italy.

CHAPTER 5

Romola:
The authority of history

Romola is George Eliot's sole historical novel: the only novel placed outside the sphere of living memory. It is also the novel which most painstakingly explores the nineteenth-century issues of organicism: the relationship between social duty and egoism, submission and rebellion, historical change and continuity. In replacing nineteenth-century English provincial life by fifteenth-century Florence George Eliot has transferred the novel's appeal for validation from the subjective realm of readers' experience to that higher court, History. The authority of history is inscribed within *Romola* both through the treatment of a recognised historical period (where period implies both a span of time, and its definite cessation), and the inclusion of actual historical figures. In weaving together the lives of Savonarola, Romola and Tito, George Eliot sought the endorsement of historical chronology and event for a story whose essence was, as her contemporaries realised, nineteenth-century experience.[1]

Replying to Frederic Harrison's proposal that she should write a Comtean novel, George Eliot referred to the "unspeakable pains" she had taken in *Romola* to capture the "Idiom" of Florence, "And there I was only trying to give *some* out of the ordinary relations. I felt the necessary idealisation could only be obtained by adopting the clothing of the past."[2] George Eliot's aim in *Romola* was "to make certain ideas thoroughly incarnate"[3] and in fifteenth-century Florence she found the perfect medium. Live social issues and contemporary confusion could be placed within the clarity of historical perspective, for the historical conclusion of the period seemed to guarantee that the issues themselves were susceptible to resolution. The temporal distance appeared to confirm the organic continuity of history: that like the unchanged river courses, "the life-currents that ebb and flow in human hearts, pulsate to the same great needs, the same great loves and terrors."[4]

The change in historical period is accompanied by alterations in

96

narrative technique: George Eliot drops the narrator's persona, and the intimacy of the moral generalisations which assume continuity between the lives of the narrator and reader. She similarly discards comments designed to create a dual perspective between the time of the novel and that of the reader. Entry into the novel does not occur through memory as in "Amos Barton" or *The Mill on the Floss*; the initial presiding consciousness is not that of the author but of the Florentine Spirit who moves, not backward, but forward in time, following the onward course of history. Thereafter George Eliot relies on the appearance of objectivity, or what Barthes terms "the referential illusion" where, in the absence of clues to the narrator, "the historian tries to give the impression that the referent is speaking for itself."[5] In her note on "Historic Imagination" George Eliot observes that "for want of such real, minute vision of how changes come about in the past, we fall into ridiculously inconsistent estimates of actual movements."[6] The wealth of scholarship behind *Romola*, and the presentation of the novel not as constructed fiction but as history, illustrate George Eliot's desire to illuminate contemporary confusion by reference to the historical past.

Renaissance Italy furnished an apt setting for the novel for, like nineteenth-century England, it was a society undergoing radical change, witnessing "the unrest of a new growth" (Proem, I, 9). Religious belief clashed with unbelief, hebraism with hellenism, and oligarchy with democracy. Clearly, it was an era in which the issues of organicism could be fully dramatised in both their personal and political aspects. Thus it is within *Romola* that George Eliot offers her most direct statement of the organic continuity of private and political life: "as in the tree that bears a myriad of blossoms, each single bud with its fruit is dependent on the primary circulation of the sap, so the fortunes of Tito and Romola were dependent on certain grand political and social conditions which made an epoch in the history of Italy" (Ch. 21, I, 313). Relations between the individual and the social whole are governed by the same principles of interdependence that determine organic life. In addition, *Romola* also dramatises a homologous relationship between the personal and the larger political sphere: the same question is fundamentally at stake in both. As George Eliot observes in a letter, the "great problem" of Romola's life "which essentially coincides with a chief problem in Savonarola's, is one that readers need helping to understand."[7]

The "great problem" is that raised by the organicist Burke, in his

Reflections on the Revolution in France. In a passage, recorded by George Eliot in her "Commonplace Book," he remarks, "The speculative line of demarcation, where obedience ought to end, and resistance must begin, is faint, obscure, not easily definable."[8] In *Romola* this dilemma is dramatised on both a personal and political level. The Florentine people confront its political dimensions when Savonarola defies the Pope, for, as George Eliot observes:

The question where the duty of obedience ends and the duty of resistance begins could in no case be an easy one; but it was made overwhelmingly difficult by the belief that the Church was – not a compromise of parties to secure a more or less approximate justice in the appropriation of funds, but – a living organism instinct with Divine power to bless and to curse (Ch. 55, II, 255).

Romola, deciding whether to leave Tito, and questioning how far she should be bound by the social institution of marriage, is faced with the same dilemma:

The law was sacred. Yes, but rebellion might be sacred too. It flashed upon her mind that the problem before her was essentially the same as that which had lain before Savonarola – the problem where the sacredness of obedience ended, and where the sacredness of rebellion began (Ch. 56, II, 273).

The question derives from Burke, but not the resolution. As one of the leaders of the conservative reaction to the French Revolution, Burke upheld the value of historical continuity, of submission not rebellion. But for George Eliot, who was writing from within the later Comtean perspective which sought to unite concern for order and continuity with the revolutionary desire for progress, the issue was not so easily resolved.

The fundamental question, of how far man should be bound by the culture of the past, is present at every level of the text. It underlies the political debate between the Mediceans and their opponents, concerning whether government should be by family loyalties and tradition or by democracy, and it also lies behind the fundamental conflict between hebraism and hellenism. George Eliot explores in the novel the relationship between the hebrastic belief in submission to the teachings of the church, and the hellenistic commitment to the free play of mind. Within the doctrines of hellenism itself, she also examines the contrast between Bardo's blind immersion in the past and Tito's bright, creative, but amoral energy which flies free from the shackles of history. In their relationship to history and language Bardo and Tito dramatise,

on a thematic level, George Eliot's own doubts about writing an historical novel. Romola's dilemma concerning her relationship to history is
also that of her author. George Eliot wrote *Romola* in full awareness
that it would not be popular,[9] it also caused her greater anxiety than
any other novel: "I began it a young woman – I finished it an old
woman."[10] Years later she was to tell Blackwood that of no other novel
did she "more thoroughly feel that I could swear by every sentence as
having been written with my best blood."[11] Both her urgency of purpose
and sense of fulfilment derive from the fact that, through the historical
setting of *Romola*, she was able to confront both the issues of organicism,
and her own role as novelist.

Throughout the novel George Eliot appears to be engaged in a dialogue with Comte, questioning his ideas by embodying abstract ideals
within the complex detail of her Florentine lives.[12] In a letter to R. H.
Hutton, George Eliot alluded to the strong self-control she exercised
over the presentation of detail, so that there was "scarcely a phrase, an
incident, an allusion, that did not gather its value to me from its sup-
posed subservience to my main artistic objects." She continues:

It is the habit of my imagination to strive after as full a vision of the
medium in which a character moves as of the character itself. The psychological causes which prompted me to give such details of Florentine life
and history as I have given, are precisely the same as those which determined me in giving the details of English village life in *Silas Marner*, or the
'Dodson' life, out of which were developed the destinies of poor Tom and
Maggie.[13]

Her "encyclopedic"[14] efforts in the composition of *Romola* stem from
her adherence to Comte's organicist conception that the individual is
the product of the medium in which he dwells. Interaction between the
individual organism and social medium establishes both character and
"destiny" – the problems concerning the individual's relation to society
which George Eliot seeks in her novels to resolve. Carole Robinson
rightly argues against any simplistic reading of the novel in terms of
egoism versus devotion: "The true conflicts within the novel occur
within the heroine, not between heroine and villain."[15] The question of
obedience and rebellion is not a simple issue of inner desire versus
external constraint; following organicist theory, constraint is inscribed
within the individual.

Romola, attempting to draw off Tito's ring, is arrested by "that force
of outward symbols by which our active life is knit together so as to
make an inexorable external identity for us, not to be shaken by our

wavering consciousness" (Ch. 36, II, 46). The movement brings "a vague but arresting sense that she was somehow violently rending her life in two" (Ch. 36, II, 46). In line with Comtean theory, the individual is not conceived as an autonomous unit: self-identity is established through the historically evolving symbolic network. Questions of individual integrity thus relate to the larger issue of historical continuity. On the second occasion of her leaving Tito, Romola is again torn, feeling that the sanctity which attached to the marriage tie was "but the expression in outward law of that result towards which all human goodness and nobleness must spontaneously tend; that the light abandonment of ties, whether inherited or voluntary, because they had ceased to be pleasant, was the uprooting of social and personal virtue" (Ch. 56, II, 272). Law is not the arbitrary creation of a nation's rulers, but the external expression of the people's historical and moral progress. The personal and political acts of rebellion are shown to be synonymous. To break the marriage tie is to institute both self-division and a pattern of behaviour which, if followed, would disrupt the historical development of the race. The observation is a theoretic formulation of the social assumptions and values underlying Maggie's allegiance to the past in *The Mill on the Floss*: "If the past is not to bind us, where can duty lie?" (Bk VI, Ch. 14). The question expresses in personal terms the political issue posed by the theorists of organicism in response to the French Revolution.

Savonarola, an embodiment of Comte's Priest of Humanity, preaches the doctrines of positivism to Romola, stressing primarily her duty not to God, but to Florence, the social organism of which she forms a part. If Romola is tied only by love of her father she is, Savonarola declares, "without religion: you are no better than a beast of the field when she is robbed of her young" (Ch. 40, II, 107). The sentiment of altruism which, Comte believed, emerged through social evolution, is expressed not in the individual emotions of personal affection, but through the observation of social law. Savonarola counsels Romola to return to her home, "My daughter, you are a child of Florence; fulfil the duties of that great inheritance" (Ch. 40, II, 111). The filial image captures the theory of organic continuity which underlies his appeal to duty. Yet Romola returns to Florence only to flee again. The repetitive pattern of doubt, flight and affirmation in *Romola* reflects George Eliot's uncertain relation to Comtean philosophy. In his *Catéchisme* Comte proclaimed the inescapable demands of duty: "Le positivisme n'admet jamais que des devoirs chez tous envers tous. Car son point de vue toujours social ne peut comporter aucune notion de droit, constamment fondée sur l'individualité."[16] In the margin against this passage George Eliot noted in her copy "How could there be duties without corresponding claims?" Unquestioning submission, whether personal or political, is an ideal whose premises are investigated and challenged within the novel.

Savonarola preaches the positivist doctrine of altruism outlined by Comte: "Toute l'étude du dogme positif conduit à conclure que notre véritable unité consiste surtout à vivre pour autrui."[17] Romola, Savonarola argues, is below the believer who "beholds the history of the world as the history of a great redemption in which he is himself a fellow-worker, in his own place and among his own people!" (Ch. 40, II, 107). Through emphasis on ideas of historical development and social membership, Comte sought, in his Religion of Humanity, to replace what he saw as the superstitions and narrowing beliefs of the nineteenth-century Catholic Church. Romola, with a mind that "had not been allowed to draw its early nourishment from the traditional associations of the Christian community in which her father had lived a life apart" (Ch. 55, II, 255), is in a state parallel to that of the Victorian intellectual who could no longer accept the authority of the church. But, as the novel demonstrates, with the loss of divine authority, there can be no simple formulation of duty, for where should allegiance lie if society is shown to be corrupt? Comte's willed creation of the Religion of Humanity scarcely solves the dilemma of a philosophy which proclaims society as an organic whole but wishes to deny the validity of one of its long-standing institutions. Romola, fleeing a second time from Florence, "despaired of finding any consistent duty belonging to that name" (Ch. 61, II, 320). The central question in *Romola*, and one which arises in all George Eliot's novels, is how, having accepted the organic values of social interdependence and duty, can an unequivocal form of duty be discerned in a conflict-ridden society? It is an issue which George Eliot was to explicitly address in her later notes on "Historic Guidance."

Comte, in stating his doctrine of the substitution of Duties for Rights, the subordination of "personal to social considerations," had argued that "the consensus of the social organism extends to Time as well as Space. Hence the two distinct aspects of the social sympathy; the feeling of Solidarity, or union with the Present; and of Continuity, or union with the Past."[18] George Eliot observes in her notes on "Historic Guidance" that "When continuity or the dependence of one generation on the preceding, & solidarity or the interdependence of co-existing men, have thoroughly entered into the human consciousness they necessarily become tests & rules of action. Continuity passes from a mere fact into a motive":[19] men actively seek to determine their lives by these values. But, for George Eliot, the question "How shall that idea or recognised fact shape our procedure?" is one that remains unresolved. Historical continuity, she argues, is not always beneficial, for "we see evil results descending from generation to generation."[20] Reconciling the two ideals of stability and change, George Eliot argues that continuity can at the most act as "a guide in the *adaptation* of systematic reforms."[21] Social transformation is at least as important as social continuity. This stance leads directly to a critique of Comte's theory of a separate priesthood, which was based on an assumption of individual passivity in regard to social change. Should we reproduce a priesthood, she asks, "which shall give forth intellectual and moral judgments as *placita* of authority & shall be liable to no control except the threat of disapprobation in minds over which it exercises the sole spiritual direction?"[22] The question is central to *Romola*. In the "Notes" George Eliot challenges this proposed system on two counts. Firstly, even priests of superior calibre will not be "exempt from the temptations or warping influences which have hitherto made corporations disposed to amplify their power even to tyranny & created in them a spirit of jealousy towards all inspirations outside their pale as 'irregularities.' "[23] Secondly, George Eliot expresses reservations concerning the abstract nature of theory: "Doctrine, no matter of what sort, is liable to putrefy when kept in close chambers to be dispensed according to the will of men authorized to hold the keys."[24] These questions concerning the social and political premises of organicism, and the role of the Comtean priesthood, are precisely those which guided the composition of *Romola*.

In her portrait of Savonarola, George Eliot dramatises the dangers of the Comtean priesthood. Trapped by the complexity of social conditions, his history is that of "the struggle of a mind possessed by a never-silent hunger after purity and simplicity, yet caught in a tangle of egoistic demands, false ideas, and difficult outward conditions, that made simplicity impossible" (Ch. 59, II, 306). Savonarola's role as priest is undermined both by uneven social conditions, and by his own egoism. The reconciliation of egoism, individualism, and social duty represents the personal form of the larger historical reconciliation Comte sought between continuity and change, order and progress. He had predicted the developing synthesis of the two:

À mesure que l'activité matérielle devient de plus en plus collective, elle tend davantage vers le caractère altruiste quoique l'impulsion égoiste doive toujours rester indispensable à son premier essor.[25]

But, in *Romola*, George Eliot translates this proposition into all its possible social complexities which the glib abstract formulation conceals, thus revealing the necessary opposition between motivating egoistic energy and altruistic goals. Romola is alienated by the conflict of altruism and egoism in Savonarola's teachings:

In that declaration of his, that the cause of his party was the cause of God's kingdom, she heard only the ring of egoism. Perhaps such words have rarely been uttered without that meaner ring in them; yet they are the implicit formula of all energetic belief (Ch. 61, II, 322).

Following *Romola*, one can see why Daniel Deronda should desire "some social captainship, which would come to me as a duty, and not be striven for as a personal prize."[26] Energetic belief, if allowed to carve its own path must, George Eliot believes, inevitably fall prey to the lures of egoism. Romola's second form of disillusionment with Savonarola stems from the same distrust of abstract theory which George Eliot expressed in her "Notes." Savonarola's refusal to aid Bernardo awakens Romola's critical response for "*she* looked with the eyes of personal tenderness, and *he* with the eyes of theoretic conviction" (Ch. 61, II, 322). Savonarola's adherence to doctrine, without consideration of the particular case, leads to both injustice and unwarranted hardness.

George Eliot challenges, in *Romola*, both Comte's belief in the unproblematic creation of a priesthood, and the ideal of unquestioning submission. As Carole Robinson has noted, Romola's life in Florence scarcely fulfils the ideal outlined by Savonarola. Romola has no "innate taste for tending the sick and clothing the ragged" (Ch. 44, II, 146); only the enthusiasm which Savonarola personally inspires sustains her. Carole Robinson sees in this discrepancy a failure in George Eliot's honesty, quoting in evidence the report of Romola's consciousness at this period:

'She was marching with a great army; she was feeling the stress of a common life. If victims were needed, and it was uncertain on whom the lot might fall, she would stand ready to her name.' The word 'stress' itself belies the pretended exaltation in a 'common life'; and 'victim' is an unfortunate epithet for a heroine of the people.[27]

Yet the term "victim" is precisely chosen: it illuminates Romola's self-dramatisation. Like Maggie Tulliver, Romola "had thrown all the energy of her will into renunciation" (Ch. 41, II, 116) which thus became a form of wilfulness, not true submission.[28] Faced with irreconcilable claims, the "labour of choice," Maggie's response had been to surrender herself to sensuality, to drift away with Stephen. Romola's courted death is a similar surrender:

The imagination of herself gliding away in that boat on the darkening waters was growing more and more into a longing, as the thought of a cool brook in sultriness becomes a painful thirst. To be freed from the burden of choice when all motive was bruised, to commit herself, sleeping, to destiny... (Ch. 61, II, 325).

Romola is unable to achieve, however, the oblivion of Maggie, where "memory was excluded," for "Memories hung upon her like the weight of broken wings that could never be lifted" (Ch. 61, II, 326). Yet this emphatic denial of the possibility of escaping the remorseless tread of historical continuity immediately precedes Romola's waking to a new life, where the past has no hold: a true Lethean bliss. Maggie awakes to an agonised consciousness of conflict between her past and present self. Romola arises from the sleep of death a fully fledged Madonna. The falsities which beset her position in Florence are no longer evident. With the child under her arm she becomes, as U. C. Knoepflmacher has pointed out, a living symbol of the positivist philosophy of history.[29] Madonna is no longer a courtesy title but the villagers' literal apprehension. Maggie attains self-unity only through the disruption of historical continuity, as she re-enters, through the agency of the flood, her childhood past. Romola, however, like the Lady of St Ogg's, becomes herself part of the mythic process, part of the growing heritage of mankind, creating through legend a bond of unity between past and present: "Many legends were afterwards told in that valley about the blessed Lady who came over the sea, but they were legends by which all who heard might know that in times gone by a woman had done beautiful loving deeds there, rescuing those who were ready to perish" (Ch. 68, II, 411).[30]

Through the "romantic and symbolical" "Drifting Away" George Eliot appears to over-rule her doubts regarding Comtean philosophy.[31] Thus Romola at the close is a true positivist, maintaining her altar for a Saint of Humanity. But the ritual seems sterile. Tito, when shown Giotto's campanile, that "prophetic symbol, telling that human life must somehow and some time shape itself into accord with that pure aspiring beauty" (Ch. 3, I, 48), had identified himself as one of George

Eliot's immoral characters by expressing nothing but scorn. Yet he is not simply a philistine; his reasons are shown by the narrative to possess a disturbing validity: "I have a shuddering sense of what there is inside – hideous smoked Madonnas" (Ch. 3, I, 49). Though men build symbols of "pure aspiring beauty" their function is to encase relics of past superstitions which have degraded original Christian principles into a worship of idols. Romola, as Madonna, can be seen in accordance with the ideas of Strauss or Comte, as a true reincarnation of the life and principles which the Virgin originally symbolised.[32] In an alternative reading, however, she can also be viewed as being trapped within a crippling Christian mythology.

Tito originally felt before Romola "that loving awe in the presence of noble womanhood, which is perhaps something like the worship paid of old to a great nature goddess, who was not all-knowing, but whose life and power were something deeper and more primordial than knowledge" (Ch. 9, I, 144). As Madonna, however, Romola is forever excluded from the life and fertility of a nature goddess, paralysed by an image of woman which places her outside the sphere of nature. In *Adam Bede*, the celebration of organic continuity was marked by the creation of a new Adam and Dinah. The later *Felix Holt* similarly concludes with the creation of a young Felix. Romola, by contrast, remains barren, charged only with the upbringing of Ninna and Lillo, who are signs not, as the Proem idealistically states, of "the eternal marriage between love and duty" (I, 12) but of amoral sensuality, which drew no guidance from the accumulated civilisation of the past. The conclusion of *Romola* does not reflect organic continuity – the perfect reconciliation of rebellion and obedience, egoistic energy and altruism, individual aspiration and duty. Though Romola expressed doubts, which her author clearly shared, concerning the egoistic basis of Savonarola's teachings, the pattern of the narrative seems to suggest that the only form of energy which will be productive of future continuity is that which is purely selfish, freed from social constraints. The contrast between Romola's barrenness and Tito's fertility dramatises, in a physical and sexual form, the questions George Eliot was asking in relation to history when she created the polarity of Bardo and Tito.

In his *Catéchisme* Comte proclaimed that women should be the object of men's worship. George Eliot notes, in the margin of her text, the reply to the next inevitable question, "What shall women worship?" The answer, it seems, is "Mother, Son, Husband."[33] But Romola has known no mother, will bear no son, and was blessed with a husband who should hardly inspire worship. There is, however, as Carole Robinson has noted, a proliferation of father figures in *Romola*, though all of them clearly fail her. Indeed, the novel tends to suppress "the disturbing masculine element." Thus the final female alliance between Tessa and Romola seems to be "peculiarly evasive, since it resolves Romola's search for a standard of authority simply by establishing her as the only authority remaining in the novel."[34] Romola, in fact, becomes the object of her own cult.

George Eliot substitutes the stasis of self-referentiality for genealogical continuity. The deaths of her father, Bernardo, Savonarola, and Tito release Romola from the conflict of irreconcilable claims and, simultaneously, from the challenge of historical continuity. The novel dramatises the impossibility of any single source of authority. Bardo's beloved history does not offer Romola an adequate guide, and her personal loyalty and affection for Bernardo cannot blind her to the questionable nature of his political stance. Similarly, the teachings of the Church, as represented by Savonarola, are obviously partial and flawed, while the sacredness of the socially instituted marriage tie is called into question by the behaviour of Tito. The novel asserts, however, not only that each of these forms of authority are inadequate by themselves, but that they are also mutually contradictory. Thus Romola believed that Bernardo was, in the political sphere, "the victim to a collision between two kinds of faithfulness" (Ch. 60, II, 316). Romola herself experiences divided allegiances: on the one hand Savonarola's moral energy is marred by fanaticism, whilst on the other Bernardo, to whom she is drawn by affection and memory, is engaged in possible crime. Romola fears that "she would be torn by irreconcilable claims" (Ch. 52, II, 237). The model of history to which George Eliot adheres in *Romola* is that of the "antagonism of valid principles," the Hegelian concept of tragedy which she outlined in her essay "The Antigone and its Moral."[35] Piero di Cosimo, who resembles the author in his gift of prophecy, possessing knowledge prior to its narrative disclosure, chooses to paint Romola not as Ariadne "in contradiction to all history and fitness" (Ch. 25, I, 355), but rather as Antigone.[36]

Darrell Mansell has argued that George Eliot dramatises in her novels Hegel's theory that tragedy was the conflict between the individual and the general life of the State; a conflict which, Hegel believed, was essential to historical development.[37] *Romola* does not conform, however, to this model of development. With the death of the four male figures in her life, all of whom represented potential sources of authority,

Romola is saved both from the inevitable conflict, and from the ensuing submission which would characterise historical progress. In the relationship of Tito and Romola one can see, through the microcosm of marriage, the larger historical forces at work. Tito's energy is represented as that of masculinity: "he had a masculine effectiveness of intellect and purpose which, like sharpness of edge, is itself an energy, working its way without any strong momentum. Romola had an energy of her own which thwarted his, and no man, who is not exceptionally feeble, will endure being thwarted by his wife" (Ch. 48, II, 187–8). In this clash of conflicting energies, Romola refuses the traditional pattern of female submission. Romola, the narrator comments, "was labouring, as a loving woman must, to subdue her nature to her husband's" (Ch. 27, I, 379). The prescriptive "must" strikes an alarming note for a female author; its strident tone in fact suggests that George Eliot, like her heroine, was struggling to reconcile the two conflicting impulses of submission and rebellion.[38] Indeed, Romola's rebellion against the marriage tie is, one feels, less a revolt against Tito's conduct than against the required female submission. Yet, as in all George Eliot's other works, rebellion is not rewarded; its consequence is historical stasis: Romola's barrenness enclosed within a self-reflexive cult.

On one level *Romola* appears to be a simple moral tale which portrays a heroine's struggle for noble life amidst "mixed conditions," and the historical consequences of wrong-doing. Attitudes to history in the novel, however, are both complex and contradictory. On the one hand, the narrative appears to endorse the idea of cumulative moral progress within history. Tito's attitude to history is that it is a stage on which many parts can be played: "Could he not strip himself of the past, as of rehearsal clothing, and throw away the old bundle, to robe himself for the real scene?" (Ch. 57, II, 286). The plot, with its remorseless movement towards poetic justice, furnishes an emphatic denial to this question. In accordance with organicist theories of cultural and physiological inheritance, the patterning of narrative events is represented as the workings of physiological law. Tito denies his stepfather, but experiences "the inward shame, the reflex of that outward law which the great heart of mankind makes for every individual man, a reflex which will exist even in the absence of the sympathetic impulses that need no law" (Ch. 9, I, 154). The physiological principles of reflex action, to which Lewes devoted much of his attention in *The Physiology of Common Life*, are used here to sustain a moral theory of social progress.[39] Developing this idea George Eliot later observes, "Our lives make a moral tradition for our individual selves, as the life of mankind at large makes a moral tradition for the race" (Ch. 39, II, 88). The individual life, like the larger historical life, is founded on the principles of organic interdependence and growth.

Tito's lack of reverence for history functions as the index of his villainy. Like those other flawed characters, Hetty and Godfrey, he relies not on the "inexorable law of consequences" but increasingly, as his moral decline progresses, on the workings of chance: "As the freshness of young passion faded, life was taking more and more decidedly for him the aspect of a game in which there was an agreeable mingling of skill and chance" (Ch. 35, II, 35). But the reflex action which determined his shame also ensures his downfall. In the absence of a God, Tito's body acts as his impartial judge, recording his deeds, waiting in readiness to confront him on the day of judgement. Tito wishes he had not denied Baldassarre, but, "he seemed to have spoken without any preconception: the words had leaped forth like a sudden birth that had been begotten and nourished in the darkness. Tito was experiencing that inexorable law of human souls, that we prepare ourselves for sudden deeds by the reiterated choice of good or evil which gradually determines character" (Ch. 23, I, 340). The moral is that of the "inexorable law of consequences" which is given, in *Romola*, a physiological base. In a passage which closely resembles this section in *Romola*, Lewes refers, in *The Foundations of a Creed*, to the moral law that " 'the habit of right action is the securest preparation for acting rightly under emergencies'. . . all men are trained to act rightly on emergencies by what is a kind of moral instinct, organised in previous habits of acting rightly."[40] For both Lewes and George Eliot, the moral instinct or habit is based upon physiological channels established in the mind by previous action. These channels then, in turn, direct future behaviour quite independently of the conscious mind.[41] Thus in Tito's conscious decision not to seek for Baldassarre "the little rills of selfishness had united and made a channel, so that they could never again meet with the same resistance" (Ch. 9, I, 153). Use of the term resistance confirms the physiological implications of channel: sensation, Lewes had argued, always takes the channel of least resistance.

The theory of psychic channels establishes scientific authority for the moral values which order the text. Romola's return to Florence, which fulfils the demands of organic continuity, is similarly attributed to the channels of her psychic history. Once her work in the Plague Village is accomplished, Romola longs to return to Florence: "the emotions that were disengaged from the people immediately around her rushed back into the old deep channels of use and affection" (Ch. 69, II, 413). Her emotions offer physiological proof of George Eliot's axiom that "in strictness there is no replacing of relations" (Ch. 69, II, 414), the past cannot be discarded. The conflict of irreconcilable claims is now referred to the integrity of the body, a "natural" guarantee of historical continuity. Tito, however, also appeals to the laws of nature to support his interpretation of history; he turns to a form of social darwinism to vindicate his self-interested actions. Why should he sacrifice his own blooming youth, he asks himself, for the "withered wintry life" of Baldassarre?: "that was the proper order of things – the order of nature, which treats all maturity as a mere nidus for youth." Thus the gems might belong to Baldassarre in a narrow sense, "but in that large and more radically natural view by which the world belongs to youth and strength, they were rather his who could extract the most pleasure out of them" (Ch. 11, I, 175–6). Tito justifies his political duplicity on this same principle of the survival of the fittest: "Men did not really care about these things, except where their personal spleen was touched. It was weakness only that was despised; power of any sort carried its immunity" (Ch. 57, II, 285). In place of respect for history, sentiment and tradition, Tito proposes a politics of naked power. Nature is not, to his eyes, a process of continuous growth where the past dominates the present. Dominance belongs rather to those who have the strength and skill to defeat their fellows: adaptability, not continuity, is the key. Tito's unfettered energy is an embodiment of that vitality in nature which proceeds to its own growth by strangling the past, the withering life of the old. The poetic justice of Tito's end reverses the natural pattern.

In the figure of Tito, George Eliot focuses her anxieties concerning the natural relation between past and present. His complete freedom from the fetters of history make him one of George Eliot's greatest villains; yet he is also a prototype for Ladislaw, the outsider whose free energy releases Dorothea from the labyrinth of Middlemarch and Casaubon's historical tomb. Politically, his role is unambiguous. A precursor of Harold Transome in his political pragmatism, Tito possesses no loyalties which might bind him to either side. Inevitably, however, like Harold, he is finally associated with the mode of government which breaks free from traditional ties – democracy. Tito's political vacillation, his lack of firm allegiance, receives its own hideous reflection in the rampaging mob who assault him. Representing force without directing control, their behaviour foreshadows that of the mob in *Felix Holt*, a novel in which George Eliot clearly articulates the ruling class fears of handing government to a class who are not imbued with respect for ruling cultural traditions. The political function of Tito's role is to affirm the conservative values of organic continuity. In relation to history itself, however, the issue is less clear cut.

If Tito, with his "bright youthfulness, as of a sun-god" (Ch. 17, I, 274), is a precursor of that solar deity Will Ladislaw, Bardo is a fore-runner of Casaubon: "For me, Romola, even when I could see, it was with the great dead that I lived; while the living often seemed to me mere spectres" (Ch. 5, I, 77). These sentiments are to be echoed by Casaubon: "I feed too much on the inward sources; I live too much with the dead" (Ch. 2, I, 23). Yet there is no simple opposition, as in *Middlemarch*, between life and sterility. Through their different rela-tionships to history and to language Bardo and Tito dramatise George Eliot's doubts about writing an historical novel. In an image which reflects George Eliot's own struggles when writing *Romola*, and the burden of scholarship which impedes the free flow of writing, Bardo asserts that "blindness acts like a dam, sending the streams of thought backward along the already-travelled channels and hindering the course onward" (Ch. 5, I, 78). The image expresses George Eliot's own doubt as to whether immersion in the history of the past could ever illuminate the present.

Bardo breaks through the dam only with the aid of Tito, whose rest-less energy is neither ordered nor controlled by veneration for the past.[42] Tito also brings release for Romola who was trapped, before his advent, in history, in a room where there was little colour or light to give "relief to the marble, livid with long burial" (Ch. 5, I, 72). Memory does not function for Romola, as for George Eliot's earlier characters, as a posi-tive force which might link past to present, and hold forth images of future growth. It is related solely to death. Only with the arrival of Tito does the possibility of light and growth occur: "It seemed like a wreath of spring, dropped suddenly in Romola's young but wintry life, which had inherited nothing but memories – memories of a dead mother, of a lost brother, of a blind father's happier time" (Ch. 6, I, 90). Tito frees both Romola and her father from subjugation to the past. Yet *Romola* does not conform to the future pattern of *Middlemarch*; historical scholarship does not simply constitute a Hades from which Persephone is released.

Romola is deliberately set in the Renaissance, a period when rediscovery of the past brought new vitality, new growth. As R. H. Hutton observed in his review of *Romola*, the portrayal of Bardo and Baldassarre gives:

that sense of large *human* power which the mastery over a great ancient language, itself the key to a magnificent literature, gave, and which made scholarship then a *passion*, while with us it has almost relapsed into an antiquarian dryasdust pursuit. We realize again, in reading about Baldo and Baldassarre, how, for these times, the first sentence of St. John, 'In the beginning was the Word,' had regained all its force, to the exclusion, perhaps, of the further assertion that the Word was with God and was God.[43]

George Eliot confirmed this reading in a letter to Hutton: "You have seized with a fulness which I had hardly hoped that my book could suggest, what it was my effort to express in the presentation of Bardo and Baldassarre."[44] The sense of directing power experienced by Renaissance men, once they felt themselves released from the trammels of theological doctrine, is precisely that outlined by Comte when he proclaimed the emergence of the Positivist era. George Eliot undoubtedly saw in Renaissance experience an analogue of contemporary history. The passiveness enjoined by Catholic mysticism is supplanted in both eras by belief in vigorous human power – creativity was no longer invested in a force external to man. Following Feuerbach, nineteenth-century theorists celebrated man's release from alienation, identifying power not with God, but with human, social creation. For Comte, this power was crystallised in the social evolution of language: "Language becomes thus the accumulating store of the wisdom of the race. The transmission of it from parents to offspring is always, even with mankind, the most precious part of their inheritance."[45]

Baldassarre offers a particularly graphic illustration of Comte's theory that human identity is constructed within and through language. Without Greek, Baldassarre is without identity; unable to pronounce his own name, retain details of the present, or memories of the past. His mind is narrowed to "one sensation." With the return of his Greek, however, he once again experiences mental empire:

he was once more a man who knew cities; whose sense of vision was instructed with large experience, and who felt the keen delight of holding all things in the grasp of language. Names! Images! – his mind rushed through its wealth without pausing, like one who enters on a great inheritance (Ch. 38, II, 68).

Personal continuity, like that of the larger social organism, is dependent on language. In analysing Baldassarre's passion for historical scholarship, and in tracing the path of his madness, George Eliot is posing the same questions which determined her representation of Romola: how far is individual identity dependent on the surrounding, historically emerging, cultural medium? Does loss of that culture, by rebellion or amnesia, destroy personal integrity? The contemporary reviewer who criticised George Eliot's "psychologico-medical study of Baldassarre"[46] failed to see the wider significance of the physiological and psychological terms she employed in character analysis. In constructing her work with such scientific precision George Eliot was consciously putting to the test Comte's and Lewes' theories concerning the relationship between the evolution of the social organism, personal identity, and cultural inheritance.

Situated within the historical past, *Romola* also takes history as its theme, questioning at both levels organicist theories of history. Through the figures of Tito, Bardo and Baldassarre, George Eliot dramatises the Victorian fear that, in the absence of God, neither the free play of mind, nor submergence in the culture of the past, can offer sufficient guidance for action. She lacks Comte's authoritative confidence in the unambivalent social creation of duty. Romola remains glad that she did not accept Dino's warning, product of that "sickly superstition which led men and women, with eyes too weak for the daylight, to sit in dark swamps and try to read human destiny by the chance flame of wandering vapours" (Ch. 36, II, 53). She trusts rather in "the large music of reasonable speech." Yet this "reasonable speech" can offer no directing aid. Tito, with his glib facility of speech, exposes the dangers of a corrupt hellenism; and Baldassarre, though regaining his linguistic inheritance, still clings with animal narrowness to his pursuit of revenge. Even Bardo's attitude to the past is barren. Though his conception of the historical process is that of growth and harvest, fertility is reserved for the ancients, "the immortals who have reaped the great harvest and left us to glean in their furrows" (Ch. 5, I, 77). Like his future embodiment, Casaubon, he sees any later attempts at production as "presumptuous" and imitative.

These Renaissance scholars, immersed in the learning of the past, find their Catholic counterparts in Dino and Savonarola. Defiant atheists and Catholic mystics are alike absorbed within philosophical systems which hinder full response to the exigencies of the present. Thus Dino returns to Florence, not to see his father, but to urge his brethren to study the Eastern tongues. And, preoccupied with his visions, he fails to make the few fraternal enquiries which could have saved Romola from her marriage. Savonarola bases his foreign policy on the mistaken belief that "in the Sacred Book there was a record of the past in which might be seen as in a glass what would be in the days to come" (Ch. 21, I, 320). Like Bardo he attempts to map out the present according to a pre-established pattern; history blinds him in his orientation to the present.

In the Proem the dawning light falls upon the student seeking "for that hidden knowledge which would break through the barrier of man's brief life, and show its dark path, that seemed to bend no whither, to be an arc in an immeasurable circle of light and glory" (I, 2). The quest, with its vision of the glorious illumination of historical continuity, stands as a possible model for George Eliot's own enterprise. Bardo, in his conception of a poet, echoes these sentiments within the novel, seeing, "that far-stretching, lasting light which spreads over centuries of thought, and over the life of nations" (Ch. 5, I, 76). Bardo's cherished self-image is, in accordance with this vision, that of Tiresias, happy in his blindness for he held in his soul the image of Minerva unveiled. But Piero di Cosimo, the novel's only true prophet, and an alternative authorial voice, casts Bardo as Oedipus in relation to Romola's Antigone. For Oedipus, blindness is neither compensated for by the powers of prophetic vision, nor delivered as punishment for the fact that he possessed the inner illumination which springs from seeing Minerva unveiled. Piero exposes the delusions of his fellow characters: Tito's that Romola could be Ariadne married to Bacchus, or Bardo's that history could unify past and present in one bright arc. Oedipus discovers only the darkness of knowledge; his blindness comes not as punishment but as sought desire. Confirming Romola in her role as Antigone, the image of Oedipus proposes a model of history which is not that of glorious unity, but rather that of a war of irreconcilable claims.

George Eliot's ambivalent attitude towards organicist theory gives rise in this, as in her two preceding novels, to two conflicting models of history. The poetic justice of Tito's end, which Romola recounts didactically to Lillo in the Epilogue, underscores the idea of history as morally ordered, cumulative growth. Yet the sole source of dynamic growth in the novel actually stems from Tito, whose bright, amoral energy is quite unshackled by veneration for the past. Tito both releases Bardo's mind from the labyrinth of history and leaves behind his own progeny . Though Romola lectures Lillo on the moral structure of history, the Epilogue itself proposes an alternative vision. Lillo, displaying his desire for dominance by attacking a fly,[47] shows no interest in history, for his concerns lie only with fame and pleasure. His behaviour and character seem to suggest that the whole historical process will once more repeat itself; the adopted child will once again repudiate his parent. History does not reveal a pattern of morally ordered growth; it seems, rather, to conform to the social darwinian battle of Tito's conception.

CHAPTER 6

Felix Holt:
Social and sexual politics

George Eliot returns in *Felix Holt* to her accustomed setting of English provincial life. She still invokes, however, the authority and clarity of historical perspective. Although the novel was written whilst the Second Reform Bill was being hotly debated, it is actually backdated to the time of the first. Like all George Eliot's earlier work, *Felix Holt* explores the possibilities of organic reconciliation between the ideals of duty and fulfilment, continuity and change; but with the heightened political anxiety of the period, the questions concerning the social validity of democracy which first emerged in *Romola* are now brought into central focus. *Felix Holt* is the one novel in which George Eliot makes the possible conservative political implications of organicism truly explicit. The celebration of organic continuity is not mirrored, however, in the narrative form for, like the later *Daniel Deronda*, *Felix Holt* is a divided novel. Felix's authoritative confidence in his own ideas and aims is matched by Mrs Transome's self-doubt and torture. The organic continuity established by the concluding wedding which makes that representative voice, Mr Wace, "feel somehow as if I believed more in everything that's good," is marred by her unassimilated misery.[1] The official meliorism of Felix's position is counterpointed by Mrs Transome's desire that all history could be erased, that her son had never been born. Progressionism, the creation of a "young Felix" to continue his father's line, is undercut by Mrs Transome's experience that a son can bring, not fulfilment, but an accentuated sterility.

In *Romola* George Eliot turned to the "idealisation" of the "clothing of the past" to resolve contemporary conflict, though the final affirmation of the Comtean values of organic continuity remains unconvincing. In *Felix Holt* she seeks resolution through character division. The self-conflict and doubt experienced by Romola and Savonarola are allotted to Mrs Transome. Felix admits the dangers of egoism which had undermined Savonarola: "If I once went into that sort of struggle for success, I should want to win – I should defend the wrong that I had once identified myself with" (Ch. 27, II, 37); but he is, without struggle, an unproblematic Christ figure. His self-unity is reflected in his political position which acknowledges none of the contradictions in organicism which Maggie or Romola had encountered. Like his predecessor, that other stalwart workman, Adam Bede, he neither acknowledges complexity nor questions his own values.

Significantly, all George Eliot's characters who possess an unproblematic relationship to organicism are male: Adam, Felix, and Daniel. Reasons for this division could be sought in George Eliot's own experiences as a woman, and thus her greater sensitivity to the struggles of her female characters; in the historical complexity of the lives of women in this era; or, finally, in the relationship between the sexual and social ideology of organicism. It is on the latter that I intend to concentrate, for it subsumes the other levels.

Study of George Eliot's letters reveals her abiding fear of egoism. Though she was obsessed, during her evangelical stage, with the dangers of egoism, her anxiety was not diminished with the later repudiation of her faith.[2] In a letter to her aunt in 1840, she disclosed the same fear of egoistic ambition that Felix later articulates: "I earnestly desire a spirit of childlike humility that shall make me willing to be lightly esteemed among men; this is the opposite of my besetting sin, which is an ever struggling ambition."[3] Many years later, when she had long forsaken her religion, she expressed the same sentiments in reference to her art. In her journal of 1861 she speaks of "the despondency that comes from too egoistic a dread of failure,"[4] and, writing to Mrs Congreve in 1870, she observes: "But my strong egoism has caused me so much melancholy, which is traceable simply to a fastidious yet hungry ambition, that I am relieved by the comparative quietude of personal cravings which age is bringing."[5] Desiring, like her later characters, to counteract her egoism, and the lack of direction she experienced in life once she had repudiated her faith, the young Marian Evans had ardently hoped "to have given to me some woman's duty, some possibility of devoting myself where I may see a daily result of pure calm blessedness in the life of another."[6] Since duty did not lie in any recognisable path of social action, it was to be sought in self-subordination. The gender qualification of duty is significant. Victorian ideals of womanhood both confirmed and strengthened the organic values of duty and submission: women were doubly the focus of organicist ideology.[7] Thus in *The Mill on the Floss* and *Romola* it is the heroines who crystallise in their lives the contradictions of organicism. In *Felix Holt*, this relationship between the politics of social organicism and those of sexuality actually leads to the polarisation of the novel.

To understand fully the structural divisions of *Felix Holt* one must place the novel in its social and political context. F. C. Thomson has argued that the politics were an afterthought; but one of his major pieces of evidence – that George Eliot began the novel in March 1865 but Reform did not become an issue in parliament until May – is unsound.[8] As Michael Wolff records, Gladstone had stated in May 1864 that "everyone not disqualified from a voice in government for some special reason was entitled to that voice."[9] Interest in Reform mounted, and in January 1865 Bright initiated a great campaign. Reform was thus very much a live issue at the time George Eliot commenced writing. Indeed, the discussion of democracy in *Romola* certainly points to George Eliot's growing interest in questions of government during the 1860s. For Thomson, the politics in *Felix Holt* seem "adventitious" for, "while they certainly underscore with good effect the private issues by enabling a projection of them on a public scale, they are not necessarily intrinsic."[10] The political issues in *Felix Holt* are not, however, merely the projection of private issues on a public scale; the private issues are themselves politically determined. The moral questions in George Eliot's works have all related centrally to the politics of organicism; but in *Felix Holt*, with the increased contemporary social anxiety concerning the question of working-class power, they are given an explicit political focus. The simplicity of *Felix Holt*'s political message must be related to the increased urgency of the external situation in 1865. All George Eliot's earlier reservations remain, however, embodied in the figure of Mrs Transome.

The political message of Felix is spelt out in all its crudeness in George Eliot's essay, the "Address to Working Men, by Felix Holt." Written in 1867, after the passage of the Second Reform Bill, and a year after the publication of *Felix Holt*, the Address was specifically designed as a political tract. While it obviously lacks, therefore, the complexity of *Felix Holt*, it does help reveal, through the repetition of similar images and arguments, the values which underlie Felix's political stance in the novel. Elements of Felix's speeches in the novel recur: the insistence on the "nature of things" and on "vain expectations," and on the fact that rationality, rather than ignorance or passion, must form the guide for action. In both texts, lip service is paid to public opinion, though a fundamental distrust of the opinion of the majority is also expressed; and primary emphasis is placed less on major social evils, than on details of political corruption. Analysis of the two works reveals the unity of theme which links the treatment of women's roles, sexuality, and political action within the novel.

One of the primary themes of the "Address" concerns the dangers of excess. Using the predominant organic model, Felix argues:

> I suppose there is hardly anything more to be shuddered at than that part of the history of disease which shows how, when a man injures his constitution by a life of vicious excess, his children and grandchildren inherit diseased bodies and minds and how the effects of that unhappy inheritance continue to spread beyond our calculation.[11]

The effects of militant action are equated with the effects of syphilis. In one, as in the other, action is in excess of rationality, not governed, that is, by careful obedience to predominant social law. Jermyn and Mrs Transome "had seen no reason why they should not indulge their passion and their vanity, and determine for themselves how their lives should be made delightful in spite of unalterable external conditions" (Ch. 21, I, 328). Mrs Transome's history is that of a woman suffering the consequences of excess, of placing passion and sensuality before the "unalterable external conditions" of social law. The law of the inheritance of disease is, Felix argues, "the law that we all bear the yoke of, the law of no man's making, and which no man can undo" (p. 419). Thus Harold, on discovering his parentage, "felt the hard pressure of our common lot, the yoke of that mighty resistless destiny, laid upon us by the acts of other men as well as our own" (Ch. 49, II, 335). The creed of organicism does not simply enforce consideration of the law of consequences; it is founded on a fear of passion, whether sexual or political, for the two are inextricably linked. To exceed the bounds of social law, either in sexual or political fervour, is to establish an ineradicable social disease.

Behind Felix's apparent optimism, his stated faith in human potential, there lies pessimism and fear. His proclaimed belief in public opinion is linked to a forcible distrust of all opinion not governed by his own conception of rationality. George Eliot here follows Comte who looked forward to "the increased influence which Public Opinion is destined to exercise"[12] in the positivist state; provided that is, that a philosophic organ was set up to interpret the positivist doctrine upon which Public Opinion was to be based.[13] Felix, with his "congregation" in Sproxton, is evidently that philosophic organ, helping to create public opinion on sound principles. There is a question, indeed, whether anything worthy of the name of opinion existed before: "Somebody must take a little knowledge and common-sense to them in this way, else how are they to get it?" (Ch. 5, I, 107). Without the enlightenment of true opinion the workers are seen to lead but an animal existence: "But while Caliban is Caliban, though you multiply him by a million, he'll worship every Trinculo that carries a bottle" (Ch. 27, II, 45). In *The Tempest*, Caliban's sensual nature represented a sexual threat to Miranda and a political threat to Prospero's government. George Eliot dramatises both aspects of this threat in *Felix Holt*: while Mrs Transome's sexual transgressions disrupt the order of her particular social sphere, the sensuality of the mob leads to a more widespread political disorder. During the election riots the crowd are excited by drink and "their action could hardly be calculated on more than those of oxen and pigs congregated amidst hootings and pushings" (Ch. 33, II, 115). Felix counts on his influence over these men "whose mental state was a mere medley of appetites and confused impressions" (Ch. 33, II, 123). The election riots do not simply illustrate the evils of political bribery or "treating"; they are a living demonstration of Felix's argument that Caliban, or the working class, should not be given the vote whilst their behaviour remains incalculable and governed by appetite; not approximating, that is, to dominant definitions of rational action.

Felix speaks in the "Address" of the "hideous margin of society" who are "the multiplying brood begotten by parents who have been left without all teaching save that of a too craving body" (p. 423). In bourgeois ideology, with its implicit identification of its own government with that of rationality, the threat of those excluded from appreciation of this rule is represented as that of the body, of sensuality. Maggie's surrender to Stephen, Romola's to Tito, Mrs Transome's to Jermyn, and Esther's potential surrender to Harold thus take on political implications. Sensuality, like militancy, is a form of action which acknowledges no higher law. Esther exchanges the "languorous haziness of motiveless ease" (Ch. 44, II, 281) of Transome Court (with its echoes of the "enchanted haze" of Maggie's drifting, and Stephen's languid exclamations of love) for the love of Felix who seemed "to bring at once a law, and the love that gave strength to obey the law" (Ch. 27, II, 45). Esther's "inward revolution" (Ch. 49, II, 340) stands as an image of the desired political revolution. Her sexual submission, in accepting Felix's rule, furnishes the pattern of the requisite political submission. Mrs Transome, however, resolutely refuses to be satisfied with the social roles of wife or mother. Like the "hard-lipped antagonism of the trades-union man" (Ch. 30, II, 86) she represents an element which remains unassimilable within this organic social ideal. Her stance, in fact, suggests that the higher law Esther has adopted is perhaps solely the liberty to renounce self-determination.

The sensuality of the "hideous margin" inspires fears of social war; it represents, Felix declares, a "persistent disobedience to the laws" and a "struggle to subvert order" (p. 423). If uncontrolled, these "degraded men" would unleash "the savage beast in the breasts of our generation" (p. 423). The direct political threat is recast ideologically into a question of moral degradation, to be resolved, therefore, not by social change, but by the moral education of the individual.

In various, rather crude, ways, the organic model is employed in the "Address" to buttress the theory of gradual, developmental change. Each group should be bound by consideration of the whole, for "society stands before us like that wonderful piece of life, the human body, with all its various parts depending on one another, and with a terrible liability to get wrong because of that delicate dependence" (p. 420). The interdependence of the whole becomes an argument for the suppression of all militant action. The idea that death of the whole might result from injury to a part fulfils a similar function. Thus precautions should be taken "so that the public order may not be destroyed, so that no fatal shock may be given to this society of ours, this living body in which our lives are bound up" (p. 422).

More subtly, the idea of scientific law is appropriated to give scientific authority to arguments for the maintenance of the *status quo*. Thus Felix suggests that "Selfishness, stupidity, sloth, persist in trying to adapt the world to their desires" (p. 429), they ignore, that is, the law of sequence revealed by the world's events, for "Wisdom stands outside of man and urges itself upon him, like the marks of the changing seasons" (p. 429). The contemporary social structure becomes personified rationality whose teachings are as unquestionable as the laws of nature. The presence of this wisdom "on our side" is "a mighty fact, physical and moral" and man's duty is "seriously to consider this outside wisdom which lies in the supreme unalterable nature of things, and watch to give it a home within us and obey it" (p. 429). The injunction echoes Felix's sentiments of the novel: "The way to get rid of folly is to get rid of vain expectations, and of thoughts that don't agree with the nature of things" (Ch. 30, II, 89). In the interests of direct political argument, society is no longer represented as a process of fluid interaction between organism and medium. The model adopted is that of Spencer who defined life as "the continuous adjustment of internal relations to external relations."[14] In her essay on "Antigone," George Eliot had spoken of the struggle "by which the outer life of man is gradually and painfully being brought into harmony with his inward needs."[15] Man should not merely try to conform to a preordained "nature of things" but should act directly on the outer world to adjust it to his needs. In Felix's doctrine of obedience there is no glimmer of the conflict dramatised in *Romola* where inner demands clashed, not with an unmodifiable external nature, but with the laws and symbols created by man, and inscribed within his own identity.

The simplicity of Felix's political creed corresponds with the simplicity of his characterisation in the novel. He undergoes neither internal conflict nor development. Indeed, the role of Comtean priest which he is destined to fulfil would clearly be vitiated by any inner self-conflict. Like Comte, Felix advocates that "Class Interests" should be transformed into "Class Duties" (p. 421). The true social solution, Comte had argued, would be "the submission of all classes to the moral requirements of their position, under the institution of a spiritual authority, strong enough to enforce discipline" thus "the vague and stormy discussion of rights would be replaced by the calm and precise determination of duties."[16] Felix takes upon himself this role of spiritual authority. Rather than social change he advocates transformations in attitudes, so that the social hierarchy will appear less a form of social oppression than a blessed inheritance. In the "Address" the composition of this inheritance is made painfully explicit.

Like her contemporary Matthew Arnold, who was similarly appalled by the threat of working-class power, George Eliot appeals to the idea of culture.[17] Culture, Arnold argued, seeks through "all the voices of human experience . . . art, science, poetry, philosophy, history, as well as that of religion" to determine the true condition of perfection. It "places human perfection in an *internal* condition, in the growth and predominance of our humanity proper, as distinguished from our animality."[18] Arnold draws on the same distinction between humanity and animality which bedevils Felix's political addresses and, like Felix, he proclaims that human perfection must be sought not through social change but through modification of the inner man. In the "Address" the social and political implications of this position are made clear. Man's chief inheritance, Felix declares, is "that treasure of knowledge, science, poetry, refinement of thought, feeling, and manners, great memories and the interpretation of great records" (p. 425). The preservation of this inheritance is dependent, however, on the preservation of the class which possesses it, despite the fact that, as Felix admits, "this fine activity, the exalted vision of many minds, is bound up at present with conditions which have much evil in them" (p. 425). To throw the classes who possess "the treasure of refined needs" out of power is to "injure your own inheritance and the inheritance of your children" (p. 426). The argument for self-culture becomes a blatant justification for class privilege.

The power of Felix's arguments should not, however, be underestimated. Frederic Harrison, himself an ardent supporter of the trade-union movement and universal suffrage, wrote to George Eliot of his admiration for the novel:

And each party and school are determined to see their own side in it – the religious people, the non-religious people, the various sections of religious people, the educated, the simple, the radicals, the Tories, the socialists, the intellectual reformers, the domestic circle, the critics, the metaphysicians, the artists, the Positivists, the squires, are all quite convinced that it has been conceived from their own point of view.[19]

Such indiscriminate power of pleasing can be partially accounted for by the mode in which the strident tones and argument of the "Address" are carefully moderated within the novel. The treatment of Mrs Transome, furthermore, gives rise to conflicting interpretations. Perhaps the most influential factor, however, in determining the novel's general popularity was the fact that radicals and conservatives alike adhered to the doctrine of self-culture. In his study of "The Intellectual Origins of Mid-Victorian Stability," T. R. Tholfsen has shown how the adoption by the working class of the ethics of self-improvement led to radicalism being coopted by the system. He cites a letter to a newspaper concerning the Gateshead Ironworkers' Lockout in 1867: "An iron worker's wife in the midst of a vehement denunciation of the perfidy of her husband's employers, concluded that 'all our salvation lies in ourselves . . . in our cultivation of those higher qualities which are lying dormant in our natures.' "[20] A similar note is sounded in an English Chartist Circular. Like Felix, the Circular opposes the evils of drink, proposing instead the ideal of self-culture, and the education of children:

Then there is the *time* wasted over the pint and the pipe – time which ought to be devoted to *Self Culture* or the *Education of Children* . . . And though we admit that *class* legislation has inflicted upon us ills innumerable, and blighted the intellect and broken the hearts of whole generations of sons of toil, we cannot shut our eyes to the truth that no state of freedom can improve the man who is the slave of his own vices.[21]

The goal of self-culture and improvement was readily received by radicals who equated it with the founding of self-respect. But it produced a commitment to self-improvement independent of, and prior to, political action, thus directing attention away from corporate action and towards self-contemplation. The motto "divide and rule" might justly be applied.

With the goal of self-improvement, the radicals imported into their own orientation the bourgeois distrust of the lower classes. They adopted, also, the assumption that a man's composition is independent of his environment; that individual change can, and must, occur independently of social change. But as David Craig has noted, Francis Place observed in 1832 that the struggle for reform "has impressed the morals and manners, and elevated the character of the working man. . . In every place as reform has advanced, drunkenness has retreated."[22] It was not inward contemplation, but corporate action towards a concrete social goal which in fact effected the most decisive change in working-class habits.

The popular science of phrenology plays, in this context, an interesting role in *Felix Holt*. As Roger Cooter has demonstrated, phrenology, with its doctrine of self-improvement, appealed widely to the radicals and working class, though it actually operated, covertly, as a mystification of the emergent social relations.[23] The motto of the Phrenological Journal was "Know Thyself," and its proclaimed doctrine, "universal democracy." Phrenology attracted radical support for it suggested a form of social distinction based, not on class and privilege, but on biological formation. The doctrine of self-knowledge and improvement was founded on the belief that each individual would, with determined effort, develop his latent faculties. The function of phrenology, however, was to supply an accessible and acceptable image of the emerging division of labour. The hierarchy of faculties mirrored the social hierarchy, whilst ideas of the harmonious functioning of the faculties naturalised the appeal for social harmony. Phrenology was, in fact, a more personalised form of the social organism metaphor employed by Felix.

Initially, it seems rather puzzling that George Eliot should make use of phrenology in *Felix Holt* since Gall's phrenological theory had, by the 1860s, been discredited by the work of Comte, Spencer and Lewes. The static faculty division proposed by Gall was replaced by an evolutionary psychology which incorporated the realm of social experience. Thus psychology formed, for Spencer, yet one more example of the law of movement from homogeneity to heterogeneity that dominated the natural and social realms. Though Spencer retained the idea of the cerebral localisation of faculties in his psychology, his faculties were not rigid categories, but the product of individual and racial experience, arising through adaptation to the environment.[24] This flexibility is not evident in *Felix Holt*. Felix reports to Mr Lyon his visit to a phrenologist:

"I'm perhaps a little too fond of banging and smashing," he went on; "a phrenologist at Glasgow told me I had large veneration; another man there, who knew me, laughed out and said I was the most blasphemous iconoclast living. 'That,' says my phrenologist, 'is because of his large Ideality, which prevents him from finding anything perfect enough to be venerated' " (Ch. 5, I, 98).

The episode offers a concise summary of the novel's politics: Felix's radicalism is an extreme form of veneration for the established order. Phrenology also supplies a quick description of Felix's unchanging character. In thus resorting to a static model of the mind, George Eliot reveals the uneasiness she feels, in this novel, with the more fluid organic model of psychological development of Spencer or Lewes.

George Eliot's disquiet with more dynamic conceptions of organic development is reflected at a personal and social level in the novel. It is evident in the Introduction, and in the early descriptions of Treby Magna, where two theories of social organicism seem to clash. The opening nostalgic lament for departed glory, and the description of the trim cheerful villages centered round the church, are based on a theory of organic community which takes as its static ideal the traditional rural village. These villages, it appears, are centres of individual crafts such as those of blacksmith, basketmaker and wheelwright. Life is bright, clean and cheerful; even the thundering of the blacksmith's anvil is a "pleasant tinkle." The gloom of the growing industrial cities does not encroach here for town and country have "no pulse in common." The villages belong to a timeless dimension of life, "the low, grey sky" overhangs them "with an unchanging stillness as if Time itself were pausing" (Introduction, I, 5, 8). The description could aptly apply to Treby Magna, but only, significantly, in its earlier stage of life when it was still "the heart of a great rural district" (Ch. 3, I, 68): "Such was the old-fashioned, grazing, brewing, wool-packing, cheese-loading life of Treby Magna, until there befell new conditions, complicating its relation with the rest of the world, and gradually awakening in it that higher consciousness which is known to bring higher pains" (Ch. 3, I, 66). In this passage Spencer's theory of organic evolution from homogeneity to heterogeneity is imposed upon the static model. Thus Treby Magna "took on the more complex life brought by mines and manufactures, which belong more directly to the great circulating system of the nation than to the local system to which they have been superadded" (Ch. 3, I, 68). The analogy is that employed by Spencer in his essay "The Social Organism" where he draws a comparison between "the blood of a living body and the circulating mass of commodities in the body politic."[25]

For Spencer, however, the coming of industrialism necessarily constitutes progress; greater complexity brings a higher form of life. George Eliot is unsure. Such changes violate both the traditional form of community, and a defined hierarchy. They admit a fluidity inconsistent with veneration which necessarily requires a fixed object. An unattributed passage in George Eliot's notebook for *Felix Holt* is of relevance here:

Democracy is not favourable to the reverential spirit. That it destroys reverence for mere social position must be counted among the good, not the bad part of its influences; though by doing this it closes the principal *school* of reverence (as to mere human relations) which exists in society. But also democracy, in its very essence, insists so much more forcibly on the things in which all are entitled to be considered equally, than on those in which one person is entitled to more consideration than another, that respect for even personal superiority is likely to be below the mark.[26]

The passage succinctly illustrates George Eliot's ambivalent attitude towards democracy. Though she appreciates intellectually the benefits democracy would bring in its destruction of reverence for mere social position, her appreciation is linked to an emotional distrust. Her preoccupation with notions of superiority reveals her underlying emotional commitment to forms of thought which are the mental reflection of the hierarchical system. George Eliot's own ambivalence clearly suggests why *Felix Holt* should have been welcomed by reformers and conservatives alike. It indicates, furthermore, the intimate connections which exist between Felix's personal qualities and character, his political message, and the mode of his characterisation. The static, phrenological presentation of Felix's fixed faculty of veneration mirrors his support for a society where the "nature of things" doesn't change. As in phrenology there can be no major reordering, merely an encouragement of latent faculties, whilst the structure must necessarily remain hierarchical.

Though class distinctions are disguised in the form of cultural distinctions, the organic model to which Felix adheres is clearly the nostalgic, static one, rather than the Spencerian model which could encompass industrial and social change. Felix's natural political partner is not his fellow "radical," the corrupt Harold, but the conservative, Philip Debarry. This conservative bias in the novel is reinforced by the issue of election "treating" which functions to equate Harold's moral corruption with his political position. Yet in portraying the election George Eliot deliberately departs from her own experience. Gordon Haight records that, in the election riots which George Eliot witnessed at Nuneaton in December 1832, it was clear that, in a fair poll, the radical would clearly win:

> But the Tories, seeing the tide going against them, suspended the poll, and called in a detachment of Scots Greys, which had been kept in readiness at Meriden; the Riot Act was read, and when the mob did not disperse, horse soldiers with drawn swords rode through the town, charging the people cutting and trampling them down. One man died of his injuries.[27]

Both the corruption and violence were on the side of the conservatives and authority. George Eliot's decision to reverse this pattern casts an interesting light on the assumptions and political perspective which lie behind *Felix Holt*.

Harold's radicalism is treated simply as an extension of his egoism and "unsympathetic" nature: "the utmost enjoyment of his own advantages was the solvent that blended pride in his family and position, with the adhesion to changes that were to obliterate tradition and melt down enchased gold heirlooms into plating for the egg-spoons of 'the people'" (Ch. 43, II, 257). The futility and absurdity concentrated in the image of gold-plated egg spoons crystallises the narrative's attitude to all attempts to obliterate tradition. Philip Debarry, the successful candidate, serves, by contrast, as a focus for moral, and hence, political excellence. He possesses neither Harold's egoism nor his disrespect for tradition, whilst his conservatism is not like that of his father, a blind prejudice, but a carefully considered position. Though he receives little direct characterisation, he is always behind the scenes, urging his relatives to correct moral action. With his conservatism and moral integrity he stands as a direct embodiment of Felix's political goals.

Felix's description of his phrenological diagnosis does not pass without challenge in the text. Rufus Lyon voices his disquiet concerning the phrenologists' heathen precept "Know thyself" which "'too often leads to a self-estimate which will subsist in the absence of that fruit by which alone the quality of the tree is made evident'" (Ch. 5, I, 99). The objection, however, serves less to question the precept "Know thyself" than to introduce, with dramatic irony, Esther into Felix's life. The sole form of development permitted Felix Holt is in his relations with Esther, and then it is solely his perception of their relationship which alters, not his character. He is gradually allowed to perceive that he could so transform Esther as to make her worthy to become his wife. The phrenological precept "Know thyself," with its correlated doctrine of self-improvement, stands as the central tenet which links the personal and political themes of the novel. Felix, in the "Address," equates wisdom not with an understanding of social organisation but with self-knowledge: "If we have the beginning of wisdom, which is, to know a little truth about ourselves" (p. 416) he observes. Political action is thus reduced to the sphere of the individual. Similar assumptions govern the novel. Introducing the political life of Treby Magna, George Eliot remarks that not all Reformers were "large-hearted patriots or ardent lovers of justice. . . Again, the Tories were far from being all oppressors, disposed to grind down the working classes into serfdom" (Ch. 3, I, 71). Politics is reduced to a question of individual personality. There is no class analysis; no sense that it is not the character of the individual, but the social position they occupy which constitutes class oppression. It is this willingness to perceive social and political issues in terms of individual character and development which enables George Eliot to offer, in Esther's development, an image of the desired social transformation.

As W. F. T. Myers has perceptively noted, *Felix Holt* follows the Comtean approach to history, for social change is represented primarily in terms of mental development.[28] The often-quoted statement that "there is no private life which has not been determined by a wider public life" (Ch. 3, I, 72) does not capture all the forms of relation between individual and society dramatised in the novel. Society does not simply exercise a formative influence on the individual; both individual and society conform to the same pattern of development. The description of the awakening of painful higher consciousness in Treby Magna is echoed in the analysis of Esther's development. Thus, if Felix were to love her, Esther's life would be exalted "into a sort of difficult blessedness, such as one may imagine in beings who are conscious of painfully growing into the possession of higher powers" (Ch. 22, I, 341). Yet Treby Magna and Esther do not display symmetry in their development. Through the history of Esther, George Eliot can illustrate her faith in meliorism and evolutionary progress without the discomfort of displaying its effects amongst the distrusted mob. Esther's inward revolution may stand as demonstration of the efficacy of Felix's teaching. Yet George Eliot's doubts about Felix's actual social effectiveness seem to surface in the narrator's elaborate refusal to reveal the secret of his final whereabouts. Like Mrs Transome's misery, which refuses assimilation within the contented organicism of the conclusion, Felix's actual relationship with the workers similarly withstands integration. The secret of Felix, like that of Mrs Transome, points to an area of disturbance, whose disclosure would disrupt the illusion of organic continuity.

The apparent resolution of class conflict through the marriage of two individuals is in line with the novel's representation of the political threat posed by the working class as a question of moral education. This mode of conclusion, however, is not just a novelistic device. It is firmly based on the homology which existed between the social ideals of organicism and Victorian theories of women's roles. Marriage was seen as a microcosm of social order: the harmonious union of the sexes, with its differentiation of functions, offered an ideal image of the social division of labour. The ideas of duty and obedience which surrounded Victorian concepts of the wife were applied, in the political sphere, to the working class. George Eliot was not alone in drawing a novelistic parallel between these two spheres. The structure of *Felix Holt* replicates that of an earlier novel, Charlotte Bronte's *Shirley*, which similarly integrates the treatment of working-class riots with a romantic courtship and concluding marriage. A comparison between the two novels will illuminate the relationship between the political and romantic themes of *Felix Holt*.

There is strong internal evidence that George Eliot was directly influenced by Charlotte Bronte's novel. Like *Felix Holt*, *Shirley* was written during a time of contemporary crisis but set within a period of earlier historical disturbance: composed in 1848 during the time of Chartist activity, it was backdated to the Luddite disturbances of 1812. The social implications of its concluding marriage are made more explicit than in the later novel. The four-way marriage between Caroline and Robert, Shirley and Louis, which unites the interests of the landed class and the rising mill and factory owners, ushers in a vision of cosy paternalism. Working-class violence no longer constitutes a problem. Caroline will have "such a Sunday-school," "such a day-school" and "the houseless, the starving, the unemployed, shall come to Hollow's mill from far and near; and Joe Scott shall give them work, and Louis Moore, Esq., shall let them a tenement, and Mrs. Gill shall mete them a portion till the first pay-day."[29] The image is that of a perfectly harmonious social division of labour. The women's acceptance of their wifely duties is replicated in the social sphere.

The parallel between the situations of women and workers, which the structure of the two novels suggests, is one that recurred frequently in mid-Victorian theory, though it was used primarily to sustain a reactionary politics. Thus in 1861 a reviewer in *Blackwood's Edinburgh Magazine* offering an account of a social science meeting, observes:

> We believe we are called upon to discuss not 'privileges,' but 'rights,' for 'social science,' we understand, takes as one of its bases the equal rights of woman side by side with man. This startling attitude on the part of ladies, analogous we presume, to the uprising of certain oppressed nationalities on the continent of Europe, has at length, we are informed, assumed the definite form of a positive organization.[30]

The audacity of women in trying to organise themselves, and their claims for "rights," rather than inferiority and the acceptance of duties, is seen by the reviewer as equivalent to the uprising of an oppressed nation. One can easily insert here Disraeli's "other nation," the working class. Charlotte Bronte in fact draws an explicit parallel, in her letters, between the role of women and "operatives," though her emphasis, unlike that of the *Blackwood's* reviewer, lies entirely on their shared suffering.[31]

Felix in his "Address" calls for "patient heroism," for the willing performance of work, whatever its nature, for the good of the "nation at large." His argument that class distinctions must represent "the varying duties of men, not their varying Interests" is expressed in the novel through his observation that "If there's anything our people want convincing of, it is, that there's some dignity and happiness for a man other than changing his station" (Ch. 45, II, 294). The *Blackwood's* reviewer, calling to women to return to the traditional virtues of womanhood, appeals to the same ideals of duty, devotion, and self-sacrifice:

> To the true glory of the female character we have, in short, every one of us, known women content to live without applause, willing to perform day by day the simple offices of home, to train up children, to watch domestic economy, and, if needs be, to work; in fine to do all which devoted self sacrifice can dictate to render our English households the abodes of happiness.[32]

Felix's arguments refer to the smooth running of the country, the reviewer's to the household – a microcosm of the country. The Victorian vision of domestic harmony did not simply offer a powerful image of social order. The socially ingrained idea of the sexual differentiation of functions facilitated acceptance of the hierarchical social division of labour. The "uprising" of women would thus threaten the fundamental principles of social order.

In George Eliot's own comments upon the role of women in her letters of this period one can see the same play of ambivalence, the same apparent acceptance of the ideology of duty which emerges in *Felix Holt.* Thus, although she acknowledges, in a letter of 1867, that women have the "worst share in existence" she argues that this situation should lead to a "sublimer resignation in women and a more regenerating tenderness in man . . . the goal towards which we are proceeding is a more clearly discerned distinction of function."[33] She sees progress not as the creation of greater equality, but, in accordance with Comte's theories of organic social development, as a more thorough demarcation of men and women's social functions. Acceptance of this theory of the division of labour, and of women's special sphere of influence, leads her to characterise women's suffrage as an "extremely doubtful good."[34] Her cautious endorsement of women's higher education is also qualified by her belief in the necessary sexual division of labour. Higher education of women should lead to,

their recognition of the great amount of social unproductive labour which needs to be done by women, and which is now either not done at all or done wretchedly.

No good can come to women, more than to any class of male mortals, while each aims at doing the highest kind of work, which ought rather to be held in sanctity as what only the few can do well. I believe – and I want it to be well shown – that a more thorough education will tend to do away with the odious vulgarity of our notions about functions and employment, and to propagate the true gospel that the deepest disgrace is to insist on doing work for which we are unfit – to do any sort of work badly.[35]

The values which underlay the representation of Adam Bede, and later of Caleb Garth, the worship of the dignity of labour, are here associated with the sexual ideology of women's duty, and the social ideology which exhorts individuals to remain in their given station, not clamour for "rights."

Perhaps the clearest statement of George Eliot's position occurs in a letter to Emily Davis, again with reference to women's education. In an argument which echoes Felix's sentiments concerning the treasure of inheritance she takes as one topic in her letter: "The spiritual wealth acquired for mankind by the difference of function founded on the other, primary difference; and the preparation that lies in woman's peculiar constitution for a special moral influence." Accepting the more "sublime resignation" women have been forced into as a spiritual gain, and holding it not as a relative, social creation, but as the now defining characteristic of the "feminine character" she remarks that "there lies just that kernel of truth in the vulgar alarm of men lest women should be unsexed."[36] The sequence of George Eliot's thought resembles that of Felix when he argues that class abuses must be maintained in order to preserve the cultural heritage with which they are associated. George Eliot would rather preserve women's greater tenderness, which she yet recognises as a product of their social hardships, than risk altering the feminine character by social change. Her discussion of the necessity of education is thus framed entirely in relation to women's roles as wives and mothers, and the benefits that would accrue to the social institution of marriage, for "The domestic misery, the evil education of the children that comes from the presupposition that women must be kept ignorant and superstitious, are patent enough."[37]

George Eliot's evident concern with the "woman question" at this time strongly affected the treatment of her heroine in *Felix Holt*. Complexity was sacrificed to broad generalisations about women's nature which reinforce the conservative political message of the novel. Thus at one stage George Eliot observes that there are some women who can be alone "But Esther was not one of these women: she was intensely of the feminine type, verging neither towards the saint nor the angel. She was 'a fair divided excellence, whose fulness of perfection' must be in marriage" (Ch. 44, II, 286). Femininity is associated with dependence, thus sanctioning the social and sexual division of labour, and the resolution of the social problems the novel portrays through the concluding marriage.

The image of society in *Felix Holt* clearly corresponds, as W. F. T. Myers has pointed out, to Comte's conception of an ideal union between philosophers, who represent the Intellect, the working class who furnish Activity, and women, who embody Feeling.[38] In instituting these divisions, Comte projected a static phrenological model onto society; thus abandoning temporarily the more radical, dynamic biological conception of the social organism which he at other times employed. George Eliot's acceptance of these inflexible categories clearly reveals the sense of political urgency which underpins *Felix Holt*. In *Romola* she had questioned, through her representation of Savonarola, the idea that one class should hold exclusive property over knowledge and intellect, whilst the idea that women should be restricted to the sphere of feeling was firmly challenged by both Maggie Tulliver and Romola. Such division is possible, however, in *Felix Holt* for the crude conservatism of Felix's political position is complemented by the stereotypical femininity of the novel's heroine. Departing from the pattern of her three preceding novels, George Eliot appears to be offering an endorsement of the conservative implications of organicism, rather than exploring its contradictions.

In both *Felix Holt* and *Shirley* phrenology plays a crucial role in linking the treatment of character with the novels' wider political themes. Charlotte Bronte describes Mr Yorke, who sympathises with the Luddites, in phrenological terms as being "without the organ of Veneration" and possessing "too little of the organs of Benevolence and Ideality" (Ch. 4, I, 62). The fixed shape of his skull reveals what Charlotte Bronte believed were the inadequacies of radical thought. Felix, with his large organs of Veneration and Ideality, appears to be conceived as the direct antithesis to Mr Yorke; the relationship is one that clearly illuminates the exact nature of Felix's "radicalism." A further parallel between the two novels, and one that again reveals the underlying politics of organicism, lies in the use of *Coriolanus*, a play that contains perhaps the most famous organic social analogy in literature.

Chapter 30 of *Felix Holt*, which contains Felix's address to the election crowd, opens with an epigraph from *Coriolanus*:

> His nature is too noble for the world:
> He would not flatter Neptune for his trident,
> Or Jove for his power to thunder. His heart's his mouth:
> What his breast forges, that his tongue must vent;
> And, being angry, doth forget that ever
> He heard the name of death.
>
> (Ch. 30, II, 75)

In the context of the chapter, where even the Duffield men are impressed by Felix's grandeur, it would appear that the epigraph is not ironic. The literal meaning of "too noble for the world" is reflected in "the human face divine" of Felix (Ch. 30, II, 87). George Eliot's characterisation contains none of Shakespeare's subtle questioning of the nature of Coriolanus' nobility. Further echoes of *Coriolanus* occur in this chapter with the trade-union member's reversal of Menenius' parable of the belly and members; he employs images of bodily interdependence not to justify government by the aristocracy but to sustain an argument for democracy and universal suffrage. Significantly, Felix voices his agreement prior to this parable. His own speech is a direct refutation of this democratic interpretation of organic interdependence.

Coriolanus furnishes both a political and character model for Felix. The chapter which contains Felix's first clear statement of his ideals also draws its epigraph from *Coriolanus*. Thus, again, I feel, the intention is not ironic:

> Custom calls me to't:
> What custom wills, in all things should we do't
> The dust on antique time would lie unswept,
> And mountainous error be too highly heaped
> For truth to over-peer.
>
> (Ch. 27, II, 30)

Felix, like Coriolanus, announces his disrespect for custom which perpetuates men's error. But the custom to which Coriolanus refers is the democratic appeal for votes: the speech displays his vehement scorn for the "mob." George Eliot's choice of epigraph exposes the strength of the distrust of the working class which lies behind the presentation of Felix's "idealism" and the politics of the novel.

Coriolanus plays a slightly different role in *Shirley*, where it explicitly links the political and sexual themes. Caroline persuades Robert to read the play with her, and escapes, momentarily, from his domination. The complexity of the play, ignored in *Felix Holt*, is brought to the fore. Caroline wishes Robert to appreciate Coriolanus' faults, as well as his greatness. Yet her plea that he treat his workers less haughtily is to become the basis for the final *rapprochement* of the novel when Caroline becomes a submissive, fulfilled wife, and Robert a paternal rather than tyrannical capitalist. Caroline's disquiet goes no further than a vague liberalism which does not question the fundamental hierarchy, just as her discontent with the expected role of women does not lead her to question the institution of marriage. Her despair thus erupts in violent imaginings which, like the violence of the workers, are soothed by the final creation of organic order within the two spheres of home and work.

In *Felix Holt* Esther is not permitted to question the quality of her Coriolanus. But the despair of Mrs Transome, herself a Coriolanian autocrat, and the negativity of her life, function as an implied questioning of patterns of hierarchical dominance, both social and sexual. Mrs Transome's bitterness stems from her continued adherence to the very social forms she had earlier defied: "Unlike that Semiramis who made laws to suit her practical licence, she lived, poor soul, in the midst of desecrated sanctities, and of honours that looked tarnished in the light of monotonous and weary suns" (Ch. 40, II, 210). Her revolt can find no legitimate form of expression. It is thus forced to smoulder inwardly, flashing out occasionally in violence parallel to that of Caroline, and the mob.

Mrs Transome fulfils a very similar function to the self-effacing Mrs Pryor in *Shirley*, for both represent an enclave of misery in the novel, where apparent outward ease and comfort are belied by inner agony. Though Mrs Pryor's experiences have been the opposite of Mrs Transome's, ruled governess rather than ruling aristocrat, her bitterness is similarly caused by her inability to defy the values of social hierarchy. She concludes her tirade to Caroline on the degradations of a governess' life with a defence of the very practices which had occasioned her torture: "Implicit submission to authorities, scrupulous deference to our betters (under which term I, of course, include the highest classes of society) are, in my opinion, indispensable to the wellbeing of every community" (Ch. 10, II, 250). Like Mrs Transome, she can find no form of expression for her revolt, but remains locked within the values which had occasioned it. The problem is that faced by Romola when attempting to cast off her cultural heritage. If one is formed through interaction with the social medium, one's sense of self becomes inseparable from external cultural forms or values. Outright rebellion can thus only create self-division.

Though *Felix Holt* and *Shirley* deal explicitly with the question of working-class rebellion, it is in the exploration of the women's situation that both novels offer their most intricate analysis of the dynamics of power. Following Harold's defeat as Radical candidate, Mrs Transome dared not ask questions, but could not resist the temptation to express her bitterness, thus "helping, with feminine self-defeat, to exclude herself more completely from any consultation by him. In this way poor women, whose power lies solely in their influence, make themselves like music out of tune, and only move men to run away" (Ch. 34, II, 136). Mrs Transome's situation is presented as that of all women. Denied the right to speech and self-expression, they are locked in a vicious circle of self-defeat: any attempt to articulate their feelings will automatically destroy their cause. The musical image, employed in *Adam Bede* and *Middlemarch* to illustrate the dignity of work, and the harmonious, organic division of labour, functions here to challenge hierarchical theories of sexual differentiation.

Charlotte Bronte offers a comparable analysis of "feminine self-defeat." Caroline, faced with Robert's coldness, is denied the right to speech:

A lover masculine so disappointed can speak and urge explanation, a lover feminine can say nothing: if she did the result would be shame and anguish, inward remorse for self-treachery. Nature would brand such demonstration as a rebellion against her instincts, and would vindictively repay it afterwards by the thunderbolt of self-contempt smiting suddenly in secret.

Caroline is doubly entrapped within the ideology which imprisons her. Rebellion quickly brings remorse and self-contempt for having dared to violate the "natural" order. The discussion which follows must surely qualify as one of the bitterest pieces of Victorian prose:

Take the matter as you find it: ask no questions; utter no remonstrances: it is your best wisdom... You held out your hand for an egg, and fate put into it a scorpion. Show no consternation: close your fingers firmly upon the gift; let it sting through your palm. Never mind: in time, after your hand and arm have swelled and quivered long with torture, the squeezed scorpion will die, and you will have learned the great lesson how to endure without a sob (Ch. 6, I, 146–7).

The ideology of resignation is exposed in all its ugly consequences. For those who are permitted no voice – whether women or workers – the only course open is that of self-suppression or, as Felix put it in his political address, "resolution and self-control" (p. 424).

Though George Eliot proclaimed the need for women's "sublimer resignation" and adopted Comte's political creed of resignation as her own, her novels suggest an underlying disquiet with this doctrine.[39] The representation of Mrs Transome clearly challenges notions of women's necessary silence and passivity, but a similar unease is also expressed within the portrayal of Esther. Like Caroline, Esther cannot express her love. Following Felix's near confession, "Esther, like a woman as she was – a woman waiting for love, never able to ask for it – had her joy in these signs of her power" (Ch. 32, II, 111). The comment aptly summarises Esther's type of power, the power of passivity which can only wait and hope, accept one of the choices offered, but never create its own. To Felix's description of his ideals Esther had replied: " 'A woman can hardly ever choose in that way; she is dependent on what happens to her. She must take meaner things, because only meaner things are within her reach' " (Ch. 27, II, 43). The statement fulfils two functions in the narrative. Superficially it is over-ruled. Esther need not take "meaner things" if Felix is available. The same statement recurs when Esther is being wooed by Harold, and the same superficial reading is possible:

After all, she was a woman, and could not make her own lot. As she had once said to Felix, 'A woman must choose meaner things, because only meaner things are offered to her.' Her lot is made for her by the love she accepts. And Esther began to think that her lot was being made for her by the love that was surrounding her with the influence of a garden on a summer morning (Ch. 43, II, 252).

In one reading, Esther's vision of woman's necessary passivity is false. She need not marry Harold, and in fact actively rejects both him, and the wealth he represents, to marry Felix. But it remains true that "a woman is dependent on what happens to her." Esther has only the power of choice between two men. She is free neither to ask for love nor to order her life apart from the love that is brought her.

The courtship of Felix and Esther is cast in terms of conventional patterns of social and sexual differentiation. Thus, following Esther's statement that she could accept hardship, "Felix was struggling as a firm man struggles with a temptation, seeing beyond it and disbelieving its lying promise. Esther was struggling as a woman struggles with the yearning for some expression of love, and with vexation under that subjection to a yearning which is not likely to be satisfied" (Ch. 27, II, 43). Felix, the firm man, is dominant, controlling the situation, placing it within the wider perspective which is at his command. Esther is imprisoned within herself, victim of a creed which dictates that women's only fulfilment should be within love, but prohibits them from asking for it. In *Shirley*, Caroline, suffering from Robert's refusal to state his love, reflects on her place in the world and forcibly rejects the creed of devotion, submission, and renunciation of self: "Does virtue lie in abnegation of self? I do not believe it. Undue humility makes tyranny; weak concession creates selfishness. . . Each human being has his share of rights" (Ch. 10, I, 255). Her rebellion is against the organicist creed of duties, in place of rights. Yet, like Robert's workers, she can find no socially recognised form for her revolt. Faced with Robert's coldness, and trapped within the social practice which denies women the fundamental right to speech, her passion, like that of Mrs Transome, becomes self-consuming, creating with her illness another form of living death.

In neither *Felix Holt* nor *Shirley* is the social ideal of submission within marriage explicitly challenged. Both novels possess a circular structure: the final dependence of the heroines on their male associates does not represent a progression but merely a new form of the emotional dependence or weakness which characterised them in the novels' opening sections.[40] Courtship and marriage in both novels follow the pattern of dominance and submission, offering a clear political model: the inferior woman submits to the teaching of her master. As Esther declares, "I am weak – my husband must be greater and nobler than I am" (Ch. 51, II, 356).

Felix, as representative of the Comtean priesthood, wishes to establish a teacher–pupil relationship with his congregation at Sproxton. The same hierarchical model, however, also determines the relationship between the sexes in both novels. The parallels between Louis and Shirley, and Esther and Felix are particularly strong. Like Esther, Shirley refuses to marry for money but marries instead her penniless tutor whose vision of the woman he would marry clearly accords with Felix's views: "To such a creature as this, I should like to be first tutor and then husband. I would teach her my language, my habits, and my principles, and then I would reward her with my love" (Ch. 13, III, 275). The arrogant assumption of superiority is only a more blatant version of Felix's sentiments when he arrives to give Esther a sermon, or wonders whether she was a woman who could make "a man's passion for her rush in one current with all the great aims of his life" (Ch. 27, II, 39). Louis literally offers Shirley a new language. Their courtship is complete when, repeating after him a poem in his native French, she finds "lively excitement in the pleasure of making his language her own" (Ch. 4, III, 105). Felix also gives Esther a new language. He replaces her romantic reading with his own vocabulary of veneration, sanctity, and duty. He demands that Esther transform herself in accordance with his ideas, or, as the text expresses it, he "asked her to be something better than she actually was "(Ch. 24, II, 4). Interestingly, George Eliot sees Esther's response to this demand as the confirmation of her femininity; she acquires "a softened expression to her eyes, a more feminine beseechingness and self-doubt to her manners" (Ch. 24, II, 4–5). George Eliot's reduction of her heroine to this stereotype of the feminine is in line with the simplistic political message of the novel. With an identity based on self-doubt and supplication, Esther conforms to the social role Comte ascribed to women in his hierarchical division of society. Marriage, Comte believed, was based on "the natural subordination of the woman." Her sphere was to be that of affectivity for, "It is indisputable that women are, in general, as superior to men in a spontaneous expansion of sympathy and sociality, as they are inferior to men in understanding and reason."[41] Esther loses her assertiveness to take on the "true" female attributes of feeling.

Comte's model of the social organism offers a resolution to George Eliot's fears that democracy would undermine respect for natural superiority. Positivism claimed to demonstrate scientifically the natural laws of subordination; the superiority of the intellectual classes to the workers, and of men to women:

Sociology will prove that the equality of the sexes, of which so much is said, is incompatible with all social existence, by showing that each sex has special and permanent functions which it must fulfil in the natural economy of the human family, and which concur in a common end by different ways, the welfare which results being in no degree injured by the necessary subordination, since the happiness of every being depends on the wise development of its proper nature.[42]

In *Felix Holt* Esther adopts Felix's Comtean values. She measures Harold against Felix's ideal, and finds him lacking, for she had "no sense of inferiority and just subjection when she was with Harold Transome" (Ch. 43, II, 249). Esther is not, like Harold's first wife, a slave. Enthralled, however, by Felix's ideas of just subjection she possesses only the illusion of freedom, and a bondage all the stronger for its chains being invisible.

For a true corrective of these images of courtship and marriage we should turn to Mrs Transome:

This girl has a fine spirit – plenty of fire and pride and wit. Men like such captives, as they like horses that champ the bit and paw the ground: they feel more triumph in their mastery. What is the use of a woman's will? – if she tries, she doesn't get it, and she ceases to be loved. God was cruel when he made women (Ch. 39, II, 202).

The imagery anticipates George Eliot's later study, in *Daniel Deronda*, of Grandcourt's social and sexual tyranny. Alone among the women characters, Mrs Transome has refused to be mastered, refused to delight in surrendering her will to another. But by refusing to submit she is left only barrenness and sterility. She exerts her will only in the autocratic authority with which she rules over petty details of village life. Those who surround her offer her the role solely of a placid, powerless, and non-thinking elderly lady. As her son Harold observes, " 'a woman ought to be a Tory, and graceful, and handsome, like you. I should hate a woman who took up my opinions, and talked for me' " (Ch. 8, I, 161). The statement is a variation on Comte's belief that "the moment that woman leaves the home, she necessarily loses her greatest strength, which is more bound up with the Heart than with Intellect or Character."[43]

Mrs Transome stands as a powerful challenge to the ideology which surrounds the images of wife and mother. Motherhood was, for Comte, the supreme symbol of organicism, for it signalled both self-abnegation and the organic continuity of society. Mrs Transome's experience puts these values into question: "It is a fact perhaps kept a little too much in the background, that mothers have a self larger than their maternity" (Ch. 8, I, 166). Try as she might, Mrs Transome's attempts to subdue her feelings to the required role only increase her frustrations. Harold's polite attentions as dutiful son only emphasise the nullity of their relationship. Mrs Transome had shared "the common dream that when a beautiful man-child was born to her, her cup of happiness would be full" (Ch. 8, I, 167). But her experience has exposed the dream. The desired plenitude and continuity are replaced by misery, non-understanding and an impenetrable barrier between the generations.

Esther's life is directly contrasted to that of Mrs Transome who had lived, since her affair, amidst "desecrated sanctities," for, "It is only in that freshness of our time that the choice is possible which gives unity to life, and makes the memory a temple where all relics and all votive offerings, all worship and all grateful joy, are an unbroken history sanctified by one religion" (Ch. 44, II, 286). The image of an unbroken sacred history captures both the historical, and social organic continuity for which Esther's love must stand as a symbol. Esther's "choice" is finally confirmed when, in the courtroom scene, she exhibits, like the later Dorothea, the "ardour" that "illuminates" history: "In this, at least, her woman's lot was perfect: that the man she loved was her hero; that her woman's passion and her reverence for rarest goodness rushed together in an undivided current" (Ch. 46, II, 313). Her achievement of organic unity is, significantly, qualified as the perfect form of "woman's lot." Her sublimity, indeed, arises from the "inspired ignorance" of her action. Even in the perfection of her lot, Esther, in accordance with Comtean principles, is debarred from the realm of knowledge and rationality. George Eliot has once again denied to her heroine her own achievements.

Yet in opposition to this perfection stands Mrs Transome, bitterly discontented that her son should refuse to grant her the right, either to opinions, or to rational control. Mrs Transome, like Esther, had hoped that her love would unify her life: "She had thought that the possession of this child would give unity to her life, and make some gladness

through the changing years that would grow as fruit out of these early
maternal caresses" (Ch. 1, I, 31). Her life does possess unity, but not
that signalled by this image of organic growth. Mrs Transome is a true
embodiment of history, a living geological record, "a breathing woman
who had numbered the years as they passed, and had a consciousness
within her which was the slow deposit of those ceaseless rolling years"
(Ch. 39, II, 199). Her consciousness retains a simultaneous record of
past and present. Yet the result of such unity is pain – "why, every fibre
in me seems to be a memory that makes a pang" (Ch. 39, II, 205). Her
suffering culminates in the desire that the past had never been, that
Harold had never been born. With Mrs Transome that derivative
organic image, the web, is reversed in its usual implications. Instead of
symbolising social and historical continuity, it stands as an image of
torture – its meshes do not gently connect but strangle: "The finest
threads, such as no eye sees, if bound cunningly about the sensitive
flesh, so that the movement to break them would bring torture, may
make a worse bondage than any fetters." Only if "all the past could be
dissolved, and leave no solid trace of itself" (Ch. 8, I, 167–8) would
she have tasted some joy. All the images which surround Esther and her
love are endowed with contrary implications in the life of Mrs Transome. Whilst Esther sits waiting for her final union with Felix she is
"not reading, but stitching" (Ch. 51, II, 352) having substituted submissive duty for the pursuit of knowledge.[44] Yet the image of Mrs
Transome stitching "as if she had to work out her deliverance from
bondage by finishing a scroll-patterned border" (Ch. 45, II, 288)
should surely stand as a direful warning.

The sexual division to which Esther submits is directly correlated
with the preservation of a traditional form of hierarchical community.
Thus the Rectory is described as "one of those rectories which are
among the bulwarks of our venerable institutions – which arrest disin-
tegrating doubt, serve as a double embankment against Popery and
Dissent, and rally feminine instinct and affection to reinforce the deci-
sions of masculine thought" (Ch. 23, I, 344). Sexual roles and social
institutions are inextricably intertwined. By agreeing to add her
feminine affection to Felix's masculine thought, Esther is agreeing to
preserve the institutions of the traditional organic community, object
of so much nostalgia in *Felix Holt*. But, once again, Mrs Transome
stands as challenge to this ideal. Her rigid autocracy deconstructs the
image of a harmonious society. In the strength of her conservatism she
achieves the same insight as the trade-union man. She believed in the

doctrines and rituals of the Church of England: "in fact, in such a view of this world and the next as would preserve the existing arrangements of English society quite unshaken, keeping down the obtrusiveness of the vulgar and the discontent of the poor" (Ch. 1, I, 41). In this vision of the union of church and social institutions in social oppression, she is echoed by the trade-union member. He extends his reversal of the belly parable to religion:

It's part of their monopoly. They'll supply us with our religion like everything else, and get a profit on it. They'll give us plenty of heaven. We may have land *there*. That's the sort of religion they like – a religion that gives us working men heaven, and nothing else (Ch. 30, II, 85).

Felix, with his creed of veneration and sanctity, actually reinforces this ideological and social suppression. His doctrine that sobriety, industry and faithfulness will bring the working class the power they desire is directly countered by Mrs Transome's dismissive response to her inferiors. She fails to notice Mr Lyon, "not from studied haughtiness, but from sheer mental inability to consider him – as a person ignorant of natural history is unable to consider a fresh-water polype otherwise than as a sort of animated weed, certainly not fit for table" (Ch. 38, II, 189). Mrs Transome's attitude stands as warranty for the inevitable failure of Felix's project. By concentrating his education programme on the working classes, Felix will not rectify, but will rather confirm social abuses. Whilst the intransigence of such as Mrs Transome remains, his ideal of organic harmony must rest a mockery.

Thus in the two related spheres of social and sexual order Mrs Transome stands as a challenge to all ideals of unity, continuity, and organic harmony. Felix's creed, based on the Comtean idea of the natural division of classes within the social organism, demanded the submission. Though the conclusion might point to a Comtean union their position."[45] Only through Esther, however, do we witness this submission. Though the conclusion might point to a Comtean union between philosophers, workers, and women, this organicist ideal is clearly undermined, both sexually and politically, by the tragic, but defiant, figure of Mrs Transome.

CHAPTER 7

Middlemarch:
An experiment in time

The problems George Eliot encountered in unifying *Felix Holt* seemed to renew her determination to explore fully the social issues of organicism. The themes that, in her earlier novels, had become evident only during the course of the narrative are deliberately asserted in the Prelude to *Middlemarch*. Dorothea's story is that of "spiritual grandeur ill-matched with the meanness of opportunity"; her goal, the "rapturous consciousness of life beyond self."[1] Dorothea exemplifies perfectly the organic ideal: she strives for a form of personal fulfilment which would transcend egoism and integrate individual desire with social demands. The thematic clarity of the novel's introduction does not herald, however, a simplistic social vision. *Middlemarch* possesses neither the political crudeness of *Felix Holt* nor the correlated naive idealisation of "woman's lot." It offers no simple endorsement of theories of organic social harmony. Rather, like the earlier novels *The Mill on the Floss* and *Romola* that also took a woman as their main protagonist, it explores the complexities and contradictions within organicist social theory.

The Prelude poses the question of how originality can survive within an environment whose essence, as the title suggests, is its middlingness. The question is not, however, an innocent one. The form in which the problem is expressed also defines the terms of its ideal resolution. These "later-born Theresas," the narrator observes, "were helped by no coherent social faith and order which could perform the function of knowledge for the ardently willing soul" (Prelude, I, 2). The passage is not simply a lament for a departed era; it simultaneously defines the values that will structure the narrative and the model of social and individual development to which George Eliot adheres. Both are drawn from an organicist perspective. The perfect state will be one in which there is no disjunction between inner consciousness and the external social medium. In *Middlemarch,* however, George Eliot applies the ideal of organic union between the individual and society to a situation that exposes its poverty. Her uncertainty about this ideal had led in

Felix Holt to a split within the novel: a radical division between the hopeless negativity of Mrs Transome's life, and the optimistic idealisation of Felix. In *Middlemarch* it leads, not to internal division, but to a greater complexity in social vision, narrative technique and structure. Faced with apparent irreconcilable contradictions within the traditional organic social model, George Eliot turned to contemporary theories in biological science and social philosophy for the principles that would structure her narrative.

Middlemarch is a work of experimental science: an examination of the "history of man" under the "varying experiments of Time" (Prelude, I, 1).[2] In *Adam Bede*, the scientific methodology of natural history had sustained the novel's static vision of social order. George Eliot brings to *Middlemarch*, however, a more questioning social vision; the Middlemarch of the Prelude is neither a static nor a harmoniously integrated society. The role of natural historian, passively transcribing a given order, will no longer suffice. George Eliot turns instead to the more dynamic methodology of experimental biology, a stance which receives paradigmatic expression in the novel in the research of Lydgate.[3] *Middlemarch* is the first novel in which science is treated as an explicit theme, and in the long discussions of Lydgate's methods and beliefs one can discern George Eliot's reflections on her own assumptions and procedures.[4]

Speaking as an experimental scientist, Lydgate summarily dismisses Farebrother's practice of natural history. He was, he declares, "early bitten with an interest in structure" (Ch. 17, I, 262). This interest in structure is expressed in his belief that living bodies "are not associations of organs which can be understood by studying them first apart, and then as it were federally" (Ch. 15, I, 223–4). Though offered only as a biological observation, Lydgate's statement in fact holds the key to George Eliot's social theory and narrative practice in *Middlemarch*. The natural historian looks at society as a collection of individuals that can be viewed first separately, and then federally, but the experimental scientist challenges this conception of individual autonomy. The characters in *Middlemarch* cannot be abstracted out from the life-processes of the town. As George Eliot tries to suggest through the complex narrative organisation of her novel, each part of Middlemarch life is related to every other part; individual identity is not only influenced by the larger social organism, it is actively defined by it.

On a more fundamental level, Lydgate's theory of organic interdependence also affects George Eliot's conception of realism. The natural historian's function is to label and classify the individual components of a fixed reality; conceptions of dynamic interdependence, however, undermine that possibility. As the experimental physiologist Claude Bernard argued, to try to discover physiological properties by isolating organs would be like trying to determine the difference between comedy and tragedy by seeing which has more 'a's and 'b's:

> En effet, les lettres ne sont rien par elles-mêmes, elles ne signifient quelque chose que par leur groupement sous telle ou telle forme qui donne un mot de telle ou telle signification. Le mot lui-même est un élément composé qui prend une signification spéciale par son mode de groupement dans la phrase, et la phrase, à son tour, doit concourir avec d'autres à l'expression complète de l'idée totale du sujet. Dans les matières organiques, il y a des éléments simples, communs, qui ne prennent une signification spéciale que par leur mode de groupement.[5]

The linguistic analogy is peculiarly apt. Ideas of organic interdependence challenge equally empiricism in science and naive realism in art. There can be no one-to-one correspondence between sign and signified, since meaning, like organic life, is a product of a total system. G. H. Lewes extends Bernard's analogy to illustrate why the new science must move beyond the empiricism of natural history to the realm of ideal construction: "It is through the manifold ideal constructions of the Possible that we learn to appreciate the Actual. Facts are mere letters which have their meaning only in the words they form; and these words again have their meaning, not in themselves alone but in their positions in the sentence."[6] The function of the scientist is no longer simply to transcribe the "real." Following the theory of organic interdependence, observations only possess meaning when placed in an ideally constructed framework. George Eliot's narrative practice in *Middlemarch* accords with these principles. She no longer adheres to the naive realism of *Adam Bede* with its apologetic image of the defective mirror, but actively accepts the creative role of author. Dexterously interweaving many strands of material, she uses the resources of both myth and symbol to create the "ideal experiment" of her novel. The image of the historian untangling the pre-existent web is complemented by that of the creative scientist; and the realism of the Garths' presentation is balanced by the mythological resonances of the story of Dorothea, Casaubon, and Will. George Eliot's method and theory of art in fact look forward to the later *Daniel Deronda* in which the visionary Mordecai's prophetic role is directly compared to that of an experimental scientist.

For Bernard, the experimental scientist was "a real foreman of creation"; in creating the conditions of his experiments, he actively engineered the appearance of phenomena.[7] His methodology, moreover, was firmly based, as Lewes also believed, on the processes of ideal construction and imaginative pre-vision[8] for, as Bernard observes, "Ideas, given form by facts, embody science."[9] Bernard held adamantly to the conviction that "We must give free rein to our imagination; the idea is the essence of all reasoning and all invention."[10] This conception of scientific method, which underpins George Eliot's "experiment in time," is articulated in the novel by Lydgate who adheres, somewhat in advance of his time, to a belief in the scientific imagination. Lydgate disdains the form of imagination present in cheap narration which he regards as

rather vulgar and vinous compared with the imagination that reveals subtle actions inaccessible by any sort of lens, but tracked in that outer darkness through long pathways of necessary sequence by the inward light which is the last refinement of Energy, capable of bathing even the ethereal atoms in its ideally illuminated space (Ch. 16, I, 249).

Like his creator, Lydgate conceives science not simply as a process of observation and classification, but rather as the pursuit of ideas and hypotheses. The object of science is not to record the already known, but to reveal hidden connections, through the creation of an "ideally illuminated space" – Lewes' "manifold ideal constructions of the Possible" that help to reveal the Actual.

In creating the experimental conditions through which to explore the possible outcome of the life of a "later-born Theresa" placed in the uncongenial social medium of Middlemarch, George Eliot follows Lydgate's scientific methodology. Her labour of imagination is not "mere arbitrariness, but the exercise of disciplined power." She combines and constructs all the multitudinous elements of Middlemarch life "with the clearest eye for probabilities and the fullest obedience to knowledge" (Ch. 16, I, 249). The purpose behind her labour also corresponds to that of scientific practice, for the aim of science, Lewes suggests, is to link together, through imaginative construction, the fragments of the phenomenal world so as to reveal an underlying order. While "Perception gives the naked fact of Sense, isolated, unconnected, merely juxtaposed with other facts, and without far-reaching significance," science reveals connections and confers significance: "The facts of Feeling which sensation differentiates, Theory integrates."[11] George Eliot tries, through the structural organisation of her work, to reveal underlying organic unity beneath apparent surface disorder. The pursuit of significant order constitutes, indeed, both the major theme and methodology of the novel, for George Eliot's characters share her goal. Thus Lydgate searches for the one primitive tissue, and Casaubon for the "Key to all Mythologies." Dorothea, in similar fashion, yearns for "a binding theory which would bring her own life and doctrine into strict connection with that amazing past" (Ch. 10, I, 128). On a more humorous level, Mr Brooke seeks, in his usual rambling way, for a means of ordering his documents other than by the arbitrary system of A to Z. Author and characters alike quest for an organising principle or theory which would bind together disparate parts and reveal unity beneath apparent chaos.

In their search, the characters often fall into the stance of natural historians, holding, mistakenly, that meaning actually inheres in external form. Thus Lydgate believes that Rosamond's physical appearance expresses her virtue "with a force of demonstration that excluded the need for other evidence" (Ch. 16, I, 248) while Dorothea is similarly misled by Casaubon: "Everything I see in him," she responds rather haughtily to Celia, "corresponds to his pamphlet on Biblical Cosmology" (Ch. 2, I, 27). Casaubon is similarly guilty of treating the world as a system of signs to be decoded. His Key is to make "the vast field of mythical constructions . . . intelligible, nay, luminous with the reflected light of correspondences" (Ch. 3, I, 33). He wishes to reveal the underlying order of history through the external correspondences of myths, though, as the narrator observes, this approach had been discredited in both mythological studies, and the related science of philology: Mr Casaubon's theory "floated among flexible conjectures no more solid than those etymologies which seemed strong because of likeness in sound until it was shown that likeness in sound made them impossible" (Ch. 48, II, 312). External correspondences can be actively misleading. Thus Lewes, in *Sea-side Studies*, confirmed Bernard's warning against "attempting to deduce a function from mere inspection of the organ" for the external resemblance of organs cannot be taken as evidence of their similar functions.[12] The same principle of organic interdependence applies to physiological life, language, social relations, or historical development. One must look beyond the details of external form to the underlying dynamic process, for, as in Bernard's linguistic analogy, each part only derives meaning from its position within the whole.

The structure of *Middlemarch* reflects this principle of interdepen-

dence. The unity of the novel is not based, as in that earlier study of
provincial life, Mrs Gaskell's *Cranford*, on spatial continuity or community of life style.[13] The life portrayed is both geographically and
socially dispersed, moving from Tipton to Frick, from the gentry to
labourers, and from the measured cadences of Casaubon's speech to the
trenchant assertions of Mrs Dollop. Unlike the earlier *Felix Holt*, or
Dickens' *Bleak House*, the plot does not revolve around the gradual
revelation of hidden connections between socially disparate groups, or
a cumbersome legal machinery. Indeed the sole links that emerge from
the past – those of Bulstrode, Raffles, and Will – seem rather to disturb
than affirm our sense of the unity of Middlemarch life. Though the
Bulstrode and Casaubon plots are connected by Will, in his capacity as
twice disinherited heir, George Eliot actively eschews, in general, the
technique of linking all her characters through relations of direct personal contact. No links, for example, are drawn between Dorothea and
Farebrother or Caleb until after Casaubon's death, while the sole direct
connection between Dorothea and Featherstone occurs with Dorothea's
distant glance at Featherstone's funeral. The structure of *Middlemarch*
conforms to Lewes' definition of organic life: "The part exists only as
part of a whole; the whole exists only as a whole of its parts."[14]

The unity of *Middlemarch* is based, primarily, not on relations of
direct effect, but on the shared community of language. In constructing
her "Study of Provincial Life" George Eliot adhered to the same social
interpretation of organicist premises as Lewes. Her representation of
Middlemarch life accords with the theory of the social medium Lewes
was concurrently defining in *The Foundations of a Creed*. Lewes
differentiates his approach from that of psychologists; his was the first
survey, he believed, to take fully into account the role of the social
medium in determining individual psychology. Thus, "The psychologist, accustomed to consider the Mind as something apart from the
Organism, individual and collective, is peculiarly liable to this error of
overlooking the fact that all mental manifestations are simply the result-
ants of the conditions external and internal."[15] These external conditions
are not simply the material or economic conditions of society but "the
collective accumulations of centuries, condensed in knowledge, beliefs,
prejudices, institutions, and tendencies," and transmitted primarily
through language.[16] The individual and social life of Middlemarch
conforms to this model. Though characters are linked in material
relations of dependency, the primary connecting bond is the shared
linguistic medium. Through language characters articulate both their

individual and communal identity: gossip, or the exchange of opinion, functions as the fundamental linking force. The structure of the individual chapters reflects this principle. Chapters move either linearly, connecting various strands of plot through an extended chain of characters' opinions about each other, or laterally, from a larger social issue to its effects upon the thoughts and reflections of a single life.[17]

A linear structure is manifest, for example, in Chapter 71 which traces the revelation, through gossip, of Bulstrode's story, and the indignant responses in each social stratum. In keeping with George Eliot's commitment to organic heterogeneity, the chapter concludes, not with Bulstrode, but with Dorothea, fervently asserting her faith in Lydgate. Though the majority of characters in this chapter scarcely know of each other's existence, they are all linked together by the connecting chain of opinion.

An example of the principles of lateral construction is furnished by Chapter 56 which moves from a general discussion of the coming of the railway to trace its effects on individual lives. George Eliot enumerates in this chapter the three social issues she employs to unite the disparate elements of Middlemarch existence: "In the hundred to which Middlemarch belonged," she observes, "railways were as exciting a topic as the Reform Bill or the imminent horrors of Cholera, and those who held the most decided views on the subject were women and landholders" (Ch. 56, III, 30). Though the three issues of railways, Reform, and Cholera engross the social organism, their unifying force lies less in their material effects than in their mobilisation of public opinion. Individual psychology is defined, in accordance with Lewes' theories, both by the accumulated beliefs and prejudices stored within language, and the contemporary functions of gossip. Indeed, the processes of gossip constitute both the dominant principles of chapter construction, and one of the novel's major themes. As George Eliot demands, in reference to Bulstrode, "Who can know how much of his inward life is made up of the thoughts he believes other men to have about him, until that fabric of opinion is threatened with ruin?" (Ch. 68, III, 238). Public opinion cannot be ignored; it actively enters into the creation of both mind and self-identity. George Eliot explores through the plot and formal structure of her novel the implications of this principle of organic interdependence.

The constant shifts in perspective within the chapters, from the social whole to the individual parts, accord with George Eliot's conception of organic form which she outlined in her notebook essay "Notes on

Form in Art" (1868). Form, she argued, "must first depend on the discrimination of wholes & then on the discrimination of parts."[18] Lydgate, translating this premise into biological practice, believed that "there must be a systole and diastole in all inquiry." Unlike Lydgate, George Eliot actually follows this method; her novel is "continually expanding and shrinking between the whole human horizon and the horizon of an object glass" (Ch. 63, III, 163). Both the chapter construction and larger structure of the work reinforce this process. Book titles, like "Old and Young" or "Waiting for Death," draw attention away from the continuity of plot to suggest a wider unity of theme, while the epigraphs, which often hold an enigmatic relation to the following material, similarly disrupt linear narration to establish a framework of expectations for the ensuing chapter. The jumps in perspective reflect the heterogeneous structure of the social organism itself, for, as George Eliot argued in her essay, "The highest Form . . . is the highest organism, that is to say, the most varied group of relations bound together in a wholeness which again has the most varied relations with all other phenomena."[19] Her definition follows Spencer's theory that the highest form of art will be "not a series of like parts simply placed in juxtaposition, but one whole made up of unlike parts that are mutually dependent."[20] The universal principle of development from homogeneity to heterogeneity to which Spencer refers here is one, George Eliot suggests in the essay, that governs equally the development of organic life, or poetic form, and the growth of mind, both in the individual and in the race.[21] Within the form of her novel she attempts to capture the organic principles that govern both historical growth and social interdependence.

In a recent study, which points to the connections between notions of organic form, narrative conventions, and "the system of assumptions which is associated with the idea of history in Western culture," Hillis Miller argues that in *Middlemarch* "in place of the concept of elaborate organic form, centered form, form organised around certain absolute generalizable themes, George Eliot presents a view of artistic form as inorganic, acentered, and discontinuous."[22] He mistakenly identifies all "Western ideas of history" with a Hegelian teleological organicism, ignoring the fact that the "unlikeness and difference" of *Middlemarch* crystallises George Eliot's conception of organic form and development. Yet in stressing the discontinuity, and the "contradictory struggle of individual human energies" within the novel, Hillis Miller does locate a source of internal narrative tension. The historical process of differentiation could, for Spencer, only be one of progress; the mutual dependence of unlike parts would necessarily be harmonious. Theoretically, according to George Eliot's own definition of organic form, the *differentiation* of opinion would actually unite Middlemarch. Her study reveals, however, the destructive functions of gossip. Mrs Bulstrode learns to her cost the meaning of "candour" in the Middlemarch vocabulary, while the dinners required to feed gossip about her husband and Lydgate suggest a decidedly cannibalistic interpretation of the social organism. The narrator's early observation that Middlemarch "counted on swallowing Lydgate and assimilating him very comfortably" (Ch. 15, I, 274) proves to be disturbingly accurate.

At every level, the interdependence of Middlemarch life seems to be based not on harmony, but on conflict. Thus Mr Brooke learns, during his lamentable experience as a political candidate, that Middlemarch is not the cosy paternalist society of his imaginings: "the weavers and tanners of Middlemarch . . . had never thought of Mr. Brooke as a neighbour" (Ch. 51, II, 349). Economically, indeed, Middlemarch society reveals the worst vices of capitalism. We discover, for instance, from Mr Vincy that Bulstrode is associated with Plymdale's house which employs dyes liable to rot the silk, while Mr Vincy himself is identified by Mrs Cadwallader as "one of those who suck the life out of the wretched handloom weavers in Tipton and Freshitt" (Ch. 34, II, 82). Though the narrator refers at one stage to the "stealthy convergence of human lots," thus seeming to offer a moral rebuke to Lydgate and Dorothea for their "mutual indifference," the description of social interaction which follows is scarcely suggestive of harmonious integration:

Old provincial society had its share of this subtle movement: had not only its striking downfalls, its brilliant young professional dandies who ended by living up an entry with a drab and six children for their establishment, but also those less marked vicissitudes which are constantly shifting the boundaries of social intercourse, and begetting new consciousness of interdependence (Ch. 11, I, 142).

Social interdependence is defined primarily by vicissitudes, while the actual process of change is marked by darwinian elements of competition. The inhabitants of Middlemarch are displaced by successful settlers who "came from distant counties, some with an alarming novelty of skill, others with an offensive advantage in cunning." In the darwinian battle for survival, success belongs to those with the highest powers of adaptation. Middlemarch life exhibits all the characteristics of a vital organism, for movement of each part affects the whole. Thus, even those who stand "with rocky firmness amid all this fluctuation" are by the surrounding changes themselves transformed, "altering with the double change of self and beholder." Yet despite this evident interdependence, town life displays none of the peaceful unity of the organic social ideal.

George Eliot adheres, in *Middlemarch*, to the moral ideal of organic unity while simultaneously demonstrating the social impossibility of attaining this goal. Such an internal contradiction does not lead her, however, to deconstruct notions of historical unity and continuity as Hillis Miller, for rather different reasons, has suggested. Though innovatory in form, *Middlemarch* is a solidly nineteenth-century text, constructed in the light of contemporary social and scientific debates concerning historical growth. In true realist fashion, the novel poses a social and moral problem which the narrative seeks to resolve. George Eliot is committed, ultimately, not to openness and discontinuity but to narrative closure. The difficulties she encounters in moving towards the desired resolution are clearly exacerbated, however, by her recognition of the social conflict which the myth of social heterogeneity actually conceals.

On a more fundamental level, her difficulties are also increased by the model of individual development to which she subscribes. Though the function of her "experiment in time" is to assess the relative claims of the individual and the social organism, she actually adheres to a dynamic theory of organic process which undermines conceptions of individual autonomy upon which such judgements must necessarily be based. Thus, Lewes, outlining the psychological implications of Lydgate's theory of organic interdependence, argued that the division between self and not-self is false; it is analytic rather than real. The individual cannot be isolated out and defined apart from the organic process, for the individual, he concludes, *is* its relations.[23] This model suggests a fluidity and openness incompatible with the traditional realist demand for moral closure. If character is treated as flux, or process, there can be no fixed points of value, no grounds for assessing individual moral responsibility for action. Nor can the narrative draw to a defined close. The dynamic theory of organic order in fact undercuts the terms of the original organic problematic. George Eliot strives in *Middlemarch* to resolve this contradiction: to reconcile the idea of individual fluidity with the need for fixed moral judgement.

The opening chapter of *Middlemarch* clearly reveals George Eliot's organicist premises. Characters are introduced not in terms of fixed personal attributes, but in terms of their social effects. Dorothea, we learn in the opening paragraph, "was usually spoken of as being remarkably clever." Public opinion defines each character: thus Mr Brooke "was held in this part of the county to have contracted a too rambling habit of mind," while "The rural opinion about the new young ladies, even among the cottagers, was generally in favour of Celia." We discover, furthermore, that Mr Brooke, though blamed by neighbouring families for not securing a companion for Dorothea, was yet "brave enough to defy the world – that is to say, Mrs. Cadwallader the Rector's wife, and the small group of gentry with whom he visited in the north-east corner of Loamshire" (Ch. 1, I, 7–13). The increased particularisation draws attention to the specificity of their environment. To comprehend Dorothea or Mr Brooke, one must bring knowledge, not of the world, but rather of that particular "north-east corner of Loamshire" which determines their lives.

Our understanding of each character is formed through the medium of his neighbours' eyes. The narrator's protest against the reader's possible response to Casaubon draws attention to her own technique:

I protest against any absolute conclusion, any prejudice derived from Mrs Cadwallader's contempt for a neighbouring clergyman's alleged greatness of soul, or Sir James Chettam's poor opinion of his rival's legs, – from Mr Brooke's failure to elicit a companion's ideas, or from Celia's criticism of a middle-aged scholar's personal appearance (Ch. 10, I, 125).

Character cannot be defined apart from social opinion, for each individual is only the sum of his, constantly changing, relations with the social organism. Such relativism, however, is more apparent than real; it is clearly undercut by the text's claim to offer authoritative judgement. We rest in little doubt concerning the "absolute conclusion" we should draw about each character. Through analysis of the three histories of Lydgate, Bulstrode, and Dorothea I will try to suggest the different ways in which George Eliot actually used the premises of organicist theory to achieve this moral closure. Drawing on the assumption, which she outlined in "Notes on Form in Art," that the same principles of organic life govern physiological, psychological, and social development, she mediates constantly between these different levels of analysis in *Middlemarch* in an attempt to impose structural and moral order on the text.

Introducing Lydgate, George Eliot observes that "character too is a process and an unfolding" (Ch. 15, I, 226). This admission of fluidity is not borne out, however, by the narrative. The statement is immediately followed by a detailed account of Lydgate's history which functions to define his character independently of his life within the social organism of Middlemarch. In the case of Lydgate, plot, or the patterning of social events, does not trace a process of dynamic interaction between the individual and the social whole. It functions, rather, as a structural analogue of the predefined composition of his mind. The history of Lydgate's association with Laure illustrates his "two selves"; his relations with Middlemarch are but an external enactment of this fixed internal contradiction. The "spots of commonness" in his nature find their reflection in the petty judgements of the Middlemarch mind, while his other, idealistic, self finds its social correlative in Dorothea's willing faith. But as the "spots of commonness" predominate in his nature, so the judgement of Middlemarch ultimately prevails. The social drama is merely that of his psychological constitution writ large. Reflecting on Lydgate's failure, George Eliot observes that "It always remains true that if we had been greater, circumstance would have been less strong against us" (Ch. 58, III, 82). Sympathy is linked to firm moral judgement, thus suggesting a strong sense of order in the world. This stance is possible, however, only because George Eliot did not adhere firmly to a fluid model of character. It is, in the final instance, Lydgate's intrinsic moral flaws, his lack of innate greatness, and not the circumstances of his interaction with Middlemarch, that create his downfall.

The need to offer moral judgement also determines the representation of Bulstrode. At its simplest level, George Eliot wants to suggest that crime does not pay. If organic social harmony is to be preserved, wrongdoing must be shown to have undesired consequences for the perpetrator. In order to enforce this moral George Eliot departs once more from the fluid model of character. Bulstrode is the only other character apart from Lydgate who is given a detailed history outside his incorporation within Middlemarch life; his relations with Middlemarch can similarly be defined as the gradual unfolding or revelation of the prior structure of his mind. The history of Bulstrode is the only one in which coincidence strains credibility; Will's presence in Middlemarch, and Raffles' re-emergence conform more to a desired moral configuration than to the laws of realistic probability. In order to naturalise these occurrences George Eliot turns once more to physiology, to the idea of a physical basis for memory:

The terror of being judged sharpens the memory: it sends an inevitable glare over that long-unvisited past which has been habitually recalled only in general phrases. Even without memory, the life is bound into one by a zone of dependence in growth and decay; but intense memory forces a man to own his blameworthy past. With memory set smarting like a reopened wound, a man's past is not simply a dead history, an outworn preparation of the present: it is not a repented error shaken loose from the life: it is a still quivering part of himself, bringing shudders and bitter flavours and the tinglings of a merited shame (Ch. 61, III, 125–6).

The final term "merited" reveals the moral bias of the whole description. George Eliot uses physiology to suggest that for the individual, as much as for the society or culture, there is a vital interdependence in history. Past history can never be "dead," never be discarded; shame must inevitably occur. All the terms employed reinforce the idea of a physical basis of memory; whether the "shudders" and "tinglings" of the sensations aroused, or the quivering vibrations which constitute the physiological response. The zone of dependence in growth and decay recalls de Blainville's theory upon which Lewes based his theory of mind: that organic life is a process of composition and decomposition in interaction with the environment.[24] George Eliot employs this physical theory, as she did with Tito in *Romola*, to suggest a moral conclusion which is by no means sure: that a man will always be called to account for his past actions. The apparent transitory nature of social experience is referred to the constancy of physiological composition.

Raffles' social ostracism mirrors his status in Bulstrode's mind. George Eliot employs the operations of the unconscious as a model for the plot and social events, thus proposing a form of homology between the social and psychic realms that appears to offer a grounding within nature for the moral patterning of the narrative. She draws, however, on contemporary theories of unconscious life which do not simply reinforce ideas of a linear, cumulative history. Thus Bulstrode:

felt the scenes of his earlier life coming between him and everything else, as obstinately as when we look through the window from a lighted room, the objects we turn our backs on are still before us, instead of the grass and the trees. The successive events inward and outward were there in one view: though each might be dwelt on in turn, the rest still kept their hold in the consciousness (Ch. 61, III, 126).

This superb image presents a model of the mind which, departing from the linear model of associationist theory, admits the simultaneity of different levels of consciousness. The analysis of Bulstrode's mental processes focuses strongly on duality, whether of past and present, or the simultaneous existence of the "theoretic phrases" he had used to justify his actions, and his actual experience of egoistic terror (Ch. 53, II, 385). Both modes are captured in Lewes' theory of the psychological subject:

> He lives a double life and has a double world – the world of Feeling and the world of Thought, that of sensations and images and that of abstract ideas. The Present is to him a complex web, with threads of the Past and threads of the Future inextricably interwoven.[25]

The web image recalls Bulstrode's inability to "unravel" his confused promptings (Ch. 70, III, 271), while the distinction between thought and image is that which occurs when he attempts to pray: "through all this effort to condense words into a solid mental state, there pierced and spread with irresistible vividness the images of the events he desired" (Ch. 70, III, 262). Although Bulstrode has interpreted history as one unified Providential order, his psychological experience of duality and contradiction exposes the falsity of this model. The representation of Bulstrode's consciousness clearly challenges linear models of the *cogito*. Yet, his experience is used, not to subvert, as Hillis Miller suggests, but rather to reinforce the continuum of history. The physiological coherence of his body appears to offer a guarantee of cumulative social order.

Bulstrode and Lydgate were both defined by their histories before they entered Middlemarch. George Eliot tries, however, in the case of Dorothea, to follow more closely her theory of dynamic development. We witness a reciprocal interaction between social organism and individual: social contradiction becomes personal. Dorothea is introduced in terms of two conflicting value systems and forms of language, suggesting two different temporal schemas. Her plain garments "by the side of provincial fashion gave her the impressiveness of a fine quotation from the Bible, – or from one of our elder poets, – in a paragraph of to-day's newspaper" (Ch. 1, I, 7). The long-standing cultural and religious traditions expressed in poetry or the Bible are contrasted with the pragmatic, ephemeral prose of a newspaper, the voice of contemporary social values. Dorothea is caught between the two. The reasons given for her dress clearly suggest this conflict; they are firstly those of economic class and status, and only secondly those of religion. The reader should not be fooled by Dorothea's self-image. She is not the embodiment of ahistorical religious values, but rather the product of a conflict between historically established religious traditions, and the rising values of her social class. The discussion of her religious proclivities is thus placed in the context of her marriageability: the two are intimately related.

Analysis of Dorothea's thoughts and actions clearly reveals her internalisation of external social contradictions. Though she enjoys riding in a "pagan sensuous way" she looks forward to renouncing it. Her religious values are revealed to be primarily social constructs that actually denature sensuous response. Indeed her imitation of Madame Poinçon betrays the role-playing her "religion" demands. In the episode with the jewels Dorothea's internal contradiction emerges as semi-conscious duplicity, finally erupting in her angry defence of her decision to keep the jewels she had earlier scorned. We are left with Celia's verdict: "But Dorothea is not always consistent" (Ch. 1, I, 19). Whereas Lydgate's inconsistencies appeared due to innate flaws in his character, Dorothea's are shown to be socially produced.

In portraying the history of Bulstrode George Eliot employed the physiological coherence of his mind as a seeming guarantee of historical continuity and social unity. Dorothea's unity of consciousness, by contrast, reflects the strange association of dissonant elements that actually constitutes the social organism. In the sole connection drawn between Dorothea and Featherstone she glances from her window at his funeral. The scene,

aloof as it seemed to be from the tenor of her life, always afterwards came back to her at the touch of certain sensitive points in memory, just as the vision of St. Peter's at Rome was inwoven with moods of despondency. Scenes which make vital changes in our neighbours' lot are but the background of our own, yet, like a particular aspect of the fields and trees, they become associated for us with the epochs of our own history, and make a part of that unity which lies in the selection of our keenest consciousness (Ch. 34, II, 79–80).

George Eliot draws on contemporary theories of physiological psychology to illuminate the composition of the social organism.[26] Her model of mind is not, however, that of the rational intelligence which, for Spencer, best explained the harmonious distribution of functions within the social organism. Middlemarch is best represented by the confused associations of the mind which are established and recalled without obvious functional reason, far beyond the control of rationality. Although the physiological unity of mind determines the selection of consciousness, there is no order or harmony in that unity. George Eliot explicitly relates this mode of association to Dorothea's position within the social organism:

The dream-like association of something alien and ill-understood with the deepest secrets of her experience seemed to mirror that sense of loneliness which was due to the very ardour of Dorothea's nature. The country gentry of old time lived in a rarefied social air: dotted apart on their stations up the mountain they looked down with imperfect discrimination on the belts of thicker life below. And Dorothea was not at ease in the perspective and chilliness of that height (Ch. 34, II, 80).

Dorothea's situation at the window, isolated and looking down, is paradigmatic of her social position; the dream-like associations of her mind capture the inharmonious connections of Middlemarch life. The Middlemarchers may be bound together in relations of vital organic interdependence but they remain "alien and ill-understood" to each other. Social unity need not be harmonious; it can equally well be founded on conflict and contradiction.

In portraying the three histories of Lydgate, Bulstrode, and Dorothea, George Eliot shifts constantly between physiological, psychological, and social levels of explanation attempting, in the case of the first two, to resolve social problems metonymically by reference to psychic structure. Only in the case of Dorothea does she portray a truly dynamic relationship between the individual and society, or employ physiology to suggest the dissonance, rather than the order, of the social organism. Yet this image of social and psychological confusion is implicitly contrasted with its ideal forms: free flow of energy on the psychic level and harmonious integration on the social. The thrust of the novel is still towards resolution, whether of historical, social, or psychological disorder. George Eliot poses the problem of integration on each of these three levels; she also supplies, however, a structure of imagery which enables her to mediate between these different levels of analysis.

Following Lewes' conviction that science is based on Ideal Construction, George Eliot employs a controlling idea, or hypothesis, to structure her experiment. The ruling idea of *Middlemarch* is that of a labyrinth. Fundamentally, a labyrinth is a structure that dissipates energy, impedes the free flow of force. With the rise of physiological psychology it was a concept that could be applied equally to social, mental, or physiological structure. Drawing on contemporary developments in scientific theory, George Eliot employs the idea of channelled, free-flowing energy to establish a value framework for her novel. The image of a labyrinth first occurs to describe Dorothea's ardour, impeded by the entanglements of Middlemarch society: "and with such a nature struggling in the bands of a narrow teaching, hemmed in by a social life which seemed nothing but a labyrinth of petty courses, a walled-in maze of small paths that led no whither, the outcome was sure to strike others as at once exaggeration and inconsistency" (Ch. 3, I, 39). Contorted social channels are reduplicated in the mind. Dorothea's natural energy is blocked, dissipated by socially created friction. Her case is like that of Lydgate whose progress towards greatness is halted by the "retarding friction" of "small temptations and sordid cares" (Ch. 15, I, 221–2). In accordance with Lewes' theory that psychology was based on the physiological flow of energy, the tendency of sensation to "discharge itself through the readiest channel," the way through the social and psychological labyrinth of Middlemarch is to establish clear channels of transmission.[27]

The central question in *Middlemarch* is whether, as the Prelude despairingly suggests, Dorothea's energy will be "dispersed among hindrances" or will attain, in the words of the Finale, "fine issues," "channels" of positive social effect. The recurrent imagery of flowing water and streams in the novel is not simply metaphoric in origin but is grounded in contemporary social and psychological theories of energy flow.[28] As Spencer remarks in the second edition of *The Principles of Psychology*:

when describing how discharges of molecular motion go along lines of least resistance, and by recurring render them lines of less resistance, it was pointed out that in this respect there is an analogy between the flow of molecular motion and the flow of a liquid; for a stream, in proportion as it is strong and continued, cuts for itself a large and definite channel.[29]

The comparison between the "full current" of Dorothea's mind and the "shallow rills" of Casaubon's has significant scientific implications. Both Spencer and Lewes were working concurrently on questions concerning the relationship between force and cause, psychological feeling and physiological motion. Their assumptions help structure George Eliot's narrative; social and psychological action is interpreted as the movement of force.

In one of her direct scientific analogies George Eliot observes: "In watching effects, if only of an electric battery, it is often necessary to change our place and examine a particular mixture or group at some distance from the point where the movement we are interested in was set up" (Ch. 40, II, 190). The image is possibly drawn from William Grove's *On the Correlation of Physical Forces* which George Eliot records rereading "with new interest, after the lapse of years" in May

1870.[30] The voltaic battery, Grove observes, "affords us the best means of ascertaining the dynamic equivalents of different forces."[31] Grove's thesis, and George Eliot's own marginal comments in the book, concern the inseparability of cause and effect, force and motion. As a scientist examining the dynamic interdependence of the social organism George Eliot analyses action in terms of the play of force. Those convenient authorial spokesmen, the two "gents" of the epigraphs, confirm this reading; they appear twice to discuss the nature of causality. Chapter 34, which contains Featherstone's funeral, opens with their observations:

1st Gent. Such men as this are feathers, chips, and straws,
            Carry no weight, no force.
2nd Gent.   But levity
            Is causal too, and makes the sum of weight:
                                        (Ch. 34, II, 75)

In a deliberate pun, George Eliot suggests that, in the complex interdependent network of the social organism, the seeming "feather" has the causal force of a weighty stone. The domestic relations of the Lydgates receive comparable analysis. To the suggestion in Chapter 64 that blame lies with power the second Gent replies that power is relative:

            All force is twain in one: cause is not cause
            Unless effect be there;
                                        (Ch. 64, III, 173)

Lydgate's action is inseparable from Rosamond's response, just as his social effect on Middlemarch is determined not by his avowed intentions but by a balance of social forces. As Lewes observes, "In a vital organism every force is the resultant of *all* the forces; it is a disturbance of equilibrium, and equilibrium is the equivalence of convergent forces."[32] Each action in Middlemarch can only be comprehended in terms of the convergence of social forces.

Psychological behaviour is also interpreted in terms of the movement of force. Thus George Eliot observes of Mr Casaubon's disappointment concerning his lack of delight in his forthcoming marriage: "It is true that he knew all the classical passages implying the contrary; but knowing classical passages, we find, is a mode of motion, which explains why they leave so little extra force for their personal application" (Ch. 10, I, 126–7). Though light-hearted in tone, the passage confirms George Eliot's adherence to Lewes' theory that "Motion is a mode of Feeling."[33] Close scrutiny of the novel reveals the frequency with which action is interpreted as the discharge and channelling of energy. Chapter 37 furnishes two apparently trivial examples. The first refers to Will: "He did not shrug his shoulders; and for want of that muscular outlet he thought the more irritably of beautiful lips kissing holy skulls and other emptinesses ecclesiastically enshrined" (Ch. 37, II, 137–8). The second refers to Mr Casaubon: "In uttering the last clause, Mr. Casaubon leaned over the elbow of his chair, and swayed his head up and down, apparently as a muscular outlet instead of that recapitulation which would not have been becoming" (Ch. 37, II, 145–6). Unimportant in themselves, the passages yet demonstrate the degree to which George Eliot has departed from the traditions of the realist novel, and the model of the rational actor in full control of his own actions. The "Thinking Principle," Lewes argues, "is not an antecedent but a resultant, not an entity but a convergence of manifold activities."[34] The self in *Middlemarch* is not a predefined entity that determines action, but, like the social organism, is only a product of the convergence of forces.

Principles of energy transmission thus establish the foundation for a theory of psychology, and of social interaction which undermines conceptions of individual autonomy and control. The same principles, however, also underpin the novel's rather conservative inheritance plot. The labyrinth is equally one of impeded ardour and mismanaged estates. In each of the separate strands of plot concerning Featherstone, Bulstrode, Will, Casaubon, and the Brookes, George Eliot explores the moral question of how the future channel of property is to be determined. The term "channel" occurs explicitly in relation to the Bulstrode inheritance plot: if the lost daughter were found "there would be a channel for property – perhaps a wide one, in the provision for several children" (Ch. 61, III, 130). Questions of issue and transmission relate not simply to abstract qualities of soul, but also to the material realm of social order. Dorothea's story, we learn in the opening chapter, is not only that of a would-be St Theresa but also that of a potential heiress for "if Dorothea married and had a son, that son would inherit Mr. Brooke's estate" (Ch. 1, I, 10). In the history of her Puritan ancestor who served under Cromwell but emerged from political troubles as "the proprietor of a respectable family estate" (Ch. 1, I, 8) one can see an encapsulation of Dorothea's own history. Her "hereditary strain of Puritan energy" (Ch. 1, I, 10) leads her into unfortunate entanglements but ultimately enables her to bequeath a respectable family estate. The story is a more prosaic version of the St Theresa problem presented in the Prelude: native energy confronted with a labyrinth must strive to create some issue, not degenerate into formlessness like the childless Mr Brooke who "will run into any mould," but "won't keep shape" (Ch. 8, I, 103).

In her marriage to Casaubon Dorothea can produce no issue, she experiences a "nightmare of a life in which every energy was arrested by dread" (Ch. 37, II, 155). Entangled in the labyrinth of history, the impotent Casaubon can produce neither Key nor child. By violating in his will, however, the rules of social propriety (a term which shares a common root with property), he releases Dorothea from her bond, thus freeing her will or energy. Significantly, it is in marriage to the vital Will that she produces the desired heir. The pun is clearly deliberate. Though Will has twice been the victim of irresponsible inheritance Dorothea, in marrying him, returns him to his rightful role of property owner. Vitality is thus restored to the social organism and history established, once more, on its true course.

The question of property is linked to both the continuity and solidarity of the social organism; just inheritance ensures the perpetuation of social order, while just administration establishes organic harmony amongst the different social strata. Unlike Mr Brooke, or Featherstone, Dorothea, on accession to her estates, demonstrates responsible administration: she appoints Mr Farebrother, releases Lydgate from his debt to Bulstrode, and engineers the reappointment of Caleb Garth. Looked at with a jaundiced eye, Caleb, preserving Mr Brooke's rule by mending his broken fences, could be seen to be patching up a broken system. The text, however, gives no explicit confirmation of this reading. Caleb's activities receive nothing but praise, while even Sir James emerges as a model figure. Dorothea had "to resolve not to be afraid of him – all the more because he was really her best friend" (Ch. 72, III, 309). The organicism of benevolent paternalism would appear to be the political stance of the novel. *Middlemarch*, however, conforms neither to the social vision nor the methodology of *Adam Bede*. Acting as a creative scientist, George Eliot offers, through the controlling experimental conception of a labyrinth, many levels of analysis of Middlemarch life. From the materialist analysis of property transmission she moves, through levels of ascending complexity, to consider questions of psychological and social structure, offering, at the highest level, an interrogation of the nature of historical understanding and mythic creation.

Though, on one level, the inheritance plot might appear to confirm Carlylean conceptions of organic harmony, the narrative is also clearly critical of the "labyrinth of petty courses" which inhibits the flow of Dorothea's "full current of sympathetic motive" (Ch. 10, I, 128). Trapped within the literal confines of Middlemarch society, Dorothea is also imprisoned mentally by her own confused notions. During courtship she gazes into the "ungauged reservoir" of Mr Casaubon's mind and sees "reflected there in vague labyrinthine extension every quality she herself brought" (Ch. 3, I, 32). She discovers on her honeymoon, however, that the work which had originally seemed of "attractively labyrinthine extent" is literally without issue: "the large vistas and wide fresh air which she had dreamed of finding in her husband's mind were replaced by anterooms and winding passages which seemed to lead nowhither" (Ch. 20, I, 300). The restricted channels of Middlemarch social life have a psychic replica in the contorted passages of Casaubon's mind. The question originally posed by the narrative concerned Dorothea's relations to her social surroundings, but this shift in imagery subtly transposes the problem to one of historical understanding. Casaubon is imprisoned, primarily, by his inability to understand the historical process.

This change in emphasis is accompanied by a change in scene; the narrative moves from the narrow world of Middlemarch to Rome, and to a wider historical perspective. While Middlemarch life in 1829 represents one moment in the historical development of the social organism, Rome is itself the embodiment of history. The bewildered Dorothea encounters "the city of visible history, where the past of a whole hemisphere seems moving in funereal procession with strange ancestral images and trophies gathered from afar" (Ch. 20, I, 295). A deliberate parallel is drawn between her relationships to Casaubon and to Rome, for the "stupendous fragmentariness heightened the dreamlike strangeness of her bridal life" (Ch. 20, I, 295). Rome becomes the material, external expression of Casaubon's historical confusion, and of Dorothea's frustration in marriage.

The impact of Rome on Dorothea is described in physiological terms:

all this vast wreck of ambitious ideals, sensuous and spiritual, mixed confusedly with the signs of breathing forgetfulness and degradation, at first jarred her as with an electric shock, and then urged themselves on her with that ache belonging to a glut of confused ideas which check the flow of emotion (Ch. 20, I, 296).

Like Middlemarch, Rome impedes the free flow of energy. By casting the problem of the labyrinth in terms of physiological response, however, George Eliot is able to offer an apparent source of resolution – the tendency of Dorothea's mind to flow in a unified current: "But in Dorothea's mind there was a current into which all thought and feeling were apt sooner or later to flow – the reaching forward of the whole consciousness towards the fullest truth, the least partial good" (Ch. 20, I, 311). Innate physiological constitution seems to hold the key to the problem of historical understanding.

George Eliot's use of physiology here is in accordance with Spencer's belief that it was both possible, and necessary, to interpret mental evolution in terms of a redistribution of Matter and Motion:

If from a corollary to the Persistence of Force we can legitimately draw the conclusion that, under certain conditions, lines of nervous communication will arise, and, having arisen, will become lines of more and more easy communication in proportion to the number and strengths of the discharges propagated through them; we shall have found a physical interpretation which completes the doctrine of psychical evolution.[35]

Spencer employs the principle of the persistence of force to demonstrate necessary psychic evolution, and thus to support his theory of history as unified progress. Mental evolution occurs as wider and wider channels of communication are carved in the mind. The same argument is offered by Lewes in *The Foundations of a Creed*. "The evolution of Mind," he observes, "is the establishment of definite paths: this is the mental organisation, fitting it for the reception of definite impressions, and their co-ordination with past feelings."[36] In *Middlemarch* the problem of the social and historical labyrinth becomes one of psychic coordination as cultural confusion is set against Dorothea's physiological tendency towards unity.

Spencer based both his social and political theories on the principle of the persistence of force. Thus in *Social Statics* he argued against government interference in the workings of the country for the administrative mechanism would only dissipate social force in friction.[37] Even in his late work *The Data of Ethics* (1879), he still maintained that "Ethics has a physical aspect; since it treats of human activities which, in common with all expenditures of energy, conform to the law of the persistence of energy: moral principles must conform to physical necessities."[38] Lewes, however, though acknowledging a physiological basis to psychology, also recognised that social interaction introduced a higher level of complexity that did not conform to the principles of energy exchange. Men, he believed, were separated from mere animal life by "the Language of symbols, at once the cause and effect of

Civilisation."[39] A study of the "redistribution of Matter and Motion" could never, for Lewes, give full insight into mental evolution since human development and interaction are primarily determined by the linguistic social medium: "The Language we think in, and the conceptions we employ, the attitude of our minds, and the means of investigation, are social products determined by the activities of the Collective Life."[40] Language both determines individual moral and cultural development and offers a symbolic system which functions, like scientific construction, to reveal connections and relations not evident to sense.

George Eliot follows Lewes' pattern, considering Dorothea's relations to the social labyrinth on both an initial physiological level, and on the more complex level of language. Dorothea's passage through the labyrinth is from the darkness of Middlemarch life and ignorance to the light of historical and linguistic comprehension. Thwarted by her lack of any sense of connection with or understanding of the people who surround her in Middlemarch, Dorothea remarks, "I don't feel sure about doing good in any way now: everything seems like going on a mission to a people whose language I don't know" (Ch. 3, I, 40). Her cultural confusion is reinforced by that miniature version of Rome, her uncle's study; his "severe classical nudities and smirking Renaissance-Correggiosities" were, to her, "painfully inexplicable" (Ch. 9, I, 109). Through her marriage to Casaubon, Dorothea hopes to find a language that will enable her to make sense of surrounding Middlemarch life, and the developing cultural history of the world. It is Will, however, who is to offer this illumination. On first meeting Will Dorothea refuses to offer judgement on his sketch, for pictures " 'are a language I do not understand. I suppose there is some relation between pictures and nature which I am too ignorant to feel – just as you see what a Greek sentence stands for which means nothing to me' " (Ch. 9, I, 117). The analogy is suggestive. While Casaubon imprisons his young bride in his labyrinthine research, forcing her to transcribe alien Greek characters she is not permitted to understand, Will brings a language that illuminates the unity lying beneath the surface chaos of history, embodied for Dorothea in the inexplicable art of Rome. Under his tuition Dorothea begins to gather

quite new notions as to the significance of Madonnas seated under inexplicable canopied thrones with the simple country as a background, and of saints with architectural models in their hands, or knives accidentally wedged in their skulls. Some things which had seemed monstrous to her were gathering intelligibility and even a natural meaning; but all this was apparently a branch of knowledge in which Mr. Casaubon had not interested himself (Ch. 22, I, 327–8).

Will breaks through Dorothea's narrow Puritanic conceptions, arousing within her an understanding of the evolving cultural language of the social organism that presages her later "awakening" to the true relations of Middlemarch life.

Amidst the chaos of Rome, Casaubon can aid Dorothea only by making a spurious distinction between "a genuine mythical product" and "the romantic invention of a literary period" (Ch. 20, I, 302). He is trapped by his theory that history is only a process of degeneration, that "all the mythical systems or erratic mythical fragments in the world were corruptions of a tradition originally revealed" (Ch. 3, I, 33). Will, on the other hand, is concerned less with origins than with the vital organic processes of historical growth; he would "prefer not to know the sources of the Nile" (Ch. 9, I, 120). His attitude corresponds to that outlined by Lewes, in a passage later praised by George Eliot, in which he likens the investigation of any phenomenon to the exploration of the sources of a river. Lewes stresses, however, not the importance of the source, but the "individuality at each stage" of the river:

the thread of light, the cloud of spray, the floating mist, and leaping cataract, the snow-flake, and the breaker, are embodied histories. Each successive form is a succession of events, each event having been determined by some prior group. This is the circulation of Cause. Causation is immanent Change.[41]

Emphasis is placed on the dynamic process of change; even seemingly static forms are in reality "successions of events," "embodied histories" in the process of "immanent Change."

Will's response to Rome partakes of this dynamic conception. While Casaubon's energy is trapped and impeded, "lost among small closets and winding stairs" (Ch. 20, I, 302), Will's, on the contrary, is released. He enjoys the miscellaneousness "which made the mind flexible with constant comparison, and saved you from seeing the world's ages as a set of box-like partitions without vital connection" (Ch. 22, I, 325). He confesses "that Rome had given him quite a new sense of history as a whole: the fragments stimulated his imagination and made him constructive" (Ch. 22, I, 325). Will's creative energy uncovers the vital organic life of history. Like George Eliot in her construction of *Middlemarch*, he reveals through constant comparison the vital interdependence of apparently fragmented parts, offering release from the labyrinth through the language of historical understanding.

Unlike Casaubon, George Eliot was actually up-to-date in her mythological research; she believed, in accordance with Feuerbach, that the creation of myth was a continual process, inseparable from the writing of history.[42] Her story of the labyrinth is thus cast on the three ascending levels of physiology, social history, and universal myth. In the mythic vision of the novel Will is presented as a solar deity. The history of Will, Dorothea, and Casaubon in fact accords with the dominant contemporary school of thought, established by Max Muller, which interpreted all myth in terms of solar symbolism.[43] Descriptions of Will centre on his irradiation of light: "The first impression on seeing Will was one of sunny brightness . . . his hair seemed to shake out light. . . Mr Casaubon, on the contrary, stood rayless" (Ch. 21, I, 320–1). The deliberate juxtaposition is indicative of the process by which Dorothea's struggles with Middlemarch are turned into a mythic battle between the forces of light and dark. Echoes of the myths of Dis and Persephone, and Orpheus and Eurydice, recur throughout the tale. Casaubon is surprised that the matrimonial path, which should have been bordered with flowers, did not "prove persistently more enchanting to him than the accustomed vaults where he walked taper in hand" (Ch. 10, I, 126). Casaubon's feelings as a husband are inseparable from his inability to find his way through the labyrinth of history. Dorothea, as the fair flower-gatherer Persephone, is imprisoned by her Dis in a tomb of dead languages, trapped at Lowick, whose very name suggests the absence of light and energy.[44] Will offers the only hope of light and release. The chance of seeing him acted "like a lunette opened in the wall of her prison, giving her a glimpse of the sunny air" (Ch. 37, II, 134). As Eurydice, Dorothea sees her final hope of social integration fade as her Orpheus turns toward her as he retreats:

She longed for work which would be directly beneficent like the sunshine and the rain, and now it appeared that she was to live more and more in a virtual tomb, where there was the apparatus of a ghastly labour producing what would never see the light. To-day she had stood at the door of the tomb and seen Will Ladislaw receding into the distant world of warm activity and fellowship – turning his face towards her as he went (Ch. 48, II, 307).

Dorothea's desire for beneficent activity links the classical myth of renewal to the social ideal of organic integration. Will, as fertility god, brings the sun and rain, and thus the possibility for organic social growth.

Casaubon's incorporation within contemporary myth acts as an implicit condemnation of his belief that all myths were corruptions of one original source. Locked within the confines of this theory, ignoring even contemporary developments in his field, he refuses to acknowledge history as a constant process of organic growth and change: "in bitter manuscript remarks on other men's notions about the solar deities, he had become indifferent to the sunlight" (Ch. 20, I, 303). Will, by contrast, actively embodies the spirit of creative renewal. In talking to Dorothea he shows "such originality as we all share with the morning and the spring-time and other endless renewals" (Ch. 22, I, 342). Will shares in the mythic process of the novel, casting himself as the rescuer of Dorothea from "fire-breathing dragons" (Ch. 47, II, 299), and giving voice to the narrative's implied underlying myth of Ariadne. George Eliot's use of the term "monstrous" to describe Dorothea's responses to Catholic art prefigures Will's own formulation of Dorothea's imprisonment:

It is monstrous – as if you had had a vision of Hades in your childhood, like the boy in the legend. You have been brought up in some of those horrible notions that choose the sweetest women to devour – like Minotaurs. And now you will go and be shut up in that stone prison at Lowick: you will be buried alive (Ch. 22, I, 337).

As Gillian Beer has pointed out, "Ladislaw's verbal energy readily shifts dead metaphor into myth: (monstrous becomes Minotaur)."[45] Will's creative vision suggests how the labyrinth of classical myth becomes the imprisoning network of nineteenth-century language and beliefs.

The key to Will's role in the novel lies in the flexibility of his responses. He possesses the qualities he attributes to a poet: "a soul in which knowledge passes instantaneously into feeling, and feeling flashes back as a new organ of knowledge" (Ch. 22, I, 341–2). Knowledge does not become a "lifeless embalment" but is fully integrated within the current of feeling. In accordance with the value structure established by physiology, energy is neither blocked nor dissipated but directly channelled.

Will's mode of expression differs markedly from that of the surrounding Middlemarch characters, whose inadequacies in social response are reflected in their choice of linguistic forms.[46] Mr Brooke's syntactic incoherence, for example, replicates his confusion in the realm of history and his social irresponsibility as a landlord; Mr Casaubon, taken on a "severe mental scamper" by Mr Brooke, remains mindful that "this desultoriness was associated with the institutions of the country," and that his host was a "landholder and *custos rotulorum*" (Ch. 3, I, 35–6). The frigid rhetoric of Casaubon's own address reflects his own particular failings in historical understanding. Thus his memory "was a volume where a *vide supra* could serve instead of repetitions, and not the ordinary long-used blotting-book which only tells of forgotten writing" (Ch. 3, I, 36).[47] In accordance with his model of history, Casaubon's mind and language proceed by a linear chain of association which denies any vital organic or emotional connections.

Both Rosamond Vincy and Mrs Garth are also guilty of unnecessary rigidity in their approach to language. In a judgement which reflects the neat propriety of her egoistic vision, Rosamond distinguishes between "correct English" and "slang" thus associating the constantly transforming social medium of language with the narrow values of her own class (Ch. 11, I, 148). The worthy Mrs Garth, for her part, displays too strict an adherence to the rules of the grammar of the past. The *Lindley Murray* which, in the wreck of society, she would hold above the waves is discarded by her daughter.

Language, George Eliot reveals, need not necessarily act as a medium for vital communication but, like the pier glass of her parable, it can act directly to enforce egoistic vision. Thus Bulstrode hides behind his language of divine intention, whilst Rosamond had "no consciousness that her action could rightly be called false" for, as George Eliot observes, "We are not obliged to identify our own acts according to a strict classification, any more than the materials of our grocery and clothes" (Ch. 65, III, 203–4). Language, when misused, actually blocks communication, creating a self-sufficient system that can remain, as Rosamond clearly shows, impervious to outside challenge or change.

In contrast to these models of language, Will's dynamic interchange between knowledge and feeling suggests a response hindered neither by egoism nor rigidity of thought. His language does not just reflect the inner world, entrapping energy like a labyrinth, but turns outwards, actively creating bonds and connections. Through conversations with Naumann, Will relates his commitment to language to his theory of history. While Casaubon believes there is only one origin to history, Naumann believes there is only one end. He assumes, in Will's words, " 'that all the universe is straining towards the obscure significance of your pictures' " (Ch. 19, I, 290). Imposing his own preconceptions on the historical process, Naumann ignores dynamic connections, and, like Casaubon, transforms history into a series of box-like partitions.

Will, however, objects to the static air of finality such paintings carry. More experimental biologist than natural historian, he insists that the changing processes of life cannot be captured through external form: " 'As if a woman were a mere coloured superficies!' " He defends, instead, language as a "finer medium" which "gives a fuller image, which is all the better for being vague" (Ch. 19, I, 292). Since women "change from moment to moment," only within the flexible medium of language could one hope to capture this process.

Under Will's creative vision Dorothea is revealed as the perfect embodiment of art and language; she is "a poem – and that is to be the best part of a poet – what makes up the poet's consciousness in his best moods" (Ch. 22, I, 342). Will shifts the definition of a poem from a static final form to a continuing process of effect; Dorothea, with her unified current of thought and feeling, has the integrative effect of art on the life of her fellow Middlemarchers. She holds the key to the labyrinth of art and history. Painting, Will believed, could never capture the changing timbre of a voice; Dorothea's impact on Middlemarch is described in terms of her voice – the external expression of the inner channels of the mind. For Caleb, who hears "sublime music" in the sounds of integrated labour, Dorothea's voice recalls the "mighty structure of tones" of parts of the *Messiah* (Ch. 56, III, 29). For Lydgate, Dorothea's voice confirms the unity of history: "That voice of deep-souled womanhood had remained within him as the enkindling conceptions of dead and sceptred genius had remained within him" (Ch. 58, III, 91). Dorothea offers a resolution to social and historical fragmentariness. As Will illuminated the chaos of Rome for her, so she illuminates the life of Middlemarch: "The presence of a noble nature, generous in its wishes, ardent in its charity, changes the lights for us: we begin to see things again in their larger, quieter masses, and to believe that we too can be seen and judged in the wholeness of our character" (Ch. 76, III, 352). Dorothea breaks through the narrowing egoism of Lydgate's vision to suggest order where he perceives only chaos. Her ardent faith leads her past the stumbling block of insular perception to a wider, integrated vision of the social whole. Dorothea follows, in fact, the unifying processes of both art and science, creating the "ideally illuminated space" of Lydgate's scientific vision.

In revealing the underlying unity of the social organism Dorothea fulfils, on a scientific plane, her mythic role of Ariadne.[48] Bernard used the image of Ariadne's thread to describe the complex interdependence of organic life which rendered experimentation, and thus scientific

medicine, possible.[49] Lewes extends the image to encompass the fundamental processes of science:

It is the greatness of Science that while satisfying the spiritual thirst for
knowledge, it satisfies the pressing desire for guidance in action: not only
painting a picture of the wondrous labyrinth of Nature, but placing in
our hands the Ariadne-thread to lead us through the labyrinth.[50]

Dorothea, with her desire for a life both "rational and ardent" is the
narrative's Ariadne thread. It is she, not Lydgate, who is the novel's
true physician; instead of searching for origins she offers, through her
vision of social interconnections, actual "guidance in action." Dorothea
fulfils, within the novel, her creator's fictional goal for, as George Eliot
observed in a letter of 1868, "the inspiring principle which alone gives
me courage to write is, that of so presenting our human life as to help
my readers in getting a clearer conception and a more active admiration
of those vital elements which bind men together and give a higher
worthiness to their existence."[51]

As creative experimenter, George Eliot weaves together the materials
of history, science and myth, attempting to find a resolution to the
social problem posed in the Prelude. Through the play of metaphor the
social labyrinth is transposed into one of mind, and then of history,
resolvable, on a physiological level, through the light of historical
understanding. Yet, though Dorothea shows Lydgate things "in their
larger, quieter masses," he is still judged by the petty Middlemarch
mind. Will might irradiate light, but Dorothea, in marrying him, becomes only "a wife and mother." On a material level, the labyrinth is
successfully traversed once property is correctly channelled; but
Dorothea's son, though inheriting the estates, declines the stifling possibility of representing Middlemarch. Though George Eliot moves into
the realm of myth and symbol, using the ideal hypothesis of a labyrinth to construct the moral framework of her novel, she is still committed to a traditional realist form of narrative resolution.

The complexities and internal contradictions within *Middlemarch*
can be traced, in large part, to the relationship between the moral and
epistemological aspects of contemporary organicist theory. Thus Lewes,
defining his dynamic theory of organic social composition observed:
"the search after the *thing in itself* is chimerical: the thing being a
group of relations it *is* what these are. Hence the highest form of existence is Altruism, or that moral and intellectual condition which is
determined by the fullest consciousness – emotional and cognitive – of
relations."[52] The passage could be taken as a scenario for *Middlemarch*.

The moral climax of the novel occurs, as Paris has noted, when Dorothea, arising from her night of sorrow, sees the far-off figures in the field: "she felt the largeness of the world and the manifold wakings of men to labour and endurance. She was a part of that involuntary, palpitating life, and could neither look out on it from her luxurious shelter as a mere spectator, nor hide her eyes in selfish complaining" (Ch. 80, III, 392).[53] Dorothea transcends the narrowing limitations of egoism to accept the full responsibilities of her social role. In thus recognising her membership of that "palpitating life" she attains the emotional and cognitive understanding of relations which, for Lewes, constitutes the state of Altruism.

There is, however, a logical jump in Lewes' argument. No essential connection exists between the epistemological statement that a thing *is* its relations, and the moral conclusion that full knowledge of these relations would create a state of altruism.[54] Lewes, in fact, assumes that the relations of mutual dependence within the social organism are, in essence, harmonious, and that increased understanding of these social relations will necessarily lead to augmented good will, and not hostility. Yet Middlemarch, as George Eliot clearly reveals, is not a harmonious whole; it possesses all the vices of a capitalist economy, and the social antagonisms of a class-ridden society. Indeed, the analysis of the functions of that primary connecting medium, language, or gossip, does not augur well for a Middlemarch blessed in the future with increased understanding of mutual relations. George Eliot's ambivalent response to organic theory is reflected in the novel in her treatment of Dorothea. Although Dorothea ardently desires full social integration her stature as heroine in fact arises from her social aloofness, her blindness to the petty courses of the Middlemarch mind. Following her awakening George Eliot promptly removes her from the town. The theory of growing social altruism is not put to the test.

Like Lewes, George Eliot is torn between intellectual allegiance to a radical, dynamic theory of organic life, and emotional commitment to a moral vision of social order. Although Lewes formulated a model of organic life which could encompass conflict and contradiction, he yet attempted to wed this conception to his moral belief in evolving social harmony. George Eliot adopts, in Lydgate's biological theories of organic interdependence, a theoretical model which forms the basis, in the novel, for a dynamic social theory, and a radical conception of fictional method. Yet her commitment to fluidity and ideal construction is undercut by her simultaneous allegiance to the idea of narrative resolution. Thus, as I argued earlier, in portraying the histories of her characters she employs physiology to create moral closure. The admission that "character is process" is counteracted by the fact that Lydgate's relations with Middlemarch are merely the analogue of his prior psychic structure. In the case of Bulstrode, George Eliot uses the physiological unity of the unconscious mind to suggest moral order and coherence in external social events. Although more openness is evident in the representation of Dorothea, her innate physiological constitution, the one ardent channel of her mind, functions as a locus of value. Flexibility is over-ruled amidst the imperative need for a fixed basis for moral judgement.

George Eliot's dual allegiances are clearly revealed in the Finale which opens with the observation that the fluidity of social life actually prohibits narrative closure for "Every limit is a beginning as well as an ending." There can be no final moral judgements since the fragment examined will not be necessarily "the sample of an even web." Yet this statement of continuing process is immediately followed by an atemporal vision of Fred and Mary's future: "On inquiry it might possibly be found that Fred and Mary still inhabit Stone Court – that the creeping plants still cast the foam of their blossoms over the fine stone-wall into the field where the walnut-trees stand in stately row" (III, 459). Instead of organic process we are presented with a vision of life in which there is no possibility of change. The technique recalls the Epilogue of *Adam Bede* where apparent changes were referred to the constants of light, and the unchanging house. Here again we are referred to the solidity of objects in a natural landscape; the eternal natural rhythms guarantee the unchanging order of Fred and Mary's style of life. This ending is in keeping with the treatment of the Garths throughout the novel for, within the harsh social world of Middlemarch, they seem to represent an enclave of pastoral organicism. Caleb, with his worship of the divinity of labour, is a later embodiment of Adam Bede. Despite references to mechanisation and the encroaching town, he still seems to live within an unchanging rural order. Indeed the Garths' house, "a homely place with an orchard in front of it" (Ch. 24, I, 369), clearly belongs to the world of Hayslope. *Middlemarch*, however, differs fundamentally from the earlier novel. While the Epilogue of *Adam Bede* merely reaffirmed the values and model of society which ran throughout the book, the Finale of *Middlemarch* creates internal contradiction. The atemporality and affirmation of pastoral organicism which characterises the portrait of Fred and Mary's future lives consorts strangely with the dynamic representation of society, where constant changes create fresh difficulties for social integration.

George Eliot cannot escape, in *Middlemarch*, the fundamental problem that her moral vision of organic interdependence is clearly at odds with her analysis of the harmful, destructive effects of social integration. In *The Mill on the Floss* this problem was resolved by the two endings: the idealistic, atemporal vision of Tom and Maggie's union, and the realistic assessment of the ravages of nature. A similar contradiction gives rise to a dual ending in *Middlemarch*. In marked contrast to the idyll of Fred and Mary the Finale also covers the future histories of Lydgate and Dorothea. Lydgate's future, in which he experiences an absolute contradiction between the report of his inner senses and that of the outer world, is the direct antithesis of the sentimentalised picture of Fred and Mary. The treatment of Dorothea is more complex. On the one hand, there is a tone of regret, an admission, almost, of failure: "Many who knew her, thought it a pity that so substantive and rare a creature should have been absorbed into the life of another, and be only known in a certain circle as a wife and mother" (III, 461). But, on the other hand, there is an attempt to integrate this vision of Dorothea's future with the organic ideal. The birth and inheritance of Dorothea's son is given a commanding position in the concluding paragraphs thus suggesting the continuity of the social organism on a material level. George Eliot also draws upon the psychological and social implications of the term channel to demonstrate Dorothea's impact on evolving social order: "Her finely-touched spirit had still its fine issues, though they were not widely visible. Her full nature, like that river of which Cyrus broke the strength, spent itself in channels which had no great name on the earth" (III, 465).

This concluding passage was clearly resonant for George Eliot; echoes of its imagery appear in her work eight years later. In preparing for publication the final volume of Lewes' *Problems of Life and Mind* she added the following section to explain his theory that consciousness of social interdependence awakens sympathy, "till we finally see in many highly wrought natures a complete submergence (or, if you will, a transference) of egoistic desire, and an habitual outrush of the emotional force in sympathetic channels."[55] Dorothea, with her "finely-touched spirit" literally embodies this organic ideal. Sympathy, not egoism, clearly determines the outrush of her feeling into external social channels. George Eliot draws on the organic principle of interdependence, by which movement of each part affects the whole, to suggest that Dorothea's life will determine the future development of the entire social organism.

A less positive conclusion, however, is implied by the reference to Cyrus, whose history George Eliot recorded in her "Middlemarch Miscellany": the breaking of the river's strength staved off the fall of Babylon, but only for one year.[56] George Eliot is torn, finally, between an idealistic commitment to the organic ideal, and a realistic assessment of possibilities. Her references to the vital "growing good of the world" are counteracted by the final image of the novel: "unvisited tombs." Associations with Casaubon are immediately provoked, summoning images of death in life, and casting the gloomy shadow of Casaubon's sterility over the conclusions of the novel. In the mythological battle between light and dark, the forces of darkness remain unvanquished.

CHAPTER 8

Daniel Deronda:
Fragmentation and organic union

"Men can do nothing without the make-believe of a beginning" – with this bold declaration George Eliot begins her final novel. While the Finale to *Middlemarch* questioned the absolute nature of endings, the opening words of *Daniel Deronda* draw attention to the arbitrary nature of beginnings. By suggesting that the novelist's choice of a beginning is merely a fictional construct, George Eliot challenges the dominant assumptions of the realist text. She takes direct responsibility in *Daniel Deronda* for her own constructive role as novelist. Following the developments of *Middlemarch*, *Daniel Deronda* confirms George Eliot's movement towards a more critical social vision, and a more experimental fictional method. The novel retains no vestiges of natural history; no longer is the novelist's role merely to outline a story which possesses a predefined beginning and end. George Eliot's goal in *Daniel Deronda* is not to represent a fixed "reality" but to challenge contemporary social values and conceptions. The novel presents a bitter critique of the economic and social practices of English society, and of the restrictions which it imposed on social and psychological understanding. To express this social vision, George Eliot turns not to the empiricism of natural history, but to a more radical theory of scientific method, and a more dynamic narrative structure.

The text of *Daniel Deronda* does not adhere to the conventions of spatial or temporal continuity. Starting *in medias res*, it jumps back and forth in time to recount the separate histories of Gwendolen and Daniel. It also ranges geographically throughout Europe, and socially through England's social strata. The challenging assertion of the novel's opening epigraph is reflected in the first paragraph which presents neither the solidity of objects, nor the precision of dates, but a series of questions: "Was she beautiful or not beautiful?" Gwendolen's effect on Deronda is that of "unrest rather than of undisturbed charm"; his desire to look again is "felt as coercion and not as a longing in which the whole being consents" (I, 3). Daniel is divided between longing for organic unity "in which the whole being consents," and his actual experience of unrest and coercion. The same division characterises the text. *Daniel Deronda* encompasses George Eliot's most trenchant portrayal of psychological and social contradiction, but also her most determined affirmation of the values of organic union. The narrative structure reflects these two concerns. Opening in the setting of a sordid foreign gaming saloon, the novel closes with Daniel's voyage to a mysterious destination in the East. Fragmentation is replaced by the organic unity of his visionary quest.

Since the publication of *Daniel Deronda* in 1876, the unity of the novel has formed the object of critical discussion. Although the portrait of Gwendolen Harleth is seen as one of the highest achievements of psychological realism, it is argued that, in the Jewish sections of the book, George Eliot relinquished firm control of her art and wandered off into the vagaries of mysticism.[1] Yet the same preoccupations and underlying epistemology, I will argue, structure both elements of the novel. The representation of Mordecai's visionary idealism and Gwendolen's inner conflict stem equally from organicist premises. Contemporary scientific ideas and theories of method provided a basis not only for the psychological theory, but also for the social and moral vision and narrative methodology of *Daniel Deronda*.

The underlying methodological premises of the novel are suggested by the opening epigraph which continues with a comparison that relates the practice of science to that of poetry:

Even Science, the strict measurer, is obliged to start with a make-believe unit, and must fix on a point in the stars' unceasing journey when his sidereal clock shall pretend that time is at Nought. His less accurate grandmother Poetry has always been understood to start in the middle; but on reflection it appears that her proceeding is not very different from his; since Science, too, reckons backwards as well as forwards, divides his unit into billions, and with his clock-finger at Nought really sets off *in medias res*.

George Eliot challenges inductive certitude. For men, as for planets, neither origins nor history can be fully known; the comfort of certainty must be exchanged for an openness to the unknown. Science, like poetry, cannot provide absolute surety; all findings are dependent on the constructive role of the scientist. George Eliot's conception of science here conforms to that of Bernard who, when defining experimental science, contrasted it with the science of "scholastics or systematizers [who] never question their starting point, to which they seek to refer everything; they have a proud and intolerant mind and do not accept contradiction, since they do not admit that their starting point may change."[2] Experimenters, on the contrary, never assume an immutable starting point; their more open attitude, therefore, enables them to accept contradiction.

A similar conception of relativity governs George Eliot's representation of Mordecai's idealism, and her psychological analysis of Gwendolen's self-conflict. Both are founded on an epistemology that can be related to Bernard's understanding of organic life, since his theory of the relativity of experimental science stems directly from his belief that the complex relations of determinacy in organic life do not conform to a linear sequence of cause and effect: there is no single point of origin or end. Organic interdependence, he argues, should rather be understood in terms of the old cyclical emblem of a serpent with a tail in its mouth.[3] George Eliot also rejects linear causality. Full authoritative knowledge, she asserts in the epigraph, cannot be obtained by tracing through a linear sequence of cause and effect. Through the figure of Mordecai she criticises those forms of social thought which cannot accommodate relativity or contradiction, but are predicated on an immutable starting point, and refer everything to these value-laden premises. Mordecai's idealistic social vision, and his apparently non-rational faith, challenge accepted social definitions of rationality, revealing forms of connection and association excluded by the limited sequence of thought that passes for rational social judgement. In portraying Gwendolen, and the conflict and contradiction that characterise her psyche, George Eliot likewise challenges the dominant social conception of the rational actor, and the theory of causality upon which it is based. As the fragmented narrative form suggests, Gwendolen, with all her conflicting impulses, is not a unified character, the sum of her previous experiences. Her history cannot therefore be represented through a simple temporal sequence of cause and effect.

It is impossible to divorce George Eliot's methodological reflections in *Daniel Deronda* from the narrative form of the novel or its social themes. By drawing attention to the relationship between the continuous process of the "stars' unceasing journey" and the arbitrary division introduced by scientific classification or narrative intervention, George Eliot introduces as a methodological issue the question of the relationship between part and whole that also underlies the social and moral vision of the novel. The comparison, in addition, establishes a chain of astronomical imagery, which defines both the "science" of Mordecai's idealism and the novel's fundamental values. Thus astronomical imagery, when it next occurs, illustrates the restricted nature of Gwendolen's social vision, and reveals her wounded egoism once Klesmer has delivered his devastating verdict on her singing, and on the culture that produced it: "Croyez-vous m'avoir humilée pour m'avoir appris que la terre tourne autour du soleil? Je vous jure que je ne m'en estime pas moins" (Ch. 6, I, 72).

The epigraph, which is taken from Bernard Fontenelle's *Entretiens sur la Pluralité des Mondes* (1686), captures both Gwendolen's bravado, and the relationship between self-assessment and cosmology. Fontenelle explored in his work the social and personal implications of the new Copernican astronomy. The contrast he draws between the closed self-assurance of the stable Ptolemaic universe, and the admission of infinite space, of personal insignificance, and of change in the Copernican universe is central to George Eliot's examination of nineteenth-century social experience. On the one hand, astronomy is employed to illustrate the traditional organic ideal of a stable, harmonious order. For the Meyricks, the objects in their home seemed "as necessary and uncriticised a part of their world as the stars of the Great Bear seen from the back windows" (Ch. 18, I, 294). On the other hand, however, astronomy illustrates the relativity of Gwendolen's universe, its lack of absolute order or stability. The narrator intervenes to lament Gwendolen's lack of roots and a fixed home, for she cannot therefore perceive the stars as an unchanging order, since "The best introduction to astronomy is to think of the nightly heavens as a little lot of stars belonging to one's own homestead" (Ch. 3, I, 26–7). Without this stable personal foundation, astronomy inspires Gwendolen only with terror: "The little astronomy taught her at school used sometimes to set her imagination at work in a way that made her tremble: but always when some one joined her she recovered her indifference to the vastness in which she seemed an exile" (Ch. 6, I, 90). The sense of panic, of displaced centrality, is equivalent to that created by the discovery that the sun did not move around the earth.

Fontenelle's Marchioness was horrified by the picture of an infinite and changing universe. Her philosopher companion, by contrast, found inspiration in the new astronomy, experiencing in its vision of infinite space and constant movement a sense of liberty and release.[4] The two perspectives underlie *Daniel Deronda*, encapsulating the closed, arrogant social vision of the English ruling class, and the expansive possibility envisaged by Mordecai. Gwendolen moves between these two

poles. First encountered in a foreign gaming saloon, where the only law
is that of chance, she dwells in a world without apparent fixity, whether
of place, social class, fortune, or religion. Her "Ptolemaic response" to
life has been to see herself as the centre around which all else revolves.
The novel traces the progress of her education, through which she
finally learns to accept the vastness of the universe, the earth's insignificance, and thus a horizon wider than the self. It is a process that is
accomplished through her relationship with Deronda, and contact with
the values represented by the "Jewish side" of the novel.

Imagery of astronomy is also extended to include that other element
of the Jewish story: Daniel's love for Mirah. George Eliot observes
that even in Romeo's discourse with Juliet his objections to Ptolemy
would have had an effect: "this passion hath as large scope as any for
allying itself with every operation of the soul: so that it shall acknowledge an effect from the imagined light of unproven firmaments, and
have its scale set to the grander orbits of what hath been and shall be"
(Ch. 32, II, 125). Even love is affected by breadth of vision. This
perspective raises questions concerning scientific method: the mind must
accept not simply a wider horizon but "unproven firmaments," that
which cannot be known, scientific hypotheses that cannot be proved.
The observations belong, not to the world of Paley and natural history
or theology, but to that of Darwin or Bernard; to a world in which the
certainty of fixity was renounced for the potentiality of constant change.
They can be related not to the traditional Baconian model of science
rejected by Comte, Bernard, and Lewes, but to a theory of scientific
method that stresses deduction and the role of the imagination. Thus
Lewes argued in *The Foundations of a Creed* that "Fictions are potent;
and all are welcome if they can justify themselves by bringing speculative insight within the range of positive vision."[5] As a methodological
statement it defines George Eliot's practice in *Daniel Deronda*.

Lewes, in outlining his scientific methodology, took as his model
Copernicus, a scientist who had been sneeringly dismissed by Bacon as
"the man who thinks nothing of introducing fictions of any kind into
Nature provided his calculations turn out well."[6] In an extension of
the novel's astronomical imagery, George Eliot explicitly compares the
Jewish mystic Mordecai to Copernicus and Galileo.[7] As these scientists
broke through the geocentric perspective of Ptolemaic astronomy,
changing conceptions of the universe, so Mordecai offers a vision that
leads beyond the stultifying, insular perceptions of English society. The
scientific comparison is not restricted to the revolutionary nature of

Mordecai's visions; it has extended social and methodological implications. With reference to Mordecai's possible social impact, George Eliot observes that the appearance of fanaticism should not discredit a theory: responsibility for judgements rests with each individual:

> Shall we say, 'Let the ages try the spirits, and see what they are worth?' Why, we are the beginning of the ages, which can only be just by virtue of just judgment in separate human breasts – separate yet combined. Even steam-engines could not have got made without that condition, but must have stayed in the mind of James Watt (Ch. 41, II, 354–5).

The discussion associates Mordecai's visions, not with the vagaries of mysticism, but with the concrete realm of scientific practice. Furthermore, it reintroduces, as both a social and methodological question, the novel's dominant concern with the relationship between part and whole. The process according to which Mordecai's visions are to be assessed anticipates Deronda's conception of organic social union. In embracing Judaism, Daniel accepts his grandfather's belief that "the strength and wealth of mankind depended on the balance of separateness and communication" (Ch. 60, III, 273). The organic ideal that underlies the novel – the balance of individuality and social integration – also determines the representation of Mordecai's idealism.

In a letter of this period George Eliot defines her writing as "a set of experiments in life – an endeavour to see what our thought and emotion may be capable of – what stores of motive, actual or hinted as possible, give promise of a better after which we must strive."[8] Like Bernard, who saw the experimental scientist as a "real foreman of creation," George Eliot possesses a vision of future changes made possible by the experimental creation of conditions not yet achieved in nature. Within the novel Mordecai fulfils this creative role: his visions of an alternative form of social life are based on a firm belief in human potential. In an explicit analogy George Eliot compares his thought processes directly to those of an experimental scientist. On seeing Deronda row towards Blackfriars Bridge, in accordance with the mental image he had conceived, Mordecai felt an exultation "not widely different from that of the experimenter, bending over the first stirrings of change that correspond to what in the fervour of concentrated prevision his thought has foreshadowed" (Ch. 40, II, 328). Mordecai shares Dorothea's fervour, but he also possesses the power to evoke "images which have a foreshadowing power" (Ch. 38, II, 295). As experimenter he dramatises the beliefs George Eliot expressed to Madame Ponsonby: "I shall not be satisfied with your philosophy till you have conciliated necessitarianism – I hate the ugly word – with the practice of willing strongly, willing to will strongly, and so on."[9] Mordecai's science does not simply reinforce acceptance of a given order, but actively reveals the creative, transformative power of will.[10]

George Eliot cannot, within the scope of the novel, demonstrate the scientific validity of Mordecai's visions. The narrative is structured, however, in such a way as to endorse ideas of visionary power.[11] George Eliot deliberately breaks the conventions of realism to include within the novel coincidences in plot that strain credibility, and individual visions that narrative events fulfil. Thus Gwendolen's dream of Deronda, and her feeling, as she sails towards Genoa, that "there might be some preparation of rescue for her" (Ch. 54, III, 199–200) are fulfilled when she encounters Daniel on the shore. Less positively, her fear of the painting of a death figure at Offendene foreshadows the scene of Grandcourt's death. Most significantly, however, Mordecai does turn out to be Mirah's brother, and his unshakeable faith in Deronda as his promised disciple is finally vindicated by Daniel's discovery of his Jewish ancestry. The sequence of the narrative seems to suggest that there exist forms of mental and social association, and patterns of events, that normal social judgement excludes or denies. George Eliot uses the analogy with science to validate this judgement. Although she does not, as narrator, directly endorse Mordecai's visions, she allows Daniel to reflect that, "even strictly measuring science could hardly have got on without that forecasting ardour which feels the agitations of discovery beforehand, and has a faith in its preconception that surmounts many failures of experiment" (Ch. 41, II, 358).

This theory of scientific method, in which faith in preconception is not necessarily to be over-ruled by scientific results, corresponds to that of Bernard. Rejecting the empiricist belief in fact, Bernard argues that experimentation must be guided by theory: "A fact is nothing in itself, it has value only through the idea connected with it or through the proof it supplies."[12] There are occasions, he concludes, when the scientist is justified in ignoring certain empirical "facts" that appear in contradiction to reason.[13] For Bernard "blind belief in fact, which dares to silence reason, is as dangerous to the experimental sciences as the beliefs of feeling or of faith which also force silence on reason."[14] George Eliot is not arguing, in *Daniel Deronda*, that reason should be abandoned for a vague, implausible, mystical faith, but that appearances should not be accepted unchallenged. Man must remain open to hitherto unexplored alternatives, to different forms of thought.

The consequences of this theory can be traced in *Daniel Deronda,* not only in George Eliot's use of "Ideal Construction," but also in her approach to language. Lewes, defending his belief in scientific hypothesis, quotes Laplace's "undeniable statement" that "if men had limited their efforts to the collection of facts, Science would have been only a sterile nomenclature, and would never have revealed the great laws of Nature."[15] George Eliot has no desire to offer a "sterile nomenclature"; she no longer possesses the natural historian's confidence in the power of definition. In *Daniel Deronda* she questions both the functions of language, and her own role as author. Of Gwendolen's eyes being "mysteriously" arrested by Grandcourt she comments:

mysteriously; for the subtly-varied drama between man and woman is often such as can hardly be rendered in words put together like dominoes, according to obvious fixed marks. The word of all work Love will no more express the myriad modes of mutual attraction, than the word Thought can inform you what is passing through your neighbour's mind (Ch. 27, II, 38–9).

George Eliot here implicitly rejects all modes of thought which presume that life can be known and strictly defined or quantified. Her observation arises directly from her search for a language and narrative methodology that could express her radical social vision. Thus, her distrust of "fixed marks" finds a social and thematic reflection in the novel's social critique of those worldly figures who, following the rules of liberal, discursive reason, judge all issues according to neat, predefined categories. Deronda easily envisages Sir Hugo's traditional-minded assessment of Mordecai: "In such cases a man of the world knows what to think beforehand" (Ch. 41, II, 353). The phrase "man of the world," which expresses the class assumptions of those who equate social position with authoritative knowledge, reveals the relationship between linguistic usage and social power.

The political consequences of the ruling classes' confidence in their power of definition are revealed by Grandcourt's callous attitude toward the Jamaican Negro. In supporting Governor Eyre's brutal massacre of the Jamaicans, Grandcourt dismisses the Jamaican Negro as "a beastly sort of baptist Caliban" (Ch. 29, II, 80–1). The smug assumption of authority in definition is but the linguistic correlative of the expression of assertive power in colonial rule. The species identification, which absolves the speaker from confronting the horrifying reality of the event, preserves ruling-class confidence in its own rule by blocking perception of alternative definitions.

Violence is institutionalised by language – whether that of imperialist murder or its more subtle form of expression, which George Eliot traces in the life of English high society. Her critique of the social practices which lead to Gwendolen's subjection to Grandcourt's tyranny is based on analysis of the language employed by Gwendolen's relatives. The Reverend Mr Gascoigne, Gwendolen's uncle, uses a monetary metaphor to quiet doubts about Grandcourt's past: "All accounts can be suitably wound up when a man has not ruined himself, and the expense may be taken as an insurance against future error. This was the view of practical wisdom; with reference to higher views, repentance had a supreme moral and religious value" (Ch. 13, I, 207). All religious considerations or values are subordinated to the language of the cash-nexus. Rebellion against the dominant social values thus takes the form of a challenge to its language. The heiress Catherine, wishing to marry the musician Klesmer, struggles with her parents for the power of definition. She refuses to accept both her mother's definition of duty, and the terms she applies to Klesmer, and she exposes her father's appeals to the "nation" and "public good" as merely a linguistic mask for his belief that an heiress should "carry the property gained in trade into the hands of a certain class" (Ch. 22, I, 371). Words, as Lewes and Bernard demonstrated in their organic analogies, do not hold meaning in themselves; their meaning is dependent on the system of assumptions within which they are employed.[16]

In place of the language and social vision of the English ruling class, George Eliot proposes two alternative languages: one offered by the musician Klesmer and the other by the visionary Mordecai. Klesmer, in his conversation with that representative of the English political system, the "aimiably confident" Mr Bult, challenges the lack of idealism in English politics, its dependence "on the need of a market" (Ch. 22, I, 362). He asserts instead the artist's right to rule: " a man who speaks effectively through music is compelled to something more difficult than parliamentary eloquence" (Ch. 22, I, 363). Klesmer's sentiments are echoed by Daniel who refuses to enter parliament on the grounds that politics is all opinion. Amidst the "self-satisfied folly" of English culture which, according to Klesmer's analysis, possessed "no sense of the universal" (Ch. 5, I, 67–8) the exchange of opinion could only confirm constricted forms of social judgement. Yet, within the novel, it is not Klesmer but Mordecai who offers a truly alternative language: Deronda's movement away from the values of English ruling-class society is symbolised by his study of Hebrew.

George Eliot found within Judaism an autonomous yet historically based language and culture, open to imagination and not restricted to the rules of the barren, culture-bound reasoning of nineteenth-century English thought. Jewish culture represented for her the virtues of organic historical growth without the attendant disadvantages of the corruption of the English social organism. She took great care, therefore, to base Mordecai's speeches on those of the medieval scholar Halevi, in an attempt to validate his visionary ideals through an authentic language. Mordecai acknowledges that his faith departs from philosophical conceptions, both past and present; but he asserts: "if I chose I could answer a summons before their tribunals. I could silence the beliefs which are the mother-tongue of my soul and speak with the rote-learned language of a system, that gives you the spelling of all things, sure of its alphabet covering them all" (Ch. 40, II, 343). His challenge is to the ruling-class alphabet – to the belief that all things may be defined by merely rearranging the sequence of predefined letters. This challenge has its methodological issue in the narrative pattern of *Daniel Deronda*: in the abrupt opening, and the fracturing of temporal and spatial continuity, and the repeated instances of coincidence and fulfilled visions. These narrative devices mark George Eliot's departure from the smooth sequence of cause and effect, and the manipulation of predefined themes, or figures, traditionally associated with the realist novel. "Man finds his pathways," Mordecai declares, but "has he found all the pathways yet?" (Ch. 40, II, 343).

Mordecai questions whether the language of social rationality offers an adequate description of reality. The same underlying question governs George Eliot's subtle, psychological portrait of Gwendolen, who, with her conflicting impulses and self-division, does not conform to the dominant nineteenth-century model of the rational actor. The psychological consequences of the social practices crticised in the novel are shown in the history of Gwendolen. Like her uncle, Gwendolen has no form of spiritual idealism; she falls prey to a similar confusion between religion and the economic calculus: she had "always disliked whatever was presented to her under the name of religion, in the same way that some people dislike arithmetic and accounts." In a comparison that suggests the political consequences of this attitude, George Eliot observes that Gwendolen had no more inquired into religion than into the "conditions of colonial property and banking" (Ch. 6, I, 89–90). The reference to imperialism is highly significant, for it relates not only to social practices, but also to Gwendolen's understanding of her own psyche. Gwendolen's self-image reflects the social imperialism of her class; she concentrates her ambitions on "the possibility of winning empire" (Ch. 6, I, 90). Social imperialism, however, cannot brook ambiguity, as Grandcourt's drawling dismissal of the Jamaican Negro illustrates. It effectively blocks perception of contradiction. In similar fashion, Gwendolen's imperialist goal rests on the assumption that she possesses a unified and non-contradictory ruling self. The inadequacy of her conception is revealed, however, by her "fits of spiritual dread," experiences that cannot be accommodated within her attempt to win empire, and for which the language of society could not account.

Gwendolen's image of herself as being in full control of her wishes and desires, and in a commanding social role, stems from a view of society and the self which ignores all divisive possibilities. She experiences, however, "subjection to a possible self, a self not to be absolutely predicted about, [which] caused her some astonishment and terror: her favourite key of life – doing as she liked – seemed to fail her" (Ch. 13, I, 201). George Eliot exposes the falsity of Gwendolen's self-image: in doing so she draws on contemporary psychological theory. Gwendolen, in clinging to the idea of free will, has fallen victim to the theory of causality implicit in the social conventions of language, which, as the psychologist James Sully, George Eliot's friend and contemporary, remarked, lead us to attribute actions to a dominating ego through the assumption "that the agent expressed by the subject of the verb is the adequate cause" – thus identifying the process of causation with the linear temporal ordering of language.[17] In his discussion of free will, Sully argues that forms of speech that ascribe to a person the act of choosing between contending motives imply "not only that there exists quite apart from the processes of volitional stimulation some substantial ego, but that this ego has a perfect controlling power over these processes."[18]

Sully's challenge to theories of a directing, controlling ego is founded on premises drawn from contemporary developments in physiology and psychology that were to undermine the models of man that had dominated early nineteenth-century thought – the Cartesian *cogito* or Bentham's rational actor – and the theories of social order they had sustained. His observations offer a linguistic basis for Lewes' argument that "Consciousness is not an agent but a symptom."[19] According to Lewes, all notions of unity and simplicity normally associated with the "Thinking Principle" had to be discarded since, "that Principle is not an antecedent but a resultant, not an entity but a convergence of

manifold activities.[20] Lewes' theories, which define the principles that lie
at the heart of the social and psychological vision of *Daniel Deronda,*
were based on Bernard's conception of organic life as a regulative
process of interaction between an internal and external milieu. In
developing this model Bernard had proposed a theory of causality that
transcended the old division of materialism and vitalism, and, in its
vision of the complex causal chains in the interactive process, laid the
foundations for the principles of homeostasis or feedback control and
modern communication theory. His biological theories suggested a way
of closing the split not only between materialism and vitalism, but also
between the organism and environment, and mind and body of earlier
physiology. Lewes, applying the same principles to psychology, challenged conceptions of individual autonomy, and the dualism of subject
and object, self and other. His theories also undermined the Cartesian
division of mind and matter, which had sustained the identification of
the self with conscious thought. Lewes' conception of the "Thinking
Principle" as simply "the convergence of manifold processes" had
significant social and political implications.

Descartes' psychological theory had supported a conception of
society as a mechanical association of autonomous, rational actors; a
view whose economic foundations have been aptly summarised recently
in Anthony Wilden's observation that "Every *cogito* was free to sell
his disposable energy at the best price." [21] This model formed the basis
for Spencer's social organicism, and for Gwendolen's psychological
assumptions. Gwendolen's "key of life – doing as she liked" conforms
to Spencer's "first principle" that "Every man has freedom to do all
that he wills, provided he infringes not the equal freedom of any other
man."[22] Subjection to a self "not to be absolutely predicted about"
exposes, however, the falsity of such assumptions of individual autonomy, and the economic model of free exchange to which they are
related.

With its emphasis on the principles of energy exchange, Spencer's
organicism had remained within the epistemological atomism of social
physics, whose premises Bernard had overturned. As Buckley, writing
to define the basis of modern communication theory, observes: "after
Spencer it became clearer that whereas the relations of parts of an
organism are physiological, involving complex physio-chemical *energy*
interchanges, the relations of parts of society are primarily psychic,
involving complex communicative processes of *information* exchange."[23]
It is within this latter framework that *Daniel Deronda* primarily be-

longs: Daniel is eventually incorporated not within the economic organism of English society but within a symbolic language community. In representing Mordecai's idealism and Gwendolen's psychological conflict George Eliot clearly departs from the linear causality of Spencer's mechanistic interpretation of the social organism. Spencer's social philosophy is directly opposed to George Eliot's belief in the efficacy of will, and to her commitment to social change within *Daniel Deronda*. No pattern of action, Spencer believed, could alter the sum total of injustice for,

It is impossible for man to create force. He can only alter the mode of its manifestation, its direction, its distribution. . . This is as true in ethics as in physics. Moral feeling is a force – a force by which men's actions are restrained within certain prescribed bounds; and no legislative mechanism can increase its results one iota.[24]

The morality and epistemology of *Daniel Deronda* are directed precisely against the economic and political assumptions which underpin such crass uses of conceptions of energy transfer.

Daniel, like his creator, dreads "that dead anatomy of culture which turns the universe into a mere ceaseless answer to queries" (Ch. 32, II, 132). He rejects the dominant social belief that the universe could be parcelled out into segments of certainty – the assumption, implicit in the question "Why?", that there is only one chain of causation. Reflecting on Mordecai's faith in their relationship, Daniel cannot dismiss it as an illusion. For Daniel "the way seems made up of discernible links" (Ch. 41, II, 360); but he refuses to accept the principles of associationism that had sustained earlier mechanistic interpretations of the social organism, to assume that because one causal chain has been traced there cannot be another. Mordecai's conception of society cannot be expressed in terms of quantitative analysis; it is rather, as in Bernard's conception of the organism, a non-linear homeostatic system: the same starting point may lead to many different ends, and different initial states may produce the same end. In terms of the symbolic system of society this may be expressed through the concept of over-determination developed by Freud to explain the function of language in the Unconscious: because of the freedom of association that language permits, many causal chains may have led to the same symptom.[25] This principle of causation underlies both the representation of Mordecai's idealism, and the psychological analysis of Gwendolen.

Gwendolen's social ambitions and her conception of a unified, directing self are synthesised in her Phaeton-like desire to "mount the chariot and drive the plunging horses herself" (Ch. 13, I, 202). The horses Grandcourt had brought to support his marriage proposal had represented for Gwendolen the social control she would assume: they were "the symbols of command and luxury, in delightful contrast with the ugliness of poverty and humiliation at which she had lately been looking close" (Ch. 27, II, 43). Yet once she has entered her economic bargain with Grandcourt, her engagement, the horses come instead to represent her failure to command either her self or her destiny: "it was as if she had consented to mount a chariot where another held the reins" (Ch. 29, II, 76). George Eliot's analysis of Gwendolen's self-division and loss of directing social power is founded on an implicit critique of theories of the self that stress rational, unified control, and the concomitant theories of society that are based on a conception of free interaction between autonomous entities.

The imagery of this analysis is drawn directly from contemporary psychological debate in which Lewes was involved. The analogy between the soul and the charioteer and his horses dates back to the *Phaedrus* of Plato, but in the nineteenth century the imagery of the horse and its commander was recast to take account of a newly-perceived problem in psychology. The discovery of the physiological basis of reflex action had threatened to disturb the model of a unified, controlling psyche. William Carpenter countered this problem in *Principles of Mental Physiology* (1874 – which Lewes records reading in March of that year), by using the analogy of a horse and skilful rider to explain the relationship between the body's automatic activity and volitional direction. Although the muscles furnish the power, Carpenter argues, "the role and direction of the movement are determined by the Will of the rider, who impresses his mandates on the well-trained steed with as much readiness and certainty as if he were acting on his own limbs."[26] In its reliance on the concept of a dominant will, Carpenter's argument is based on a vitalist biology that Bernard, in his biological theory, and Lewes, in his psychology, had transcended. Although Carpenter's argument is introduced purely in a physiological context, its political consequences can be traced in the work of Eduard von Hartmann. In *Philosophy of the Unconscious* Hartmann argues that the organisation of the human organism, which he views as a hierarchy dominated by a guiding intelligence, supplies a perfect model for political government. His political stance is directly reflected in his theories of physiological psychology: reflex action occurs in response to "commands coming from above," thus proving, the artistic and purposive organization of the nervous system, in which the lower energies are kept, it is true, prepared and always ready for action, but at the same time are held in check by the superior authorities as a squadron of skilful riders and snorting steeds by the will of the leader until the moment seems to have arrived for unchaining these energies by a nod.[27]

In rejecting the conception of a dominating will, the self as a rider in firm control of his steed, George Eliot is also challenging the theory of social order it sustains: the conception of society as a harmonious system, wonderfully coordinated by the guiding intelligence of its rulers.

It should not be assumed, however, that George Eliot employed physiological psychology in *Daniel Deronda* solely in support of radical argument. Like her previous novels, *Daniel Deronda* was written within the moral framework of organicism, and, following her earlier pattern, George Eliot employs the resources of physiological psychology to give an apparent scientific force or validity to her moral propositions. Thus, Mordecai's plans for the Jewish race are couched in language that combines the sentiments and expressions of the medieval visionary Halevi with the precision of contemporary physiological theory. He proposes that the Jews draw on "the heritage of Israel" beating in their veins, the "inborn half of memory" (Ch. 42, II, 393). Physiologically the Jews represent a cultural and religious unity, a historical continuity, that is lacking in fragmented European society: European culture was "an inheritance dug from the tomb. [The Hebrew culture] is an inheritance that has never ceased to quiver in millions of human frames" (Ch. 42, II, 394). "Where else," Mordecai exclaims, "is there a nation of whom it may be as truly said that their religion and law and moral life mingled as the stream of blood in the heart and made one growth" (Ch. 42, II, 385). The theory of psychic and cultural evolution proposed is that of Spencer's Lamarckian vision: "Every one of the countless connections among the fibres of the cerebral masses, answers to some permanent connection of phenomena in the experiences of the race."[28] This theory underlies the opposition dramatised in the text between Mirah, whose "religion was of one fibre with her affections, and had never presented itself to her as a set of propositions" (Ch. 32, II, 128), and Gwendolen, whose lack of hereditary roots is associated with her psychic disunity, her lack of an unquestioned centre of value. Yet it is this reliance on purely biological factors that creates the division experienced by the reader in the novel's conclusion: the potentiality of Deronda's future contrasted with the barrenness of Gwendolen's.

George Eliot also employs physiological concepts to reinforce the moral distinction between Mordecai and Grandcourt. Deronda is made to reflect on the role of ardent men: "the men who had visions which, as Mordecai said, were the creators and feeders of the world – moulding and feeding the more passive life which without them would dwindle and shrivel into the narrow tenacity of insects, unshaken by thoughts beyond the reaches of their antennae" (Ch. 55, III, 213). The power of vision is related to the ardour of its possessor; an opposition is thus proposed between creative force and insect-like tenacity. This opposition is enacted in the text by Mordecai and Grandcourt.

Mordecai's desires were those of "the passionate current of an ideal life straining to embody itself, made intense by resistance to imminent dissolution" (Ch. 38, II, 300). As the terms "current" and "resistance" suggest, George Eliot follows here her practice in *Middlemarch* of equating physiological force with emotional strength. Grandcourt, by contrast, is defined by his "small expense of vital energy," which does not yet preclude tenacity. A man,

may be obstinate or persistent at the same low rate, and may even show sudden impulses which have a false air of daemonic strength because they seem inexplicable, though perhaps their secret lies merely in the want of regulated channels for the soul to move in – good and sufficient ducts of habit without which our nature easily turns to mere ooze and mud, and at any pressure yields nothing but a spurt or a puddle (Ch. 15, I, 232).

In default of defined psychic channels, energy is non-productive.

The mud imagery, which synthesises the reptilean epithets applied to Grandcourt, indicates his low position within the evolutionary scale, and associates channelled force with evolutionary development. Grandcourt seems to rise no higher up the scale than an insect. It would be quite hopeless, George Eliot suggests, for Grandcourt's servant Lush to try and figure out the reasons for his master's actions for "Of what use . . . is a general certainty that an insect will not walk with his head hindmost, when what you need to know is the play of inward stimulus that sends him hither and thither in a network of possible paths?" (Ch. 25, II, 9). Without strong directing motives, Grandcourt's energy, like that of an insect, is dissipated in response to immediate stimuli: "How trace the why and wherefore in the mind reduced to the barrenness of a fastidious egoism, in which all direct desires are dulled, and have dwindled from motives into a vacillating expectation of motives . . ?" It is a condition that belongs to a life "unmoulded by the pressure of obligation" (epigraph, Ch. 25, II, 3). Grandcourt refuses the responsibilities of social duty. His actions are therefore unpredictable, merely a listless response to the changing demands of egoism. George Eliot correlates Grandcourt's egoism with vacillation, and Deronda's sense of obligation with directed energy. The contrast between the two men reveals the underlying organic ideal that informs George Eliot's use of physiological metaphors.

Early in the novel, Daniel, questing for organic union, had been paralysed by "a too reflective and diffusive sympathy." He longed for "some external event, or some inward light, that would urge him into a definite line of action, and compress his wandering energy" (Ch. 32, II, 132). Unlike Grandcourt, his problem is not lack of energy but misuse of that precious resource, a consequence which stems from his lack of a definitive role within the social organism:

But how and whence was the needed event to come? – the influence that would justify partiality, and make him what he longed to be yet was unable to make himself – an organic part of social life, instead of roaming in it like a yearning disembodied spirit, stirred with a vague social passion, but without fixed local habitation to render fellowship real? (Ch. 32, II, 133).

Daniel is spared the conflict between egoism and social duty which characterised the life, for example, of Savonarola. He had "always longed for some ideal task, in which I might feel myself the heart and brain of a multitude – some social captainship, which would come to me as a duty, and not be striven for as a personal prize" (Ch. 63, III, 315). He does not, however, undergo any of the struggles George Eliot's other protagonists experienced in their quest for social integration. The desired organic union is given to him unproblematically through biological filiation. Following the discovery of his Jewish birth, "There was a release of all the energy which had long been spent in self-checking and suppression because of doubtful conditions" (Ch. 63, III, 307). Daniel's Jewish ancestry enables him to attain, through Mirah, the goal that always eluded Dorothea: "the blending of a complete personal love in one current with a larger duty" (Ch. 50, III, 118). In *Middlemarch* George Eliot used the unified vocabulary of social and psychological channels of energy to suggest a way through the labyrinth. In *Daniel Deronda* her desire to resolve the social questions raised by organicism leads to an over-reliance on ideas of energy transmission and biological inheritance. Though biological filiation offers the perfect model of organic continuity, the notable exclusion of Gwendolen undercuts its effectiveness as a moral resolution.

The principles of physiological psychology are not only employed, however, to support moral argument; they are also used to undermine the conception of a unified, integrated character, which had sustained the traditional linear development of the realist novel. "We mortals," George Eliot observes of Grandcourt, "have a strange spiritual chemistry going on within us." The comment introduces her reflections on the absence of any correlation between intelligence and rational action; the description of mind that follows conforms to Lewes' theory: "Grandcourt's thoughts this evening were like the circlets one sees in a dark pool continually dying out and continually started again by some impulse from below the surface" (Ch. 28, II, 63). In Lewes' favourite image the mind is like a lake: consciousness is the interaction between the stationary waves below the surface and fresh incoming waves.[29] In both illustrations it is the ceaseless action of the waves below the surface of consciousness that determines behaviour.

Jean Sudrann, in her study of *Daniel Deronda*, has argued that whereas twentieth-century psychologists have given contemporary novelists a vocabulary by which to describe the descent into the self, George Eliot was forced to use the idiom available to her: that of melodrama.[30] George Eliot did have available, however, the idiom of Lewes' psychology, which anticipated in many ways twentieth-century developments in psychological theory. An alternative image of the mind employed by Lewes is that of the palimpsest:

the sensitive mechanism is not a simple mechanism, and as such constant, but a variable mechanism, which has a *history*. What the Senses inscribe on it, are not merely the changes of the external world; but these characters are commingled with the characters of preceding inscriptions. The sensitive subject is no *tabula rasa*: it is not a blank sheet of paper, but a palimpsest.[31]

The metaphor of the palimpsest, indicating the coexistence of many psychic levels, was to be employed by Sully to describe the dream process, and later borrowed by Freud to define his distinction between manifest and latent content.[32] In all three writers the image signifies a conception of mind that is neither that of conscious control nor a hierarchy of levels dominated by a directing will. Gwendolen's history is not one which can be captured by the chronology of social time; as the narrator observes, "There is a great deal of unmapped country within us which would have to be taken into account in an explanation of our gusts and storms" (Ch. 24, I, 416). The cartography of that region, however, cannot be that of visible surface, but must represent the simultaneity of conflicting desires. George Eliot found, in the work of Lewes, a theory adequate to her purpose.

In her descriptions of Gwendolen's psyche, George Eliot skilfully interweaves terminology from the Romantic–Gothic literary tradition with an interpretation of the mind's processes that accords with Lewes' psychological theory: "Fantasies moved within her like ghosts, making no break in her more acknowledged consciousness and finding no obstruction in it: dark rays doing their work invisibly in the broad light" (Ch. 48, III, 94). Lewes argued in *The Physical Basis of Mind* (which he was working on while George Eliot wrote *Daniel Deronda*) that the operations of the mind were composed equally of sensations within consciousness and the unconscious; there was no absolute distinction between the two levels, merely one of gradation, such as that between light and dark: "The nervous organism is affected as a whole by every affection of its constituent parts . . . the thrill which any particular stimulus excites will be unconscious, sub-conscious, or conscious, in proportion to the extent of the *irradiated* disturbance."[33] In George Eliot's description, the "rays" of the unconscious operate concurrently with conscious processes, never rising to the surface of consciousness.

At issue is the question of polar opposition: whether of a mode of judgement that would divide all into black and white ("in such cases a man of the world knows what to think beforehand"), or of a theory of the self that would institute a rigid division between rational thought and other psychic phenomena. Gwendolen is far from being Carpenter's rider in firm control of his steed. Conscious and unconscious thought patterns coexist without forming one unified stream, while the rigid division between the self and the external world predicated upon the notion of a rational actor or controlled rider is also dissolved. Gwendolen recalls that, seeing Grandcourt drowning in the water, "I only know that I saw my wish outside me." In her jump into the water beside him, she was "leaping from my crime, and there it was – close to me as I fell – there was the dead face – dead, dead" (Ch. 56, III, 231–2). The external action, the leap away from self, only becomes a new entry into the self, the external embodiment of her crime. It functions as a symbolic demonstration of the fact that the self cannot be identified with the narrow limits of rational consciousness.[34]

George Eliot describes Gwendolen when on the yacht as being "at the very height of her entanglement in those fatal meshes which are woven within more closely than without, and often make the inward torture disproportionate to what is discernible as outward cause"

(Ch. 54, III, 188). The image of the web is one employed by Lewes to define the psyche; to demonstrate the impossibility of a division between organism and environment, self and other, consciousness and the unconscious.[35] In George Eliot's illustration the complex interlocking social and psychic meshes do not exhibit linear causality, one-to-one correspondence between external cause and inner effect, but rather overdetermination. The individual cannot be comprehended, in Lockean fashion, as the *sum* of his previous experiences – a quantitative mode of assessment that cannot account for complexity or contradiction. George Eliot contrasts the linear, social time of language with the actual simultaneity of conflicting experience. The contradictory feelings Gwendolen inspires George Eliot attributes to:

the iridescence of her character – the play of various, nay, contrary tendencies. For Macbeth's rhetoric about the impossibility of being many opposite things in the same moment, referred to the clumsy necessities of action and not to the subtler possibilities of feeling. We cannot speak a loyal word and be meanly silent, we cannot kill and not kill in the same moment; but a moment is room wide enough for the loyal and mean desire, for the outlash of a murderous thought and the sharp backward stroke of repentance (Ch. 4, I, 57).

Rational, syntactic progression cannot readily capture both conscious and unconscious complexity.

George Eliot describes Gwendolen's psychic conflicts using a variety of techniques. Gwendolen's speech after Grandcourt's death is punctuated by gaps which, like the lapses in speech investigated by Freud, signify an underlying unarticulated disturbance: "for I was very precious to my mother – and he took me from her – and he meant – and if she had known —" (Ch. 65, III, 341). The literal transcription is also accompanied by explicative commentary as George Eliot seeks not merely to present, but to offer as well theoretical explanations of Gwendolen's behaviour: "the question had carried with it thoughts and reasons which it was impossible for her to utter, and these perilous remembrances swarmed between her words, making her speech more and more agitated and tremulous" (Ch. 65, III, 341).

George Eliot, as author, confronts the same problem as Daniel when faced with the inadequacy of language to aid Gwendolen:

Words seemed to have no more rescue in them than if he had been beholding a vessel in peril of wreck – the poor ship with its many-lived anguish beaten by the inescapable storm. How could he grasp the long-growing process of this young creature's wretchedness? – how arrest and change it with a sentence? (Ch. 48, III, 100).

Language appears mere surface gloss when called upon to transform the overdetermined effects of a lifetime. Deronda's problem is that of explication or articulation, and as such is identical with the project of the novel: that of rendering in language the complex network of determinate processes that constitute the conflicts and contradictions of the psyche. Like Mordecai, who challenged the language of "a system that gives you the spelling of all things, sure of its alphabet covering them all," George Eliot is seeking in *Daniel Deronda* a narrative structure and language that could encompass complexity and contradiction: a form that would disrupt the association of the temporal sequence of language with a theory of causality. Linguistic convention, as Sully demonstrated, had led men to attribute actions to a dominating ego through the assumption "that the agent expressed by the subject of the verb is the adequate cause." George Eliot attempts in *Daniel Deronda* to break this convention, to undermine, through manipulation of the language and structure of the novel, conceptions of the self as a unified directing force, and of society as the free interaction of autonomous entities.

The inner "furies" which defy Gwendolen's attempt at rational control are also the social furies she encounters in the "Satanic masquerade" who transform the world into a battle for economic wealth and power.[36] In questioning ideas of individual coherence and autonomy George Eliot also explicitly challenges the correlated social theories of free exchange. The story of Gwendolen offers a critique both of dominant conceptions of the self and of correlated social practices. The marriage market into which Gwendolen enters is, George Eliot stresses, one of commodity exchange:

1st Gent.   What woman should be? Sir, consult the taste
Of marriageable men. This planet's store
In iron, cotton, wool, or chemicals –
All matter rendered to our plastic skill,
Is wrought in shapes responsive to demand:
The market's pulse makes index high or low,
By rule sublime. Our daughters must be wives,
And to be wives must be what men will choose:
Men's taste is women's test.

(epigraph, Ch. 10, I, 144)

Women, like raw materials, are shaped to the needs of the market, while social relations are reduced to relations between isolated objects or commodities. This process receives symbolic expression in the recurrent mirror imagery of the novel.

In Chapter 2 we see Gwendolen posing before the mirror, reducing the fullness of her being to the dimensions of her bodily image. Moved by her own reflection she "leaned forward and kissed the cold glass which had looked so warm" (Ch. 2, I, 21). In mistaking the cold glass for living warmth, the limited coherence of the bodily image for the complex network of relations which compose the self, Gwendolen falls prey to the illusions sustained by the economic practices of her society. Mirrors in *Daniel Deronda* are but a secondary form of reflection, a physical representation of social practices. Gwendolen was "a girl who had every day seen a pleasant reflection of that self in her friends' flattery as well as in the looking-glass" (Ch. 2, I, 20). Friends and family confirm her identification of self with bodily image. Gwendolen aspires to self-determination, to be unlike others who "allowed themselves to be made slaves of, and to have their lives blown hither and thither like empty ships in which no will was present" (Ch. 4, I, 53). She desires to "achieve substantiality for herself and know gratified ambition without bondage" (Ch. 23, I, 378), but she is doomed to failure. Enslaved by the idea of self as reflected image, the only career she can conceive, acting, is based on a marketing of her beauty. Far from achieving freedom, she is merely following the market's pulse, treating herself as a commodity to be shaped according to social demand. Following Klesmer's refusal to accept the values of the market, and to judge Gwendolen in terms of her physical appearance, Gwendolen's self-image takes its rank amongst other worthless commodities: "All memories, all objects, the pieces of music displayed, the open piano – the very reflection of herself in the glass – seemed no better than the packed-up shows of a departing fair" (Ch. 23, I, 394). Once the circle of exchange has been broken all elements lose their value. Even memories take on the qualities of objects, alien and external, for Gwendolen lacks any wider conception that could integrate her life.

The world Gwendolen enters on her marriage to Grandcourt is one of mirrors. At Ryelands, in their London home, or on the yacht, the walls are hung with mirrors whose endless repetition of images reflects the enclosed system in which Gwendolen is entrapped. On receiving Lydia's diamonds, her symbolic purchase price, Gwendolen is overcome with terror: "She could not see the reflections of herself then: they were like so many women petrified white" (Ch. 31, II, 124). Gwendolen has entered the ceaseless round of commodity exchange in which women are reduced to non-individuated elements of exchange value. Grandcourt's world is epitomised by the luxury of his boat: "the cabin fitted up to perfection, smelling of cedar, soft-cushioned, hung with silk, expanded with mirrors" (Ch. 54, III, 190). Such mirrors offer, however, only an illusion of depth and truthful representation; restricted to the field of surface appearance they cannot capture complexity or contradiction but reflect an image of the world dominated by material objects. The self-referentiality of their endless repetition is designed to deny the possibility of conflict, of a world outside that cannot be captured with such symmetry.

Grandcourt's judgement is of a piece with this world of mirrors: "in dog fashion, Grandcourt discerned the signs of Gwendolen's expectation, interpreting them with the narrow correctness which leaves a world of unknown feeling behind" (Ch. 54, III, 202). Grandcourt exists only within the world of the sign, incapable of comprehending the complexity of symbolic language. In a naive theory of signification, which George Eliot was attempting to transcend in *Daniel Deronda*, he believes that, mirror-like, there is a one-to-one correspondence between sign and signified. His judgements are purely quantitative; he fails to understand that "the bent of a woman's inferences on mixed subjects which excite mixed passions is not determined by her capacity for simple addition" (Ch. 48, III, 78). Like Spencer in his mechanistic social theory, Grandcourt does not allow for the introduction of a higher level of complexity in social communication than simple energy exchange. His mode of judgement thus reinforces the psychological atomism of a mirror world.

The figure of Grandcourt is counterbalanced by Gwendolen's "terrible-browed angel," Daniel. Like Klesmer, Daniel refuses to enter the circle of exchange, to treat Gwendolen as a commodity, or to accept the false values and distortions employed as currency there. He offers "Not one word of flattery, of indulgence, or dependence on her favour" (Ch. 54, III, 195–6). Stimulating Gwendolen's impulse to complete honesty and confession, he holds up a mirror capable of capturing not just surface illusion, but the multi-levelled layers of psychic confusion. While Grandcourt binds Gwendolen ever tighter in the isolation of his alienated world, trapping her within the distortions of his own vision, Daniel enables her to break through these barriers, to transcend the socially created division between self and other. Thus Gwendolen "learned to see all her acts through the impression they would make on Deronda" (Ch. 54, III, 195). Daniel becomes for her an "outer conscience," and, in an image that captures the organic process, the "breathing medium" of her joy (Ch. 64, III, 334). "In this way,"

George Eliot observes, "our brother may be in the stead of God to us" (Ch. 64, III, 335). In the transfer and interdependence that characterise their association, Gwendolen and Deronda epitomise the "I and Thou" relationship that Feuerbach saw as the foundation of true religion – a religion that would not constitute a self-alienation by situating itself within God, but one firmly founded in humanity.[37] In *The Essence of Christianity* Feuerbach criticised the "exaggerated subjectivity of Christianity," which, knowing only individuals and not species, is forced to resort to God as supernatural mediator. The more natural reconciliation, he suggested, is that in which "my fellow-man is *per se* the mediator between me and the sacred idea of the species."[38] Deronda, breaking down Gwendolen's sense of autonomous individuality, fulfils this function. Through his influence Gwendolen "was for the first time feeling the pressure of a vast mysterious movement, for the first time being dislodged from her supremacy in her own world, and getting a sense that her horizon was but a dipping onward of an existence with which her own was revolving" (Ch. 69, III, 399). Like Mordecai, Deronda has played the role of Copernicus, displacing Gwendolen's Ptolemaic sense of cosmology. Feuerbach was to be criticised by Marx for abstracting the human essence from the historical process, situating it in contemplation rather than sensuous activity, but George Eliot's study corrects this deficiency. The relationship between Gwendolen and Daniel is placed firmly within the context of social and economic relations of power in nineteenth-century England.

In a letter to Frederic Harrison, who was to read a paper on Lewes' psychology, George Eliot observed: "It is melancholy enough that to most of our polite readers the Social Factor in Psychology would be a dull subject. For it is certainly no conceit of ours which pronounces it to be the supremely interesting element in the thinking of our time."[39] More clearly than in any of her previous novels, George Eliot demonstrates in *Daniel Deronda* the social determination of psychic currents, and reveals the correlation that exists between models of the self and society. Both the idealism of Mordecai, and the psychological intricacy of Gwendolen's portrait stem, as I have argued, from the same source. Through Mordecai, George Eliot questions atomistic and inductive science, and theories of linear causality; through Gwendolen, she questions social and psychological atomism, the opposition between self and other, consciousness and the unconscious. In both cases George Eliot challenges dominant modes of social categorisation – the identification of thought with a restricted form of rationality. The ideals of organicism which underpin the novel are those which have determined George Eliot's earlier work – the protagonists still strive for the intergration of individual fulfilment and social duty, historical change and continuity. But the underlying model is now firmly that of Bernard and Lewes: the organism is conceived not as fixed structure, but as interactive process. Yet, despite this unity of conception, one is aware of an impasse at the conclusion of the novel: the potentiality of Deronda's future contrasts markedly with the barren resignation which defines Gwendolen's. While Daniel finds, through Mirah, a union of personal love and social duty, Gwendolen experiences only "that peaceful melancholy which comes from the renunciation of demands for self" (Ch. 69, III, 385).

Through the figure of Daniel George Eliot affirms the central organicist value of duty. It is an affirmation which is undermined, however, by the text itself. The narrative clearly reveals the ideological functions the term could fulfil. Both Mrs Arrowpoint and Mr Gascoigne invoke "duty" in a blatant defence of materialist values: "A woman in your position," observes Mrs Arrowpoint to her daughter, "has serious duties. Where duty and inclination clash, she must follow duty." But, as Catherine so aptly retorts, "People can easily take the sacred word duty as a name for what they desire any one else to do" (Ch. 22, I, 370).[40] A more positive image of the concept of duty is offered by Mirah who was "capable of submitting to anything in the form of duty" (Ch. 45, III, 17). Yet her meek compliance contrasts strongly with the Princess' vehement defence of her right to self-definition. The Princess, a recreation of Armgart, issues a challenge which cannot be answered in the novel: "you can never imagine what it is to have a man's force of genius in you, and yet to suffer the slavery of being a girl. To have a pattern cut out – 'this is the Jewish woman. . .' " (Ch. 51, III, 131). Though the selfishness of the Princess earns the narrator's disapproval, the fundamental question, with its challenge to ideas of unquestioning submission, is one that was framed by Maggie, by Romola, and by Dorothea. Perhaps the strength of *Daniel Deronda* lies in George Eliot's willingness to leave it unresolved.

In Judaism George Eliot found an integrated religion and culture, distinct from the English pattern and values; yet the isolation which guarantees its purity also ensures that its efficacy is restricted to a chosen few. Despite George Eliot's attempt to give Daniel's movement social goals and a geographical locus it remains, within the context of the novel, an esoteric possibility: the narrowness of English social judgement is exchanged for that of an idealism divorced from a determinate social base. Gwendolen is forever excluded from the cultural potential of Judaism – a division which represents yet another form of the sexual demarcation to be found in all George Eliot's novels. Dinah, Esther, and Dorothea, unlike their male counterparts, found social integration only in marriage. George Eliot invests, within the separate figures of Mirah and Gwendolen, the conflicting desires which normally characterise her heroines – the struggle between individual aspiration and the desire for duty. In *Daniel Deronda*, however, she finally refuses the compromise of marriage: Mirah may have complete fulfilment but Gwendolen is left in resigned despair. The concluding tone of *Middlemarch* was ambiguous, regret for Dorothea's wasted potential mingled with affirmation of organic continuity. The persistent disjunction between the lives of Daniel and Gwendolen which fragments the narrative of *Daniel Deronda* plays out that conflict, and exposes the social inadequacy of the metaphoric reconciliation of organicism.

Conclusion

Abandoning the constraints of realism and the conventions of textual unity, George Eliot adopted, in *Daniel Deronda*, a more open narrative form than in her earlier work. The divided structure of the text, however, is a result both of conscious experimentation, and of the final breakdown of the organic ideal. While the cyclical structure of *Adam Bede* had reflected George Eliot's allegiance to the values of pastoral organicism, to a stable model of society, and a static conception of the psychological subject, the narrative form and stance in *Daniel Deronda* are perhaps best defined by the radical uncertainty which characterises the novel's interrogative opening. The text both actively affirms the values of organic union, and displays the conditions of their impossibility. George Eliot's movement away from realism to idealism, and from traditional modes of character representation to one which stresses the operation of the unconscious, is directly correlated with the development of her more critical social perspective. English society in *Daniel Deronda* does not conform to the conflict-free, harmonious whole of organic ideology, nor character to the idea of the unified rational actor which had sustained this social vision. Yet the moral and social values of organicism still furnish the framework of the narrative, thus forcing the novel into a radical divide.

Analysis of George Eliot's novels reveals the variety of narrative strategies which she employed in her attempt to overcome the inherent social contradictions concealed by the organic metaphor. Thus she turned, in *The Mill on the Floss* and *Silas Marner*, to conflicting models of social and psychological development, and, in *Romola*, to the authority of history and a wealth of historical detail. In response to the increased sense of political urgency in the 1860s George Eliot explored, in *Felix Holt*, the conservative political implications of organic thought. She produced a text, however, which is characterised less by unity than by division. Far from displaying the delicate balance of reconciliation, the novel actually anticipates, in its polarisation between affirmation and despair, the later *Daniel Deronda*. *Middlemarch* also looks forward, in rather different fashion, to *Daniel Deronda*, for the increased complexity of George Eliot's social analysis in this work is reflected in her methodology. Adopting for the first time the role of active experimenter, she attempts, through the use of the resources of myth and language, to achieve narrative resolution of the problems of organicism. Yet, in *Middlemarch,* and in the more radical *Daniel Deronda* which perfects this experimental technique, the desired resolution proves elusive.

To understand fully *Daniel Deronda,* and its relation to George Eliot's earlier novels, it is perhaps best to turn to her final published work, *Impressions of Theophrastus Such,* whose essay structure suggests that in *Daniel Deronda* George Eliot had, given the framework of organicism, pushed the novel form to its limits.[1] There is no hint in *Theophrastus Such* of either the radical social or psychological vision of *Daniel Deronda.* In its place we find an affirmation of the past (particularly in "Looking Backward") which, in its nostalgic evocation, recalls passages in *Adam Bede* and *The Mill on the Floss.* The Judaism of *Daniel Deronda* is now developed to a near-hysterical nationalism. Thus the narrator argues, in "The Modern Hep! Hep! Hep!," that it is necessary to moderate the fusion of races, "Because there is a national life in our veins. Because there is something specifically English which we feel to be supremely worth striving for, worth dying for, rather than living to renounce it."[2]

The radical testing of the constraints of realism and narrative convention in *Daniel Deronda* is replaced by an almost morbid self-consciousness, displaced on to the persona of a failed writer. Indeed, the first essay "Looking Inward" focuses almost exclusively on questions of self-concealment and revelation within autobiography. Like George Eliot's previous first-person narrative, "The Lifted Veil," the essays are centrally concerned with the issues of writing, a self-reflexive preoccupation which clearly suggests the doubts George Eliot entertained concerning the creative authority she claimed in her novels. In "The Lifted Veil" this questioning stance underscores a relentlessly pessimistic social vision which counterbalanced the idealistic elements of *The Mill on the Floss.* Latimer's despair was so nihilistic, however, that he was rendered quite untrustworthy as a narrator. Theophrastus, by contrast, plays a more ambiguous role since his pessimism stems from a moral vision which corresponds closely to that of the novels. The danger of egoism is a theme which recurs throughout the essays, while the morally directed pieces ("Looking Backward," "Debasing the Moral Currency," "Moral Swindlers," and "The Modern Hep! Hep! Hep!") stress the value of cultural inheritance. Morality, in accordance with the perspective of the novels, is defined as the "thorough appreciation of dependence in things" (p. 241). In the dogmatic assertions of "The Modern Hep! Hep! Hep!" the narrator actively endorses the ideology of organicism which had, in the novels, always been subject to critical examination: "Our dignity and rectitude are proportioned to our sense of relationship with something great, admirable, pregnant with high possibilities, worthy of sacrifice, a continual inspiration to self-repression and discipline by the presentation of aims larger and more attractive to our generous part than the securing of personal ease or prosperity" (p. 267). The declaration conforms, in its stress on the necessity of self-repression, to Dowden's characterisation of George Eliot's work, in which "self-surrender" is "sternly enjoined." It was a formulation, however, which, as we have seen, could not capture the complexity of the novels.

George Eliot appears to have gone almost full circle in her work, for the narrative tone of *Theophrastus Such* is perhaps closer to "The Natural History of German Life" than to that of the later novels.[3] Both works offer the same declaration of moral intent, the same unequivocal definition of the real and the true. Yet the later work does not possess the authority of the earlier essay for the surety of address now belongs not to George Eliot, but to her narrator. Although George Eliot deliberately distances herself from her creation, Theophrastus' own self-consciousness, and the elaborate attention paid to the construction of this eccentric persona, necessarily draw the reader's attention back to the initial issue of self-revelation in autobiography. The essay title "Looking Inward" aptly summarises the whole collection; while *Daniel Deronda* looks outwards, actively exploring external social contradictions, *Theophrastus Such* confines exploration to internal questions of individual perspective and personal projection. George Eliot thus retreats in her final work from the radical social conclusions and experimental methodology of *Daniel Deronda*, falling back on a more assertive essay style. Through the persona of her narrator she is able to present, unchallenged, sentiments and ideas which had, in the novels, been the subject of narrative interrogation.

Though the essays of *Theophrastus Such* illustrate the thematic unity of George Eliot's work, they also clearly demonstrate the importance of contextual analysis. If one focused only on the narrator's moral pronouncements, little differentiation could be made between *Adam Bede*, *Daniel Deronda*, and *Theophrastus Such*; similar passages on the value of rootedness, for example, could be abstracted from each work. Yet this comparison would reveal little about the actual social perspective, or attitude to organicism in each text since narrative developments frequently undercut the social vision proposed within narrational commentary. Conflicts and divisions within the narrative structure of the novels expose the social contradictions of organic social theory. Furthermore, though George Eliot retains the moral vocabulary of organicism throughout her work, her social and psychological interpretation of the organic idea changes; she moves from the static organic model of *Adam Bede* to the dynamic conception of *Daniel Deronda*.

In tracing these changes in George Eliot's work I have sought to demonstrate the complex ways in which science was assimilated into her fiction. Science did not, as some of her contemporaries proposed, merely supply her with a source of esoteric imagery. Nor, as more recent critics have argued, was its function merely to lend validation and authority to established views of social order. As I suggested in the opening chapter, nineteenth-century scientists and social philosophers shared certain fundamental concerns; mainly, a preoccupation with the relationship between part and whole within an historically changing field. George Eliot addressed the social dimensions of this question, employing a biological model of organic interdependence to resolve the ideological conflict between theories of individualism and social integration and, on a historical plane, the demands of continuity and change. The dynamic model of the organism to which she eventually turned, however, disturbed the delicate balance between holism and individualism which the organic metaphor had originally sustained in social ideology.

Pushed to its logical conclusion, the organicist theory of Comte, Bernard, and Lewes undermined theories of individual autonomy, and related conceptions of the rational actor which had furnished a pattern for notions of linear historical growth. The "thinking subject," as Said has observed, guaranteed "ideas, methods, and schemes of continuity and achievement, endowing them libidinally with a primal urgency underlying all patterns of succession, history, and progress."[4] Lewes, in extending the theories of Comte and Bernard to the psychological realm, undercut ideas of a unified consciousness, and thus effectively challenged notions of historical continuity. Far from sustaining traditional organicist conceptions of evolving social and psychological order, the biological premises to which George Eliot turns in her later works actually reinforce images of conflict and contradiction.

Study of George Eliot's involvement with organicist theory suggests the complex ways in which nineteenth-century social and scientific thought were intertwined. Clearly, evolutionary theory was not the sole ground of interconnection; nor was the relationship between science and social philosophy manifest only in the realm of explicit social ideas. As we have seen, biological theories of the organic influenced not only the social theory, but also the narrative methodology of George Eliot's work. Her shift from a static to a dynamic model of the organism, and from the role of passive observer to that of active experimenter reflects the nineteenth-century decline in natural history and the rise of experimental science. This movement in the field of science found parallel expression in the development of nineteenth-century fiction. As interest in the sciences moved from the order of nature to its history, so novelists turned their attention to the historical growth of the social whole and the inner workings of the mind. With the decline of natural history, conventions in realism also shifted: the task of the novelist, like that of the scientist, was no longer merely to name the visible order of the world. George Eliot's fiction encapsulates these changes, foreshadowing subsequent developments in the Victorian novel.

Although I have focused in this study on the fiction of George Eliot, the implications of the arguments are clearly more extensive. Other Victorian novelists, less directly preoccupied with science than George Eliot, were yet inevitably influenced by the scientific assumptions entering into the discourse of their times. Thus George Eliot's interpretation of realism, and her increasingly complex model of psychology, anticipate, for example, the later Meredith and James. Whether writers sought, like George Eliot and Hardy, to incorporate science directly into their work or, like James, attempted rigidly to demarcate the realms of art and science all were, nonetheless, affected by the mutual interaction of literary, social, and scientific thought. Within the broad framework of change which I have sketched, the specific relations of each author to the realm of science varied in accordance with individual perspectives. The direct appropriation of the vocabulary of phrenology in Charlotte Bronte's fiction, for instance, contrasts sharply with the more subtle connection between James' narrative practice and contemporary developments in scientific methodology. Such divergent responses confirm our understanding of the manifold ways in which scientific theory penetrated literary practice.

Nineteenth-century science, as this study has shown, was not a monolithic structure. As different physiological themes of the organic gave rise to conflicting social interpretations, so too, throughout nineteenth-century thought one can see scientific diversity reflected in the spheres of literary and social analysis. The relations between science and literature were, I would suggest, more subtle and complex than we have previously suspected. Science permeated not only the social and psychological theory, but also the language, structure and fictional methodology of the Victorian novel.

Notes

Preface

1 Unsigned review, *Galaxy*, 15 (March, 1873), 424–8, reprinted in David Carroll, ed., *George Eliot: The Critical Heritage* (London, 1971), 353–9 (p. 359).

2 Richard Simpson, unsigned article "George Eliot's Novels," *Home and Foreign Review*, 3 (1863), 522–49, reprinted in Carroll, ed., *The Critical Heritage*, 221–50 (p. 235).

3 Sidney Colvin, review, *Fortnightly Review*, 13 (1873), 142–7, reprinted in Carroll, ed., *The Critical Heritage*, 331–8 (p. 334).

4 The publication of Bernard J. Paris' *Experiments in Life: George Eliot's Quest for Values* (Detroit, 1965), in fact coincided with that of U. C. Knoepflmacher's *Religious Humanism and the Victorian Novel: George Eliot, Walter Pater, and Samuel Butler* (Princeton, 1965) which also offered an important, if less extended, discussion of George Eliot's relationship to science. Another crucial analysis of this issue, which actually ante-dates these two works, is to be found in Michael Wolff, "Marian Evans to George Eliot: The Moral and Intellectual Foundations of her Career" (Diss., Princeton, 1958). Since 1965 numerous articles have appeared which consider the influence of social and scientific theory on George Eliot's fiction. Two articles which deal specifically with the impact of science are: Robert A. Greenberg, "Plexuses and Ganglia: Scientific Allusion in *Middlemarch*," *Nineteenth-Century Fiction*, 30 (1976), 33–52; and Michael Y. Mason, "*Middlemarch* and Science: Problems of Life and Mind," *Review of English Studies*, 22 (1971), 151–69. Though Mason's article touches on the relationship between the work of George Eliot and G. H. Lewes, this area of study has, until recently, remained relatively unexplored. Three articles have appeared in the last few years, however, which go a long way towards rectifying this omission: K. K. Collins, "G. H. Lewes Revised: George Eliot and the Moral Sense," *Victorian Studies*, 21 (1978), 463–92, and "Questions of Method: Some Unpublished Late Essays," *Nineteenth-Century Fiction*, 35 (1980), 385–405; and George Levine, "George Eliot's Hypothesis of Reality," *Nineteenth-Century Fiction*, 35 (1980), 1–28. The article by George Levine is closest in approach to my own work in that it investigates the relationship between George Eliot's conception of science and her narrative method. Indeed, there are significant parallels between this article and my own "The Language of Science and Psychology in George Eliot's *Daniel Deronda*," in James Paradis and Thomas Postlewait, eds., *Victorian Science and Victorian Values: Literary Perspectives*, Annals of the New York Academy of Sciences, 360 (1981), 269–98, which forms the basis of the final chapter in this work.

5 For an important discussion of Henry James' relations to nineteenth-century scientific theory see Alexander Welsh's excellent article, "Theories

of Science and Romance, 1870–1920," *Victorian Studies*, 17 (1973), 135–54 (pp. 145–9). A more unusual approach to this issue is offered in Strother B. Purdy's *The Hole in the Fabric: Science, Contemporary Literature, and Henry James* (Pittsburgh, 1977).

6   Although I am indebted to the two very distinct studies of Paris and Knoepflmacher my work differs from theirs in varying respects and degrees. In focusing on the narrative structure of George Eliot's fiction I depart from the methodology of Paris who (as Knoepflmacher has pointed out in *George Eliot's Early Novels: The Limits of Realism* (Berkeley, 1968), p. 5) is concerned primarily with the moral philosophy rather than the form of the novels. My interpretation of the function of science in George Eliot's fiction differs from that of both critics. Despite their differences in methodology, both writers attribute to science a relatively fixed and unchanging role in George Eliot's novels. Paris, indeed, interprets her work in the light of her attempt to overcome a fundamental conflict between the teachings of science and her moral vision of the universe. My own work suggests a rather closer inter-relationship between the spheres of moral, social and scientific thought. In the course of George Eliot's fictional development, I argue, one can see radical changes in her social theory and fictional methods which can be directly correlated with transformations in contemporary scientific theory.

7   As David Carroll recently observed, "It is a commonplace of criticism that George Eliot's thinking is pervaded by ideas of the organic, whether she is writing about the psychology of character, society, religion or art" (" 'Janet's Repentance' and the Myth of the Organic," *Nineteenth-Century Fiction*, 35 (1980), 331–48 (p. 331). Carroll offers in this article a very perceptive analysis of the relationship between George Eliot's theories of the organic and the form of her fiction. Although his interpretation of organicism is quite similar to my own, he does not relate these theories to the sphere of physiological thought.

8   G. H. Lewes, *Comte's Philosophy of the Sciences* (London, 1853), p. 234.

9   George Eliot, *Daniel Deronda*, Cabinet Edition, 3 vols. (Edinburgh, 1878–80), Ch. 321, II, 133. References to this edition will be cited hereafter in the text.

10 I am adapting here a simile, originally employed by Lionel Gossman in *Medievalism and the Ideologies of the Enlightenment* (Englewood Cliffs, New Jersey, 1972) which Maurice Mandelbaum later adopted in *History, Man, and Reason: A Study in Nineteenth-Century Thought* (Baltimore, 1971) to describe his own approach to nineteenth-century thought (p. x).

11 The critique of organicism is evident in many fields of contemporary theory; it lies, for example, behind Louis Althusser's rejection of interpretations of Marx which accredit him with an evolutionary, organic theory of history. Marx, Althusser argues, did not merely invert Hegel, for inversion would still imply an acceptance of linear theories of evolution. (See *For Marx*, trans. Ben Brewster (Harmondsworth, 1969), pp. 197–9.) Althusser draws support from Marx' later work for his thesis that history is "punctuated by radical discontinuities" (see Louis Althusser and Etienne Balibar, *Reading Capital*, trans. Ben Brewster (London, 1970, 2nd edn, 1977), p. 44). A similar critique of organic theory also lies behind Michel Foucault's rejection of the idea of history as chronology, and his refusal of the theory of the unified subject. He proposes to replace theories of genesis, continuity and totalisation with concepts of

discontinuity and rupture, and to take "discourse" as the object of his study. "Discourse is not the majestically unfolding manifestation of a thinking, knowing, speaking, subject but, on the contrary, a totality in which the dispersion of the subject and his discontinuity with himself may be determined" (*The Archaeology of Knowledge,* trans. A. M. S. Smith (London, 1972), p. 55). Within literary theory itself the critique of organicism has been focused in the attack, by Pierre Macherey and his followers, on Lukacs' theory of organic form in art. In its place they propose a model founded on notions of conflict, gaps, and contradictions. (See Pierre Macherey, *A Theory of Literary Production,* trans. Geoffrey Wall (London and Boston, 1978).) Macherey's theories have strongly influenced the work of Terry Eagleton who undertakes, in *Criticism and Ideology: A Study in Marxist Literary Theory* (London, 1976), to study the inter-relations between social and aesthetic theories of organicism in Victorian England, taking "the concept of 'organic form' as one crucial nexus between history and literary production" (p. 104).

12 Letter to Francois D'Albert-Durade, 29 January, 1861. Gordon S. Haight, ed., *The George Eliot Letters,* 9 vols. (New Haven, 1954–78), III, 374; cited hereafter as *Letters.* This collection contains letters written by both George Eliot and G. H. Lewes.

1 *Science and social thought: The rise of organic theory*

1 Thus Hobbes observes that:
> Everything is best understood by its constituent causes. For as in a watch, or some small engine, the matter, figure and motion of the wheels cannot be well known except it be taken asunder and viewed in parts; so to make a more curious search into the rights and duties of subjects, it is necessary, I say, to take them asunder, but yet that they may be so considered as if they were dissolved.

Quoted in John Burrow, *Evolution and Society: A Study in Victorian Social Theory* (Cambridge, 1966), p. 26.

2 Walter Buckley, *Sociology and Modern Systems Theory* (Englewood Cliffs, New Jersey, 1967), p. 8.

3 For an extended treatment of this argument see Georges Canguilhem, *La Connaissance de la Vie* (Paris, 1969), p. 57.

4 A good analysis of the changes in biological and social theory of this period which focuses on Kant's role is that of Ernst Cassirer, *The Problem of Knowledge: Philosophy, Science and History since Hegel,* trans. W. H. Woglom and C. W. Hendel (New Haven, 1950). Other helpful studies include, Oswei Temkin, "Basic Science, Medicine and the Romantic Era" in *The Double Face of Janus and other Essays in the History of Medicine* (Baltimore, 1977); François Jacob, *The Logic of Life: A History of Heredity,* trans. Betty E. Spillman (New York, 1973); and Michel Foucault, *The Order of Things: An Archaeology of the Human Sciences,* translated (London, 1974).

5 There is a considerable amount of debate as to who should be considered the founders of biology. T. H. Huxley in his essay "On the Study of Biology" in *The Scientific Memoirs of T. H. Huxley,* eds. M. Foster and E. R. Lankester, 4 vols. (London, 1898), IV, pp. 248–64 claims as an epoch the moment when biology, the study of living matter, was dif-

ferentiated from natural history. His chosen originators are Bichat, Lamarck, and Treviranus. François Jacob, writing from the perspective of this century, chooses Pallas, Lamarck, Vicq d'Azur, De Jussieu, Goethe, Treviranus, and Oken, while Cassirer focuses on Cuvier and Goethe since both were demonstrably influenced by Kant. The names matter less, however, than the realisation that the same transformation was occurring, simultaneously, in the natural sciences, in France and Germany.

6   See Auguste Comte, *System of Positive Polity or Treatise on Sociology, Instituting the Religion of Humanity,* trans. J. H. Bridges, Frederic Harrison, E. S. Beesly, Richard Congreve, 4 vols. (London, 1875–7), I, Chap. 11 "The Social Aspect of Positivism, as shown by its Connection with the General Revolutionary Movement of Western Europe," pp. 50–1. For an analysis of Burke's impact on German *Naturphilosophie* see Heinz Maus, *A Short History of Sociology* (London, 1962), p. 24.

7   Thomas Pinney, ed., *Essays of George Eliot* (London 1963), p. 287; cited hereafter as *Essays.*

8   *Essays,* p. 287.

9   *Essays,* p. 287.

10 T. Pinney, "More Leaves from George Eliot's Notebook," *Huntington Library Quarterly,* 29 (1966), 371. The notebook was written, Pinney suggests, between 1872 and 1879.

11 Comte, *System of Positive Polity,* I, 291.

12 Quoted in F. W. Coker, *Organismic Theories of the State* (New York, 1910), p. 22.

13 Auguste Comte, *The Positive Philosophy of Auguste Comte,* trans. and ed. H. Martineau, 2 vols. (London, 1853), II, 472.

14 G. H. Lewes, *Comte's Philosophy of the Sciences* (London, 1853), p. 9.

15 *Essays,* p. 31.

16 *Essays,* p. 31. For a detailed study of George Eliot's belief in the moral force of physical law see Paris, especially pp. 25–30, and Michael Wolff "Marian Evans to George Eliot."

17 Quoted in Gordon S. Haight, *George Eliot: A Biography* (Oxford, 1968), p. 464.

18 John Stuart Mill, *Nature, The Utility of Religion and Theism,* 2nd edn (London, 1854), p. 15.

19 For information on Bernard's relationship to Comte I have drawn on the work of Georges Canguilhem. In *Essai Sur Quelques Problèmes Concernant le Normal et le Pathologique* (Paris, 1950), Canguilhem draws attention to Comte's considerable influence on the biology as well as the philosophy and literature of the nineteenth century, and particularly his direct influence on Bernard. In "Auguste Comte: La Philosophie Biologique d'Auguste Comte et son influence en France au XIX Siècle," in *Études d'Histoire et de Philosophie des Sciences* (Paris, 1968), he argues:

> Ce serait une tout autre tâche que de rechercher dans quelle mesure la plupart des théories que les historiens de la physiologie attribuent à Claude Bernard, pour lui en faire honneur, trouvent en réalitité leur origine dans la philosophie biologique de Comte. Au moins est il certain que, même sans *l'Introduction à l'Étude de la Médicine Expérimentale,* le XIX siècle aurait été familiarisé avec les théories du déterminisme des phénomènes biologiques, et l'identité de nature des phénomènes physiologiques et pathologiques, de la spécificité irréductible des êtres organiques (p. 73).

20   Edward Dowden, *Studies in Literature: 1789–1877* (London, 1878), p. 100.
21   See John Passmore, *A Hundred Years of Philosophy* (London, 1957), p. 35.
22   Dowden, p. 119.
23   Dowden, p. 119.
24   Dowden, p. 119.
25   George Eliot, "Armgart," *The Legend of Jubal and Other Poems*, Cabinet Edition (Edinburgh, 1878–80), p. 133.
26   Eliot, "Armgart," p. 133.
27   This theory of metaphor is advanced by Max Black in *Models and Metaphors: Studies in Language and Philosophy* (Ithaca, New York, 1962).
28   Comte, *Positive Philosophy*, II, 508.
29   Comte, *Positive Philosophy*, II, 130.
30   John Stuart Mill, *A System of Logic*, 9th edn, 2 vols. (London, 1875), II, 492–3.
31   Mill, *A System of Logic*, II, 469.
32   John Stuart Mill, *Auguste Comte and Positivism*, London, 1865; rprt (Ann Arbor, 1961), p. 123.
33   Mill, *Auguste Comte and Positivism*, p. 138.
34   Herbert Spencer, *Social Statics* (London, 1851), p. 455.
35   Spencer, *Social Statics*, p. 103.
36   Spencer, *Social Statics*, p. 448.
37   Spencer, *Social Statics*, p. 16.
38   Letter to Sara Hennell, 9–10 July 1860, *Letters*, III, 319.
39   George Eliot, *The Mill on the Floss*, Cabinet Edition, 2 vols. (Edinburgh, 1878–80), Bk VI, Ch. 14, II, 329.
40   Spencer, *Social Statics*, p. 1.
41   George H. Lewes, *Problems of Life and Mind. First Series: The Foundations of a Creed*, 2 vols. (London, 1874–5), I, 2.
42   Jacob, p. 74.
43   Thus Lewes observes in *Sea-side Studies* (London, 1858), that,

In the earliest forms of Life, as in the earliest states of society, all do everything, each does all. There is no separate digestive system, no separate respiratory system, no muscular system, no nervous system. Every part of the animal assimilates, respires, contracts, moves; just as in barbarian tribes every man is his own tailor, his own purveyor, his own architect, and his own lawyer. At last the principle of Division of Labour emerges; then that which is true of the whole organism ceases to be true of an organ; and we have no more right to demand that an arm should digest food, than that Moses & Son should preside over the deliberations of Downing Street, or cook the Whitebait dinner; we have no more right to ask the lungs to produce offspring, than to ask Mr. Cobden to take command of the Baltic Fleet, and Mr. Bright to perform the operation for stone (p. 60).

44   I. Dollinger, *Grundzuge der Physiologie*, translated and quoted by Temkin, in "Ontogeny and History around 1800," *The Double Faces of Janus*, p. 379.
45   Thus Maurice Mandelbaum in *History, Man and Reason* defines historicism as "the belief that an adequate understanding of the nature of any phenomenon and an adequate assessment of its value are to be gained through considering it in terms of the place it occupies within a process of development" (p. 42).

46   T. H. Buckle, *History of Civilization in England*, 2 vols. (London, 1857–61), II, 601.

47   *Essays*, p. 413.

48   Herbert Spencer, "Progress: its Law and its Cause," in *Essays: Scientific, Political and Speculative*, First Series (London, 1858).

49   *Essays*, p. 31.

50   Her notebooks for *Middlemarch*, for instance, suggest the wide diversity of her source material; notes from W. R. Grove's *On the Correlation of Physical Forces* (London, 1855) occur alongside lengthy extracts from works on mythology, anthropology, and mythological criticism. See John Clark Pratt and Victor A. Neufeldt, eds., *George Eliot's Middlemarch Notebooks* (Berkeley, 1979).

51   Letter to Sara Hennell, 14 January 1862. *Letters*, IV, 8.

52   F. Max Muller, *Lectures on the Science of Language*, First Series (London, 1861), p. 25.

53   The term "morphology" was actually first introduced by Goethe. See Philip C. Ritterbush, "Organic Form," in *Organic Form: The Life of an Idea*, ed., G. S. Rousseau (London, 1972), p. 37.

54   Muller, *The Science of Language*, p. 262.

55   Letter to Mme Bodichon, 5 December 1859. *Letters*, III, 227.

56   Charles Darwin, *On the Origin of Species by Means of Natural Selection*, ed. John Burrow from 1st edn (London, 1859; Harmondsworth, 1968), p. 459.

57   Charles C. Gillispie, "Lamarck and Darwin in the History of Science," in *Forerunners of Darwin*, eds. B. Glass *et al.* (Baltimore, 1968).

58   Darwin, *Origin*, p. 173.

59   Thus Darwin states in the *Origin*; "As buds give rise by growth to fresh buds, and these, if vigorous, branch out and overtop on all sides many a feebler branch, so by generation I believe it has been with the great Tree of Life, which fills with its dead and broken branches the crust of the earth, and covers the surface with its ever branching and beautiful ramifications" (p. 172). The image recalls the idealist organicism of Carlyle for whom it forms a constant refrain: "For the Present holds in it both the whole Past and the whole Future: – as the Life Tree Igdrasil, wide-weaving, many-toned has its roots down deep in the Death King-doms, among the oldest dead dust of men, and with its boughs reaches always beyond the stars; and in all times and places is one and the same Life-tree!" (*Past and Present*, London, 1843; rprt, ed. A. M. D. Hughes, Oxford, 1918), p. 34.

60   "The tree of life should perhaps be called the coral of life, base of branches dead; so that the passages cannot be seen" (Notebook of 1837). Francis Darwin, ed., *The Life and Letters of Charles Darwin*, 2 vols. (New York, 1919), I, 368. I am indebted to Gillian Beer for first drawing my attention to this point.

61   *Fortnightly Review*, 3 n.s. (April 1868), p. 356.

62   George Eliot, Autograph manuscript notebook, No. 7, Beinecke Rare Book and Manuscript Library, Yale University.

63   Max Muller, *The Science of Language*, Second Series (London, 1864), p. 306.

64   Dowden, p. 98.

65   Buckle, I, 822.

66   Temkin has argued that the social outcry against Lawrence should be seen against the background of a fear of Jacobinism in the Post-

Revolutionary era. See "Basic Science, Medicine and the Romantic Era," in *The Double Face of Janus.*

67 Thomas Carlyle, "The Nigger Question," first pub. in *Fraser's Magazine,* Dec. 1849, rprt in *Selected Essays,* ed. Ian Campbell (London, 1972), p. 318.

68 See Collins, "G. H. Lewes Revised." In the appendix to this article Collins cites the original, and George Eliot's own version, of certain key passages in Lewes' work.

69 G. H. Lewes, "Spiritualism and Materialism," *Fortnightly Review,* 19 n.s. (1876), pp. 479–93, 707–19 (715–16).

70 Lewes, "Spiritualism and Materialism," p. 717.

71 Comte, *Positive Philosophy,* II, 4.

72 This statement was preceded by the following observation: "L'électricité est, par exemple, le résultat de l'action du cuivre et du zinc dans certaines conditions chimiques; mais si l'on supprime la relation de ces corps, l'électricité étant une abstraction et n'existant pas par elle-même, cesse de se manifester." *Introduction à l'Étude de la Médicine Expérimentale* (Paris, 1865), p. 129. The quotation was taken from a passage marked by Lewes in his own copy of the book which is now held in Dr Williams's Library, Gordon Square, London. For a full catalogue of the Eliot and Lewes holdings in this library see William Baker, *The George Eliot–George Henry Lewes Library: An Annotated Catalogue of their Books at Dr. Williams's Library, London* (London, 1977).

73 Lewes, *The Foundations of a Creed,* I, 125fn.

74 Lewes, *The Foundations of a Creed,* I, 124.

75 Lewes, *The Foundations of a Creed,* I, 124.

76 Letter to Frederic Harrison, 10 June 1879. *Letters,* VII, 161.

77 Lewes, "Spiritualism and Materialism," p. 716.

78 Lewes, "Spiritualism and Materialism," p. 481.

79 Lewes, *The Foundations of a Creed,* I, 144–5.

80 Lewes, *Problems of Life and Mind. Third Series,* 2 vols. (London, 1879), II, 365.

81 Lewes, "Spiritualism and Materialism," p. 716.

82 See L. L. Whyte, *The Unconscious before Freud* (London, 1962), pp. 63–6, 165–70.

83 Eduard von Hartmann, *Philosophy of the Unconscious: Speculative Results According to the Inductive Method of Physical Science,* trans. W. C. Coupland, 2nd edn, 3 vols. (London, 1893), I, 19.

84 E. S. Dallas, *The Gay Science,* 2 vols. (London, 1866), I, 217.

85 Herbert Spencer, *The Principles of Psychology* (London, 1855), p. 374.

86 See Spencer, *Psychology,* pp. 495–6.

87 Lewes, *Problems of Life and Mind. Second Series: The Physical Basis of Mind* (London, 1877), p. 363.

88 My analysis of George Eliot's organicism differs from that of Paris who assumes that organicist premises suggested only one model of society, and that George Eliot's relations to organic theory were static and unchanging. I argue, however, that her social and psychological interpretation of organic theory changes radically during her career; she does not retain the "social-political conservatism" of her early response (see Paris, p. 47).

89 Claude Bernard, *An Introduction to the Study of Experimental Medicine,* trans. Henry Copley Green (New York, 1949), p. 18.

90 Lewes, *The Foundations of a Creed,* I, 288.

91 Lewes, *The Foundations of a Creed*, I, 289. For a further analysis of Lewes' theories of the scientific imagination, see Levine, "George Eliot's Hypothesis of Reality," pp. 12–14.
92 Lewes, *The Foundations of a Creed*, I, 289.
93 George Eliot, *Middlemarch*, Cabinet Edition, 3 vols. (Edinburgh, 1878–80) Ch. 16, I, 249; Levine, "George Eliot's Hypothesis of Reality," p. 12. Gillian Beer offers an excellent discussion of the relationship between Lydgate's practice and Claude Bernard's theories of scientific method in "Plot and the Analogy with Science in Later Nineteenth-Century Novelists," in *Comparative Criticism: A Yearbook*, ed. E. S. Shaffer, 2 (1980), 131–49 (p. 144). A more general survey of the rise of theories of scientific methodology which stress the role of the imagination is to be found in Welsh who focuses primarily, however, on the realm of physics, rather than on the biological sciences.

2   *Adam Bede*: Natural history as social vision

1 A. O. Lovejoy, *The Great Chain of Being* (Cambridge, Mass., 1942), p. 244.
2 G. Canguilhem, "Du Développement à l'Évolution au XIX Siècle," in *Thalès: Recueil des Travaux de l'Institut d'Histoire des Sciences et des Techniques de l'Université de Paris* (Paris, 1962), p. 3.
3 George Eliot, "The Natural History of German Life," *Westminster Review*, 66 (July, 1856), 51–79, in *Essays*, pp. 266–99 (p. 287). Immediately before this passage George Eliot inserted a footnote to the effect that in her statement of Riehl's opinions "we must be understood not as quoting Riehl, but as interpreting and illustrating him" (p. 287). The views and terminology that follow are those of Comte. All references to this essay will be cited hereafter in the text.
4 See Comte, *Positive Philosophy*, I, 360–2.
5 Examination of *Modern Painters* reveals the bias which George Eliot brought to her reading of Ruskin. The theory of realism she outlines is more nearly her own than that of Ruskin. Though Ruskin employed the term "realism" he chose to characterise his own approach as "idealism." He is less concerned with the truth of external form than with that of inner essence. In *Adam Bede* George Eliot relates her concept of realism explicitly to the Dutch school of painting, yet Ruskin dismisses the Dutch school as not even third rate (*Modern Painters*, 5 vols. (London, 1873), III, 33). It is Turner whom he designates as "master of the science of *Essence*" (III, 314). The crucial distinction between his own theory of art, and the one to which George Eliot adheres at this stage in her career is illustrated by his argument that, "There are some truths, easily obtained, which give a deceptive resemblance to nature, others only to be attained with difficulty, which cause no deception, but give inner, and deep resemblance" (III, 131). The verisimilitude of external form which George Eliot values so highly conveys for Ruskin, only a "deceptive" resemblance to nature. For further discussion of George Eliot's relations to Ruskin see Wolff, "Marian Evans to George Eliot," p. 344.
6 George Eliot, "Art and Belles Lettres," *Westminster Review*, 65 (April, 1856), pp. 625–50 (p. 626).
7 Comte, *Positive Philosophy*, II, 97.
8 Comte, *Positive Philosophy*, II, 491.

9   Comte, *Positive Philosophy*, II, 99.
10 See Ch. 1, Note 71.
11 George Eliot, *Adam Bede*, Cabinet Edition, 2 vols. (Edinburgh, 1878–80), Ch. 17, I, 265. All references to this edition will be cited hereafter in the text.
12 Though the author is a woman I have chosen to refer to the narrator in this novel as "he" since the persona projected appears to be that of a man.
13 Lewes, in a discussion of Bacon in *The Biographical History of Philosophy, From its Origin in Greece down to the Present Day*, offers the following quotation: " 'The mind,' he observes, 'is not like a plane mirror, which reflects the images of things exactly as they are; it is like a mirror of an uneven surface, which combines its own figure with the figures of the objects it represents' " (London, 1857), p. 339.
14 C. Buffon, *De la manière d'étudier et de traiter l'histoire naturelle*, in *Oeuvres complètes* (Paris, 1774–9), I, 17. Quoted in Jacob, p. 47.
15 John Goode, "Adam Bede," in *Critical Essays on George Eliot*, ed. Barbara Hardy (London, 1970), p. 22. I am particularly indebted to this article for its excellent analysis of George Eliot's approach to history in *Adam Bede*.
16 Spencer, *The Principles of Psychology*, pp. 577–8.
17 John Goode (p. 36) notes that Adam's maxim is from Franklin's Preface to *Poor Richard's Almanack* entitled "The Way to Make Money Plentiful in Every Man's Pocket."
18 Spencer, *Social Statics*, pp. 323, 322.
19 Spencer, *Social Statics*, p. 345.
20 Spencer, *Social Statics*, p. 16.
21 Herbert Spencer and George Eliot were close associates during the period in which he was writing *The Principles of Psychology*. Spencer, indeed, acknowledges, in a footnote to a relatively minor point, that he was indebted to discussion with "a distinguished lady – the translator of Strauss and Feuerbach" (p. 162). As Gordon Haight has suggested in his biography, however, Spencer's work probably owed a good deal more to George Eliot than the single phrase he cites (p. 116).
22 Thus Lewes offers the following definition of the "Law of Sensibility": "No sensation terminates in itself; it must either discharge its excitation in some secondary sensation, or in some motor-impulse. Generally it does so in both together". *The Physiology of Common Life*, 2 vols. (London, 1859–60), II, 55.
23 See *Middlemarch*, Ch. 24, I, 382.
24 For Lewes' discussion of "nerve-fibres" see *The Physiology of Common Life*, II, pp. 15–18.
25 Spencer, *The Principles of Psychology*, p. 275. For information on the role of concepts of muscular sense, the will, and the impression of resistance, in nineteenth-century philosophy I have drawn on Roger Smith, "Physiological Psychology and the Philosophy of Nature in Mid-Nineteenth-Century Britain" (Diss., Cambridge, 1970). Smith observes that both Alexander Bain and Spencer, "argued with professional physicists over the nature of physical force and refused to accept force as merely a mathematical function devised by physicists to aid understanding of matter in motion" (p. 217). The same error, I would argue, underlies George Eliot's equation of sensation with the fulfilment of the will.
26 Spencer, *The Principles of Psychology*, p. 472.
27 Spencer, *The Principles of Psychology*, p. 620.

28 Smith (see Note 25 above) points out that Bain "viewed the scientific principle of the conservation of energy as reinforcing the philosophical principle of the uniformity of nature" (p. 219). This mistaken identification also occurs in the work of Dowden who argues that there is a moral order in the universe on the basis of the principle of the conservation of energy: "But not only is nature everywhere constant, uniform, orderly in its operations; all its parts constitute a whole, an *ensemble*. Nothing is added: nothing can be lost" (p. 100). See Ch. 1, note 20.

29 See U. C. Knoepflmacher, *George Eliot's Early Novels: The Limits of Realism*, p. 111. Knoepflmacher argues that Adam, "like Milton's more culpable Adam, . . . must overcome despair by recognizing the paradox of a fortunate fall." In his perceptive analysis, Knoepflmacher reveals the pervasive influence of Milton's epic in *Adam Bede*.

30 *Letters*, III, p. 374.

31 In employing the term "organic" here I am drawing on traditional critical definitions of an "organic" text as one that is fully integrated and unified. This concept is suggested by George Eliot's own image of "balance."

32 See Ch. 16, I, 246, where Adam rebukes Arthur for believing he could forget the past, and Ch. 33, II, 97, which refers to Adam's love for Hetty and suggests that love binds together "your whole being past and present in one unspeakable vibration."

33 Pre-eminent examples in George Eliot's work are Godfrey in *Silas Marner*, Tito in *Romola*, Mrs Transome in *Felix Holt* and Gwendolen in *Daniel Deronda*.

34 *Essays*, p. 31. See Ch. 1, Note 16.

35 See Note 28.

36 The static conception of character lying behind this assurance can best be illustrated by reference to the later *Romola*. Describing Tito shortly before his death the narrator observes he was "not the same Tito, but nearly as brilliant as on the day when he had first entered that house" (Ch. 67, II, 389). (Cabinet Edition, 2 vols. Edinburgh, 1878–80.) The "different conditions" have actually created a transformation in his character.

37 Spencer, *Social Statics*, p. 415.

3 *The Mill on the Floss*: The shadowy armies of the unconscious

1 George Eliot, *The Mill on the Floss*, Cabinet Edition, 2 vols. (Edinburgh, 1878–80), Bk I, Ch. 1, I, 3. All references to this edition will be cited hereafter in the text.

2 For an interesting analysis of George Eliot's use of historical narrative in this work, see Steven Marcus, *Representations: Essays on Literature and Society* (London, 1975), pp. 182–213.

3 L. A. Bisson, "Proust, Bergson and George Eliot," *Modern Language Review*, 40 (1945), 104–14 (p. 109).

4 C. C. Gillispie, "Lamarck and Darwin in the History of Science," p. 284.

5 Edward W. Said, *Beginnings: Intention and Method* (New York, 1975), p. 66.

6 Said, p. 10. See also pp. 160–82.

7 Said, p. 11.

8 As Barbara Hardy has observed, "even though *The Mill on the Floss* is

a very Darwinian novel, its debt to Darwin is to be found in its hard and pessimistic look at struggle and survival, rather than in its optimistic treatment of personal evolutions" ("The Mill on the Floss" in *Critical Essays on George Eliot* (London, 1970), pp. 42–58 (p. 53)). See also Gordon Haight's introduction to the Riverside edition of *The Mill* (Boston, 1961) in which he traces the echoes of Darwin's Struggle for Existence in the novel (pp. xii–xiii).

9 E. S. Dallas, unsigned review, *The Times* (19 May 1860), pp. 10–11, reprinted in Carroll, ed., *The Critical Heritage*, p. 133.

10 *Letters*, III, 299. To William Blackwood, 27 May 1860.

11 *Essays*, p. 264.

12 Charles Darwin, *Origin*, p. 175.

13 The *Bridgewater Treatises* (1833–40) were a series of works commissioned by the eighth Earl of Bridgewater, which were designed to show "the power, wisdom, goodness of God as manifested in the creation."

14 Darwin, *Origin*, p. 23.

15 Darwin, *Origin*, pp. 459–60.

16 See Ch. 1, Note 59.

17 Darwin, p. 142.

18 Manuscript Notebook, Parrish Collection, Princeton University Library. This notebook has recently been published by K. K. Collins in his article "Questions of Method: Some Unpublished Late Essays." See p. 390.

19 Barbara Hardy has also speculated on the relationship between *The Mill on the Floss* and a *Bildungsroman* in an attempt to account for Maggie's failure to progress. She suggests, with respect to the final "Providential" flood, that "It may have been Maggie's refusal to be a tragic and evolutionary heroine . . . that brought about the final swing into wishing and dreaming" (p. 56). Though the terms of my analysis differ from those of Barbara Hardy, I point to a similar relationship between the dual structure of the plot and Maggie's psychological history.

20 Anthony Wilden, *System and Structure: Essays in Communication and Exchange* (London, 1972), p. 95. See also Said, p. 293.

21 G. H. Lewes, *The Physiology of Common Life*, I, 64.

22 See Comte, *System of Positive Polity*, II, 240.

23 Lewes, *The Physiology of Common Life*, II, 344.

24 Lewes, *The Physiology of Common Life*, II, 59.

25 Said, p. 293.

26 Lewes, *The Physiology of Common Life*, II, 436.

27 Walter Benjamin, *Illuminations*, trans. Harry Zohn, ed. with introduction by Hannah Arendt (London, 1973), p. 206.

28 Lewes, *The Physiology of Common Life*, II, 421; II, 59; II, 58.

29 Lewes, *The Physiology of Common Life*, II, 68.

30 Lewes, *The Physiology of Common Life*, II, 55.

31 Lewes, *The Physiology of Common Life*, II, 55.

32 See Lewes, *The Physiology of Common Life*, II, 58–9.

33 Lewes, *The Physiology of Common Life*, II, 366.

34 Though Lewes does not dwell on the implications of this theory in *The Physiology of Common Life* concerning the possible determining action of dreams upon waking life, they are drawn out in the final volume of *Problems of Life and Mind*:

> To imagine an act is to rehearse it mentally. . . Hence it is that a long-meditated crime becomes at last an irresistible criminal impulse. Indulgence in the imagination of the act has grooved a pathway of

discharge, and set up an abnormal excitability in this direction, which, like a neuralgia, is for ever irritating by its restless impulses, and can only be quieted by discharge on the motor organs.
Problems of Life and Mind: Third Series, II, 459.

35   Eagleton in *Criticism and Ideology*, sees the river as a "symbol of moral drifting and wayward desire" and Maggie's drifting as "a mindless yielding to natural appetite" (p. 113).

36   Lewes, *The Physiology of Common Life*, II, 58.

37   See *Letters*, II, 220. This information is contained in a letter to Sara Hennell, 16 October 1855.

38   William B. Carpenter, *Principles of Mental Physiology* (London, 1874), p. 542. This was an expanded version of the "Outline of Psychology" contained in the 4th and 5th editions of *Principles of Human Physiology* (London, 1852 and 1855).

39   Carpenter, *Principles of Mental Physiology*, p. 543.

40   The review, entitled "The Influence of Rationalism," first appeared in the *Fortnightly Review*, 1 (1865), 43–55, and has since been republished in *Essays*. George Eliot expresses disquiet in this essay with Lecky's treatment of rationalism, for his definition is either too narrow, or too vague. Her severest objections, however (which were expressed in a passage later omitted in the 1884 reprinting) relate to the model of psychology suggested by Lecky's theory of historical development, for he equates the rise of rationalism with the decline of motives for disinterested action. His image of man thus closely resembles that of the rational actor of utilitarian economic theory.

41   Quoted in Bisson, p. 105.

42   Bisson, p. 107.

43   Bisson, p. 108.

44   See Paris, pp. 162–3.

45   Gillian Beer offers a strong feminist reading of the novel's final breakdown of continuity. The concluding flood allows Maggie, she suggests, to escape the pressures of determinism: "For women under oppression such needs can find no real form within an ordering of plot which relies upon sequence, development, the understanding and renunciation of the past, the acceptance of the determined present. The end of *The Mill* is symbolic outcry" ("Beyond Determinism: George Eliot and Virginia Woolf," in *Women Writing and Writing About Women*, ed. Mary Jacobus (London, 1979), pp. 80–99 (pp. 88–9)).

4   *Silas Marner*: A divided Eden

1   *Letters*, III, 41. To John Blackwood, 31 March 1859.

2   Eliot, *"The Lifted Veil," Silas Marner and "Brother Jacob,"* Cabinet Edition (Edinburgh, 1878–80), Ch. 1, p. 287. All references to this edition of the tale will be cited hereafter in the text.

3   See Knoepflmacher, *George Eliot's Early Novels*, pp. 160–1. In this illuminating study, which helped rescue "The Lifted Veil" from the critical oblivion into which it had fallen, Knoepflmacher analyses in depth the role played by "The Lifted Veil" in George Eliot's fictional development.

4   *Letters*, III, 382. To John Blackwood, 24 February 1861.

5   Ch. 1, p. 7. The edition used is the Cabinet edition cited in Note 2.

6 Thus Lecky, Mackay, Comte and Spencer all associated social progress with the increasing growth of rational control. Spencer, indeed, placing these evolutionary beliefs on a physiological basis, argued that the "ever advancing *consensus*" of the mind exemplified the universal Law of Progress governing all natural and social development (*The Principles of Psychology*, p. 485).

7 Knoepflmacher similarly links Maggie's passivity in Stephen's boat to Silas' paralysis which leads to his victimisation by William Dane. Although my conclusions concerning the symmetry of *Silas Marner* differ from those of Knoepflmacher, I am indebted to his discriminating analysis of the ways in which this tale "is a reaction to, as well as a continuation of, *The Mill on the Floss*" (*George Eliot's Early Novels*, pp. 229, 227).

8 Catalepsy, as Oswei Temkin has shown in *The Falling Sickness* (2nd edn, revised, Baltimore, 1971), was confused with forms of epilepsy from ancient times onwards, and the Victorians seemed no nearer than their predecessors to finding an explanation for its occurrence. Although catalepsy was a common term in mid-century psychological discussions (occurring, for example, in the works of Carpenter and Spencer) it was usually introduced as an inexplicable phenomenon. I have been unable to trace any detailed discussion of its causes. It's inexplicable nature seems, indeed, to persist to this day. Thus Robert Simon concludes his technical discussion of Silas' malady with the observation that "Narcolepsy is a baffling illness that defies elucidation by the disciplines of neurology and psychiatry. The precise etiology of this malady remains a mystery today as during the lifetimes of Eliot, Melville and Poe" ("Narcolepsy and the Strange Malady of Silas Marner," *American Journal of Psychiatry*, 123 (Nov. 1966), 601–2, p. 602.

9 Unsigned review in *The Times*, 29 April 1861 in Carroll, ed., *The Critical Heritage*, p. 182.

10 Carroll, ed., *The Critical Heritage*, p. 182.

11 Carroll, ed., *The Critical Heritage*, pp. 183–4.

12 "Demythologizing *Silas Marner*," *English Literary History*, 37 (1970), 226–44 (p. 236). An excellent analysis of the operation of the religion of chance within both Lantern Yard and Raveloe life is offered by Knoepflmacher, *George Eliot's Early Novels*, pp. 238–41, and David R. Carroll, "*Silas Marner*: Reversing the Oracles of Religion," *Literary Monographs*, 1 (Madison, Wisconsin, 1967), 165–200 (pp. 171–8).

13 Carroll's formative study reveals how profoundly George Eliot was influenced by the doctrines of Feuerbach in her writing of *Silas Marner*. James McLaverty traces the impact of Comte on the novel in "Comtean Fetishism in *Silas Marner*," *Nineteenth-Century Fiction*, 36 (1981), 318–36.

14 Comte distinguished his theory from that of earlier historians according to the respect with which he treated the past stages of history: "For that spirit consists in the sense of human continuity, which had hitherto been felt by no one, not even my illustrious and unfortunate predecessor Condorcet" (*System of Positive Polity*, I, 50).

15 See *Letters*, IV, 96–7 for George Eliot's description of her aims.

16 Unsigned review, *Westminster Review*, 76 (July, 1861), 280–2, reprinted in Carroll, ed., *The Critical Heritage*, pp. 186–8 (p. 187).

17 See the discussion of "our instructed vagrancy" (Bk VI, Ch. 9, I, 414).

18 Alexander Bain, *The Emotions and the Will*, 3rd edn (New York, 1876), pp. 534, 537.

19   Summarising his objections to Lewes' theories Bain concluded: "It seems
      to me, therefore, that what determines the unity of consciousness, as show-
      ing which local currents have found means to activate the collective
      currents, is the unity of the *executive*" (*The Emotions and the Will*, p.
      591).

20   Lewes, *The Physiology of Common Life*, II, 5.

21   Karl Marx, *Selected Writings*, ed. David McLellan (Oxford, 1977), p. 442.

22   David Friedrich Strauss, *The Life of Jesus, Critically Examined*, trans.
      from 4th German edn Marian Evans (London, 1846), I, 64.

23   *Letters*, III, 382. To John Blackwood, 24 February 1861.

24   Spencer, *The Principles of Psychology*, p. 532.

25   Spencer, *The Principles of Psychology*, p. 526.

26   Spencer's theories of progressive social evolution were founded on the
      premise that unconscious association formed the basis of the individual's
      adaptation to the environment, and thence of the race's progressive
      development as these "forms of thought" were transmitted to offspring.
      Since relations to the environment once established are he argues, "uniform,
      invariable, incapable of being absent, or reversed, or abolished, they must
      be represented by irreversible, indestructible connections of ideas" (*The
      Principles of Psychology*, p. 580). The physiological unity of mind is
      taken as a guarantee of essential social continuity and development.
      George Eliot also believed, in a more moderate way, that physiology played
      a role in social evolution. Thus she was vehemently opposed to Buckle's
      theories in *History of Civilization in England* for he held that "there is
      no such thing as *race* or hereditary transmission of qualities" (*Letters*,
      II, 415). Without this physiological transmission of experience, she
      believed, there could be no intrinsic moral advance in history.

27   Lewes, *The Physiology of Common Life*, II, 58.

28   Lewes, *The Physiology of Common Life*, II, 58.

29   Her procedure in this matter does not represent a departure from scientific
      precision, but rather an extension of the principles of linguistic analogy
      that lay behind the development of physiological psychology. In founding
      their science, physiological psychologists did not create an entirely new
      vocabulary but rather drew on existing terms like current, channel, or
      groove, that often carried with them concealed assumptions concerning
      the formation of the natural and social worlds.

30   Lewes, *The Physiology of Common Life*, II, p. 59.

31   In her letter to R. H. Hutton concerning the writing of *Romola* George
      Eliot observed, "I believe there is scarcely a phrase, an incident, an
      allusion, that did not gather its value to me from its supposed subservience
      to my main artistic objects" *Letters*, IV, 96–7.

32   For detailed analysis of the parallels between the lives of Godfrey and
      Silas see Carroll, "*Silas Marner*: Reversing the Oracles of Religion,"
      Knoepflmacher, *George Eliot's Early Novels*, Wiesenfarth, and Bruce K.
      Martin, "Similarity within Dissimilarity: The Dual Structure of *Silas
      Marner*," *Texas Studies in Language and Literature*, 14 (1973), 479–89.

33   Knoepflmacher, *George Eliot's Early Novels*, p. 250.

34   Thus Knoepflmacher sees in *Silas Marner* a "reconciliation through
      fable." He concludes that "In *Silas Marner* it is the 'glue' of George
      Eliot's artistry which resolves the conflicts that had divided her pre-
      viously" (*George Eliot's Early Novels*, p. 254). Although the two dis-
      parate perspectives are finely balanced within the structure of the novel,
      I would argue they are not ultimately resolved.

5 *Romola*: The authority of history

1 R. H. Hutton writing for the *Spectator* observed: "The great artistic purpose of the story is to trace out the conflict between liberal culture and the more passionate form of the Christian faith in that strange era, which has so many points of resemblance with the present" (*Spectator*, 36 (18 July 1863), 2265–7, reprinted in Carroll, ed., *The Critical Heritage*, 198–205 (p. 200)). The reviewer for the *Westminster Review* argued that it was George Eliot's greatest work, but regretted that it had been placed in the fifteenth century since the moral conflicts were those of the other novels. Romola's character was that of the modern English woman (80 (October 1863), 344–52, reprinted in Carroll, ed., *The Critical Heritage*, 213–21 (pp. 214–17)).

2 *Letters*, IV, 300–2 (p. 301). To Frederic Harrison, 15 August 1866.

3 *Letters*, IV, 300.

4 George Eliot, *Romola*, Cabinet Edition, 2 vols. (Edinburgh, 1878–80), I, 2. All references to this edition will be cited hereafter in the text.

5 Roland Barthes, "Historical Discourse," in *Structuralism: A Reader*, ed. Michael Lane (London, 1970), p. 149.

6 *Essays*, p. 447. The "Notes" are taken from Charles Lewes, ed., *Essays and Leaves from a Notebook* (Edinburgh, 1884), and were probably composed, as the editor suggests, sometime between the appearance of *Middlemarch* and *Theophrastus Such*.

7 *Letters*, IV, 96–7. To R. H. Hutton, 8 August 1863.

8 Unpublished manuscript, No. 6, in the Beinecke Rare Book and Manuscript Library, Yale University, p. 310.

9 *Letters*, IV, 49. To Sara Hennell, 14 July 1862. "Of necessity, the book is addressed to fewer readers than my previous works, and I myself have never expected – I might rather say intended – that my book should be as 'popular' in the same sense as the others. If one is to have the freedom to write out one's own varying unfolding self, and not to be a machine always grinding out the same material or spinning the same sort of web, one cannot always write for the same public."

10 J. W. Cross, ed., *George Eliot's Life as Related in her Letters and Journals*, 3 vols. (Edinburgh, 1885), II, 352.

11 *Letters*, VI, 335–6. To John Blackwood, 30 January 1877.

12 The impact of Comtean theory on *Romola* has been studied by J. B. Bullen in "George Eliot's *Romola* as a Positivist Allegory," *Review of English Studies*, 26 (1975), 425–35, and, more extensively, by Felicia Bonaparte in *The Triptych and the Cross: The Central Myths of George Eliot's Poetic Imagination* (New York, 1979). Bullen argues convincingly that Romola's moral growth represents Comte's three stages of humanity, but he fails to take into account George Eliot's own critical questioning of Comte's ideas, and the internal conflicts within the novel which render this image of progression ambiguous. I am in general agreement with Felicia Bonaparte's assessment of Comte's influence, though I feel that, at one stage, she underestimates Comte's respect for the historical past. George Eliot, when insisting "that we must not entirely repudiate our heritage," (p. 117) was not in disagreement with Comte. For Lewes' assessment of Comte's responses to history see Note 16.

13 *Letters*, IV, 96–7. To R. H. Hutton, 8 August 1863.

14 *Letters*, III, 473–4. 4 December 1861. Lewes, writing to Blackwood of

the depth of George Eliot's historical research advises him, "When you see her mind your care is to discountenance the idea of a Romance being the product of an Encyclopedia."

15 Carole Robinson, "*Romola*: A Reading of the Novel," *Victorian Studies*, 6 (1962), 29–42 (p. 30).

16 Comte, *Catéchisme Positiviste* (Paris, 1852), p. 289. George Eliot's copy is in Dr Williams's Library, London. It is impossible to date the annotations in this book, but the back end pages contain details of Comte's life in George Eliot's handwriting, ending with the "Synthèse Subjective 1856." Lewes refers to the *Catéchisme*, in 1860, in sentiments which George Eliot would wholeheartedly have endorsed. Writing to Sara Hennell he advises her that she has misconstrued Comte's attitude to history: "with regard to history I venture to say that no philosopher has ever placed so much emphasis on it, no one has more clearly seen and expressed the truth, that the past rules the present, lives in it, and that we are but the growth and outcome of the past" (*George Eliot Letters*, III, 319, 9–10 July 1860).

17 Comte, *Catéchisme*, p. 228. This passage was marked by George Eliot in her edition.

18 Comte, *System of Positive Polity*, I, 289, 291.

19 Taken from George Eliot's notebook written between 1872–9. T. Pinney, "More Leaves from George Eliot's Notebook," *Huntington Library Quarterly*, 29 (1966), 371.

20 "More Leaves," p. 372.

21 "More Leaves," p. 373.

22 "More Leaves," p. 375.

23 "More Leaves," p. 375.

24 "More Leaves," p. 375.

25 Comte, *Catéchisme*, p. 20. A passage marked by George Eliot in her edition.

26 George Eliot, *Daniel Deronda*, Ch. 63, II, 315.

27 Robinson, p. 39.

28 "From what you know of her, you will not be surprised that she threw some exaggeration and wilfulness, some pride and impetuosity, even into her self-renunciation: her own life was still a drama for her, in which she demanded of herself that her part should be played with intensity" (*The Mill on the Floss*, Bk IV, Ch. 3, II, 38).

29 The portrayal of Romola, Knoepflmacher observes in *Religious Humanism and the Victorian Novel*, "bears some parallels to the emblematic banner of the Positivists" (p. 40). In her copy of the *Catéchisme* George Eliot makes the marginal note, "Symbol of Humanity; Madonna and Child" (p. 207).

30 For a complex analysis of the mythological structure of the entire novel, see Felicia Bonaparte, *The Triptych and the Cross*.

31 *Letters*, IV, pp. 103–4, 23 August 1863. George Eliot wrote to Sara Hennell that "The various strands of thought I had to work out forced me into a more ideal treatment of Romola than I had forseen at the outset – though the "Drifting Away" and the Village with the Plague belonged to my earliest vision of the story and were by deliberate forecast adopted as romantic and symbolical elements."

32 Strauss in his biblical criticism, and Comte, in his Religion of Humanity, tried to return to the original animating spirit which lay behind the creation of the biblical "myths," or "legends" as Strauss terms them.

See *The Life of Jesus*, I, 43.
33 Comte, *Catéchisme*, p. 187.
34 Robinson, p. 41.
35 *Essays*, p. 264.
36 For George Eliot's use of the story of Antigone in *Romola*, see Bonaparte, *The Triptych and the Cross*, particularly pp. 74–5.
37 Darrell Mansell Jr., "A Note on Hegel and George Eliot," *Victorian Newsletter*, 27 (1965), 12–15 (p. 13).
38 In the original *Cornhill* and first and second editions of the novel this passage had read "as every loving woman must." George Eliot's substitution, in the Cabinet edition, of the weaker form "as a loving woman must" perhaps suggests her ambivalent response to the sentiments expressed. I am indebted to Andrew Brown, editor of the forthcoming Clarendon edition of *Romola*, for this information.
39 See *The Physiology of Common Life*, II, 55–9, in which Lewes elaborates his theory of Reflex Action and Reflex Feeling.
40 Lewes, *The Foundations of a Creed*, I, 306.
41 Tito's history confirms Lewes' argument that, "Habits, Fixed Ideas, and what are called Automatic Actions, all depend on the tendency which a sensation has to discharge itself through the readiest channel." (*The Physiology of Common Life*, II, 58.)
42 Thus Bardo observes to Tito that "my mind, as I have often said, was shut up as by a dam; the plenteous waters lay dark and motionless; but you, my Tito, have opened a duct for them, and they rush forward with a force that surprises myself" (Ch. 12, I, 181).
43 Carroll, ed., *The Critical Heritage*, p. 206.
44 *Letters*, IV, 96–7.
45 Comte, *System of Positive Polity*, I, 583.
46 Richard Simpson, "George Eliot's Novels," unsigned review, *Home and Foreign Review*, III (October 1863), 522–49, reprinted in Carroll, ed., *The Critical Heritage*, pp. 221–50 (p. 235).
47 The image recalls that of Tom shooting peas at a "superannuated blue-bottle." Though the darwinian commentary is absent in *Romola*, the implications of the recurrent image are clear.

6 *Felix Holt*: Social and sexual politics

1 George Eliot, *Felix Holt*, Cabinet Edition, 2 vols. (Edinburgh, 1878–80), Epilogue, II, 358. All references to this edition will be cited hereafter in the text.
2 For a discussion of George Eliot's references to egoism in her early letters see Gail Eason Milder, "Sublime Resignation: George Eliot and the Role of Women" (Diss., Harvard, 1973), and *Letters*, I, 6, 12, 23, 42, 52, 90, 93.
3 *Letters*, I, 73. To Mr and Mrs Samuel Evans, 5 December 1840.
4 *Letters*, III, 428, 19 June 1861.
5 *Letters*, V, 125. To Mrs Richard Congreve, 2 December 1849.
6 *Letters*, I, 322. To Mr and Mrs Charles Bray, 4 December 1849.
7 In "Sublime Resignation" Milder explores George Eliot's responses to contemporary theories of women's roles in her letters and essays, and shows how George Eliot came to adopt the theory that women's lives should be characterised by renunciation and duty.

8   F. C. Thomson, "The Genesis of *Felix Holt*," *Proceedings of the Modern Language Association*, 74 (1959), 576–84 (p. 576).

9   M. Wolff, "The Uses of Context: Aspects of the 1860's," *Victorian Studies*, 9, Suppl. (1965), 47–63 (p. 54).

10 Thomson, "The Genesis of *Felix Holt*," p. 577.

11 George Eliot, "Address to Working Men, by Felix Holt," *Blackwood's Edinburgh Magazine*, 103 (January, 1868), 1–11, reprinted in *Essays*, pp. 415–30 (pp. 418–19). All references to this essay will be cited hereafter in the text.

12 Comte, *System of Positive Polity*, I, 109.

13 Comte, *System of Positive Polity*, I, 116.

14 Spencer, *The Principles of Psychology*, p. 472.

15 *Essays*, p. 264.

16 Comte, *Positive Philosophy*, II, 472.

17 Arnold's articles, which were to form *Culture and Anarchy*, appeared in 1866. In "The Uses of Context: Aspects of the 1860's" Wolff draws a parallel between *Felix Holt*, *Culture and Anarchy* and Carlyle's *Shooting Niagara: and After?* (London, 1867) which was also published at this time. All three authors were concerned with the replacement of religion by faith in liberty, and all looked to the creation of a spiritual authority "embodied in certain people whose ideals set them above and beyond the limitations of ordinary life" (p. 56). All "were united in their efforts to substitute for the threatened and fatal egalitarian license some sort of aristocratic authority which would revive the old hierarchic values of reverence, obedience, and perfection; and they were willing, if they had to, to fall back on any sort of aristocratic authority" (p. 56).

18 Matthew Arnold, *Culture and Anarchy* (London, 1869), p. 12.

19 *Letters*, IV, 285, 19 July 1866.

20 T. R. Tholfsen, "The Intellectual Origins of Mid-Victorian Stability," *Political Science Quarterly*, 86 (1971), 57–91 (p. 66).

21 *English Chartist Circular*, 1 : 9 (1861), cited in Tholfsen, p. 84.

22 David Craig, "Fiction and the Rising Industrial Classes," *Essays in Criticism*, 17 (1967), 64–73 (p. 70).

23 Roger Cooter, "The Cultural Meaning of Popular Science: Phrenology and the Organization of Consent in Nineteenth-Century Britain" (Diss., Cambridge, 1978). See also "Phrenology: The Provocation of Progress," *History of Science*, 14 (1976), 211–34.

24 See Robert M. Young, *Mind, Brain and Adaptation in the Nineteenth Century: Cerebral Localization and its Biological Context From Gall to Ferrier* (Oxford, 1970), Ch. 5 "Herbert Spencer: Phrenology, Evolutionary Associationism and Cerebral Localization."

25 Spencer, *Essays, Second Series* (London, 1863), p. 168.

26 Eliot, *Felix Holt, the Radical*, Autograph Manuscript Notebook, No. 10, Beinecke Rare Book and Manuscript Library, Yale University.

27 Haight, *George Eliot, A Biography*, p. 382.

28 W. F. T. Myers, "Politics and Personality in *Felix Holt*," *Renaissance and Modern Studies*, 10 (1966), 5–33.

29 Charlotte Bronte, *Shirley*, 3 vols. (London, 1849), Ch. 14, III, 314. All references to this edition will be cited hereafter in the text.

30 Anon., "Social Science," *Blackwood's Edinburgh Magazine*, 90 (1861), 463–78 (p. 468).

31 A point noted by the Marxist–Feminist Literature Collective in "Women's Writing: *Jane Eyre, Shirley, Villette*, and *Aurora Leigh*," in *Ideology and*

Consciousness, 3 (Spring, 1978), 27–48. See T. J. Wise and J. A. Symington, eds., *The Brontes: Their Lives, Friendships and Correspondence,* 4 vols. (London, 1932), II, 202 : "At the same time, I conceive that when patience has done its utmost and industry its best, whether in the case of women or operatives, and when both are baffled, and pain and want triumph, the sufferer is free, is entitled at last to send up to Heaven any piercing cry for relief, if by that cry he can hope to obtain succour."

32   "Social Science," p. 470.

33   *Letters,* VIII, 402–3. To John Morley, 14 May 1867. This letter is a more complete version of that printed in *Letters,* IV, 364. In the earlier printing the quotation had read : "And in the thorough recognition of that worse share, I think there is a basis for a sublimer recognition in women and a more regenerating tenderness in man." In the second printing "sublimer recognition" is altered to "sublimer resignation," though Gordon Haight does not draw attention to this change.

34   *Letters,* IV, 390. To Sara Hennell, 2 October 1867.

35   *Letters,* IV, 425. To Mme Eugene Bodichon, March 1868.

36   *Letters,* IV, 467–8. To Emily Davies, 8 August 1868.

37   *Letters,* IV, 468.

38   Myers, "Politics and Personality," p. 27.

39   She observes, for example, in a letter to Mrs Henry Houghton in 1853 that she has become happier "because I have better learned that as Comte and other wise men said, 'Notre vraie destinée se compose de *resignation* et *d'activité*'" (*Letters,* II, 134). She still endorses these sentiments 25 years later. Writing to Charles Ritter in 1878 she argues that "The great division of our lot is that between what is immodifiable and is the object of resignation and that which is modifiable by hopeful activity – by new conceptions and new deeds" (*Letters,* VII, 56). Resignation, however, seems to play the dominant role, whether in the "sublimer resignation" she prescribes for women, or in the "*absolute* resignation" which she recommends to Clifford Allbut as a substitute for religion (*Letters,* IV, 499).

40   This argument was made by Milder in relation to *Scenes of Clerical Life.*

41   Comte, *Positive Philosophy,* II, 136.

42   Comte, *Positive Philosophy,* II, 135–6.

43   Comte, *System of Positive Polity,* II, 256.

44   In *Shirley,* sewing for the Jew basket stands as a symbol of the enforced pettiness and futility of women's required role. Shirley, summoned by Louis, arrives with sewing in hand, in "neat indoor dress and silk apron. This was no Thalestris from the fields, but a quiet domestic character from the fireside. Mr. Moore had her at advantage." The very act of sewing creates the required submissive character.

45   See Note 16.

7   *Middlemarch*: An experiment in time

1   George Eliot, *Middlemarch,* Cabinet Edition, 3 vols. (Edinburgh, 1878–80), Prelude, I, p. 2. All references to this edition are cited hereafter in the text.

2   In Lewes' *The Study of Psychology,* which George Eliot prepared for publication, there occurs the observation that we may "term History an experiment instituted by Society, since it presents conspicuous variations

of mental reactions under varying social conditions" (p. 152). In writing the history of *Middlemarch,* George Eliot was instituting her own experiment, creating her own experimental conditions.

3   My interpretation of George Eliot's fictional methodology differs from that of Paris who views her as a "militant empiricist" throughout her career (p. 73). I would argue that the theory of realism which she defined in her review of Ruskin's *Modern Painters* (see Paris, p. 26 and Chapter 4) only applies to her earlier work. Although Paris views all George Eliot's novels as "experiments," I would suggest that the term should perhaps be more narrowly applied to *Middlemarch* and *Daniel Deronda* in order to distinguish the radical changes which occur in her methodology in these works.

4   For discussion of this point see Mason, *"Middlemarch* and Science," pp. 151, 162; Beer, "Plot and the Analogy with Science," pp. 138, 144–5; Levine "George Eliot's Hypothesis of Reality," pp. 12–13.

5   Claude Bernard, *Leçons de Physiologie Expérimentale Appliquée à la Médicine,* II, 12. This passage was marked by Lewes in his copy which is now held in Dr Williams's Library. In *Sea-side Studies,* he refers the reader to it, observing that Bernard "warns us against attempting to deduce a function from mere inspection of the organ, without seeing that organ in operation, and applying to it the test of experiment" (p. 153). As this quotation might suggest, Lewes' own theories were extensively influenced by Bernard, who forms a constant point of reference throughout Lewes' work. Lewes' diaries and journals in the Beinecke Rare Book and Manuscript Library at Yale University illustrate his extensive reading of Bernard throughout his career. Thus, though we by no means have a full record, we can glean the following pattern of his reading in Bernard.

   1858, 24 April, *Leçons de Physiologie Expérimentale Appliquée à la Médicine,* 2 vols. (Paris, 1855–6).

   1859, 29 Jan. *Leçons sur les Properiétés Physiologiques et les Altérations Pathologiques des Liquides de l'Organisme,* 2 vols. (Paris, 1859).

   1859, 20 March, *Leçons sur la Physiologie et la Pathologie du Système Nerveux,* 2 vols. (Paris, 1858).

   1869, 15 June, Bernard, title unclear.

   1871, 23 March, *Introduction à l'Étude de la Médicine Expérimentale* (Paris, 1865).

   1872, 6 September, *Système Nerveux.*

   1875, 15 Jan., *Leçons sur les Propriétés des Tissus Vivants* (Paris, 1866).

   1875, 28 Feb., Bernard, title unclear.

   1875, 22–25 July, *Système Nerveux.*

   All these books are amongst the collection of Bernard books in the George Henry Lewes collection in Dr Williams's Library and are all extensively marked by Lewes (see William Baker's *Catalogue,* pp. 17–18). Others which are heavily marked included, *La Science Expérimentale* (Paris, 1878) (these markings are not noted by Baker), and *Leçons sur les Effets des Substances Toxiques et Médicamenteuses* (Paris, 1857).

6   G. H. Lewes, *The Foundations of a Creed,* I, 296. Lewes was working on this volume while George Eliot was writing *Middlemarch.*

7   Bernard, *Experimental Medicine,* p. 18.

8   See *The Foundations of a Creed,* I, 26.

9   Bernard, *Experimental Medicine,* p. 26.

10 Bernard, *Experimental Medicine*, p. 34.

11 Lewes, *The Foundations of a Creed*, I, 296; II, 28.

12 See Note 5.

13 George Eliot observes, in a letter to Mrs Gaskell written in 1859, that, "I was conscious, while the question of my power was still undecided for me, that my feeling towards Life and Art had some affinity with the feeling which had inspired *Cranford* and the earlier chapters of *Mary Barton*" (*Letters*, III, 198). The spirit of *Cranford*, which George Eliot read for the first time in 1857, lies behind *Scenes of Clerical Life* and *Adam Bede*.

14 Lewes, *The Foundations of a Creed*, II, 18.

15 Lewes, *The Foundations of a Creed*, I, 128.

16 Lewes, *The Foundations of a Creed*, I, 124.

17 For an extended analysis of chapter construction in *Middlemarch* see John Holloway, "Narrative Process in *Middlemarch*," in *Narrative and Structure: Exploratory Essays* (Cambridge, 1979), pp. 38–52.

18 George Eliot, "Notes on Form in Art (1868)," in *Essays*, pp. 431–6 (p. 432).

19 *Essays*, p. 433.

20 This theory was first outlined in "The Philosophy of Style," published in the *Westminster Review* (October, 1852), whilst George Eliot was editor. Spencer, *Essays*, First Series, p. 261.

21 *Essays*, pp. 435–6.

22 J. Hillis Miller, "Narrative and History," *English Literary History*, 41 (1974), 455–73 (p. 468).

23 See Lewes, *The Foundations of a Creed*, II, 27. Levine also discusses this point ("George Eliot's Hypothesis of Reality," p. 8).

24 Lewes had adopted De Blainville's definition from Comte. See *Comte's Philosophy of the Sciences*, pp. 171–3.

25 Lewes, *The Foundations of a Creed*, II, 122–3.

26 Thus Lewes argued that perception of the external world will always be influenced by the individual's general stream of sensation at that time. "Of two men looking from the same window, on the same landscape, one will be moved to unutterable sadness, yearning for the peace of death; the other will feel his soul suffused with serenity and content: the one has a gloomy background of Consciousness, into which the sensations excited by the landscape are merged; the other has a happy background of Consciousness, on which the sensations play like ripples on a sunny lake. The tone of each man's feeling is determined by the state of his general consciousness. . . Consciousness, in the general sense, is the sum total of all our sensibilities, the confluence of many streams of sensation." And, following associationist theory, repetition of the emotion will also recall the scene with which it is associated in memory. *The Physiology of Common Life*, II, 68.

27 See Lewes, *The Physiology of Common Life*, II, 58.

28 In his article "Optic and Semiotic in *Middlemarch*," J. Hillis Miller traces the "family of intertwined metaphors and motifs – the web, the current, the minutely subdivided entity" which occur in the novel and inquires, in a footnote, "What, exactly, is the nature of the resemblance which binds together the members of this family and makes it seem of one genetic stock? Why, if Eliot's goal is to describe what is 'really there,' objectively, must there be more than one model in order to create a total picture?" J. H. Buckley, ed., *The Worlds of Victorian Fiction*, Harvard

English Studies (Cambridge, Mass., 1975), pp. 125–45 (pp. 134–5, fn. 7). I would suggest that all these metaphors can be traced back to the same source in contemporary physiological and psychological theory.

29   Herbert Spencer, *The Principles of Psychology*, 2nd edn, 2 vols. (London, 1870–2), I, 585.

30   Diary entry for 30 May 1870; Manuscript diary, July 1861–December 1877, No. 3, Beinecke Rare Book and Manuscript Library, Yale University.

31   Grove, *On the Correlation of Physical Forces*, p. 211. George Eliot has placed marks and commentary in her copy of this work which is now in Dr. Williams's Library. On p. 213 she has marked Grove's conclusion to this argument: "Thus, matter and force are correlates, in the strictest sense of the word."

32   Lewes, *The Foundations of a Creed*, I, 114.

33   Lewes, *The Foundations of a Creed*, II, 457.

34   Lewes, *The Foundations of a Creed*, I, 144–5.

35   Spencer, *The Principles of Psychology*, 2nd edn, I, 509.

36   Lewes, *The Foundations of a Creed*, I, 121.

37   Spencer, *Social Statics*, p. 279.

38   Herbert Spencer, *The Data of Ethics* (London, 1879), p. 62.

39   Lewes, *The Foundations of a Creed*, I, 156.

40   Lewes, *The Foundations of a Creed*, I, 174.

41   Lewes, *The Foundations of a Creed*, I, 360. In their copy of the work George Eliot has written the marginal comment "Admirable here" beside this passage.

42   George Eliot, or rather, Marian Evans, had published her translation of Feuerbach's *The Essence of Christianity* in 1854, before she embarked on her career as novelist. All her novels, however, as Paris has argued, reveal the impact of Feuerbach's ideas.

43   For an analysis of the role of myth in *Middlemarch* see Gillian Beer, "Myth and the Single Consciousness: *Middlemarch* and 'The Lifted Veil,' " in Ian Adam, ed., *This Particular Web: Essays on Middlemarch* (Toronto, 1975), pp. 91–115; Brian Swann, "*Middlemarch* and Myth," *Nineteenth-Century Fiction*, 28 (1973–4), 210–14; and U. C. Knoepflmacher, "Fusing Fact and Myth: The New Reality of *Middlemarch*," in Adam, ed., *This Particular Web*, pp. 43–72. I am indebted to all these articles in my discussion of myth.

44   A point made by Swann, "*Middlemarch* and Myth," p. 213.

45   Beer, "Myth and the Single Consciousness," p. 105.

46   For a good analysis of the function of language and dialogue in *Middlemarch* see Robert Kiely, "The Limits of Dialogue in *Middlemarch*," in J. H. Buckley, ed., *The Worlds of Victorian Fiction*, pp. 103–24.

47   Lewes, in describing his conception of the mind, used the image of a palimpsest. For discussion of this point see Chapter 8, Notes 31 and 32.

48   Dorothea, when first encountered in Rome, is standing next to a statue of Ariadne (Ch. 19, I, 288).

49   Le déterminisme du phénomène initial une fois saisi sera le fil d'Ariane qui dirigera l'expérimentateur, et lui permettra toujours de se retrouver dans le labyrinthe en apparance si obscur des phénomènes physiologiques et pathologiques.
Bernard, "Du Progrès dans les Sciences Physiologiques," *Revue des Deux Mondes*, 58 (1865), 653. The quotation is taken from a section marked by Lewes in his copy.

50 Lewes, *The Foundations of a Creed*, I, 26.

51 *Letters*, IV, 472. To Clifford Allbutt, August 1868.

52 Lewes, *The Foundations of a Creed*, II, 27.

53 See Paris, p. 190.

54 My interpretation of the Lewes passage differs from that of George Levine who argues that: "Such a theory of perception and of the quest for scientific truth is simultaneously intellectual and moral. 'Altruism,' that Comtean ideal, is both a condition of organic relationship and a moral category; the discovery of the reality of that relationship – the quest for which impels the organization of novels like *Bleak House*, as well as *Middlemarch* – is a moral discovery" ("George Eliot's Hypothesis of Reality," p. 8). I would suggest, however, that, like Lewes and Eliot, Levine is imposing a moral interpretation on an epistemological principle. There is, in *Middlemarch*, an internal conflict between the underlying moral premises of altruism and the form of the social relations actually portrayed.

55 Collins, "G. H. Lewes Revised: George Eliot and the Moral Sense," p. 491. Collins prints here Lewes' own original draft of this section and George Eliot's final version. The imagery is all George Eliot's own.

56 See Pratt and Neufeldt, eds., *George Eliot's Middlemarch Notebooks*, p. 101, n. 4.

8 *Daniel Deronda*: Fragmentation and organic union

1 The most famous example of this form of assessment is to be found in F. R. Leavis' *The Great Tradition* (London, 1948).

2 Bernard, *Experimental Medicine*, trans. Green, p. 50.

3 Bernard, *Experimental Medicine*, p. 88.

4 Bernard Fontenelle, *Entretiens sur la Pluralité des Mondes*, 4th edn (Paris, 1866), p. 129. A heavily marked copy of this edition is in the George Eliot – George Henry Lewes Collection in Dr Willliams's Library.

5 Lewes, *The Foundations of a Creed*, I, 47.

6 Lewes, *The Foundations of a Creed*, I, 317–18. See also I, 339.

7 See Ch. 41, II, 354.

8 *Letters*, VI, 216–17. To Dr Joseph Frank Payne, 25 January 1876. See Paris, pp. 116–17 for discussion of this passage which, he argues, "is the most revealing statement George Eliot ever made about the role of art in her quest for values." Implicit in Paris' statement is the assumption that George Eliot's observation applies equally to all her novels. I would suggest, however, that, in its emphasis on ideal construction, and future possibility rather than present reality, it most closely defines George Eliot's perspective in her final works.

9 *Letters*, VI, 166; 19 August 1875.

10 Levine links this transformative power directly to scientific practice. Mordecai, he argues, has "a working hypothesis: that Deronda is a Jew. Like a good scientist, he experiments as though the hypothesis were true, and he awaits a final verification. The hypothesis, meanwhile, helps create the conditions that make it true" ("George Eliot's Hypothesis of Reality," p. 5). Though Mordecai does not actually create the conditions that make Daniel a Jew, he does help create Daniel's predisposition to accept his role as disciple.

11 Gillian Beer has suggested that plot, within all nineteenth-century novels, is self-verifying: "It projects the future and then gives real form to its

predictions. Thus, it is self-verifying: its solutions confirm the validity of the clues proposed" ("Plot and the Analogy with Science," p. 137). In *Daniel Deronda* this process holds true not only at the level of narrative organisation, but also for the characters themselves, since George Eliot deliberately endows them with second sight.

12   Bernard, *Experimental Medicine*, p. 53. Comte had made a similar theoretical pronouncement. See Chapter 2, Note 9.

13   Bernard, *Experimental Medicine*, p. 54: "It follows from the above that if a phenomenon in an experiment had such a contradictory appearance that it did not necessarily connect itself with determinate causes, then reason should reject the fact as non-scientific."

14   Bernard, *Experimental Medicine*, p. 53. See Beer, "Plot and the Analogy of Science," p. 138.

15   Lewes, *The Foundations of a Creed*, I, 317.

16   See Chapter 7, Notes 5 and 6.

17   The quotation is from a passage underlined in George Eliot and Lewes' copy of James Sully, *Sensation and Intuition: Studies in Psychology and Aesthetics* (London, 1874), p. 138. It is taken from the essay entitled "The Genesis of the Free-Will Doctrine" which has been heavily annotated. In his record of their reading Lewes lists Sully's *Sensation and Intuition* on 12 July 1874, and then on many subsequent dates (Diary, 1874, Beinecke Rare Book and Manuscript Library, Yale University). A strong bond existed between George Eliot, Lewes, and Sully, giving rise to close interconnections in their work. In *Sensation and Intuition* Sully evinces admiration both for George Eliot and Lewes. In the essay "On some elements of Moral Self-Culture" he observes: "However systematic his ethical studies may have been, one will pretty certainly discover a new grandeur in virtue and a new foulness in base living after reading a play by Shakespeare or a story by Eliot" (p. 152). In "The Relation of the Evolution Hypothesis to Human Psychology" he states that he hopes to solve "a question recently raised by Mr. Lewes in his *Problems of Life and Mind*, namely, that of the dependence of psychology on sociological data" (p. 12). The question he addresses is that with which I am here concerned – the relationship between the individual and the social medium. Sully was to help George Eliot to prepare the Third Series of *Problems of Life and Mind* for publication, and he was also to write a tribute to Lewes on his death which was published in the *New Quarterly*.

18   Sully, p. 138.

19   Lewes, *Problems of Life and Mind: Third Series*, II, 365.

20   Lewes, *The Foundations of a Creed*, I, 144–5.

21   Wilden, p. 214.

22   Spencer, *Social Statics*, p. 103.

23   Walter Buckley, *Sociology and Modern Systems Theory*, p. 42.

24   Spencer, *Social Statics*, pp. 267–8.

25   For an analysis of the theory of causality underlying Freud's concept of overdetermination see Wilden, p. 35.

26   Carpenter, *Principles of Mental Physiology*, p. 24.

27   Hartmann, III, 284. Lewes records reading this work (in the original German edition) on 15 December 1869 and again in April 1872 (Diary, 1869 and 1872, Beinecke Rare Book and Manuscript Library, Yale University).

28   Spencer, *The Principles of Psychology*, 1st edn, p. 581.

29   Lewes, *The Foundations of a Creed*, I, 150n.

30 Jean Sudrann, *"Daniel Deronda* and the Landscape of Exile," *English Literary History*, 37 (1970), 433–55 (p. 446). Despite this reservation I have found that this article offers an excellent analysis of Gwendolen's psychology.

31 Lewes, *The Foundations of a Creed*, I, 162.

32 In *The Interpretation of Dreams*, Freud quotes the following passage from Sully to illustrate this distinction: "The chaotic aggregations of our night-fancy have a significance and communicate new knowledge. Like some letter in cypher, the dream-inscription when scrutinised closely loses its first look of balderdash and takes on the aspect of a serious intelligible message. Or to vary the figure slightly we may say that like some palimpsest, the dream discloses beneath its worthless surface characters traces of an old and precious communication." *Complete Psychological Works of Sigmund Freud*, trans. J. Strachey (London, 1953–66) IV, 135n.

33 Lewes, *The Physical Basis of Mind*, p. 359.

34 For an interesting discussion of this issue from the perspective of psychoanalysis see Laurence Lerner, "The Education of Gwendolen Harleth," *Critical Quarterly*, 7 (1965), 355–64 (p. 359).

35 In *The Foundations of a Creed* Lewes employs the image of a web to illuminate the ways in which his theory of organism and medium interaction challenged the traditional division drawn between subject and object: "I regard the Subject in no such alienation from the Object; and regard Perception as the assimilation of the Object by the Subject, in the same way that Nutrition is the assimilation of the Medium by the Organism. Out of the general web of Existence certain threads may be detached and rewoven into a special group – the Subject, – and this sentient group will in so far be different from the larger group – the Object; but whatever different arrangement the threads may take on, they are always threads of the original web, they are not different threads" (I, 188–9).

     In the final volume of *Problems of Life and Mind* Lewes, uses the image of a web to express his theory that the processes of the mind do not obey the seriation of conscious thought: "We have seen that the discriminated experiences comprised under Attention must be regarded as a *series*; but the true comparison for sensorial reaction is that of a *web*. The attitude of the Sensorium is a fluctuating attitude which successively traverses and retraverses all the positions of the sensorial field, and which thus successively brings now one and now the other point into the daylight, leaving the others momentarily obscured though still impressing the sentient organism" (*Third Series*, II, 217).

36 See Ch. 54, III, 208; and Ch. 64, III, 333.

37 Elinor Shaffer in *"Kubla Khan" and The Fall of Jerusalem: The Mythological School of Biblical Criticism, and Secular Literature 1770–1880* (Cambridge, 1975), draws attention to George Eliot's use of Feuerbach's conception of the "I and Thou" relationship in *Daniel Deronda*. In emphasising ideas concerning the sexual basis of religion, and George Eliot's critique of Daniel's delusions, however, she draws conclusions which differ from my own.

38 L. Feuerbach, *The Essence of Christianity*, trans. Marian Evans (London, 1854), p. 158.

39 *Letters*, VII, 161; 10 June 1879.

40 Mr Gascoigne, when advising Gwendolen to marry, observes, "you hold your fortune in your own hands – a fortune such as rarely happens to a girl in your circumstances – a fortune in fact which almost takes the

question out of the range of mere personal feeling, and makes your acceptance of it a duty. If Providence offers you power and position – especially
when unclogged by any conditions that are repugnant to you – your course
is one of responsibility, into which caprice must not enter" (Ch. 13, I,
210). Mr Gascoigne has clearly appropriated religious conceptions of
Providence and duty into his own materialistic world view. The ambiguity
surrounding the term "fortune" is significant: fortune in life seems
inseparable from monetary wealth.

Conclusion

1   Though there is, of course, evidence of other projected novels (notably
    one dealing with the Napoleonic war) I would suggest that, actually to
    complete them, George Eliot would have had either to discard the frame-
    work of organicism, or to retreat from the radical social vision and
    methodology of *Daniel Deronda*.
2   George Eliot, *Impressions of Theophrastus Such*, Cabinet Edition (Edin-
    burgh, 1878–80), p. 286. All references to this edition will be cited here-
    after in the text.
3   Compare George Eliot's statement of artistic purpose in "The Natural
    History of German Life," with Theophrastus' scorn of falsity in "Debas-
    ing the Moral Currency."

      It is not so very serious that we should have false ideas about evanescent
      fashions – about the manners and conversation of beaux and duchesses;
      but it *is* serious that our sympathy with the perennial joys and struggles,
      the toil, the tragedy, and the humour in the life of our more heavily-
      laden fellow-men, should be perverted, and turned towards a false
      object instead of the true one (p. 271).

      It is a small matter to have our palaces set aflame compared with the
      misery of having our sense of a noble womanhood, which is the
      inspiration of a purifying shame, the promise of life-penetrating affec-
      tion, stained and blotted out by images of repulsiveness (p. 153).
4   Said, p. 293.

Select bibliography

The bibliography is divided into two sections.
1 A Primary Sources.
   B Works Consulted in the George Eliot–George Henry Lewes Collection in Dr Williams's Library, London.
2 Secondary sources.

PRIMARY SOURCES

Baker, William. *Some George Eliot Notebooks: An Edition of the Carl H. Pforzheimer Library's George Eliot Holograph Notebooks Mss. 707, 708, 709, 710, 711. Vol. 1, Ms. 707 and Vol. 3, Ms. 711*, Salzburg, 1976 and 1980.

The George Eliot–George Henry Lewes Library: An Annotated Catalogue of their Books at Dr. Williams's Library, London, London, 1977.

Cross, J. W., ed. *George Eliot's Life as Related in Her Letters and Journals*, Cabinet edn, 3 vols., Edinburgh, 1885.

Eliot, George. Review of R. W. Mackay, *The Progress of the Intellect*. *Westminster Review*, 54 (January 1851), 353–68.

"The Creed of Christendom." *Leader*, 2 (20 September 1851), 897–9.

Review of Carlyle, *Life of John Sterling*, "Contemporary Literature of England." *Westminster Review*, 57 (January 1852), 247–51.

"Woman in France: Madame de Sablé." *Westminster Review*, 62 (October 1854), 448–73.

"The Romantic School of Music." *Leader*, 5 (28 October 1854), 1027–8.

"The Art of the Ancients." *Leader*, 6 (17 March 1855), 257–8.

"Memoirs of the Court of Austria." *Westminster Review*, 63 (April 1855), 303–35.

"Westward Ho!" *Leader*, 6 (19 May 1855), 474–5.

"Three Months in Weimar." *Fraser's Magazine*, 51 (June 1855), 699–706.

"Meander and the Greek Comedy." *Leader*, 6 (16 June 1855), 578–9.·

"Liszt, Wagner, and Weimar." *Fraser's Magazine*, 52 (July 1855), 48–62.

"Belles Lettres." *Westminster Review*, 64 (July 1855), 288–307.

"Lord Brougham's Literature." *Leader*, 6 (7 July 1855), 652–3.

"The Morality of Wilhelm Meister." *Leader*, 6 (21 July 1855), 703.

"The Future of German Philosophy." *Leader*, 6 (28 July 1855), 723–4.

"Life and Opinions of Milton." *Leader*, 6 (4 August 1855), 750.

"Love in the Drama." *Leader*, 6 (25 August 1855), 820–1.

"Heine's Poems." *Leader*, 6 (1 September 1855), 843–4.

"Michelet on the Reformation." *Leader*, 6 (15 September 1855), 892.

"German Mythology and Legend." *Leader*, 6 (22 September 1855), 917–18.

"Evangelical Teaching: Dr. Cumming." *Westminster Review*, 64 (October 1855), 436–62.

"Belles Lettres." *Westminster Review*, 64 (October 1855), 596–615.

"Margaret Fuller and Mary Wollstonecraft." *Leader*, 6 (13 October 1855), 988–9.

"Translations and Translators." *Leader*, 6 (20 October 1855), 1014–15.

"Thomas Carlyle." *Leader*, 6 (27 October 1855), 1034–5.

"Life of Goethe." *Leader*, 6 (3 November 1855), 1058–61.

"German Wit: Heinrich Heine." *Westminster Review*, 65 (January 1856), 1–33.

"Belles Lettres." *Westminster Review*, 65 (January 1856), 290–312.

"The Shaving of Shagpat." *Leader*, 7 (5 January 1856), 15–17.

"Rachel Gray." *Leader*, 7 (5 January 1856), 19.

"Introduction to Genesis." *Leader*, 7 (12 January 1856), 41–2.

"History of German Protestantism." *Leader*, 7 (9 February 1856), 140.

"The Poets and Poetry of America." *Leader*, 7 (1 March 1856), 210.

"The Antigone and Its Moral." *Leader*, 7 (29 March 1856), 306.

"Art and Belles Lettres." *Westminster Review*, 65 (April 1856), 625–50.

"Church History of the Nineteenth Century." *Leader*, 7 (5 April 1856), 331–2.

"The Court of Austria." *Leader*, 7 (12 April 1856), 352–3.

"Who Wrote the Waverley Novels?" *Leader*, 7 (19 April 1856), 375–6.

"Story of a Blue-Bottle." *Leader*, 7 (26 April 1856), 401–2.

"Heine's Book of Songs." *Saturday Review*, 1 (26 April 1856), 523–4.

"Margaret Fuller's Letters from Italy." *Leader*, 7 (17 May 1856), 475.

"Pictures of Life in French Novels." *Saturday Review*, 2 (17 May 1856), 69–70.

"The Art and Artists of Greece." *Saturday Review*, 2 (31 May 1856), 109–10.

"The Natural History of German Life." *Westminster Review*, 66 (July 1856), 51–79.

"Belles Lettres and Art." *Westminster Review*, 66 (July 1856), 257–78.

"A Tragic Story." *Leader*, 7 (19 July 1856), 691.

"The Lover's Seat." *Leader*, 7 (2 August 1856), 735–6.

"Ferny Combes." *Leader*, 7 (16 August 1856), 787.

"Recollections of Heine." *Leader*, 7 (23 August 1856), 811–12.

"Felice Orsini." *Leader*, 7 (30 August 1856), 835.

"Sight-seeing in Germany and the Tyrol." *Saturday Review*, 2 (6 September 1856), 424–5.

"Silly Novels by Lady Novelists." *Westminster Review*, 66 (October 1856), 442–61.

"Belles Lettres." *Westminster Review*, 66 (October 1856), 566–82.

"Worldliness and Other-Worldliness: The Poet Young." *Westminster Review*, 67 (January 1857), 1–42.

"History, Biography, Voyages and Travels." *Westminster Review*, 67 (January 1857), 288–306.

"Belles Lettres." *Westminster Review*, 67 (January 1857), 306–26.

"A Word for the Germans." *Pall Mall Gazette*, 1 (7 March 1865), 201.

"Servants' Logic." *Pall Mall Gazette*, 1 (17 March 1865), 310–11.

"Futile Falsehoods." *Pall Mall Gazette*, 1 (3 April 1865), 470–1.

"Modern Housekeeping." *Pall Mall Gazette*, 1 (13 May 1865), 880.

"The Influence of Rationalism." *Fortnightly Review*, 1 (15 May 1865), 43–55.

"The Grammar of Ornament." *Fortnightly Review*, 1 (15 May 1865), 124–5.

"Address to Working Men, by Felix Holt." *Blackwood's Edinburgh*

Magazine, 103 (January 1868), 1–11.

Manuscript Notebook, Parrish Collection, Princeton University Library.

Manuscript Collection, Beinecke Rare Book and Manuscript Library, Yale University:

1 Autograph Journal 1854–61.
2 Autograph Journal of a trip to Germany, April 14th–October 27th 1858; and Recollections of Italy, 1860.
3 Diary, July 1861–December 1877.
4 Journal of Journeys to Normandy in 1865 and Italy in 1864.
5 Diary: January 1st–December 4th, 1880.
6 Autograph Commonplace Book, with index.
7 Autograph Manuscript Notebook containing poetry and prose written between 1865 and 1869 but copied into this notebook between 1873 and 1876.
8 Autograph Manuscript Notebook, 1880.
9 Autograph Manuscript Notes, probably for a projected novel, January 1876.
10 *Felix Holt, the Radical*; autograph manuscript notebook of memoranda etc. (1861).
11 *Ethica* by Benedictus de Spinoza, parts I–V, autograph manuscript translations (1855).
12 Manuscript Address Book.

The Works of George Eliot, Cabinet Edition, 20 vols., Edinburgh, 1878–80.

Haight, Gordon S., ed. *The George Eliot Letters*, 9 vols., New Haven, 1954–78.

Kitchel, Anna Theresa, ed. *Quarry for Middlemarch*, Berkeley, 1950. Supplement to *Nineteenth-Century Fiction*, 4 (1950).

Lewes, Charles Lee, ed. *Essays and Leaves from a Notebook*, Edinburgh, 1884.

Lewes, George Henry. Manuscript Collection, Beinecke Rare Book and Manuscript Library, Yale University:

1 Autograph Manuscript Notebook (1850–1860).
2 Journal X.
3 Journal XI.
4 Journal XII.
5–12 Eight Autograph Manuscript Diaries 1869–1876.
13 Commonplace book labelled "Extracts."
14 Autograph Manuscript Notebook labelled "Thoughts of G. H. Lewes."

Pinney, Thomas, ed. *Essays of George Eliot*, London, 1963.

"More Leaves from George Eliot's Notebook," *Huntington Library Quarterly*, 29 (1966), 353–76.

Pratt, John Clark and Victor A. Neufeldt, eds. *George Eliot's Middlemarch Notebooks: A Transcription*, Berkeley, 1979.

WORKS CONSULTED IN THE GEORGE ELIOT–GEORGE HENRY
LEWES COLLECTION IN DR WILLIAMS'S LIBRARY LONDON

Agassiz, Louis Jean Rodolphe. *An Essay on Classification*, 1859.

Andrews, James. *The Psychology of Scepticism and Phenomenalism*, Glasgow, 1874.

Aurelius, Antonius Marcus. *The Meditations of the Emperor Marcus Aurelius Antoninus*, trans. from the Greek, 4th edn, 2 vols., Glasgow, 1764.

Bain, Alexander. *The Emotions and the Will*, 2nd edn, London, 1865.
    Mental and Moral Science, London, 1868.
    The Emotions and the Will, 3rd edn, London, 1875.
Bastian, Henry Charlton. *On the 'Muscular Sense' and on the Physiology of Thinking*, London, 1869.
Bernard, Claude. *Leçons de Physiologie Expérimentale Appliquée à la Médicine*, 2 vols., Paris, 1855–6.
    Leçons sur les Effets des Substances Toxiques et Médicamenteuses, Paris, 1857.
    Leçons sur la Physiologie et la Pathologie du Système Nerveux, 2 vols., Paris, 1858.
    Leçons sur les Propriétés Physiologiques et les Altérations Pathologiques des Liquides de l'Organisme, 2 vols., Paris, 1859.
    "Étude sur la Physiologie du Coeur," *Revue des Deux Mondes*, 56 (1865), 236–52.
    "Du Progrès dans les Sciences Physiologiques," *Revue des Deux Mondes*, 58 (1865), 640–63.
    Introduction à l'Étude de la Médicine Expérimentale, Paris, 1865.
    Leçons sur les Propriétés des Tissus Vivants, Paris, 1866.
    La Science Expérimentale, Paris, 1878.
Bray, Charles. *The Philosophy of Necessity; or, Natural Law as Applicable to Moral, Mental and Social Science*, 2nd edn, revised, 1863.
    On Force: its Mental and Moral Correlates; and on that which is supposed to underlie all Phenomena: with Speculations on Spiritualism, London, 1866.
Bridges, John Henry. *The Unity of Comte's Life and Doctrine. A Reply to Strictures on Comte's later writings, addressed to John S. Mill*, London, 1866.
Broughman, Henry. *Dissertations on Subjects of Science Connected with Natural Theology; being the concluding volumes of the new edition of Paley's works*. 2 vols., London, 1839.
Cairnes, John Elliott. *Some Leading Principles of Political Economy Newly Expounded*, London, 1874.
Comte, Auguste. *Catéchisme Positiviste, ou Sommaire Exposition de la Religion Universelle, en onze Entretiens Systematiques entre une Femme et un Prêtre de l'Humanité*, Paris, 1852.
Condillac, Etienne Bonnot de. *La Langue des Calculs*, Paris, 1798.
Drysdale, John James. "Life and the Equivalence of Force," London, 1870.
Dupuy, Eugene. *Examen de Quelques Points de la Physiologie du Cerveau*, Paris, 1873.
Faraday, Michael. *A Course of Six Lectures on the Various Forces of Matter, and their Relations to Each Other*, ed. W. Crookes, New York, 1860.
Fontenelle, Bernard Le. *Entretiens sur la Pluralité des Mondes*, 4th edn, Paris, 1866.
Forbes, Edward. "Shell-Fish: Their Ways and Works," *Westminster Review*, 57 (Jan. 1852), 42–61.
Graham, William. *Idealism: An Essay, Metaphysical and Critical*, London, 1872.
Gray, Asa. *Natural Selection not inconsistent with Natural Theology: A Free Examination of Darwin's Treatise on the Origin of Species, and of its American Reviewers*, London, 1861.
Grove, W. R., *On the Correlation of Physical Forces*, 3rd edn, London, 1855.
Helmholtz, H. "On the Conservation of Force by Dr. H. Helmholtz," un-

identified article.

Hughlings, J. P. *The Logic of Names. An Introduction to Boole's Laws of Thought*, London, 1869.

Huxley, T. H. "The Cell Theory," *The British and Foreign Medico-Chirurgical Review*, October 1853.

Kaufman, David. *George Eliot and Judaism: An Attempt to appreciate Daniel Deronda*, trans. J. W. Ferrier. Edinburgh, 1877.

Lefort, César. *La Méthode de la Science Moderne; est-elle Réelement Positive et Définitive? Introduction à la Construction du Dogma Positiviste par la Découverte de l'Origine Organique de l'Intelligence*, Paris, 1864.

Lewes, G. H. *Aristotle: A Chapter from the History of Science, including Analyses of Aristotle's Scientific Writings*, London, 1864.

Problems of Life and Mind, 5 vols., London, 1874–9.

Littré, Emile. *Conservation, Révolution et Positivisme*, Paris, 1852.

"La Philosophie Positive : M. Auguste Comte et M. J. Stuart Mill," *Revue des Deux Mondes*, 64 (1866), 829–66.

Lloyd, E. M. *The Freedom of the Will, Stated Afresh*, London, 1868.

Locke, John. *An Essay Concerning Human Understanding*, 26th edn, London, 1828.

Ludlow, Harvey. "The Physiological Discoveries of Claude Bernard," January 1854, 54–76. Source of offprint not known.

Maimonides, Moses. *Principles*, ed. H. H. Bernard, Cambridge, 1832.

Maudsley, Henry. *The Physiology of Mind*, London, 1876.

Mill, John Stuart. *Auguste Comte and Positivism*, London, 1865.

Milton, John. *The Poetical Works*, ed. David Masson, 3 vols., London, 1874.

Muller, F. Max. Unsigned review entitled "The Evolution of Language," of Muller's *Lectures on the Science of Language* (London, 1861), E. Renan's *De l'Origine du Langage* (Paris, 1859), H. Spencer's *First Principles* (London, 1862), source unknown.

Unsigned review entitled "Problems in Language and Mythology," of Muller's *Lectures on the Science of Language* delivered at the Royal Institution of Great Britain, 1862 (New York, 1865). Source unknown.

Owen, Richard. "Lyell – On Life and its Successive Development," Review of *The Principles of Geology, A Manual of Elementary Geology*, and the Anniversary Address to the Geological Society. Source unknown.

Rabelais, François. *Oeuvres de François Rabelais*, 2 vols., Paris, 1870–3.

Ribadénéyra, Le Pedro de, S.J. *Les Vies des Saints et fêtes de toute l'Année*, trans. français Abbé E. Duras. 2nd edn, 12 vols., Paris, 1857.

Riche, F. *De l'organicisme*, Paris, 1869.

Salverte, Eusèbe de. *Des Sciences Occultes ou Essai sur la Magie, les Prodiges et les Miracles*, 2 vols., Paris, 1829.

Spencer, Herbert. *First Principles*, London, 1862.

The Classification of the Sciences; to which are added Reasons for dissenting from the Philosophy of M. Comte, 3rd edn, London, 1871.

The Principles of Psychology, 2nd edn, 2 vols., 1870–2.

The Study of Sociology, London, 1873.

The Data of Ethics, London, 1879.

Sully, James. *Sensation and Intuition: Studies in Psychology and Aesthetics*, London, 1874.

Transon, Abel. *De l'Infini ou Metaphysique et Géométrie à l'Occasion d'une Pseudo-Géométrie*, Evreux, 1871.

Tyndall, John and William Francis, eds. *Natural Philosophy*, London, 1853.

Verity, R. *Subject and Object, as Connected with our Double Brain, and a New Theory of Causation,* London, 1870.

Virchow, Rudolf. *Cellular Pathology as based upon Physiological and Pathological Histology: Lectures at Berlin 1858,* trans. Frank Chance, London, 1860.

Wollstonecraft, Mary. *A Vindication of the Rights of Woman. With Strictures on Political and Moral Subjects,* 3rd edn, London, 1796.

SECONDARY SOURCES

Abrams, M. H. *The Mirror and the Lamp. Romantic Theory and the Critical Tradition,* New York, 1953.

Adam, Ian. "A Huxley Echo in *Middlemarch,*" *Notes and Queries,* 209 (1964), 227.

Ed. *This Particular Web: Essays on Middlemarch,* Toronto, 1975.

Allott, Miriam and Geoffrey Tillotson. "*Romola,* and *The Golden Bowl,*" *Notes and Queries,* 198 (1953), 124–5, 223.

Althusser, Louis. *For Marx,* trans. Ben Brewster, Harmondsworth, 1969.

and Etienne Balibar. *Reading Capital,* trans. Ben Brewster, London, 1970, 2nd edn, 1977.

Anon. "The Progress of Fiction as an Art," *Westminster Review,* 4 ns. (1853), 342–74.

Anon. "Social Science," *Blackwood's Edinburgh Magazine,* 90 (1861), 463–78.

Anon. "Review of Max Muller's Second Series," *Blackwood's Edinburgh Magazine,* 96 (1864), 400–16.

Anon. "Mr. Lewes and Metaphysics," *Westminster Review,* 102 (1874), 104–37.

Anon. "George Eliot and Comtism," *London Quarterly Review,* 47 (1876–7), 446–71.

Arnold, Matthew. *Culture and Anarchy,* London, 1869.

Bachelard, Gaston. *The Philosophy of No,* trans. G. C. Waterston, New York, 1968.

Bagehot, Walter. *Physics and Politics: or Thoughts on the application of the Principles of "Natural Selection" and "Inheritance" to Political Society,* London, 1873.

Bain, Alexander. *The Senses and the Intellect,* London, 1855.

The Emotions and the Will, London, 1859; 3rd edn, New York, 1876.

"Mr. G. H. Lewes on the Postulate of Experience," *Mind,* 1 (1876), 146.

Baker, William. "George Eliot's Readings in Nineteenth-Century Jewish Historians: A Note on the Background of *Daniel Deronda,*" *Victorian Studies,* 15 (1972), 463–73.

" 'A Problematic Thinker' to a 'Sagacious Philosopher'; some Unpublished George Henry Lewes–Herbert Spencer Correspondence," *English Studies,* 56 (1975), 217–21.

George Eliot and Judaism, Salzburg, 1975.

Barbour, Ian G. *Myths, Models and Paradigms: The Nature of Scientific and Religious Language,* London, 1974.

Barnes, Barry. *Scientific Knowledge and Sociological Theory* (Monographs in Social Theory), London, 1974.

Barnes, H. E. "Representative Biological Theories of Society," *Sociological Review,* 17 (1925), 120–30; 182–94.

Barthes, R. "Historical Discourse," in *Structuralism: A Reader,* ed. Michael Lane, London, 1970.

Beaty, Jerome. "History by Indirection: The Era of Reform in *Middlemarch*," *Victorian Studies,* 1 (1957), 173–79.

"Visions and Revisions: Chapter 81 of *Middlemarch*," *Proceedings of the Modern Language Association,* 72 (1957), 662–79.

"The Forgotten Past of Will Ladislaw," *Nineteenth-Century Fiction,* 13 (1958), 159–63.

Middlemarch from Notebook to Novel: A Study of George Eliot's Creative Method, Illinois Studies in Language and Literature, Vol. 47, Urbana, Illinois, 1960.

Beer, Gillian. "Myth and the Single Consciousness: *Middlemarch* and 'The Lifted Veil,' " in Adam, ed., *This Particular Web: Essays on Middlemarch,* pp. 91–115.

"Beyond Determinism: George Eliot and Virginia Woolf," in *Women Writing and Writing about Women,* ed. Mary Jacobus, New York, 1979.

"Plot and the Analogy with Science in Later Nineteenth-Century Novelists," in *Comparative Criticism: A Yearbook,* ed. E. S. Shaffer, 2 (1980), 131–49.

Belaval, Yvon. *Philosophers and their Language,* trans. N. Gutersman, Athens, Ohio, 1966.

Bell, C. G. "Mechanistic Replacement of Purpose in Biology," *Philosophy of Science,* 15 (January, 1948), 47–51.

Benjamin, Walter. *Illuminations,* trans. Harry Zohn, ed. with introduction by Hannah Arendt, London, 1973.

Benson, James D. " 'Sympathetic' Criticism: George Eliot's Response to Contemporary Reviewing," *Nineteenth-Century Fiction,* 29 (1975), 428–40.

Benziger, James. "Organic Unity: Leibnitz to Coleridge," *Proceedings of the Modern Language Association,* 66 (1951), 24–48.

Bernard, Claude. *An Introduction to the Study of Experimental Medicine,* trans. Henry C. Green, New York, 1949.

Bisson, L. A. "Proust, Bergson and George Eliot," *Modern Language Review,* 40 (1945), 104–14.

Black, Max. *Models and Metaphors,* Ithaca, New York, 1962.

Blake, Kathleen. "*Middlemarch* and the Woman Question," *Nineteenth-Century Fiction,* 31 (1977), 285–312.

Bock, K. E. "Darwin and Social Theory," *Philosophy of Science,* 22 (1955), 123–34.

Bonaparte, Felicia. *Will and Destiny: Morality and Tragedy in George Eliot's Novels,* New York, 1975.

The Triptych and the Cross: The Central Myths of George Eliot's Poetic Imagination, New York, 1979.

Boutroux, Emile. *The Contingency of the Laws of Nature* (1874), trans. F. Rothwell, London, 1916.

Braudy, Leo. *Narrative Form in History and Fiction: Hume, Fielding and Gibbon,* Princeton, New Jersey, 1970.

Bray, Charles. *The Philosophy of Necessity; or, The Law of Consequences; as applicable to Mental, Moral and Social Science,* 2 vols., London, 1841.

Brecht, Bertolt. "Against Georg Lukacs," *New Left Review,* 84 (March, 1974).

Breck, A. D., and W. Yourgrau, eds. *Biology, History, and Natural Philosophy*: based on the second International Colloquium held at the University of Denver, New York, 1972.

Bronte, Charlotte. *Shirley*, 3 vols., London, 1849.

Brown, John Crombie. *The Ethics of George Eliot's Works*, 1879, rprt Port Washington, New York, 1969.

Bruford, W. H. "Goethe and some Victorian Humanists," *Publications of the English Goethe Society*, 18 (1948), 34–67.

Buckle, T. H. *History of Civilization in England*, 2 vols., London, 1857–61.

Buckley, J. H. *The Triumph of Time: A Study of the Victorian Concepts of Time, History, Progress and Decadence*, Cambridge, Mass., 1967.

Ed. *The Worlds of Victorian Fiction*, Harvard English Studies, Cambridge, Mass., 1975.

Buckley, W. *Sociology and Modern Systems Theory*, Englewood Cliffs, New Jersey, 1967.

Bullen, J. B. "George Eliot's *Romola* as a Positivist Allegory," *Review of English Studies*, 26 (1975), 425–35.

Burke, Edmund. *Reflections on the Revolution in France*, Dublin, 1790.

Burrow, John W. *Evolution and Society: A Study in Victorian Social Theory*, Cambridge, 1966.

Butwin, Joseph. "The Pacification of the Crowd: From 'Janet's Repentance' to *Felix Holt*," *Nineteenth-Century Fiction*, 35 (1980), 349–71.

Canguilhem, Georges. *Essai Sur Quelques Problèmes Concernant le Normal et le Pathologique*, Publications de la Faculté des Lettres de l'Université de Strasbourg, 100, Paris, 1950.

"Du Développement à l'Évolution au XIX Siècle," in *Thalès: Recueil des Travaux de l'Institut d'Histoire des Sciences et des Techniques de l'Université de Paris*, Paris, 1962.

"The Role of Analogies and Models in Biological Discovery," in *Scientific Change* (Symposium on the History of Science, University of Oxford, 1961), ed. A. C. Crombie, London, 1963.

Études d'Histoire et de Philosophie des Sciences, Paris, 1968.

La Connaissance de la Vie, Paris, 1969.

Cannon, Walter F. "History in Depth: The Early Victorian Period," *History of Science*, 3 (1964), 20–38.

Carlyle, Thomas. *Past and Present*, London, 1843; rprt ed. A. M. D. Hughes, Oxford, 1918.

Selected Essays, ed. Ian Campbell, London, 1972.

The Collected Works, Centenary edn, 30 vols., London, 1896.

Carpenter, William B. *Principles of Human Physiology*, 4th edn, London 1852; 5th edn, 1855.

Principles of Mental Physiology, London, 1874.

Carroll, David R. "Unity through Analogy: An Interpretation of *Middlemarch*," *Victorian Studies*, 2 (1959), 305–16.

"*Felix Holt*: Society as Protagonist," *Nineteenth-Century Fiction*, 17 (1962), 237–52.

"*Silas Marner*: Reversing the Oracles of Religion," *Literary Monographs*, 1 (1967), 165–200.

" 'Janet's Repentance' and the Myth of the Organic," *Nineteenth-Century Fiction*, 35 (1980), 331–48.

Ed. *George Eliot: The Critical Heritage*, London, 1971.

Cassirer, Ernst. "Structuralism in Modern Linguistics," *Word*, 1: 2 (1945), 99–120.

The Problem of Knowledge: Philosophy, Science and History since Hegel, trans. W. H. Woglom and C. W. Hendel, New Haven, 1950.

Chalmers, Thomas. *The Bridgewater Treatises on the Power, Wisdom and*

Goodness of God as manifested in the Creation, 11 vols., London, 1833–6. Vols. I and II.

Charlton, D. G. *Positivist Thought in France during the Second Empire, 1852–1870,* Oxford, 1959.

Chase, Cynthia. "The Decomposition of the Elephants: Double-Reading *Daniel Deronda*," *Proceedings of the Modern Language Association,* 93 (1978), 215–25.

Cockshutt, A. O. J. *The Unbelievers: English Agnostic Thought, 1840–90,* London, 1964.

Coker, F. W. *Organismic Theories of the State: Nineteenth-Century Interpretations of the State of Organism or as Person,* Columbia University Studies in History, Economics etc. 38 (ii), New York, 1910.

Coleridge, Samuel Taylor. *Hints towards the formation of a more comprehensive Theory of Life,* ed. Seth Watson, London, 1848; rprt Farnborough, 1970.

Collingwood, R. G. *The Idea of Nature,* ed. T. M. Knox, Oxford, 1945.

The Idea of History, ed. T. M. Knox, Oxford, 1946.

Collins, K. K. "G. H. Lewes Revised: George Eliot and the Moral Sense," *Victorian Studies,* 21 (1978), 463–92.

"Questions of Method: Some Unpublished Late Essays," *Nineteenth-Century Fiction,* 35 (1980), 385–405.

Comte, Auguste. *The Positive Philosophy of Auguste Comte,* trans. and ed. H. Martineau, 2 vols., London, 1853.

System of Positive Polity or Treatise on Sociology Instituting the Religion of Humanity, trans. J. H. Bridges, Frederic Harrison, E. S. Beesly, Richard Congreve, 4 vols., London, 1875–7.

Cooke, George Willis. *George Eliot: A Critical Study of her Life, Writings and Philosophy,* Boston, 1883.

Cooter, R. J. "Phrenology: The Provocation of Progress," *History of Science,* 14 (1976), 211–34.

"The Cultural Meaning of Popular Science: Phrenology and the Organization of Consent in Nineteenth-Century Britain," Diss., Cambridge, 1978.

Couch, John Philip. *George Eliot in France: A French Appraisal of George Eliot's Writings: 1858–1960,* Chapel Hill, North Carolina, 1967.

Craig, David. "Fiction and the Rising Industrial Classes," *Essays in Criticism,* 17 (1967), 64–73.

Creeger, George R. "An Interpretation of *Adam Bede,*" *English Literary History,* 23 (1956), 218–38.

Dale, P. A. *The Victorian Critic and the Idea of History: Carlyle, Arnold, Pater,* Cambridge, Mass., 1977.

Dallas, E. S. *The Gay Science,* 2 vols., London, 1866.

Darwin, Charles. *On the Origin of Species by Means of Natural Selection, or the Preservation of Favoured Races in the Struggle for Life,* ed. John Burrow from 1st edn, London, 1859; Harmondsworth, 1968.

Darwin, Francis, ed. *The Life and Letters of Charles Darwin,* 2 vols., New York, 1919.

Dickens, Charles. *Bleak House,* Household Edition, London, 1873.

Doody, Margaret Anne. "George Eliot and the Eighteenth-Century Novel," *Nineteenth-Century Fiction,* 35 (1980), 260–91.

Dowden Edward. *Studies in Literature: 1789–1877,* London, 1878.

Duncan, J. S. *Analogies of Organized Beings,* Oxford, 1831.

Eagleton, Terry. *Criticism and Ideology: A Study in Marxist Literary Theory,* London, 1976.

Marxism and Literary Criticism, London, 1976.

Eiseley, Loren C. *Darwin's Century: Evolution and the Men who Discovered it*, London, 1959.

Ellegard, Alvar. *Darwin and the General Reader: The Reception of Darwin's Theory of Evolution in the British Periodical Press, 1859–1872*, Göteborg, 1958.

Ermath, Elizabeth. "Incarnations: George Eliot's Conception of 'Undeviating Law'," *Nineteenth-Century Fiction*, 29 (1975), 273–86.

Espinas, Alfred. *Des Sociétés Animales*, 2nd edn, Paris, 1878.

Everett, Edwin M. *The Party of Humanity: The "Fortnightly Review" and its Contributors 1865–1874*, Chapel Hill, North Carolina, 1939.

Feltes, N. N. "George Eliot and the Unified Sensibility," *Proceedings of the Modern Language Association*, 79 (1964), 130–6.

"George Eliot's 'Pier Glass': The Development of a Metaphor," *Modern Philology*, 67 (1969), 69–71.

Feuerbach, Ludwig. *The Essence of Christianity*, trans. from 2nd German edn, Marian Evans, London, 1854.

Figlio, Karl. "Theories of Perception and the Physiology of Mind in the late Eighteenth Century," *History of Science*, 13 (1975), 177–212.

"The Metaphor of Organization: An Historiographical Perspective on the Bio-Medical Sciences of the early Nineteenth Century," *History of Science*, 14 (1976), 17–53.

Foucault, Michel. *The Archaeology of Knowledge*, trans. A. M. S. Smith, London, 1972.

The Order of Things: An Archaeology of the Human Sciences (translation of *Les Mots et Les Choses*), London, 1974.

Freud, S. *Complete Psychological Works of Sigmund Freud*, trans. J. Strachey, London, 1953–66.

Gallagher, Catherine. "The Failure of Realism: *Felix Holt*," *Nineteenth-Century Fiction*, 35 (1980), 372–84.

Garrett, Peter K. *Scene and Symbol from George Eliot to James Joyce: Studies in Changing Fictional Mode*, New Haven, 1969.

Gaskell, Elizabeth C. *Cranford*, London, 1864.

Gillispie, Charles C. *Genesis and Geology: A Study in the Relations of Scientific Thought, Natural Theology, and Social Opinion in Great Britain, 1790–1850*, Cambridge, Mass., 1951.

"The Encyclopédie and the Jacobin Philosophy of Science: a Study in Ideas and Consequences," in *Critical Problems in the History of Science*, ed. Marshall Clagett, Madison, Wisconsin, 1959.

"Lamarck and Darwin in the History of Science," in H. B. Glass, O. Temkin, W. L. Strauss, Jr, eds., *Forerunners of Darwin: 1745–1859*.

Glass, H. B., O. Temkin, W. L. Strauss, Jr, eds. *Forerunners of Darwin: 1745–1859*, Baltimore, 1968.

Goldberg, Hannah. "George Henry Lewes and Daniel Deronda," *Notes and Queries*, 202 (1957), 356–8.

Goode, John. "*Adam Bede*," in Barbara Hardy, ed., *Critical Essays on George Eliot*.

Goodfield, G. J. *The Growth of Scientific Physiology*, (Nuffield Foundation Unit for the History of Ideas), London, 1960.

Gossman, Lionel. *Medievalism and the Ideologies of the Enlightenment*, Englewood Cliffs, New Jersey, 1972.

Gottlieb, Aviah H. "George Eliot: A Biographical and Intellectual Study," Diss., Cambridge, 1971.

Grabo, Carl. "Science and the Romantic Movement," *Annals of Science*, 4 (1939), 191–205.

Greenberg, Robert A. "Plexuses and Ganglia: Scientific Allusion in *Middlemarch*," *Nineteenth-Century Fiction*, 30 (1976), 33–52.

Greene, John C. "Biology and Social Theory in the Nineteenth Century: Auguste Comte and Herbert Spencer," in *Critical Problems in the History of Science*, ed. Marshall Clagett. Madison, Wisconsin, 1959.

Hagan, John. "*Middlemarch*: Narrative Unity in the Story of Dorothea Brooke," *Nineteenth-Century Fiction*, 16 (1961), 17–32.

Haight, Gordon S. *George Eliot. A Biography*, Oxford, 1968.

"The George Eliot and George Henry Lewes Collection," *Yale University Library Gazette*, 46 (1971), 20–3.

Ed. *The Mill on the Floss*, Riverside edn, Boston, 1961.

Ed. *A Century of George Eliot Criticism*, London, 1966.

Hardy, Barbara. "The Image of the Opiate in George Eliot's Novels," *Notes and Queries*, 4 n.s. (1957), 487–90.

The Novels of George Eliot: A Study in Form, London, 1959.

The Appropriate Form, London, 1971.

Ed. *Middlemarch: Critical Approaches to the Novel*, London, 1967.

Ed. *Critical Essays on George Eliot*, London, 1970.

Harrison, Frederic. "Industrial Co-operation," *Fortnightly Review*, 3 (1866), 477–503.

"The Positivist Problem," *Fortnightly Review*, 6 (1869), 469–93.

Hartmann, Eduard von. *Philosophy of the Unconscious: Speculative Results According to the Inductive Method of Physical Science*, trans. W. C. Coupland, 2nd edn, 3 vols., London, 1893.

Harvey, W. J. "George Eliot and the Omniscient Author Convention," *Nineteenth-Century Fiction*, 13 (1958), 81–108.

The Art of George Eliot, London, 1961.

Hearnshaw, L. S. *A Short History of British Psychology, 1840–1940*, London, 1964.

Henkin, Leo J. *Darwinism in the English Novel, 1860–1910*, New York, 1963.

Herschel, J. F. W. "On the Origin of Force," *Fortnightly Review*, 1 (1865), 435–42.

Hesse, Mary B. *Models and Analogies in Science*, Notre Dame, Indiana, 1970.

Higdon, David L. "George Eliot and the Art of the Epigraph," *Nineteenth-Century Fiction*, 25 (1970), 127–51.

Time and English Fiction, London, 1977.

Hirst, P. Q. *Durkheim, Bernard and Epistemology*, London, 1975.

Social Evolution and Sociological Categories, London, 1976.

Holloway, John. *The Victorian Sage: Studies in Argument*, London, 1953.

"Narrative Process in *Middlemarch*," in *Narrative and Structure: Exploratory Essays*, Cambridge, 1979.

Holmes, F. L. "Claude Bernard and the Milieu Interieur," *Archives Internationales d'Histoire des Sciences*, 16 (1963), 369–77.

Holstrom, John and Laurence Lerner, eds. *George Eliot and Her Readers: A Selection of Contemporary Reviews*, London, 1966.

Hughesdon, P. J. "Spencer, Darwin and the Evolution Hypothesis," *Sociological Review*, 17 (1925), 31–43.

Hulme, Hilda. "*Middlemarch* as Science-Fiction: Notes on Language and Imagery," *Novel*, 2 (1968), 36–45.

Hutton, R. H. *Essays: Theological and Literary*, 2 vols., London, 1871.

Huxley, Thomas Henry. "On the Methods and Results of Ethnology," *Fortnightly Review*, 1 (1865), 255–77.

Lay Sermons, Addresses and Reviews, London, 1870.

Science and Culture and Other Essays, London, 1881.

Evolution and Ethics, London, 1893.

Method and Results: Essays, London, 1894.

The Scientific Memoirs of T. H. Huxley, eds. M. Foster and E. R. Lankester, 4 vols., London, 1898.

Hyde , William J. "George Eliot and the Climate of Realism," *Proceedings of the Modern Language Association*, 72 (1957), 147–64.

Isaacs, Neil D. "*Middlemarch*: Crescendo of Obligatory Drama," *Nineteenth-Century Fiction*, 18 (1963), 21–34.

Jacob, François. *The Logic of Life: A History of Heredity*, trans. Betty E. Spillman, New York, 1973.

Jones, Howard M., I. B. Cohen, eds. *Science before Darwin: a Nineteenth Century Anthology*, London, 1963.

Kaminsky, Alice R. "George Eliot, George Henry Lewes, and the Novel," *Proceedings of the Modern Language Association*, 70 (1955), 997–1013.

George Henry Lewes as Literary Critic, New York, 1968.

Kaminsky, Jack. "The Empirical Metaphysics of G. H. Lewes," *Journal of the History of Ideas*, 13 (1952), 314–32.

Kant, Immanuel. *Critique of Judgment*, trans. with introduction J. H. Bernard, 2nd edn, London, 1914.

Kendrick, Walter M. "Balzac and British Realism: Mid-Victorian Theories of the Novel," *Victorian Studies*, 20 (Autumn, 1976), 5–24.

Kermode, Frank, "Novel, History and Type," *Novel*, 1 (1967), 231–8.

Kiely Robert. "The Limits of Dialogue in *Middlemarch*," in J. H. Buckley, ed., *The Worlds of Victorian Fiction*, pp. 103–24.

Kissane, James. "Victorian Mythology," *Victorian Studies*, 6 (September, 1962), 5–28.

Kitchel, Anna Theresa. "Scientific Influences in the Work of Emile Zola and George Eliot," Diss., Wisconsin, 1921.

George Lewes and George Eliot: A Review of Records, New York, 1933.

Knoepflmacher, U. C. *Religious Humanism and the Victorian Novel: George Eliot, Walter Pater, and Samuel Butler*, Princeton, 1965.

George Eliot's Early Novels: The Limits of Realism, Berkeley, 1968.

"Fusing Fact and Myth: The New Reality of *Middlemarch*," in Adam, ed., *This Particular Web: Essays on Middlemarch*, pp. 43–72.

"*Middlemarch*: An Avuncular View," *Nineteenth-Century Fiction*, 30 (1976), 53–81.

and G. B. Tennyson, eds. *Nature and the Victorian Imagination*, Berkeley, 1977.

and George Levine, eds. "Special Issue: George Eliot, 1880–1980," *Nineteenth-Century Fiction*, 35 (1980), iii.

Kriefall, Luther Harry. "A Victorian Apocalypse: A Study of George Eliot's *Daniel Deronda* and its Relation to David F. Strauss' *Das Leben Jesu*," Diss., Michigan, 1966.

Kroeber, Karl. *Styles in Fictional Structure: The Art of Jane Austen, Charlotte Bronte, George Eliot*, Princeton, 1971.

Lacan, Jacques. *The Language of the Self: The Function of Language in Psychoanalysis*, trans. and notes A. Wilden, London, 1965.

Larkin, Maurice. *Man and Society in Nineteenth-Century Realism: Determinism and Literature*, London, 1977.

Leavis, F. R. *The Great Tradition: George Eliot, Henry James, Joseph Conrad*, London, 1948.

Lecky, W. E. H. *History of the Rise and Influence of the Spirit of Rationalism in Europe*, 2 vols., London, 1865.

Lecourt, Dominique. *Marxism and Epistemology: Bachelard, Canguilhem and Foucault*, trans. Ben Brewster, London, 1975.

Lerner, Laurence. "The Education of Gwendolen Harleth," *Critical Quarterly*, 7 (1965), 355–64.

Levine, George. "Determinism and Responsibility in the Works of George Eliot," *Proceedings of the Modern Language Association*, 77 (1962), 268–279.

"George Eliot's Hypothesis of Reality," *Nineteenth-Century Fiction*, 35 (1980), 1–28.

The Realistic Imagination: English Fiction from Frankenstein to Lady Chatterley, Chicago, 1981.

and W. Madden, eds. *The Art of Victorian Prose*, London, 1968.

Levitt, Ruth. *George Eliot: The Jewish Connection*, Jerusalem, 1975.

Lewes, George Henry. *Comte's Philosophy of the Sciences; Being an Exposition of the Principles of the Cours de Philosophie Positive of Auguste Comte*, London, 1853.

The Biographical History of Philosophy, From its Origin in Greece down to the Present Day, London, 1845; revised edn 1857.

Sea-side Studies at Ilfracombe, Tenby, the Scilly Isles, and Jersey, Edinburgh, 1858.

The Physiology of Common Life, 2 vols., London, 1859–60.

Studies in Animal Life, London, 1862.

Aristotle: A Chapter from the History of Science, including Analyses of Aristotle's Scientific Writings, London, 1864.

The History of Philosophy from Thales to Comte, 3rd edn, 2 vols., London, 1867.

Problems of Life and Mind, 5 vols., London, 1874–9.

    First Series: The Foundations of a Creed, 2 vols., 1874; 1875.

    Second Series: The Physical Basis of Mind, 1877.

    Third Series: 2 vols.; I : *The Study of Psychology: Its Object, Scope and Method*, 1879; II (untitled). 1879.

Literary Criticism of G. H. Lewes, ed. Alice R. Kaminsky, Nebraska, 1964.

"Hegel's Aesthetics: Philosophy of Art," *British and Foreign Review*, 13 (1842), 1–49.

"The Character and Works of Goethe," *British and Foreign Review*, 14 (1843), 78–135.

"The Modern Metaphysics and Moral Philosophy of France," *British and Foreign Review*, 15 (1843), 353–406.

"Spinoza's Life and Works," *Westminster Review*, 39 (1843), 372–407.

"The State of Historical Science in France," *British and Foreign Review*, 16 (1844), 72–118.

"The State of Criticism in France," *British and Foreign Review*, 16 (1844), 327–62.

"The Lady Novelists," *Westminster Review*, 58 (1852), 129–41.

"Life in its Simpler Forms," *Fraser's Magazine*, 55 (1857), 194–203.

"Realism in Art: Recent German Fiction," *Westminster Review*, 70 (1858), 488–518.

"Voluntary and Involuntary Actions," *Blackwood's Edinburgh Magazine*, 86 (1859), 295–306.

"Great Wits, Mad Wits?" *Blackwood's Edinburgh Magazine*, 88 (1860), 302–11.
"Seeing is Believing," *Blackwood's Edinburgh Magazine*, 88 (1860), 381–95.
"Uncivilized Man," *Blackwood's Edinburgh Magazine*, 89 (1861), 27–41.
"Mr. Buckle's Scientific Errors," *Blackwood's Edinburgh Magazine*, 90 (1861), 582–96.
"A Box of Books," *Blackwood's Edinburgh Magazine*, 91 (1862), 434–51.
"The Heart and the Brain," *Fortnightly Review*, 1 (1865), 66–74.
"Reviews of Comte's *A General View of Positivism*, trans. J. H. Bridges and J. S. Mill, *An Examination of Sir William Hamilton's Philosophy*," *Fortnightly Review*, 1 (1865), 280–1, 507–9.
"Auguste Comte," *Fortnightly Review*, 3 (1866), 385–410.
"Spinoza," *Fortnightly Review*, 4 (1866), 395–406.
"Causeries," *Fortnightly Review*, 4 (1866), 246, 506, 637.
"Review of Bain *The Senses and the Intellect* and *The Emotions and the Will*," *Fortnightly Review*, 4 (1866), 767–8.
"Comte and Mill," *Fortnightly Review*, 6 (1866), 385–406.
"Causeries," *Fortnightly Review*, 6 (1866), 759–61, 894.
"The Reign of Law," *Fortnightly Review*, 2 n.s. (1867), 96–111.
"Mr. Darwin's Hypothesis," *Fortnightly Review*, 3 n.s. (April, 1868), 353–73, 611–28, 4 n.s. (1868), 61–80, 492–501.
"Dickens in Relation to Criticism," *Fortnightly Review*, 11 n.s. (1872), 141–54.
"Spiritualism and Materialism," *Fortnightly Review*, 19 n.s. (1876), 479–93, 707–19.
"What is Sensation?" *Mind*, 1 (1876), 157–61.
"The Uniformity of Nature," *Mind*, 1 (1876), 283–4.
"Consciousness and Unconsciousness," *Mind*, 2 (1877), 156–67.
"On the Dread and Dislike of Science," *Fortnightly Review*, 23 n.s. (1878), 805–15.
Lovejoy, A. O. "The Meanings of 'Emergence' and its Modes," *Proceedings of the Sixth International Congress of Philosophy, 1926*, New York, 1927.
"The Meaning of 'Romanticism' for the Historian of Ideas," *Journal of the History of Ideas*, 2 (1941), 257–78.
The Great Chain of Being, Cambridge, Mass., 1942.
Lyell, Charles. *Principles of Geology, Being an Attempt to Explain the Former Changes of the Earth's Surface, by Reference to Causes Now in Operation*, 3 vols., London, 1830–3.
Macherey, Pierre. *A Theory of Literary Production*, trans. Geoffrey Wall, London and Boston, 1978.
Mandelbaum, Maurice. *History, Man and Reason: A Study in Nineteenth-Century Thought*, Baltimore, 1971.
Mansell, Darrell, Jr. "A Note on Hegel and George Eliot," *Victorian Newsletter*, 27 (1965), 12–15.
Manuel, F. E. "From Equality to Organicism," *Journal of the History of Ideas*, 17 (1956), 54–67.
The Prophets of Paris, New York, 1965.
Marcus, Steven. *Representations: Essays on Literature and Society*, London, 1975.
Martin, Bruce K. "Similarity within Dissimilarity: The Dual Structure of *Silas Marner*," *Texas Studies in Language and Literature*, 14 (1973), 479–89.

Marx, Karl. *Capital: a Critique of Political Economy*, Vol. 1. Intro. Ernest Mandel, trans. Ben Fowkes, Harmondsworth, 1976.

Selected Writings, ed. David McLellan, Oxford, 1977.

Marxist–Feminist Literature Collective. "Women's Writing: *Jane Eyre, Shirley, Villette*, and *Aurora Leigh*," *Ideology and Consciousness*, 3 (Spring, 1978), 27–48.

Mason, Michael Y. "*Middlemarch* and History," *Nineteenth-Century Fiction*, 25 (1971), 417–31.

"*Middlemarch* and Science: Problems of Life and Mind," *Review of English Studies*, 22 (1971), 151–69.

Maus, Heinz. *A Short History of Sociology*, London, 1962.

McCabe, Colin. *James Joyce and the Revolution of the Word*, London, 1978.

McGowan, John P. "The Turn of George Eliot's Realism," *Nineteenth-Century Fiction*, 35 (1980), 171–92.

McLaverty, James. "Comtean Fetishism in *Silas Marner*," *Nineteenth-Century Fiction*, 36 (1981), 318–36.

Mendelsohn, E. "Cell Theory and the Development of General Physiology," *Archives Internationales d'Histoire des Sciences*, 16 (1963), 419–29.

"The Biological Sciences in the Nineteenth Century: Some Problems and Sources," *History of Science*, 3 (1964), 39–59.

"Physical Models and Physiological Concepts. Explanation in Nineteenth-Century Biology," *British Journal for the History of Science*, 2 (1965), 201–19.

Milder, Gail Eason. "Sublime Resignation: George Eliot and the Role of Women," Diss., Harvard, 1973.

Mill, John Stuart. *A System of Logic, Ratiocinative and Inductive being a Connected View of the Principles of Evidence and the Methods of Scientific Investigation*, 9th edn, 2 vols., London, 1875.

Nature, The Utility of Religion and Theism, 2nd edn, London 1854.

Auguste Comte and Positivism, London, 1865; rprt Ann Arbor, 1961.

Autobiography, London, 1873.

Essays on Literature and Society, ed. J. B. Schneewind, New York, 1965.

"The Subjection of Women," in *Essays on Sex Equality: J. S. Mill and Harriet Taylor Mill*, ed. Alice S. Rossi, Chicago, 1970.

Miller, J. Hillis. *The Form of Victorian Fiction: Thackeray, Dickens, Trollope, George Eliot, Meredith, and Hardy*, Notre Dame, Indiana, 1968.

"Narrative and History," *English Literary History*, 41 (1974), 455–73.

"Optic and Semiotic in *Middlemarch*," in J. H. Buckley, ed., *The Worlds of Victorian Fiction*, pp. 125–45.

"Ariadne's Thread: Repetition and the Narrative Line," *Critical Inquiry*, 3 (1976), 57–77.

Morley, John. *On Compromise*, London, 1874.

Mozley, Anne. "Egoism," *Blackwood's Edinburgh Magazine*, 102 (1867), 342–52.

Mulhern, Francis. " 'Ideology and Literary Form' – a Comment," *New Left Review*, 91 (1975), 80–7.

Muller, Herbert J. *Science and Criticism*, New Haven, 1943.

Muller, F. Max, *Lectures on the Science of Language*, First and Second Series, London, 1861–4.

Myers, William F. T. "Ideas of Mental Evolution in the Treatment of Character in George Eliot's Novels," B. Litt. Diss., Oxford, 1964.

"Politics and Personality in *Felix Holt*," *Renaissance and Modern Studies* (University of Nottingham), 10 (1966), 5–33.

Needham, J. "Coleridge as a Philosophical Biologist," *Science Progress*, 20 (1926), 692–702.

Newton, K. M. "George Eliot, G. H. Lewes and Darwinism," *Durham University Journal*, 66 (1973–4), 278–93.

Ockenden, R. E. "George Henry Lewes (1817–1878)," *Isis*, 32 (1940), 70–86.

Owens, R. J. "The Effects of George Eliot's Linguistic Interests on her Art," *Notes and Queries*, 5 n.s. (1958), 311–13.

Paley, William. *Natural Theology; or Evidence of the Existence and Attributes of the Deity*, London, 1802.

Paradis, James and Thomas Postlewait, eds., *Victorian Science and Victorian Values: Literary Perspectives*, Annals of the New York Academy of Sciences, 360, New York, 1981.

Paris, Bernard J. *Experiments in Life: George Eliot's Quest for Values*, Detroit, 1965.

Passmore, John A. *A Hundred Years of Philosophy*, London, 1957.

Pattison, Mark. "The Religion of Positivism," *Westminster Review*, 13 (1858), 305–50.

Peckham, Morse. "Towards a Theory of Romanticism," *Proceedings of the Modern Language Association*, 66 (1951), 5–24.

Peel, J. D. Y. *Herbert Spencer: the Evolution of a Sociologist*, London, 1971.

Pepper, Stephen C. *World Hypotheses: A Study in Evidence*, 4th rprt, Berkeley, 1961.

Phillips, D. C. "Organicism in the late Nineteenth and early Twentieth Centuries," *Journal of the History of Ideas*, 31 (1970), 413–32.

Pinney, Thomas. "George Eliot's Reading of Wordsworth: The Record," *Victorian Newsletter*, 24 (1963), 20–2.

  "The Authority of the Past in George Eliot's Novels," *Nineteenth-Century Fiction*, 21 (1966), 131–47.

Politi, G. J. *The Novel and its Presuppositions: Changes in the Conceptual Structure of Novels in the Eighteenth and Nineteenth Centuries*, Amsterdam, 1976.

Preyer, Robert. "Beyond the Liberal Imagination: Vision and Unreality in *Daniel Deronda*," *Victorian Studies*, 4 (1960), 33–54.

Purdy, Strother B. *The Hole in the Fabric: Science, Contemporary Literature, and Henry James*, Pittsburgh, 1977.

Ribot, T. A. *English Psychology*, trans. J. Fitzgerald, London, 1873.

Ricoeur, Paul. *The Rule of Metaphor: Multi-disciplinary Studies in the Creation of Meaning in Language*, Toronto, 1977.

Riese, Walter. "Romanticism and the Experimental Method," *Studies in Romanticism*, 2 (1962), 12–22.

Ritterbush, P. C. *Overtures to Biology: The Speculations of Eighteenth-Century Naturalists*, New Haven, 1964.

Rendall, Vernon. "George Eliot and the Classics," *Notes and Queries*, 192 (1947), 544–6; 564–5; 193 (1948), 148–9, 272–4.

Robbins, Larry M. "Mill and *Middlemarch*: The Progress of Public Opinion," *Victorian Newsletter*, 31 (1967), 37–9.

Robinson, Carole. "*Romola*: A Reading of the Novel," *Victorian Studies*, 6 (1962), 29–42.

Roppen, George. *Evolution and Poetic Belief*, Oslo, 1956.

Rousseau, G. S., ed. *Organic Form: The Life of an Idea*, London, 1972.

Ruesch, Jurgen and Gregory Bateson. *Communication: The Social Matrix of Psychiatry*, New York, 1951.

Ruskin, John. *Modern Painters,* 5 vols., London, 1873.

Said, Edward. *Beginnings: Intention and Method,* New York, 1975.

Salomon, G. "Social Organicism," *Encyclopedia of the Social Sciences,* ed. E. Seligman, 15 vols., London (1930–5), 14, pp. 138–41.

Schon, Donald. *The Displacement of Concepts,* London, 1963.

Scott, James F. "George Eliot, Positivism and the Social Vision of *Middlemarch,*" *Victorian Studies,* 16 (1972), 59–76.

Shaffer, Elinor S. *"Kubla Khan" and The Fall of Jerusalem: The Mythological School in Biblical Criticism, and Secular Literature, 1770–1880,* Cambridge, 1975.

Shuttleworth, Sally. "The Language of Science and Psychology in George Eliot's *Daniel Deronda,*" in Paradis and Postlewait, eds., *Victorian Science and Victorian Values: Literary Perspectives,* pp. 269–98.

Simmons, James C. "The Novelist as Historian: An Unexplored Tract of Victorian Historiography," *Victorian Studies,* 14 (1971), 293–305.

Simon, Robert. "Narcolepsy and the Strange Malady of Silas Marner," *American Journal of Psychiatry,* 123 (November 1966), 601–2.

Simon, W. M. "Herbert Spencer and the 'Social Organism,' " *Journal of the History of Ideas,* 21 (1960), 294–9.

European Positivism in the Nineteenth Century: An Essay in Intellectual History, New York, 1963.

Smalley, Barbara. *George Eliot and Flaubert: Pioneers of the Modern Novel,* Athens, Ohio, 1975.

Smith, Roger. "Physiological Psychology and the Philosophy of Nature in Mid-Nineteenth-Century Britain," Diss., Cambridge, 1970.

"The Background of Physiological Psychology in Natural Philosophy," *History of Science,* 11 (June, 1973), 75–123.

Smith, R. E. "George Henry Lewes and his *Physiology of Common Life,* 1859," *Proceedings of the Royal Society of Medicine,* 53 (1960), 569–74.

Snelders, H. A. M. "Romanticism and Naturphilosophie and the Inorganic Natural Sciences 1797–1840," *Studies in Romanticism,* 9 (1970), 193–215.

Spear, Jeffrey L. "Filaments, Females, Families and Social Fabric: Carlyle's Extension of a Biological Analogy," in Paradis and Postlewait, eds., *Victorian Science and Victorian Values: Literary Perspectives,* pp. 69–84.

Spencer, Herbert. *Social Statics: Or, The Conditions Essential to Human Happiness Specified, and the First of Them Developed,* London, 1851.

The Principles of Psychology, London, 1855.

Essays: Scientific, Political and Speculative; First Series, London, 1858; *Second Series,* 1863; *Third Series,* 1874.

Education: Intellectual, Moral and Physical, London, 1861.

First Principles, London, 1862.

The Principles of Biology, 2 vols., London, 1864.

"Mill versus Hamilton–The Test of Truth," *Fortnightly Review,* 1 (1865), 531–50.

The Principles of Psychology, 2nd edn, 2 vols., London, 1870–2.

The Data of Ethics, London, 1879.

The Factors of Organic Evolution, London, 1887.

Spinoza, Benedict de. *The Ethics of Benedict de Spinoza,* trans. W. H. White and A. H. Stirling, Oxford, 1910.

Stang, Richard. "The Literary Criticism of George Eliot," *Proceedings of the Modern Language Association,* 72 (1957), 952–61.

The Theory of the Novel in England, 1850–1870, London, 1959.

Strauss, David Friedrich. *The Life of Jesus, Critically Examined*, trans. from 4th German edn Marian Evans, 3 vols., London, 1846.

Strong, E. W. "William Whewell and John Stuart Mill: their Controversy about Scientific Knowledge," *Journal of the History of Ideas*, 16 (1955), 209–31.

Sudrann, Jean. "*Daniel Deronda* and the Landscape of Exile," *English Literary History*, 37 (1970), 433–55.

Sullivan, William J. "Piero di Cosimo and the Higher Primitivism in *Romola*," *Nineteenth-Century Fiction*, 26 (1972), 390–406.

Swann, Brian. "Eyes in the Mirror: Imagery and Symbolism in *Daniel Deronda*," *Nineteenth-Century Fiction*, 23 (1969), 434–45.

"*Middlemarch*: Realism and Symbolic Form," *English Literary History*, 39 (1972), 279–303.

"*Middlemarch* and Myth," *Nineteenth-Century Fiction*, 28 (1973–4), 210–14.

"George Eliot's Ecumenical Jew, or The Novel as Outdoor Temple," *Novel*, 8 (1974), 39–50.

Taine, H. A. *History of English Literature*, trans. H. van Laun, 2 vols., Edinburgh, 1871.

Temkin, Oswei. *The Falling Sickness: A History of Epilepsy from the Greeks to the Beginnings of Modern Neurology*, 2nd edn, revised, Baltimore, 1971.

The Double Face of Janus and other Essays in the History of Medicine, Baltimore, 1977.

Tholfsen, T. R. "The Intellectual Origins of Mid-Victorian Stability," *Political Science Quarterly*, 86 (1971), 57–91.

Thomson, Fred C. "The Genesis of *Felix Holt*," *Proceedings of the Modern Language Association*, 74 (1959), 576–84.

"*Felix Holt* as Classic Tragedy," *Nineteenth-Century Fiction*, 16 (1961), 47–58.

Tjoa, H. G. *George Henry Lewes: A Victorian Mind*, Cambridge, Mass., 1977.

Toulmin, S. E. and J. Goodfield. *The Architecture of Matter: The Ancestry of Science 2*, Nuffield Foundation Unit for the History of Ideas, London, 1962.

The Discovery of Time. The Ancestry of Science 3, Nuffield Foundation Unit for the History of Ideas, London, 1963.

Troughton, Marion. "Elections in English Fiction," *Contemporary Review*, 180 (1951), 280–4.

Tulloch, John. "Modern Scientific Materialism," *Blackwood's Edinburgh Magazine*, 116 (1874), 519–39.

Turbayne, Colin M. *The Myth of Metaphor*, Columbia, South Carolina, 1970.

Turner, Frank M. *Between Science and Religion: The Reaction to Scientific Naturalism in Late Victorian England*, New Haven, 1974.

Tylor, Edward B. "On the Origin of Language," *Fortnightly Review*, 4 (1866), 544–9.

Tyndall, John. "The Constitution of the Universe," *Fortnightly Review*, 3 (1865), 129–44.

Fragments of Science, 5th edn, London, 1876.

Waddell, Margot. "The Idea of Nature: George Eliot and her Intellectual Milieu," Diss., Cambridge, 1977.

Wallace, William A. *Causality and Scientific Explanation*, 2 vols. Vol. II, *Classical and Contemporary Science*, Ann Arbor, 1974.

Ward, James. "Naturalism," *The Encyclopedia Britannica*, 11th edn, Cambridge, 1910–11, Vol. 19, 274–5.
Welsh, Alexander. "Theories of Science and Romance, 1870–1920," *Victorian Studies*, 17 (1973), 135–54.
Wheelwright, Philip. *The Burning Fountain*, U.S.A., 1964.
Whewell, William, *The Philosophy of the Inductive Sciences, Founded upon their History*, 2 vols., London, 1840.
White, Hayden, ed. *The Uses of History*, Detroit, 1968.
Metahistory: The Historical Imagination in Nineteenth-Century Europe, Baltimore, 1973.
Whyte, L. L. *The Unconscious before Freud*, London, 1962.
Wiesenfarth, Joseph. "Demythologizing *Silas Marner*," *English Literary History*, 37 (1970), 226–44.
Wilden, Anthony. *System and Structure: Essays in Communication and Exchange*, London, 1972.
Willey, Basil. *The Eighteenth-Century Background: Studies on the Idea of Nature in the Thought of the Period*, London, 1940.
Nineteenth-Century Studies; Coleridge to Matthew Arnold, London, 1949.
More Nineteenth-Century Studies; A Group of Honest Doubters, London, 1956.
Williams, Raymond. *Culture and Society*, London, 1958; 2nd edn, Harmondsworth, 1963.
The Long Revolution, London, 1961.
The English Novel from Dickens to Lawrence, London, 1971.
The Country and the City, London, 1973.
Marxism and Literature, Oxford, 1977.
Wilson, Walter J. "Biology Attains Maturity in the Nineteenth Century," in *Critical Problems in the History of Science*, ed. M. C. Clagett, Madison, Wisconsin, 1959.
Winslow, Forbes, ed. *The Journal of Psychological Medicine and Mental Pathology*, London, 1848–83.
Wise, T. J. and J. A. Symington, eds. *The Brontes: Their Lives, Friendships and Correspondence*, 4 vols., London, 1932.
Witemeyer, Hugh. "George Eliot, Naumann, and the Nazarenes," *Victorian Studies*, 18 (1975), 245–58.
Wolf, Emily Vaughan. "George Eliot's Liberal Menagerie: Natural History, Biology, and Value in the Early Novels," Diss., Harvard, 1968.
Wolff, Michael. "Marian Evans to George Eliot: The Moral and Intellectual Foundations of her Career," Diss., Princeton, 1958.
"The Uses of Context: Aspects of the 1860's," *Victorian Studies* 9, suppl. (1965), 47–63.
Yonge, Charlotte Mary. *A History of Christian Names*, 2 vols., London, 1863.
Young, Robert M. "Malthus and the Evolutionists: The Common Context of Biological and Social Theory," *Past and Present*, 43 (1969), 109–45.
Mind, Brain and Adaptation in the Nineteenth Century: Cerebral Localization and its Biological Context From Gall to Ferrier, Oxford, 1970.
"The Historiographic and Ideological Contexts of the Nineteenth-Century Debate on Man's Place in Nature," in *Changing Perspectives in the History of Science: Essays in Honour of Joseph Needham*, eds. M. Teich and R. M. Young, London, 1973, pp. 344–438.
"The Role of Psychology in the Nineteenth Century Evolutionary Debate," in *Historic Conceptions of Psychology*, eds. Mary Henle, Julian Jaynes, John S. Sullivan, Springer, New York, 1973.

Index

Published works other than George Eliot's major books are listed under the name of the author.